Richard Rohmer

E. P. Taylor

The Biography of
Edward Plunket Taylor

McClelland and Stewart

The Canadian Publishers
McClelland and Stewart Limited
25 Hollinger Road, Toronto M4B 3G2

Manufactured in Canada by Webcom Limited

CANADIAN CATALOGUING IN PUBLICATION DATA

Rohmer, Richard, 1924-
    E. P. Taylor

Includes index.

ISBN 0-7710-7709-2 bd.   ISBN 0-7710-7710-6 pa.

1. Taylor, Edward Plunket, 1901-
2. Businessmen – Canada – Biography.   3. Capitalists
and financiers – Canada – Biography.

HC112.5.T39R65   338'.092'4   C77-001816-5

To Winnie

Contents

Acknowledgements

The writing of a biography of a man such as E.P. Taylor, who has diverse interests, carries on many activities, and has enjoyed a life full of accomplishments, requires an enormous amount of research, reading, sifting, sorting, and then putting it all together.

I am grateful to both Winnie and Eddie Taylor for their co-operation, and to their son Charles Taylor for his counsel; and to Thomas D'Arcy and Beth Heriot, who have been associated with E.P. Taylor for so many years.

In addition, I note the value of the extensive taped interviews by Professor Maurice Hecht, of the University of Toronto, during 1972 and 1973. The record of his well-researched discussions with E.P. Taylor, George Black, Jr., and others who have had close contact with Mr. Taylor over the years, was of great assistance in the preparation of this book.

Chapter I

Friday, December 13, 1940

The British passenger ship, *Western Prince*, pitched through heavy North Atlantic seas, bound for England. Not a light was showing as she struggled through the frigid wind-blown ocean, 200 miles south of Iceland and some 550 miles west of Ireland.

The day was Friday the 13th, but that was not the only reason that the 169 passengers and crew aboard were uneasy. The *Western Prince* was in U-boat waters. The German submarine packs, ranging out into the Atlantic from their Baltic lairs, were creating deadly havoc among the plodding British merchant ships huddled in their slow-moving convoys, and were picking off lone passenger ships attempting to cross the ocean alone, relying on their speed for survival.

The 496-foot *Western Prince* of the Furness, Withy Line had been built in 1929 at Port Glasgow for trade between the British Isles and New York and South America. After the war began she was armed with two defensive guns aft and placed in transatlantic service, carrying hundreds of refugees from Great Britain to New York. On this voyage, the ship carried a 10,000 ton general cargo and a large quantity of mail. Four twin-engined bombers were lashed to her deck. Her cargo, worth $30 million, was the most valuable yet to be carried across the Atlantic.

To keep their minds off the U-boats, four Canadian passengers, comfortable in the elegant main salon, played a friendly game of bridge. The four men were part of a mission to Great Britain. One of the players, the Minister of Munitions and Supply, the Honourable C.D. Howe, was the leader of the mission. The others around the table were three of his top "dollar-a-year" men who were accompanying him to the United Kingdom to attempt to convince the British that they should utilize the substantial unused capacity of Canada's industry to produce guns, ships, aircraft, and armaments of all kinds. Since it was a selling job that had to be done, Howe had brought his best salesmen. Coincidentally they were also good bridge players.

Colonel William C. Woodward was president of Woodward Stores Limited of Vancouver, then and now one of the most successful department store enterprises in western Canada. Billy Woodward was C.D. Howe's executive assistant.

The second man was Gordon W. Scott of Montreal. A chartered accountant and a partner in the firm of P.S. Ross and Sons, Scott had been provincial treasurer of Quebec and at one time a minister in the Taschereau Cabinet. He was C.D. Howe's financial adviser. Howe was his bridge adviser that evening as they played "to see Friday the 13th out," as Howe later put it.

The third man was Howe's director of munitions production, a tall, robust, balding man with an easy smile, a deep voice, and a rumbling laugh. E.P. Taylor was a young man, not yet forty, who in the short space of ten years had built a remarkable entrepreneurial empire in Canada. He had joined Howe's team just a few months before.

About an hour after midnight, with Friday the 13th successfully behind them, the four finished their card game. Then, braving the cutting wind, they took a walk around the heaving deck for a breath of fresh air before turning in.

In his state room, Taylor changed into his pajamas. The master of the *Western Prince*, Captain Reid, had instructed his passengers to remain dressed at all times in order to be ready to abandon the ship in the event of a torpedoing. But this did not suit Taylor, who had been outfitted in New York with what he considered to be appropriate survival clothing. The wives of the four men had accompanied them by train to New York to see them off. All the women were apprehensive about the long and dangerous mid-winter voyage, particularly on this slow vessel, which would have to cross the Atlantic without an escort. They would have preferred to see their men go across by bomber, which had now become the usual, but highly uncomfortable, means of getting government officials across the ocean.

But Howe would have none of this. He was tired, worn out by

the enormous pressures of gathering together the industrial and production resources of Canada in the presence of a governmental and military structure that was not geared to cutting red tape but rather to making it. What Howe wanted was a slow voyage, away from telephones, constant meetings, and the drain of tough decision-making; away from the frustrations of the restraining net of bureaucracy. He needed this time, and he was going to go across on this ship, and that was all there was to it. Furthermore, the *Western Prince* was the only ship available.

When the couples got together on the way to New York, Winifred Taylor soon discovered that all the other wives had made sure their husbands were equipped with heavy clothing for survival in a lifeboat. Winnie's husband hadn't given a thought to this. So far as he was concerned, it wouldn't be needed anyway. But the sailing of the *Western Prince* was delayed one day. The next morning the infamous Lord Haw Haw, an Englishman named William Joyce who had turned traitor-broadcaster for the Germans,* let it be known in a radio broadcast that C.D. Howe and his party were in New York preparing to depart for England on the *Western Prince,* which had been delayed for one day. A German U-boat, he announced, would sink the vessel on the way across. This news convinced several of the passengers to wait for another crossing, but not Howe and his group. Winifred Taylor did, however, march Eddie down to Abercrombie & Fitch where he bought a heavy Grenfell survival suit. He had tried on the jacket, but not the pants. With that, the purchase was made and Winnie was satisfied.

In the first hour of Saturday, December 14, 1940, when Eddie Taylor was preparing for bed in his private room on the *Western Prince,* he changed into his silk pajamas. He met part way the order the captain had given by laying out his Abercrombie & Fitch survival suit on a chair close to his bunk. Then, ever-present pipe put aside, Taylor climbed into his bunk and read for a while before he went to sleep.

Taylor vividly remembers being awakened by the thud of the torpedo. It struck near the bow of the vessel some distance from where he and the other members of the Howe party were quartered. Immediately the alarm bells sounded throughout the ship.

---

*Joyce was hanged by the British in 1946.

The lights dimmed. In his room, Taylor shot out of bed and, in the faint glow of light, reached for his survival suit. On went the heavy protective Grenfell jacket. Then he picked up the untried trousers. He had to open the zipper before he could put them on. But the zipper wouldn't work. It wouldn't budge. Amidst the sounds of alarm, Taylor worked furiously on that zipper trying to get it to move. He spent three or four minutes at it, but a "definite feeling that the ship was getting lower down"* prompted him to move. He had no choice now. Pajama bottoms still on, clutching his reluctant survival pants, his faithful pipe stuck in his coat pocket, feet now in socks and shoes, Taylor quickly made his way through the settling ship.

He came out on deck into the cold, biting wind of the grey early morning darkness. "The ship had settled quite a bit. The waves were breaking over the deck and it was very wet. Everything was under control and the officers were all at their posts. The captain was directing operations from the bridge. There was absolutely no panic or confusion. Everybody just quietly waited until told what to do." The lifeboat drills had prepared them well.

Then came the captain's final decision. The order was given to abandon ship.

Into his assigned lifeboat went Taylor. With him were Woodward and some thirty other passengers and crew, including some women, children, and an infant in a ventilated cardboard box. When its mother fainted, Taylor carried the boxed baby into the lifeboat. "They then told us to lower away. The boat kept grinding against the side of the ship as it went down. It finally reached the bottom. All the time we were holding our breath, wondering if the boat would be smashed. Even when we got to the bottom, it was difficult to keep it off the side of the ship until the ropes were loosened. There seemed to be about one hundred ropes binding the lifeboat to the ship, and none of them would loosen. Two or three of the crew had knives. They whipped them out, cut the ropes, and eventually we got clear of the ship. Then we had the annoying experience of drifting under No. 3 lifeboat–we were No. 1–which was being lowered on top of us. It came down to within six feet of us.

"The next thing was to keep the boat away from the ship. There

---

*All unattributed quotes in this book are those of E.P. Taylor.

14

seemed to be some extraordinary attraction of the lifeboat to the ship. It continually swung back, banging on the side of the ship. We were also afraid of getting into the suction if the ship should sink."

Howe was in another lifeboat. Like Taylor's, it had no motor, but oars to be manned. Gordon Scott was in yet another lifeboat. His had an engine. It was the only one so equipped on the *Western Prince*. Scott had asked to be assigned to it because he had a bad heart condition and knew that he would not be able to row. The selection of this craft was to cost Scott his life because, as his lifeboat hit the water, it capsized, spewing its passengers into the frigid ocean. For a moment, Scott was seen hanging on to the overturned lifeboat, between it and the side of the ship. Then his head, bobbing between the two, was hit, his grip released, and he was swept away.

The first torpedo had struck at 6:10 A.M. Forty minutes later, when all the people except the master and two crewmen were off the *Western Prince*, there were flashes from the submarine as its crew photographed its victim for proof of the kill. Then the U-boat captain took dead aim at the wallowing vessel and put a second torpedo into her, this time, lethally amidships. Captain Reid, still on his bridge, saw it coming and gave two farewell blasts on the ship's whistle just as the torpedo struck with a tremendous explosion that tore the ship apart. The *Western Prince* went down within a minute and a half, her captain with her. Still partly surfaced, the submarine passed within fifty feet of Howe's lifeboat and disappeared into the darkness.

At that moment Taylor had no knowledge of an inflexible Admiralty order that, unless instructed by a warship, no British merchant vessel was to stop to pick up survivors in an area where U-boats were known to be present. The logic of such an order could not be questioned. The U-boats were decimating Britain's merchant marines, and inflicting heavy losses on its navy. These precious vessels were the lifeline of the United Kingdom, for without them the food, supplies, equipment, and armaments necessary for the survival of the people of Great Britain could not be carried from North America. Therefore, in balance, the lives of those driven into the sea by the torpedoes of German submarines were less valuable than any ship capable of their rescue. Had he known that no ship would stop for them, Taylor's perception of their chances of survival would have been different. In any event, "we were just too busy rowing and bailing to think about surviving."

Howe, Taylor, Woodward, and all the souls adrift that morning on the cruel waters of the North Atlantic were as good as dead. Nevertheless, the crewmen in the lifeboats followed the drills and procedures they had been taught. From the survival kit in each lifeboat they dug out distress flares which soon arched high into the darkness, a beacon call for help which any sailor would instantly recognize.

Some ten miles away, a British merchant ship, the *Baron Kinnaird*, without cargo and westbound for New York, had fallen behind and lost her convoy in the darkness. Her master was Captain L. Dewar, an Englishman in his late fifties who had spent his adult life at sea. He saw the flares. There were people there who would surely die unless to save them the master of a ship was prepared to heave to and lay his vessel's belly open to the periscope and lethal torpedo of a hungry submarine captain. Dewar had full knowledge of the Admiralty order against picking up survivors. He knew there were U-boats in the area. And he knew that under those flares were fellow countrymen who would perish if he did not act.

Dewar then did a rather unusual thing for a ship's captain. He called in his officers, some of whom, like his crew, were Lascars. He outlined the situation and asked them whether they should alter course and rescue the survivors. Captain Dewar told them he was prepared to go if they agreed. The decision was made quickly. There was no question. They would do it. They would worry about the Admiralty order later if, indeed, they themselves survived.

Soon after the *Baron Kinnaird* altered course, she was picked up by a destroyer from the convoy from which she had been separated. It was a Town Class ship, an aged American First World War destroyer which had been taken out of mothballs by the United States, and with some fifty others put in the hands of the Royal Navy. After an exchange of signals, the captain of the destroyer decided to escort the *Baron Kinnaird* during its rescue attempt. If the destroyer had not appeared, or if its captain had come to the conclusion that the safety of his convoy was of more importance than the *Baron Kinnaird* and the survivors it was pursuing in the North Atlantic darkness, it is likely the *Baron* too would have been lost.

As the morning of December 14 wore on and the grey, sub-arctic, overcast dawn emerged, Taylor and the others in the lifeboats were sick and desperately cold, yet they rowed and bailed, their rough course set for remote Iceland, some 200 miles away. There was no possibility that they would ever reach land. The winds and the high seas continued unabated. All were thoroughly uncomfortable and beginning to feel the effects of exposure. Taylor, in his pajama bottoms, was among those suffering most. About 1:00 in the afternoon, one of the survivors saw the *Baron Kinnaird* on the horizon. C.D. Howe described the announcement of the sighting in this way:

"We were in the lifeboat several hours in the cold and wet when somebody remarked conversationally: 'There's a ship.'

"Another replied: 'That's not a ship.'

"Said a third: 'I think it is.'

"Then somebody stood up and said quietly: 'Yes. It's a ship all right.'

"After that they sat down. Nobody said another word. They just calmly waited–as if they did this kind of thing every day."

With the first sighting of the *Baron Kinnaird*, the people in the lifeboats could also see the much faster destroyer cutting through the high waves circling protectively in a wide area around the *Baron Kinnaird*. The warship's crew were at battle stations, ready to pounce on any submarine that might show its periscope or launch a torpedo at the rescue ship. Captain Dewar brought his craft to a halt between the lifeboats and the wind. Oil was dumped on the lee side of the ship to calm the heaving waters so the lifeboats could get up safely against her hull. As the small bobbing boats, crammed with their human cargo, edged up to the *Baron Kinnaird*, rope ladders were thrown down for the able-bodied to make their way up, and baskets were lowered to receive and lift those unable to climb.

Within half an hour all the survivors were on board Captain Dewar's ship, still under the watchful eye of the destroyer. Dewar set course back to England, but by a circuitous route, northerly by the Hebrides. After four days, the ship arrived at Greenock, where Howe and his party were given a hero's welcome. By this time Taylor had been warmed not only by a pair of the captain's trousers (which demonstrated that he must have been a large man because Taylor was over six feet tall and weighed about 210 pounds and they were baggy on him), but also by his scotch whisky. Captain Dewar had turned over his own small cabin to C.D. Howe, Woodward, Taylor, and eight others. When the captain visited the Howe group, he would summon his steward by pounding on the floor with his walking stick. The steward would then appear bearing a bottle of scotch. Taylor later complained that when the captain was absent, he and Howe tried to raise some scotch using the same method, but without luck.

On their arrival in England a record of the rescue was made, signed not only by Captain Dewar, but also by C.D. Howe, Billy Woodward, E.P. Taylor, and the other occupants of the captain's cabin. For his efforts, Captain Dewar was relieved of his command by the Admiralty, which at that time had all British merchant vessels under its command, and was permanently beached. Taylor, Howe, and the other passengers took up a collection for the crew, but there was no adequate way to compensate Dewar for the sacrifice he had made. Later, Taylor arranged for an expensive marine radio receiver to be sent to Dewar as a small token of his appreciation.

Looking back on the sinking of the *Western Prince*, two questions can now be asked. The first is this: if Captain Dewar and the crew of the *Baron Kinnaird* had obeyed Admiralty orders and had not altered course to rescue the survivors of the *Western Prince*, and if the destroyer had not turned up to protect the *Baron Kinnaird*, and the dynamic, powerful, aggressive C.D. Howe had died on December 14, 1940, what would Canada be like today?

Second, what would Canada and international horseracing be like today if Edward Plunket Taylor had died with him?

Chapter II

Childhood and Early Years
1901-1922

On January 29, 1901, Edward Plunket Taylor was born in Ottawa, the first child of Plunket Bourchier Taylor and Florence Magee Taylor. The recently wed Plunket Taylors led a comfortable life in the conservative, high-Victorian capital city where they lived under the watchful eyes of their respective parents. It was a slow-paced period, with horses clopping through the streets, pulling behind them wagons or elegant carriages. Most streets were yet unpaved. Tall oaks, maples, and elms shaded the majestic brick houses which were springing up everywhere. The architectural imprint of Victorian times was on each of them. The long-lined, tall windows of these stately homes were capped with rich stained glass to convert the rays of the winter sun into a shifting kaleido-scope of warm colours in the high-ceilinged parlours and dining rooms and upon the finely carpeted foyers and entrance halls. The third floor usually housed the help, always in plentiful supply in those days of massive immigration, particularly from the United Kingdom.

The economy was stable but expansionary. Immigration from western Europe, the Ukraine, and the United Kingdom continued at a high rate. The prairies of western Canada were newly laced with life, and the railways were still burgeoning and highly profit-able, their building made possible by massive investments from a wealthy England whose vast overseas empire had been spilling riches into her coffers for many decades. It was a period when the prairies were being turned into a cornucopia of grain, new metal deposits were being discovered in Ontario, and the economy throughout southern Ontario and Quebec, while agriculturally based, was becoming more and more industrialized. The country was quite British and very much the obeisant, yet self-governing (within firm limits) English colony.

The motor-car was just beginning to be seen, and the telephone just making its way into urban society. Hydro electricity was in its early stages of development and the magic electrical lightbulb, born from the inventive mind of Thomas Alva Edison just a little more than a quarter of a century before, was finding its way into most city homes, but had not yet displaced gas and kerosene lamps by any means. In the cities, such as Ottawa, for many of the senior businessmen, professional people, and politicians, normal dress was a waistcoat, high, starched collar, a formal black, long-tailed frock, grey striped trousers and a black stovepipe hat. Ladies wore enormous wide-brimmed, plumed hats, their bodies encased in corsets and high-necked, long-skirted dresses, never showing an immodest ankle, at least in public, their all-covering gowns a symbol of the closely monitored morality of the small city. It was a community in which everyone in the upper classes of society knew everyone else. Charles Magee, as a successful entrepreneur, was part of that closely structured Ottawa society. He had allowed his daughter Florence to marry Plunket Bourchier Taylor only after her suitor had a clear $1,000 in the bank. He was then in his early thirties and a mere clerk in the postal service when he began to court the sixteen-year-old Magee daughter.

Taylor was born in Kingston on August 11, 1863. His father was Thomas Dixon Taylor, an Irish civil engineer who had come to Canada to work on the building of canals and railways and had married Lucy Bourchier, whose father, a colonel in the British army and a veteran of Waterloo, had been sent to Canada as commander of the Fort George garrison at Kingston.

The Christian names of their son, Plunket Bourchier, came from Lucy's family line, which included a host of English admirals and generals stretching back as far as King Edward III, from whom it has been speculatively assessed the Bourchier family is descended–E.P. Taylor hopes it is legitimately. Plunket attended Trinity College School, Port Hope, and later the Ottawa Collegiate Institute entering the Post Office Department in Ottawa as a clerk after graduating from high school. He played football and hockey for Ottawa, and became a well-known athlete.

In 1879 he joined the militia as a private in the Governor General's Footguards and served with the Guards' Sharpshooters throughout the Riel Rebellion in the Northwest Territories in 1885 where he took part in the relief of Battleford and in operations against Big Bear. In 1887 he was commissioned, rising to the rank of major by 1896. By this time he was engaged to Florence Magee, but with the wedding date still a long way off because of the condition laid down by her father.

During the following years, Plunket Taylor worked hard, lived frugally, scrimped and saved, until finally he had his $1,000. Then, in 1899, Frances Magee married Plunket Bourchier Taylor, whose long bachelorhood came to an end at the age of thirty-six. With his bride, Taylor acquired a formidable father-in-law, and a job at the Bank of Ottawa, arranged by Charles Magee, its founder and president.

Family legend has it that Magee retired at the age of thirty-two, having made his fortune. At that age he left the dry-goods firm in which he had become senior partner, but he went on to devote the rest of his life to a series of entrepreneurial achievements. He took part in the development of the Hull Electric Railroad, which ran between Ottawa and Aylmer, in the organization of the Gatineau Power Company, and in many other enterprises.

Edward Taylor's early childhood years and those of his brother Fred, who arrived five and a half years after Edward, would have to be described as normal. There were no family crises, no upsets, no hostilities (at least that are recorded) between his mother and father or between them and their own parents. Everything appears to have been smooth, orderly, and prosperous, and everybody abided by the family rules. As Fred Taylor remembers it, "My paternal grandparents, particularly my grandmother, were terribly proud of their family. Their guiding precepts were: public opinion—you must keep your nose clean at all times and be the pillar of society; respectability and security; and the church. My father's guiding principles were community service, public opinion, respectability, and financial security. It didn't matter whether you were wealthy or not, you must not only be a good citizen, you must not have anything said about you. What people said was of terrific importance."

When it came time for his education to begin, Edward Taylor was sent to Ashbury College for Boys in Ottawa, which was then presided over by its originator, Reverend George P. Woolcombe.

21

During the years he attended that school, young Edward was quite often outside the office of the good reverend on a Friday night, when punishment was administered. Being an energetic, rambunctious lad, he was in for his share of the strap. Taylor remembers those days very well. "If you'd put newspapers in your pants, he'd say, 'Take those out. Take down your pants!'"

Each weekend had a ritual. The Plunket Taylor family would have lunch with Grandfather Magee. "He had a very big house on Lisgar Street in Ottawa. He loved building houses. He'd sell one and move to another. We'd go to lunch there every second Sunday. Of course, we all had to go to Sunday School. After Sunday School, which was from 3:00 Sunday afternoon until about 4:30, we would go to my grandfather and grandmother Taylor's house. They lived on Lewis Street in a house my mother owned. Grandfather Taylor was a fine old gentleman. My grandmother was a bustling little lady, very active and keen, except that she was almost completely deaf. There was no electric gear in those days, so she had a big horn, and one grandchild after another would go up and talk to her. She would ask us what we were doing during the week, and what we were going to do the next week, and if we'd been good children."

Sunday School at the Saint George's Church was presided over by Archdeacon Snowdon, Edward Taylor's uncle by marriage to Carrie Magee. The Anglican Church, and in particular the archdeacon, had a forceful impact upon the lives of both the Taylor and Magee families. It was church and Sunday School every weekend without fail—perhaps too much for the young child, Edward Taylor, who now acknowledges that he is not a very religious person, although he remains a member of the Anglican Church.

To use Edward's word, life in general was "standard," happy, and comfortable, even though his parents were never wealthy. Taylor points out that "When my father first got married, he had a very small salary." As a bank employee he would have to wait for a long time before his fortunes would improve.

Edward entered into his first entrepreneurial activity at the age of twelve, when he went into the business of breeding and selling rabbits. He had put together a workshop in his basement with drills, a lathe, and other tools he had acquired. He built a rabbit hutch, bought a special pedigree stock, and soon captured the local market. However, after a period of two years of genetic expansionary success, one of his competitors from the Lewis Street gang (Taylor's was the Gilmour Street gang) stole into his hutches one night and mixed up the breeds with the result that the females began turning out bastard bunnies, causing young Taylor to give up the business. He was becoming tired of being a rabbit raiser anyway, so in another Taylor first, he gave away his assets. This was the beginning of a charitable habit which has multiplied over the years.

When the war broke out in 1914, the former militiaman, Plunket Taylor, who had served as sharpshooter in the Northwest Rebellion, wasted no time getting back into the military. In 1915, he became second in command of the 77th Battalion with the rank of major, even though he was by this time fifty-two years of age. Edward recalls the whole unit turned out to help the firemen fight the blaze when the Parliament Buildings burned down on February 4, 1916, just before the battalion left for England. Edward, like almost everyone in Ottawa that day, saw the blaze that destroyed the entire Centre Block, with the exception of the library. He also recalls his grandfather being present in his stovepipe hat when General Sir Sam Hughes presented the colours to the unit. A picture of that event shows Grandfather Thomas Taylor, Sir Sam Hughes, and the adjutant of the battalion, the father of the renowned Canadian broadcaster and publisher, John Bassett.

Soon after the arrival of the 77th Battalion in England, the unit was broken up. Taylor, being the senior major, and having been a banker, was given the job of mustering the Canadian troops all over England and France, work that entailed keeping records, a sort of running inventory of who and where everyone was. This assignment was with the Canadian Pay Corps, a position that gave Taylor the rank of lieutenant colonel and the title by which he was to be known for the rest of his life–Colonel.

In those days it was acceptable for senior army officers to take their families across to England, and soon after he arrived in Britain, the new lieutenant colonel completed arrangements for his wife and two young sons to join him.

Thus, during the First World War, at the age of fifteen, Edward Plunket Taylor made his first voyage across the Atlantic Ocean with his mother, his brother Fred, and Grandfather Charles Magee, who was still going strong at the age of seventy-five. A regular visitor to London, where he raised money for his various enterprises, Magee stayed only a few days, saw the Taylor family settled in a house in Hampstead, then returned to Canada.

The family arrived in London in time to witness the spectacular night-time destruction of a Zeppelin which crashed close by, providing the two Taylor boys with scavengers' souvenirs. Over the next few months they were to witness many bombings of London by the hated "Huns."

Edward went to the City & Guilds College in London. "I completed my entrance examinations for McGill University while in London. I was really too young to go to university, and I wanted to join the British army after having served for a short time in an Officers' Training Corps." On more than one occasion, contrary to his father's instructions, Edward attempted to join the British army. In order to put a stop to this, his father sent Edward back to Canada in the fall of 1917. He wanted him to stay until he was eighteen when, so far as the Colonel was concerned, Edward would be entitled to join the army.

The next year was to be a significant one for the now six-foot-tall young Edward. Even though he had qualified to enter McGill, his parents felt that at sixteen he was too young to do so. Instead he went to Ottawa Collegiate and took what was then known as fifth form, now grade thirteen. During the next few months, however, the impressionable young man was to receive an important part of his practical education outside of school. He had the good fortune to be living with his grandfather, Charles Magee. The old man apparently saw his young grandson's potential, his interest in the world of business, and in what he, Magee, had accomplished over the years. So he took the time and trouble to tell Edward about the intricacies of some of the banking, trust company, railway, and other corporate deals he had made, and how he obtained his financing, especially in England. "In those days British money was pouring into Canada as American money is pouring into Canada today, and as it used to pour into the United States. British money built up the United States, and American money is now building up Canada." Young Edward took it all in. "My ambition was to do the same kind of thing that he had done."

Charles Magee died during the summer of 1918, quite a blow to Edward who had become very close to him. While Magee made no provision for Edward in his will, he had given his grandson a year

24

of attention and instruction which had fixed Edward's goals and ambition. More than a decade later, it would be an element of his grandfather's estate, Brading Breweries, that would be the keystone to Edward Plunket Taylor's entrepreneurial empire.

That same summer Edward took his first job. He worked in the Ottawa Car and Foundry Company as a toolmaker's apprentice, making twenty-five cents an hour. "We were making jigs and fixtures. The factory was making 4.5 Howitzer guns. I was given very simple jobs by the toolmakers. They are the greatest machinists in the world, the toolmakers." This basic knowledge was to stand Taylor in good stead when in 1940, at the age of thirty-nine, he was responsible to the Minister of Munitions and Supply, C.D. Howe, for pulling together Canada's capacity to produce rifles, machine guns, artillery, tanks, and a host of other weaponry and equipment.

Edward had to earn money each year in order to pay his way through university. His father contributed half his tuition and living expenses, and he was responsible for the other half. "My father gave me an allowance but couldn't afford a very big one. If you had about $1,500 a year, you could pay your fees and subsist. I worked in the summer every university year to supplement what my parents could afford toward an education. In those days there were no government grants of any consequence to universities and so you had to have the money to pay your fees and your keep, which I think should be the system today. I don't believe that because a fellow has a certain I.Q. he should get a free education."

In the fall of 1918, shortly after Edward started his first semester at McGill, his father, mother, and brother returned from England. Colonel Taylor was now fifty-five and quite deaf. Even though the war was not over, his superiors had decided it was time for him to return to civilian life. When he had gone into the service at the beginning of the war, he had been manager of the Northern Crown Bank. By 1918 it had been taken over by the Royal Bank of Canada. On arriving back in Canada, Colonel Taylor expected to be appointed manager of the main Ottawa branch on Sparks Street, but when he disembarked at Halifax with his family, he was presented with a telegram from the Royal Bank advising him that he would be in a lesser position; manager of the Rideau Street branch of the Royal in Ottawa. The job he wanted went to a younger man. However, there was little choice but to accept. After the family arrived back in Ottawa, they lived for a brief time in the old Magee house with Uncle Fred Magee, a bachelor, until they bought their own house.

In Montreal, at McGill University, Edward, after a brief trip to Ottawa to greet his family, settled into the university routine and began his engineering studies. During the 1918/19 academic year, he roomed in a boarding house on Mansfield Street which was run by a Miss Heward. In order to cut expenses, his cousin, George Grout, who was also going to McGill, roomed with him.

Taylor made the first football team as a flying wing, a position in Canadian football that has long gone. "There was no forward passing in those days. The flying wing was supposed to have speed. As soon as the play started, or the kick was given, he would run like hell down the field. He was supposed to get to the ballcatcher first. On the defensive, he is the secondary defenceman. He stays behind the line."

In the 1918 football season McGill played only one game, an exhibition match against Hamilton. Then disaster struck in the form of a flu epidemic which caused so many deaths that the university had to shut down. "All universities closed. The hearses were going through the streets; it was a very ugly time." Ugly indeed. His roommate and cousin George was a victim. Like everyone else, Edward was afraid that he might get the killer disease. His fear led him to take his first drink of hard liquor, this as a preventative against the flu. "I was only seventeen years of age. I'd had a little wine, a little beer, but I never had any liquor. I always heard that when you got a severe cold you should take whisky. In those days prohibition was on in Quebec, but there was a doctor at the door of every liquor store. He just said 'two dollars please' when you went in. He wrote a prescription. He didn't ask you if there was anything wrong with you or not. So I went in and gave the doctor two dollars. He said, 'What do you want?' and I said, 'A bottle of whisky.' He said, 'What kind?' I said, 'I don't know. What do you recommend?' He said, 'Corby's.' So I took a bottle of whisky, went back to my boarding house and drank half of it neat. I've never been so sick in my life. The university closed that day, and I went home. I was still violently ill. My mother got hold of the family doctor. He came and he said, 'This boy hasn't got the flu. I don't know what's wrong with him.' I didn't dare tell them what I had done. I have never had flu in my life so I must be immune to

26

it. I needn't have bothered to drink the whisky."

When the flu epidemic subsided, the universities re-opened and Edward returned to McGill to continue his studies. One day that winter, while making a piece of toast for himself at breakfast, Edward's inventive light went on. The standard toaster at that time browned only one side of the bread at a time. He conceived of the feasibility of making a toaster that could brown both sides at the same time. Instead of forgetting about the idea, Taylor went on to translate it into a reality. He sat down and made some drawings, then took them to a patent attorney. On February 14, 1919, just a little more than two weeks after his eighteenth birthday, Edward Plunket Taylor filed an application for a patent for his electric toaster. The patent was subsequently granted.

The application having been filed, Edward then had something to sell. He approached the Thos. Davidson Manufacturing Co. Limited, a Montreal company which manufactured toasters, among other things. Not only did Edward sell them the exclusive right to manufacture his electric toasters and sell them within Canada, he also talked them into giving him a job for the coming summer. The licensing agreement with the Davidson firm was signed on May 15, 1919. It provided that young Taylor would receive, "a royalty of forty cents ($.40) upon every electric toaster sold by the party of the second part containing the said improvement, said royalty payable by the party of the second part to the party of the first part on the 15th day of the following month for sales of each month." Edward, being a minor, could not lawfully make a binding contract by himself, so the agreement was signed not only by him, but also by his father. The Colonel had encouraged him to apply for the patent and, as always, stood behind his aggressive son.

With the bonanza of royalties in hand, Edward was flush enough to make his first visit to a racetrack and make a wager. "That was at Blue Bonnets, which was in its element then. It and Woodbine were the two main racetracks in Canada. On Saturday afternoon, I would go out to the races if I wasn't doing something else, which explains how I became interested in horses and racing."

Having passed his first year of engineering comfortably, he was invited to join the Delta Upsilon Fraternity, an offer he quickly accepted. In the fall of 1919 he moved into the fraternity house on

McTavish Street where he was to live for the next three years.

His football activity continued that fall, this time on the second team. His place on the first team had been taken by the boys who came back from the war that year. "They were war veterans and they were tough boys. McGill won the intercollegiate championship in 1919." Taylor also started to play interfraternity hockey, picking up a nickname in the process that aptly describes one of his principal characteristics. "They called me 'Lone Rush Taylor' because I never passed the puck."

At university, "I didn't really engage in anything like the debating society or the dramatic society, nor was I interested in the *McGill News*. I read it every day but I didn't participate in it. I wasn't active in the Students' Council. I just led my ordinary life and got a little exercise and had a good time whenever time permitted. We used to have tea dances in those days, and it was the day of the hip flasks, too. You weren't socially acceptable unless you had a hip flask when you went to a party." And Edward went to lots of parties. "We'd go out with girls at night, or we'd play tennis." Needless to say, Eddie Taylor had his own hip flask which, of course, made him socially acceptable. And, about the female sex, "Yes, I liked girls. But I played the field and got to know lots of them."

By 1920 Edward had come to a basic conclusion about his future. "I realized halfway through university that I wasn't cut out to be an engineer, and I didn't want to be an engineer. My principal interest was dabbling in a minor way in stocks and in business and finance. But I decided I'd better continue my engineering course, so I did just enough work to pass the exams except in one subject I really enjoyed and did well in–that was economics. I had no trouble heading the class in that. I passed just a little above mid-centre of the class. I could have done better if I had taken it more seriously."

Taylor's summer job in 1920 taught him a lesson about unexpected job pressures. "I heard that the city of Montreal was looking for inspectors in connection with road building. So I went to see the appropriate official and I was hired to be an inspector in a quarry where curbstones were cut out of limestone by a private contractor. I was given a blueprint regarding the proper conformation of the part of the curbstone that is buried below the ground. It had to be a certain size and a certain shape so that the curbstone would be firmly embedded and would resist pressures and the frost of winter. I wanted to keep my job so I insisted that every stone that I approved for sale to the city came within the specifications. Those that didn't, I would discard. The contractor became very upset about the number I was discarding. He offered me inducements to be less severe in my approval. I turned him down.

"Two days passed and then I noticed the blastings of the rock were coming closer and closer to where I was working. One day a blast blew me off my feet. Then one of the workmen tipped me off that the boss was trying either to frighten me away or to kill me. He said in broken English, 'The boss, he says you must be killed. You costing him too much money.' At that point I discovered that one of my fraternity brothers had unfortunately not found a summer job so I told him that I had found a better job, which happened to be the truth. But I did warn him that he had better not be too strict in his approval or rejection of any of these curbstones. Well, he managed to last through the summer. I don't know whether he took anything from the contractor or not. I didn't ask any questions."

At the beginning of his third year of university, the brothers of Delta Upsilon Fraternity made Edward the house steward, which meant that he had to collect the bills from the members, which he acknowledges was sometimes hard to do. He authorized the staff to buy the food, was responsible for paying them, and generally conducted the business affairs of the group. It is recorded that under his stewardship the Delta Upsilon Fraternity flourished financially.

The extent of the impression he made on his fraternity brothers can be seen in this poem written for the occasion of a fraternity dinner. The author could have had little understanding of how close to the mark he really was–either that or he had a crystal ball.

Our Edward

We have heard of men of London town who gained undying fame
And men from New York City who make other men look tame,
But don't forget Old Bytown or call it Slow and Dead
When it brings forth men like Edward, brilliant Edward, famous Ed.

29

A shining light is Edward amongst high financial minds,
A man of budding promise in these scientific times,
An inventor known to every race that feeds on toasted bread,
A clever youth, mechanically, our Edward, brainy Ed.

A man among the ladies, bless their little hearts, why not
For Edward in his square lapels is passing handsome what?
An example of why girls leave home–a caveman born and bred
He's a devil with the women is our Edward, dashing Ed.

If he's often absent minded why should that be called a fault?
For he gives his friends enjoyment when he fills his tea with salt.
When the finance of a nation is being settled in his head
Is it strange that Ed would pass a spoon when asked to pass the bread?

If a brother from his study should desire to clear his mind
And seek for entertainment of an inexpensive kind,
He need only knock at Edward's room where Edward lies in bed
And a book will hit the window–Edward's window smashed by Ed.

If you wish to place some money on the Derby or King's Plate
And the papers give the odds upon your horse as one to eight,
Don't believe the sporting circles for they'll do you every time
Go to Edward, he'll compute the odds at "ten to eighty-nine."

Our Edward's at his highest form on Sunday afternoon
When the hostesses await him in the large front drawing room,
When he nonchalantly spills his tea on some fair damsel's head,
They'll never be dull moments at a tea with dashing Ed.

But laugh, you simple brothers, laugh your loudest one and all
At his "outside reading" and a "par with military ball,"
When we engineers are drawing down our seven per and bed,
Our Edward will have millions, clever Edward, lucky Ed.

Chapter III

The Ottawa Years
1922-1927

Friday, May 12, 1922. On that day, Edward Plunket Taylor received his Bachelor of Applied Science in Mechanical Engineering at a convocation for over 200 McGill University graduates held at the Capitol Theatre in Montreal. He would never practise as an engineer, but the knowledge gained during the McGill years would stand him in good stead throughout his life, especially in the late 1970s as he enlarged his worldwide house-building operations, the latest of his endeavours.

Back in Ottawa, and again living with his parents, Edward could not find employment. "There had been a sharp deflationary period and the country was in a depressed state. Jobs were not available for university graduates. To keep myself busy, I played some golf and met some people." In fact, he became an excellent golfer.

"One of the people I met was complaining about the bad streetcar service from Westboro to Ottawa. Westboro is only about five or six miles away. So I said, 'Well, why don't you get a bus line?' This older man said to me, 'Why don't you form a bus line? You can drive a motor-car and you're an engineer. You want something to keep you busy.' I had no money but I had a friend who had some who was at McGill with me, Lawrence Hart. He was a year ahead of me and he hadn't been able to get a job. So I said to Lawrie, 'You can put up the money and I'll organize this thing.' He had been born with very bad eyesight. As a matter of fact, he wore very thick glasses, and couldn't see across the room. He agreed. We bought two Ford truck chassis, and we designed a bus that looked like the old open summer streetcars. We had curtains that came down the side if the weather was wet. We had them made at the Ottawa Car and Foundry where I used to work. We each drove one of the buses, even Lawrie with his bad eyesight. There were no police inspections or tests as there are today. None at all. We had to start out in Westboro in the morning because we had dealings with people in that town. We'd run our buses into Ottawa at various intervals during the day. The people we carried were nearly all civil servants going into work. We were able to charge a little more than the streetcar fare because of the convenience we offered. We would take them right up to the front door of their building. It was successful and we made wages out of it."

The Yellow Bus Line was operated by Edward Taylor and Lawrie Hart until mid-1923, when the partners, together with a third shareholder, a man called Cox who was in the income tax department, and who subsequently became the general manager of the Excelsior Life Company, decided to accept an offer to buy them out made by the owner of the Capital Bus Line which operated between Kemptville and Ottawa. They sold at a profit, and each of the partners went his own way. Hart was glad to get out. "And I was too. I was afraid he was going to kill somebody. We took an awful chance, I can tell you."

Not only was it in 1922 that, with the exception of his childhood rabbit foray, Edward Taylor went into his first business enterprise, it was also the year of his first direct involvement with horses, an interest that became a major part of his life. Certain of his friends who were officers in the Princess Louise Dragoon Guards suggested that Taylor should join the unit as a provisional second lieutenant and learn to ride. He was accepted into the regiment in the early summer and immediately took lessons from one of the local riding schools, just enough to get him on a horse. In short order, wearing his newly acquired khaki second lieutenant's uniform, he was off on a fourteen-mile ride to the regiment's summer camp. Taylor's lack of experience as a horseman was quickly demonstrated to the entire regiment. As they were moving through the west side of Ottawa, past a large Catholic church which had long steps up from the sidewalk, a streetcar clattered past the mounted men whereupon Taylor's horse took off and bolted right up the steps. "Fortunately I didn't fall off, but if the door of the church had been open, the horse would have gone right up to the altar, I'm sure. The colonel halted the regiment. The regimental sergeant major was detached to bring the new young officer down the steps and put him back at the head of his troop.

"When we got to camp the young officers who weren't capable of riding well were immediately put in the hands of a permanent force Canadian army sergeant major who was on loan to our regiment from the Royal Canadian Dragoons. I remember him very well. He was a Cockney by the name of Aisthorpe. He was a martinet, as all good sergeant majors are. The young officers, including me, had to ride bareback and learn all the ways to control a horse. The sergeant major would be in the middle of the ring. He'd yell instructions at us. His language wasn't very polite, but he taught us all to ride pretty well."

Provisional Second Lieutenant E.P. Taylor of the Princess Louise Dragoon Guards learned another lesson that summer of 1922: for an officer and a gentleman there are rules and regulations to be followed and one must behave responsibly and be responsible. One incident drove this home to Taylor in an unforgettable way.

On the final evening before summer camp of the Princess Louise Dragoon Guards broke up, a regimental mess dinner was held. The commanding officer of the regiment, Colonel Blue, a teetotaller, returned to his tent about 10:00, immediately after the formal dinner was finished. He went to bed. The rest of the officers made merry for at least another two hours, getting themselves well into the grog. "About midnight the second-in-command, Major Jock Inkster—I was the youngest subaltern in the regiment—said, 'Now we're going to have some fun with the colonel. I command you, Taylor, to form a firing squad of the six officers. We're drawing rifles and you are to march us to the colonel's tent. We will use blank ammunition and when the colonel emerges from his tent after he has been roused, you are to say, 'Firing squad, prepare to fire! Fire!' And we did it. I had to obey orders, you see." When the colonel came out of his tent dressed in his pajamas, he was greeted by six weaving officers dressed in their best mess kit finery and pointing their rifles at him. "When I said, 'Fire!' they fired. There was an awful blast. Of course, the blanks made just as much noise as real ammunition. The colonel was frightened out of his wits; he nearly killed us all. Here he was being attacked by his own officers. He was sure we were all dead drunk. I got a severe reprimand. I said, 'Well sir, I had to obey orders,' but I can tell you the older fellows got worse than I did."

Early in 1923 the decision was made by the Magee family, mainly by Uncle Delamere Magee of Toronto, who owned one-third of the family stock of the Brading Breweries Limited (Aunt Carrie Snowdon owned a third, as did Taylor's mother), that Carrie's son, Allen, who was just graduating as a lawyer, and Edward, should become members of the board of directors of Brading. Both the young men were delighted with the opportunity, as well as the prestige, of serving the family company in this way. And Colonel Plunket Taylor, who had been president and a director of the company since the death of Charles Magee in 1918, was most pleased to have these two young men with him. The Colonel could consult with them about the problems of operating the business, and at the same time could teach them about the difficulties of running a competitive concern. Even though he had been gone for five years, the influence of Charles Magee on Edward Taylor was alive and increasing.

Colonel Taylor's association with the Royal Bank of Canada came to an end when he retired in 1923, but he was not to be troubled for very long with the matter of inactivity. The Toronto securities firm of McLeod, Young, Weir & Co. Limited had decided to open a branch in Ottawa and made enquiries about the availability of an experienced Ottawa person who might take on the job of manager. Colonel Taylor was recommended to them. He fit the bill perfectly. He was ready to start immediately and was keen to work with them. So, late in life, the Colonel began a new career, joining the McLeod, Young, Weir firm selling stocks and bonds.

In the early days he operated from his house, later opening an office. By the end of the year the business had grown to the point that help was needed. Edward was out of the bus line by this time, a tall, good-looking young man with a most pleasant, yet forceful personality, a ready laugh, and a first-class sense of humour. As his father had found out, Edward was disarmingly persuasive as well as persistent–two main qualities of a good salesman. Furthermore, apart from his membership on the board of Brading Breweries, Edward was unemployed. When all things had been considered, the Colonel invited his son to join him as his sub-agent for McLeod, Young, Weir in Ottawa. He accepted without question, plunging energetically and enthusiastically into the tough business of selling bonds and securities, a job that suited him very well. For the next few years his talents would grow and develop under the influence of his father, the McLeod, Young, Weir firm, his involvement in the Brading Breweries, and his own driving ambition to become the kind of expansionist entrepreneur that his grandfather Charles Magee had been.

Under the push of that goal, and while embarking on his selling career, Edward put together another business: an Ottawa taxi operation which he named the Red Line Taxi Company. In Montreal he had been intrigued by the new taxi meters that gave the passenger a visible record of the bill he was running up. He reasoned that if metered taxis were available in Ottawa, they should compete very well against the taxis whose drivers gave their passengers arbitrary fare rates, often much more than a reasonable charge. While Taylor had a bit of money left from the proceeds of the sale of the Yellow Bus Line, a transportation business that he thought would give him some credibility when he was looking for money for the taxi operation, he didn't have enough money to finance the purchase of his proposed fleet of six automobiles and the expensive meters. He approached his father, but the Colonel had no funds he could risk at that time. Edward next approached a well-known Montreal figure, Commander J.K.L. Ross, a colourful person who was then the biggest man in Canadian thoroughbred horseracing and had won many important races in the United States Edward had met him through Ross's children. However, the commander declined the opportunity to finance the young man, telling him that the Yellow Bus Line wasn't impressive enough, but when he had a real track record to come back and see him. Taylor never did go back. He obtained the money from several older well-to-do Ottawa people whom he and his family knew. E.P. Taylor had started to do what he has been best at all his life, conceiving ideas then persuading others to buy them.

And so, in 1923 the Red Line Taxi Company of Ottawa started into business with six units, all meter-equipped. But its founder, Edward Plunket Taylor, did not do what he had done in the Yellow Bus Line enterprise. He did not drive a taxi; he was too busy selling securities. For promoting the company and putting it together, young Taylor received a percentage of the equity. Within a short period of time Charlie Garland came along and bought the company. Taylor was taken out with the rest of the shareholders. There wasn't much money involved, but there was a profit. The firm is still in existence after forty-three years, but under a different name–the Blue Line.

The Taylor family's "bread and butter" business was selling securities. "We did quite a lot of business in real estate bonds, of which McLeod, Young, Weir were pioneers. In Toronto we did an issue on the Metropolitan Building at the corner of Adelaide and Victoria, one on the Alexandra Apartments on University Avenue, and an issue on the Granite Club on St. Clair [which was torn down in 1975 to make way for redevelopment]. We did an issue on a building in Montreal on St. Denis Street. And we had industrial companies as well as real estate companies."

In those days if a customer wanted to buy or sell shares, Taylor would see that the transaction was made but not through the books of the McLeod, Young, Weir company. They were not stock exchange members. Instead it was done through a firm in the stock brokerage business. An appropriate commission went, of course, into the McLeod coffers to Taylor's credit.

One of Edward Taylor's prime bond customers was the Capital Life Insurance Company from which he received some quite big orders. Civil servants also bought from Taylor. "Their orders were small, but there were many who saved, say, $500. I had many orders for $500 or $1,000 worth of securities. On a $500 sale, I would probably make $5 or $10. And if I made ten or twelve business calls a day, I found I could do pretty well. The percentage of sales against calls was fairly high, but sometimes I'd have to go back three or four times while they studied the literature I had left with them."

During this period Taylor didn't own a car. He travelled either on foot or by streetcar. "I found out very quickly that my earnings were in direct proportion to the amount of footwear I wore out, but I did an awful lot of business. On several occasions I sold $100,000 worth of bonds. I made plenty of cold calls. I'd look up who the senior civil servants were and then I'd appear at their offices. I'd do the same with doctors. Successful doctors are always good prospective bond buyers. The average sales went up and kept rising, and so finally I bought a motor-car at the end of 1926. It was a little green, open Pontiac. My wife and I sailed away to our honeymoon spot in it."

With sales increasing, the Colonel and Edward decided to take on additional sales people to share the load, which was now almost totally carried by Edward. "I brought in two salesmen. One was a fellow called Bill Garvock, whose uncle was a prominent contractor in Ottawa. Bill was a very industrious man, older than I was. He had a myriad of small clients, but did a very good business. Another one was a chap who had a different kind of social background, called Meredith Jarvis. He was one of my fellow officers in the Princess Louise Dragoon Guards. He knew all the social set in Ottawa and I knew them too." A new golf course was started in Ottawa by a man by the name of Corrigan, the head of the Capital Life Insurance Company. The club was called the Chaudière.

"My grandfather Magee and my father had both been members of the Royal Ottawa golf course which, in those days, was a very expensive golf course to belong to. I hadn't been put up for membership but I was very keen on golf. So this new golf course was started. Mr. Corrigan invited me, not to put any money into it, but to become the captain of the club. He had, among his directors, Sir Robert Borden, the former Prime Minister of Canada, and several other people like that who were all members of one of the other golf courses as well."

Taylor confesses that he was playing golf well in those days. "I never had very good style but I was getting pretty good scores and I was very keen." As the club captain, he was able to take advantage of all the social events that took place at the clubhouse, including the dances. It was at one of these in the late spring of 1926 that a petite, blonde, blue-eyed girl caught Edward's eye. As quickly as he could, he presented himself, asked for a dance, and was accepted. The young girl was Winifred Duguid. As she recalls this first meeting, she was wearing a green dress covered with sequins. The orchestra played "My Heart Stood Still" and her partner didn't dance very well.

A few days later, an intrigued Edward Taylor invited Winifred to play golf with him. She normally played at the Rivermead Club where her father was a member. Again she accepted. The two of them played their round and discovered that they enjoyed each other's company very much. From that point they began to see a great deal of each other.

Winifred Duguid was born in Lancashire, England, on September 28, 1903. Her Scots father, Charles, was employed as a marine architect by the shipbuilders Vickers at Barrow-on-Furness. Her mother was a Lancashire girl whom Charles Duguid had met shortly after joining Vickers. In 1908, Charles Duguid had accepted his firm's offer to send him to Canada to a senior marine architect's position in their Canadian subsidiary. Uncertain as to whether or not he would stay in Canada, he left his family in England, returning there regularly to visit them. By 1913, he had made his decision to stay in Canada and brought his wife and two children, Winifred and her younger brother, to Ottawa, which had been his headquarters since his arrival five years earlier.

Winifred, only ten years old, was put in the Carleton School for Girls where she completed her education. As was customary, she then continued to live with her family and took part in the active social life of Ottawa, playing golf regularly and becoming accomplished at it. This, of course, made her all the more attractive to Edward.

About six weeks after their first meeting–Edward had been courting Winifred with typical Taylor energy and persuasion–he decided the time had come to propose. Winifred recalls how he asked. "Winnie, I have two questions to ask you. The first question is 'Will you marry me?' and the second question is 'When?' "

Winifred said yes to the first question. The second could not be settled until Edward had asked Charles Duguid for his daughter's hand. Both of Winnie's parents had become quite fond of Edward. Duguid gave his consent, and at the same time the date was settled, June 15, 1927. It was a somewhat longer wait than Edward had hoped for, but there was little choice: he had no money. Even though he was selling bonds and securities, and doing very well at it, the young bachelor had not accumulated any savings. Until then there had not been any reason to put money aside. During the year before the wedding he would have to work twice as hard and save every cent he could so when they were married they could set up housekeeping without any worries about money. During their lifetime together Winifred has never questioned Edward about money. Earlier on he told her that he would never bother her with business matters. As Winifred acknowledges, she went along with his decisions without question, even when they involved her personally.

Winifred Duguid Taylor had a profound effect on Edward Taylor's attitude and outlook from the time she agreed to marry him. Her calm, stabilizing influence has always been a strength to her husband. While it is true that she has never become involved in any of his business transactions, she has participated fully in their life with horses, owning and racing many of them under her own colours.

The wedding took place as scheduled on June 15, 1927, in a ceremony performed by Archdeacon Snowdon in Christ Church Cathedral in Ottawa. It was not a lavish wedding by any means. Afterwards there was a reception at the home of Mr. and Mrs. Duguid. Then the newlyweds climbed into Edward's green Pontiac and took off to Lake Placid for their honeymoon. Nine days later, they were back in Ottawa and into their first residence at the Strathcona Apartments at 4 Laurier Avenue East.

While his career as a bond and security salesman flourished, the new resolve and impetus given to Edward Taylor by his marriage also produced an aggressive, increasing involvement and interest in the affairs of the Brading Breweries Limited, even though he had no ownership interest in the company.

During the twenties, Ontario had embraced the anti-beer, alcohol and spirits movement which had caught up the United States and Canada. Beer and liquor could not be purchased anywhere in the province except, of course, through bootleggers. Fortunately for Brading, Quebec had not joined the prohibition trend. The beer market in that province was therefore still open. The Ontario prohibition was not against the manufacture of beer, but against its purchase. So although the Brading firm was located in Ottawa, it sold only to Quebec.

Brading thus had a good market, but there were no prospects for expansion. But the provincial election in late 1926 changed all that, and sparked E.P. Taylor's interest in the Brading prospects. In the hard fought provincial election held in December, the Conservatives, campaigning on an anti-Temperance Act platform, soundly defeated the incumbent prohibitionist Liberals. Looking beyond the expected abolition of the Temperance Act, Taylor could see that the opportunity for growth of the Brading Breweries could be unlimited. During the spring of 1927, he carefully monitored the new legislation brought down by the Conservatives which once again made it legal for Ontario citizens to buy beer and liquor.

So far as E.P. Taylor was concerned, what was needed was a bold new approach to take advantage of the new marketplace for beer. By the time the new legislation was effective, June 1, 1927,

Edward Taylor had already been hard at work studying the operations of the Brading plant in Ottawa, ferreting out costs in all sectors of the plant, checking the capacity limits, the break-even point of production, the financial statements of the company, talking with the brewmaster, and discussing the cost of new plant and equipment with suppliers, all in preparation for a proposal he wanted to make to the directors. E.P. Taylor was getting down to the business of being a businessman.

After much research, a great deal of calculation of figures and projections, and an analysis of market trends and financing opportunities, E.P. Taylor produced his first major corporate proposal and placed it before the directors of the Brading Breweries Limited in the form of a lengthy letter, which is an example of the persuasive entrepreneurial thinking of this twenty-six-year-old. The method he proposed for financing the expansion was the basic plan he was to use over and over again, especially in the mid-forties. The plan was simple–borrow from the public and the banks and retain the equity yourself.

The concluding part of Taylor's optimistic letter of proposal summarizes what was in the young man's mind and invokes the spirit of his grandfather, Charles Magee.

The plan that I wish to support is that we borrow a sum of $200,000 on a fifteen year debenture issue, the proceeds from which would be sufficient to rebuild our plant (see Schedule A for estimates) giving us an annual capacity of 1,000,000 gallons of bottled beer and a plant modern and economical in every respect. The principal reasons why I favour this course are as follows:

1. The interest on this loan, even at present production, can be found entirely from operating economies as scheduled on the attached Exhibit 'B'.
2. There will be available for the shareholders for the next eight years all profits the Company is capable of earning after, of course, a suitable reserve which would have to be made under either plan of procedure.
3. Production will not be interfered with through annual construction activities around the plant.
4. The ever-present fire hazard will completely disappear.

40

5. The publicity that we would receive through such a large expansion programme would bring us thousands of dollars additional business. It would also turn our plant from a not-too-imposing sight into a splendid group of buildings, which would favourably impress our local customers and transients.

6. Lastly and most important of all is that we will be ready to step right in and make the big money that additional business means. Under present conditions that prevail with such a plant and with sales of 1,000,000 gallons of beer per annum, we could show a profit well in excess of $300,000.

Let us, therefore, as the Boy Scouts say, "Be prepared" for this opportunity. I have shown you that our operating costs are reduced by as much as the interest on this loan and that we have everything to gain by so doing. It would simply be following the time old practice of our leading successful financiers of "Trading on the Equity" namely to borrow money on senior securities for a fixed rate of say 7% in order to make large profits on the junior investment. This was the practice adopted by the late Charles Magee when he re-organized this business and formed a new company in 1914. Let us repeat his procedure, as the future never looked so bright.

His fellow directors accepted Taylor's enthusiastic advice, but being more conservative by nature, they went along with a 50 per cent increase in capacity, following his proposed method of debenture financing. Debt money was plentiful, cheap (between 2 and 4 per cent), and deductible.

During the summer, Taylor pressed on with continuing success selling bonds and securities for McLeod, Young, Weir but with the growing realization that he was more interested in producing the merchandise than in selling it. He wanted to get into the business of originating underwriting and financing deals. He wanted to be an entrepreneur like Charles Magee, not just a salesman, although his huge capacity for the persuasive selling of business propositions, especially mergers, has been Edward Taylor's major strength.

Lieutenant Edward Plunket Taylor's continuing membership in the Princess Louise Dragoon Guards during the 1924-1927 period

41

provided him with a major outside interest. It also brought him in contact with new people. One of them, Viscount Carol Hardinge, was to become his closest lifelong friend. Hardinge, who is five years younger than Taylor, was a professional cavalry officer, trained at Sandhurst. He had come to Ottawa from England as military aide to the Marquis of Willingdon, a relative of Hardinge, who was then Governor General of Canada.

To open and close Parliament, the Governor General would travel some two and a half miles from Government House to the Parliament Buildings, riding in an elegant, open, horse-drawn carriage, escorted by two mounted troops of the Princess Louise Dragoon Guards, their officers with swords drawn, spurs polished, their plumed brass helmets bobbing up and down with the movement of their cantering horses. It was a spectacular sight.

During the opening of Parliament in 1927, Second Lieutenant Taylor was second in command of the travelling escort. "In good weather–it was an open carriage in the summer–Hardinge would sit in the carriage opposite me and opposite the Governor General and his wife and would be grinning and smirking at me. In the winter we'd be in an open sleigh, if the weather was fine enough, and we'd have on fur caps instead of the brass helmet. There'd be some troopers ahead of the carriage or sleigh and some behind. When we'd get to the Parliament Buildings there would be a company of my father's regiment, the Governor General's Footguards, drawn up as a guard of honour. As soon as we got there, the captain of the guard would say, 'Guard of Honour, slope arms!' and then the band behind them would start playing 'God Save the King.' With that our horses would raise hell. My horse bolted just as the band struck up. He wheeled around and I ended up in the back of the Parliament Buildings looking over E.B. Eddy's paper mill. But Hardinge didn't see that and I've kept it a secret from him because by that time the Governor General was out in front to take the salute and inspect the guard. Hardinge had to go with him and he didn't see me."

Assessing his situation in late 1927, Taylor saw only two ways to improve his position in the securities business: he could organize his own firm in Ottawa with his father, or he could attempt to negotiate a partnership in the McLeod, Young, Weir company. While he didn't have much hope of talking the senior members into allowing a man as young as he into a partnership, it was nevertheless worth a try. He would have to deal with them from a position of strength, and that strength was that he was prepared to set up his own company. If he did so the Ottawa operation of McLeod, Young, Weir would suffer not only serious transition difficulties, but also effective new competition from the locally entrenched Taylors.

Edward discussed the situation at length with his father and eventually obtained his agreement to participate in a new company. It would take all their resources and then some. The risk would be great, but the two of them would be working for themselves. There would be the five partners, Colonel Taylor, Edward, Meredith Jarvis, Bill Lyons, and another young Ottawa friend of Taylor's, G.A. (Pete) Bate. The name P.B. Taylor & Company Limited was chosen.

On November 28, 1927, Taylor wrote Harry Ratcliffe, a senior partner in the firm, a man who was to remain a close friend of Eddie Taylor's during all of Ratcliffe's life. The letter was short, but it amply displayed both the single-mindedness and the persuasiveness of this determined young man.

Since our chat two weeks ago certain developments have taken place which make it imperative for me to decide before the middle of December whether I will go into business in partnership with my father and others or continue with the firm. To be perfectly frank, we have practically decided to make the change and it would require some definite proposal from the firm to make my future more attractive to alter our decision.

If Dad and I leave you, we will feel making the break very keenly as our association with the firm extending over nearly five years has been most happy. The treatment we have received from you in every way has been fair and generous, and we have had the satisfaction of regarding the partners not only as our chiefs but as close friends.

You know, from your own experience, that the necessity of making such a decision as this comes sooner or later to everyone in our business who is ambitious to succeed. While I have found my selling experience extremely interesting I have now come to the time when, to be happy, I must spend my time and energies, in part at any rate, to origination work.

I am addressing this letter to you because it was with you that I discussed the possibility of this question arising. Would you please explain my position to Ewart and Gordon and to D.I. [McLeod] when he returns. If there is anything that you can offer me now to induce me to change my mind I will be only too happy to give it my consideration. In this connection, if anything to my advantage can be arranged, my father will only be too glad to step aside and leave the Ottawa Office to Bill Garvock or anyone else you would appoint as manager.

The next day Ratcliffe replied that he was very anxious for Taylor to defer definite action until December 12 because the other partners were most anxious to consult with D.I. McLeod, who would be in Europe until that time. Taylor did not wait, however. His next letter in the negotiations with the McLeod, Young, Weir firm, dated November 30, 1927, again was directed to Harry Ratcliffe. Its forceful and blunt approach was characteristic of Taylor's entire business career.

I do not wish to remain any longer as a branch manager in a district where the work involves solely the retailing of securities. I naturally would like to remain in Ottawa owing to the fact that my family and my wife's family and most of our friends are here. I have decided that if I remain here I shall form my own organization. To leave Ottawa would be a big step and I would only undertake it if there was a job which interested me and which carried with it a partnership in the firm. Naturally, in the latter connection, with such a firm as ours which has grown so much and in which the working capital must now be very considerable, I could only expect to be a small shareholder and would expect to have to pay for any shares I received in some manner or other.

Perhaps I have put my ideas a little bluntly, but I know that I can do so with you without conveying the impression that I have acquired a swelled head. If I were in the position of the partners, I believe, owing to the nature of our business, that I would inaugurate a plan whereby the likely and keen chaps in the organization would be admitted to partnership, in order to hold them with the firm and to spur them on to greater efforts to further the firm's interest. On going over the branch manager's representatives and others on our staff it strikes me that there would be less than half a dozen chaps who would come in this category. If you sold to each of these say a 5% interest in the business, this interest to be paid for by these men over a period of say five years, it would mean that you could hold them permanently. I understand that in firms of the nature of ours the senior partners usually hold an option to buy out the stock of the smaller partners, which protects the larger partners against any junior partner not proving to be a success.

Ratcliffe may well have recognized a swelled head when he read that letter. But he also knew that Taylor had performed exceptionally well and that he was a comer whose special talents were worth negotiating for.

While this correspondence was going on, the arrangements for the organization of P.B. Taylor & Company Limited were proceeding rapidly. On December 8, Edward Taylor wrote to Brian Heward of Jones, Newton & Heward of Montreal, stockbrokers, setting out terms and conditions whereby the Taylor company, which would specialize in bonds and debentures, would operate as a branch of the Heward firm insofar as their stock business was concerned. "Under this plan we could share in any profits that were made under some sort of an understanding worked out beforehand whereby you would pay us bonuses and we would be direct employees of yours. Later, if we should decide to buy a seat, we could assume the overhead and split the commissions on the basis that the exchange allowed." Taylor enclosed a monthly estimate of expenses of the branch, with the suggestion that "if you will agree to assume this on a trial period of a year and make us a satisfactory offer as to bonuses if our business goes over a certain amount, we shall consider the deal closed and shall make all arrangements to commence operations on the 1st of May next." The total monthly cost of running the operation, including the salary of the manager and operators, direct wire tickers, and rent of premises Taylor estimated to be $1,500.

In the middle of these negotiations with the McLeod, Young, Weir firm on the one hand, and with his intended partners in P.B. Taylor & Company Limited on the other, Taylor was considering buying a horse for his personal use, not as part of the pool of the Princess Louise Dragoon Guards' horses. In fact, Taylor had been looking at a filly owned by T. McCallum of Sunbury, Ontario. The deal was never closed because Edward had been "very much engaged in other matters." Indeed he was.

On December 13, 1927, Edward Taylor went to Toronto by train and met with D.I. McLeod, Ratcliffe, and other partners in the firm. The miracle did happen. They made him the "wonderful offer" which he had told Bill Lyons would be necessary to induce him to change his mind about forming the Ottawa firm. Taylor did not accept on the spot, but went back to Ottawa to talk over the offer with his father. Winnie would agree to whatever Eddie wanted to do. On December 15, he wrote to Ratcliffe accepting the proposal and confirming the arrangement that he would "come to Toronto to do origination work under the direction of D.I. and the other partners and that my salary will be $6,000 per annum together with bonuses from time to time which the firm will pay me on the merit of my work." And to E.P. Taylor the next proviso was all important: "In addition, granted my work is satisfactory, that at the end of 1928, I shall be admitted to partnership in the firm."

P.B. Taylor & Company Limited never did come into being. The intended partners carried on in their previous employment, including Colonel Taylor who stayed as co-manager with Bill Garvock of the Ottawa branch of McLeod, Young, Weir.

For the Taylor clan in Ottawa it was a happy Christmas with the prospect of new horizons opening up for Edward and Winnie who were preparing to move to Toronto where the financial action and opportunities were. If ever E.P. Taylor was going to be a successful entrepreneur like his grandfather, Charles Magee, the opportunity was now in his hands. It had not come by luck but through hard, shrewd negotiation by a determined twenty-six-year-old who knew exactly what he wanted and was prepared to work for it.

Chapter IV

The Grand Design – The First Steps 1928-1934

On January 5, 1928, Winifred and Edward Taylor arrived in Toronto, moving into the Alexandra Apartments on University Avenue. The manager, whom he knew, had been able to let them have a suite on short notice.

In those days, Sam McBride was the mayor of Toronto, a city about five times the size of Ottawa and already the financial centre of a then very British Canada outside of Quebec. University Avenue was elm-lined. The low buildings sitting on each side of the wide boulevard were dominated at the northern extremity by the red sandstone Ontario Legislature buildings.

The Alexandra Apartments building was convenient for Taylor's business purposes, located as it was just a few blocks to the west of the offices of McLeod, Young, Weir in the new Metropolitan Building. "You know, it's an ugly building by present standards, but there it is. It's still there. I had sold a great many of the first mortgage bonds on the building. It was customary for the McLeod, Young, Weir firm to give the salesman who sold the most bonds in any issue an extra bonus. I won the prize on the Metropolitan Building and on the Granite Club."

As Eddie Taylor settled into the demanding business of digging up underwriting deals–he was to originate and participate in several during 1928 and 1929–he was also working hard on research into every brewery in operation in Ontario and examining carefully the experience of National Breweries in Quebec.

When Taylor looked at the 1928 brewing industry in Ontario, he could see that there were far too many small breweries–thirty-seven–and far too many different brands. Most of the plants were not operating at capacity, nor were they sufficiently modernized. Much of the equipment was old and needed replacement. If profits were made they were slim. *Financial Post* figures showed that all the operating breweries in Ontario had combined assets of $24 million, but net sales of less than $12 million.

In Quebec the picture was quite different. With lower assets, the net sales were higher than in Ontario. The reason was obvious. There were only three brewing companies operating in Quebec. Before the First World War there were sixteen firms in operation. But the Dawes family, through its National Breweries Limited, had consolidated fourteen of them into one. The breweries had fewer brands, better advertising, and, most important, high volume, which allowed them to penetrate the Ontario market to the extent that 12 per cent of the Quebec brewery sales volume was in Ontario.

"Two-thirds of the brewing business in Canada was in the hands of old established companies. Labatt's was the strongest in Ontario; National Breweries was the strongest in Quebec; and Molson's was very strong. Those three were the only really large companies except Carling Breweries, which had run into some misfortunes. So I studied the whole brewing industry going back a hundred years in England and the United States, and I found the whole trend, as it was in any consumer goods business, was toward large companies. Although all companies have to start small, large ones have tremendous advantages over small companies, particularly in the consumer products fields."

Taylor was impressed by the National pattern of amalgamation and merger followed by the closing down and disposing of the small unprofitable plants and the creation of a better one. Such consolidation would provide for better management, better financial control, an overall advertising policy, reduction in the number of brands, the upping of the quality of product, and an increase in volume. Taylor knew that Labatt's, Molson's, and National would fight any corporate newcomer who threatened their hold on the market, but that was not to deter Eddie Taylor.

The plan he formulated in 1928 was to use the Brading Breweries Limited as the starting point. After he convinced the directors to begin a program of acquisition and mergers, he would start with the Kuntz Brewery in Kitchener. The targets would be O'Keefe, Canada Bud, Dominion and Cosgrave's in Toronto; then the

Regal in Hamilton, Carling in London, Taylor & Bate in St. Catharines, British American in Windsor, Kakabeka Falls at Fort Frances, and the Sudbury Brewery in Sudbury. Combined, those plants produced half of the total sales of beer in Ontario.

Under Taylor's scheme he would acquire and close breweries that accounted for approximately 20 per cent of all Ontario sales: Budweiser, Copland, City Club, Heather, Reinhardt, Rock Springs, Grant's, Cronmiller and White, Bixel, Perth, Walkerville, Riverside, Hofer, Tecumseh, Formosa Spring, Gold Belt, Port Arthur, Soo Falls, Lake-of-the-Woods, and Fort Frances.* Capital Breweries of Ottawa would be left out, as would the northern breweries owned by the Doran family. If the plan was successful, Brading would be Labatt's chief competitor.

Taylor's master merger plan did not emerge as a sudden flash of light, but developed as a result of an enormous amount of research, calculation, and analysis of financial statements.

In the summer of 1928, Edward decided that it was time to move out of the Alexandra Apartments, and he rented a house at the southwest corner of Duplex and Glencairn.

In his first months with McLeod, Young, Weir, Taylor worked mainly with two senior partners, D.I. McLeod and Harry Ratcliffe. They were sufficiently impressed with his origination work that by Christmas of 1928 he had earned the junior partnership they had promised him a year earlier against good performance.

Since the time he moved to Toronto in January 1928, and into 1929, Taylor had either originated or done the "dog work" in a number of important underwritings and mergers. "I had a very early connection with Standard Broadcasting. I put together the underwriting of what was then Rogers-Majestic Corporation Limited." The company was manufacturing and distributing the famous Rogers Batteryless and Majestic Electric radio sets and had not yet started into the broadcasting business. That came later, with the establishment of what is probably the most successful radio broadcasting station in Canada, CFRB, and the change of name of the company to Standard Broadcasting Limited, which Argus Corporation later controlled.

During this period, Taylor began to deal with a young man in the Toronto law firm of Fraser, Beatty, the lawyers for McLeod,

---

*The list did not include Welland Brewery, acquired in 1934.

Young, Weir. He was Henry Borden whom Taylor had known earlier at McGill University. Borden says, "Taylor was the promoter par excellence in putting companies together. He had an excellent personality and he had a quick mind. I would call him somewhat of a genius in resolving financial difficulties, putting companies together, that sort of thing. But he had a great partner. It was very difficult for me at that time to differentiate between the two. Harry Ratcliffe, to me, right up until he died, was one of the financial genii of this country." (It was to Henry Borden that Edward Taylor was to go in early 1930 to incorporate Brewing Corporation of Ontario Limited, the holding company which would eventually become Canadian Breweries Limited.)

Even though he was working night and day finding new underwriting deals and working them through with his partners at McLeod, Young, Weir, Edward Taylor was also pushing the Brading board of directors to begin to implement his grand plan of expansion. He knew that the Kuntz Brewery in Kitchener was in trouble. Edward could see enormous potential in the Kuntz three million gallon capacity, only 11 per cent of which was being used. With the approval of his father, he negotiated with the owners of the Kuntz plant on behalf of Brading, finally persuading them to sell. It gave Brading ownership of a plant close to the heart of the Ontario market. The Kuntz acquisition set the pattern that Taylor wanted to follow in his master plan. No cash changed hands, it was simply an exchange of shares.

Then, in November, came the great stock market crash of 1929. At that time Taylor was at work on a deal with John Morrow Screw & Nut Company for a merger with Ingersoll Machine Tool, also the underwriting of an issue by Appleford Paper Products, and one for the John A. Lang Tanning Company in Kitchener. These deals involved the McLeod, Young, Weir firm in underwritings to the extent of between $6 and $8 million, commitments that would have wiped them out when the crash came except for the fact that the firm had put a clause in its underwriting agreements that if the Montreal *Financial Times'* average of stocks dropped to a certain point, McLeod, Young, Weir would be relieved of its underwriting commitment. "It was an 'out clause' as we used to call it. You couldn't sell anything after the crash. So we got out. Incidentally, the firm in subsequent years revived all three transactions and did them successfully."

The stock market collapse brought disaster to the underwriting business. For Taylor it was a mixed blessing. With the disappearance of origination opportunities, he was able to concentrate on his development plan for brewery acquisitions, using its solid assets behind its common shares as a base from which to acquire other breweries. Neither Taylor nor Brading Breweries had access to money, nor as the year 1930 opened would there be any reasonable prospect that they could find any. It was virtually impossible to raise money by the sale of shares, bonds or debentures.

The Great Depression was moving rapidly toward its depths. The unemployment rate had tripled to 9 per cent from the year before and was to go to 19 per cent in 1933. The soup kitchens and the long lines of unemployed looking for jobs, which no one could have envisaged in Canada a year earlier, had made their dismal appearance. And the beer market was hit as hard as any other part of the economy. In 1929, the per capita consumption of beer in Canada was six gallons, but by early 1930 that figure was dropping rapidly, to bottom out in 1933 at 3.5 gallons.

With this kind of black scenario in front of him, the average man would have turned his back on the beer business and waited for signs of good economic times before attempting to launch the kind of plan that Taylor had in mind. But Taylor is not an average man; he would press on regardless. He knew that the sale of beer was going to expand. He knew that the market was there to be taken. He knew there would have to be a consolidation of the multitude of breweries in Ontario, and he knew that if many of the smaller breweries were available for acquisition prior to the crash, they would be highly vulnerable now. But in order to get at some of them he would have to have money as well as shares to trade. Even so, he would do the best he could using the only bartering device he had–shares of Brading for shares of the seller's company.

Luck and incredible coincidence combined to put young Taylor together with a stranger who had money. From their first meeting he has never looked back.

One of Taylor's main prospects for a merger was Toronto's Canada Bud Breweries which was prospering. In mid-February 1930, he called on Duncan McLaren, the company president, and asked whether he and his associates would be interested in selling their interest to the Brading firm in exchange for shares. McLaren was not interested in selling at that time, but in the process of the discussion he told Taylor that he had been approached by a man named Clark Jennison about the possibility of Jennison's principals purchasing McLaren's minority interest in five breweries in northern Ontario owned by the Doran family. According to McLaren, Clark Jennison, an American, was acting as an agent for English interests and had been given over half a million dollars to purchase brewing companies for them in Canada.

Jennison had what Taylor did not—cash. They had one interest in common and that was the acquisition of breweries. And Taylor had the master plan. He asked McLaren to introduce him to Jennison.

Two days later Taylor and Jennison met at McLaren's Canada Bud office. As Taylor remembers him, he was about five foot eight, with reddish hair, "He was older than I was. I would think he was probably fifty. He had had rather a checkered financial career. He was an opportunist and he was an honest man. There was nothing against him except that he was a wanderer. It was very fortuitous for me that I met him because he helped me over a very difficult period. He was a friendly man who expressed himself quite well, but a quiet man."

By this time Taylor had run a check on Jennison and found his credentials to be acceptable. He represented the Industrial General Trust Company and the Atlas Investment Trust Company, both of London, England. They were separate companies but had a common chairman. The funds that the two firms had given Jennison were in a bank in Montreal, and Jennison had full authority to use them to purchase breweries for his principals.

At that first meeting, Taylor explained what his overall objective was. Jennison's mandate, however, was to acquire brewing companies, not merely to invest in one, no matter what its prospects. During the discussions that followed, both men consulted with Henry Borden on the legal questions. Jennison was in touch with his principals, and Taylor was in contact with his father. By the beginning of March, a plan had been worked out and Borden was given instructions to draw the agreement between the two men and to proceed with incorporation of Brewing Corporation of Ontario Limited.

The agreement, dated March 5, 1930, recognized that Taylor had been negotiating with various brewing companies for the purpose of acquiring options in outstanding shares in those companies and had acquired options to purchase controlling shares of British American Brewing Company Limited of Windsor and of Taylor & Bate Limited, a brewery in the Niagara Peninsula. These negotiations had been carried on by Taylor since October 15, 1929, and his expenses in relation to those successful dealings were recognized as part of the monies to be credited to him in the agreement. The value of his time was $3,750, together with travelling expenses of $500. The new company, which was to have an authorized capital stock of 250,000 preference shares and one million common shares without nominal or par value, was incorporated by Letters Patent dated March 8, 1930. Colonel P.B. Taylor was to be president. All family-held shares of Brading Breweries and Kuntz Brewery would be acquired by the new corporation in an exchange of shares. The English investors' money, in the equivalent amount of $545,460 (Canadian), would be put into the new company in exchange for preferred and common shares, providing it with the essential cash which, when combined with the other assets (Brading and Kuntz), would give the new brewing corporation a most attractive financial base.

A later two-year agreement between the Brewing Corporation of Ontario Limited and Jennison and Taylor allowed them to purchase from the company one common share at the price of one dollar each for each two preference shares sold by the corporation in order to raise capital. As to compensation, the two would be paid at the rate of one dollar for each ten preference shares and one dollar for each five common shares issued by the company in exchange for shares or securities of other brewing companies. Any profits accruing to Taylor or Jennison as a result of the transactions they would conduct for and on behalf of the Brewing Corporation would be divided equally between them, whether paid by shares or in cash. It was this agreement that later enabled Edward Taylor personally to gain operating control of Brewing Corporation of Ontario.

As soon as the Brewing Corporation was set up and the English money was in the treasury, the energetic, optimistic Edward Taylor plunged on with his plan to expand the Brading holdings. There was no way he could commit the Brading board of directors to any deal, so his plan of action was to acquire options to purchase and then go back to his board for its approval. During this period he approached several brewery owners after having done a thorough investigation of their sales volumes, cash flow capacity, and all the other factors that made them relevant to the Brading operation.

The Taylor & Bate firm, located in St. Catharines, had a capacity of over a million gallons a year, but was selling only one eighth of it. The firm was owned by E.T. Sandell, formerly a Toronto police sergeant who eventually put his savings into a retail store selling alcoholic beverages in pre-prohibition days. He opened more stores and eventually bought the Taylor & Bate firm which had been established in 1834. Sandell had paid $120,000 cash for that acquisition. With prohibition, the retail stores had long since disappeared, leaving Sandell with the restricted operation of his brewery. When Taylor approached him to negotiate an option for the purchase of the Taylor & Bate shares in exchange for shares of Brading, Sandell was interested but his wife was not, except on a cash basis. The economy had collapsed and Mrs. Sandell would only agree to an option which returned to the family the same amount of cash they had originally put in, $120,000, plus shares for the balance. She was prepared to go that far. With the option in his pocket, Taylor had no idea where he or the Brading firm would find the cash, but that was another part of his function, and with the appearance of Jennison he brought it off.

The other option exercised by the new Brewing Corporation of Ontario was that negotiated by Taylor for the British American Brewing Company Limited in Windsor. It had a one million gallon capacity and was selling about a third of that.

Jennison, Taylor's partner in the Brewing Corporation venture, became chairman of the board of the new company, but knowing little about the brewing industry, or finance, he was prepared to leave the initiatives and decisions to Taylor.

With the Brewing Corporation of Ontario well launched and four breweries under its control, Edward Taylor moved the fledgling company toward its next acquisition, a group of five breweries that had been brought together by K.S. "Dick" Barnes of the Montreal brokerage firm of Flood, Barnes & Company. In 1926, Barnes had started to accumulate breweries under the name of Canadian Brewing Corporation Limited. By 1930, his company operated the Dominion Brewery in Toronto, with a 1.5 million gallon capacity, and the Regal Brewery in Hamilton, which with a subsidiary, had double that capacity. The Barnes firm also had in

Hamilton another company called Grant Springs Brewery. Taylor was aware that Dominion was operating at about one-third its capacity and the others well below that. The other Canadian brewing operations were the Empire Brewery at Brandon and the Kiewel Brewing Company at St. Boniface, each with a capacity of about 250,000 gallons.

Control of Canadian Brewing Corporation Limited was part of the Taylor master plan for the Brewing Corporation of Ontario. In August of 1930, an offer was made to the shareholders of Canadian Brewing Corporation for an exchange of shares. The bid was successful. By the end of October, the Brewing Corporation had acquired control of Canadian Brewing, and Taylor had acquired a new friend, adviser and sometimes partner in Dick Barnes who joined the board of the Brewing Corporation.

But that was not the end of the fortunes and plans of Edward Taylor in this incredible year, 1930. He was now in full stride. Now Taylor set his acquisition sights on Carling Breweries Limited of London, which had a 3.5 million gallon brewery, but was operating at only 20 per cent of its capacity. Carling's had been originated in 1840 by Sir John Carling and had been a successful operation from the beginning. In the 1920s it had expanded and modernized its plant, which was serving the export market, and had even entered the Quebec market, opening a bottling plant in Montreal. But, like many other breweries, it had been badly hit both by the federal government's ban on beer exports to the United States and by the 1929 stock market collapse. As a result of the severe depression, the three owners of the shares in Carling's had had to pledge their shares to the Dominion Bank as collateral for money advanced to the company to allow it to continue in operation. By the late fall of 1930, the partners retained only 16,-000 shares, while the bank held 60,000. Taylor and Jennison went after the bank's holdings.

Taylor assessed the market value of the shares at about $2, and was prepared and made an offer to the bank using that figure. However, the bank refused to sell. It had a going concern on its hands, management was in place, and it could take its chances on a possible turn-around which would eventually get them out without a loss. The Dominion Bank gave the Brewing Corporation a "take it or leave it" counter offer of $10 per share. Taylor quickly agreed to that price, if the bank would take another kind of paper instead of shares in Brewing Corporation. The bank bought Taylor's proposal and agreed to accept $600,000 of Brewing Corporation's unsecured notes, paying 5 per cent and repayable at $100,000 a year. As part of the deal, the Dominion were given the right to appoint a director to represent their interests so long as the loan was outstanding. Their nominee was a brilliant young lawyer, Wallace McCutcheon, who eventually became a partner of Taylor's, and one of the most significant Canadians of his time. Taylor cleaned up the Carling situation settling with the three original owners for cash for their shares and by trading shares with the remaining stockholders. At year's end, approximately 92 per cent of Carling's was owned by the Brewing Corporation, which by that time had almost 100 per cent ownership of all the brewing companies of which it had acquired control in that hectic, explosive year.

Taylor then decided that it was time to make the name of the corporation much more descriptive of his true objectives. Instructions were given to lawyer Henry Borden, who now acted for both McLeod, Young, Weir and Taylor and Jennison's holding company, that the name be changed to Brewing Corporation of Canada Limited. On October 9, 1930, that became the new name.*

During that pivotal year in the life of E.P. Taylor, the underwriting business came to a grinding halt as the full effect of the Depression took hold. Taylor's time and efforts, however, were now almost totally consumed by the accelerating merger and acquisition program of the Brewing Corporation in which both Taylor and Jennison were now entitled to thousands of common shares as payment for their efforts. In September, Taylor negotiated a leave of absence from the firm, a situation he claims is still outstanding. As part of the leave-of-absence agreement, he gave back to the partners his shares in the firm, and in turn, McLeod, Young, Weir gave him the shares of Brewing Corporation of Ontario that he had earned under his and Jennison's agreement with the company they had formed and which Taylor had used as part payment for his McLeod, Young, Weir shares. While the securities firm had accepted them at a 50 cent per share value, by the time Taylor got them back, they had been knocked down to 12½ cents. This was the beginning of E.P. Taylor's accumulation of Canadian Brewer-

---

*The name was changed to Canadian Breweries Limited by Letters Patent dated April 21, 1937.

ies Limited stock which continued until he formed Argus Corporation in 1946 and put into that corporation all of his holdings of Canadian Breweries.

Edward Taylor was now working seven days a week. But for him work was, and still is, a pleasure not a task. Rather than be left at home while Edward travelled around the province visiting breweries, contacting prospective sellers of shares, negotiating and making deals, Winnie often accompanied him. As she saw it, her role was to help him in every way possible, even though she found it difficult spending time by herself in small hotels and eating meals alone while her husband was negotiating deals for the Brewing Corporation. But when Louise was born in 1930,* Winnie's ability to travel with her husband was severely curtailed. She never complained though, since she knew Edward was doing what he wanted to do and doing it successfully.

Toward the end of 1930 the newly enlarged family sold their 18 Douglas Drive residence, which they had acquired a little more than a year earlier, and moved to a large sandstone house on the north side of Lawrence Avenue, just west of Bayview. This was a Sifton family house in which the Taylors stayed for three years until their new home was built on Bayview Avenue, about half a mile north. The Lawrence Avenue house had a stable, and while there, E.P. Taylor purchased his first horse and again took up riding, having given it up when he left the Princess Louise Dragoon Guards some three years earlier. At the beginning of the thirties, virtually the entire area around Bayview and Lawrence was farm country, in which "I was able to hack freely and I occasionally followed the Eglinton Hunt hounds." Ever since then Taylor has maintained his interest in riding.

As the final 1930 acquisition piece, Carling's, fell into place, the major problems that confronted Edward Taylor were centralization, standardization, and, above all, management. It was one thing to negotiate and purchase a bag of brewing companies and to become overnight one of the major forces in the brewing industry in Canada. It was quite another to run them all profitably. Taylor was and is a promoter and an entrepreneur. What he needed then, and has always required during his business career, were people who could run the day-to-day operations and look after the orga-

*Taylor's first child Judith was born in November 1928.

nization and management–things he is not inclined to do.

Taylor soon found the management help he desperately needed. He persuaded his cousin and fellow Brading director, Allen Snowdon, then a successful Ottawa lawyer, to leave his practice to manage the Dominion Brewery operation. It was a difficult decision for Snowdon and his family to make, but the Depression had cut heavily into his practice and the offer from his cousin and close friend could not be refused. Snowdon's stable presence in Toronto was to be of enormous value to Taylor over the coming years, particularly when he needed a confidential friend, wise in the world of business, to listen to his problems and give him sound advice.

The takeover of the Canadian Brewing Corporation also brought with it some much-needed executive talent. Taylor was able to convince Dick Barnes, from whom he had bought control, to leave his stock brokerage firm in Montreal and become vice-president and chairman of the executive committee of the Brewing Corporation. Barnes, a highly respected man in financial circles and a few years older than Taylor, brought with him considerable prestige which did much to enhance the stature of the new brewing firm. In addition, three older and experienced members of the board of Canadian Brewing Corporation moved to the Brewing Corporation directorate, also bringing experience and stature with them. One of these was Duncan McDougald, the father of J.A. "Bud" McDougald, who was to be E.P. Taylor's partner immediately after the Second World War in the firm of Taylor, McDougald & Company, and who in 1955 became a "partner" in Argus Corporation Limited, which Taylor formed in 1945. E.P. Taylor had a high regard for Duncan McDougald, a successful Toronto investment dealer to whom Taylor turned for advice, counsel, and friendship through the years until McDougald's death in 1939.

With the Carling deal in hand, Jennison and Taylor thought it would be wise for Taylor to go to England to make a full report to their London backers, who had yet to meet him. Taylor was most anxious to explain to them the details of the acquisitions made during the year and his plans for the future. He sought more than their approval; he hoped to gain their confidence and to meet other people who might be sources of additional money. Looking ahead, he could see that money would be required not only for the acquisitions he had in mind, but also to cover the operating losses of the Brewing Corporation. The breweries were losing money and would continue to do so. At this point Taylor had no idea when they would turn the profit corner, but he was confident that they would do so not too far down the road. In the meantime, he had payrolls to meet and an enormous need for cash, a commodity impossible to find in an economically crushed Canada.

In London he met L.E. Stride, managing director of the Industrial General Trust Company, and A.C. Whitmee, who held the same position with Atlas Investment Trust Company. These two men had jointly made the decision to pool funds and invest them in the Canadian brewing industry. Being most anxious to maintain their continued involvement and increasing investment, Taylor convinced Stride and Whitmee to form an advisory committee to counsel him and Jennison on the future activities of the Brewing Corporation. They agreed and so the London Committee was established. Taylor and Jennison were to report to it regularly in writing and frequently in person. To do this Taylor was to make the trip across the Atlantic once a year, which he did until the Second World War began. It was this English connection, along with the funds from other British investors whom Taylor was to find, that allowed the fledgling Brewing Corporation of Canada to survive more than one financial crisis during that decade.

On all counts, Taylor's trip to London was a success. He impressed those he met with his genial personality and impressive knowledge of his field. His visit laid the foundations for a lasting and profitable association with the London Committee. Now the fight was to keep the master plan going.

But the battle had only begun. Keeping it all together and operating would take all of young Taylor's imagination, persuasiveness, salesmanship, and judgement—qualities he had inherited from Charles Magee. As the year 1930 ended, the difficulties facing the optimist Edward Plunket Taylor were staggering. But then, so were the opportunities for growth and expansion of the Brewing Corporation of Canada Limited, not yet one year old, but already a major force in the Canadian brewing industry.

Taylor was now able to concentrate fully on the implementation of his grand scheme, a key part of which was the intended closure of the redundant breweries. In a memorandum to the London Committee in early 1931, Taylor commented on the underlying principle of his plan. "The scattered plant operation of your corporation [Brewing Corporation of Canada Limited] cannot result in the same degree of profit as if the total volume could be concentrated in a few plants." Such a concentration was his goal, but the crippled economy and depressed market conditions thwarted him (by 1934 only three had been shut down with a total capacity reduction of over 60,000 barrels; by 1939 a further 370,000 barrels had been closed). It was clear to Taylor that in the bad times in which he was operating, he would have to time his closeouts carefully. In the same memorandum he said the goal was "to concentrate in the fewest number of plants the volume of business now enjoyed by too great a number of plants. On the other hand, it is not possible to accomplish this result until the corporation has such a control over its market that it can be sure that the closing of any specific plant will not mean a reduction of its total volume."

During 1931 Taylor acquired, again by an exchange of shares, the Budweiser Brewing Company of Canada, whose plant at Belleville, Ontario, was operating at one-sixth of its half million gallon capacity.

By now the Brewing Corporation of Canada was the largest beer company in Ontario, but it was still making a loss. Undaunted and confident of financial support from England, Taylor decided to proceed with the acquisition of Cosgrave Export Brewing Company. With great care, he drafted a letter to J.F. Cosgrave, the president and principal shareholder of the target brewery, attempting to persuade him to sell. It was a classic Taylor letter, thoroughly researched, precisely worded and edited, detailed, and persuasive. To give it an added touch of weight, it was signed by both Taylor and Jennison. The thesis was that by concentrating production into fewer plants, there could be an increase in profits due to economies of operation, a better product and more uniform quality at lower cost, economies in purchasing, better personnel, economies in transportation, lower per unit overhead costs, all by-products at more favourable prices. In such a consolidated, centralized brewing organization the shareholders would not be dependent on sales in only one province; nor would they face the possibility of a suspension of a licence by the Liquor Control Board of Ontario, or the consequences of accidental production of an unsuitable product. They would gain better management, a better market for brewery stock, and greater influence over liquor legislation.

Having recited all of the benefits, Taylor left the heavy pressure and the crunch to the last paragraph. One can only speculate on the reaction of J.F. Cosgrave when he read this message:

> The cost of production and financial position of Brewing Corporation of Canada Limited are now such that it could meet a price war at any time and outlive practically all but a very few competitors. It could afford to sell its products at a price for a year which would either cause the failure or seriously cripple all but a very few of its competitors in the province of Ontario. We believe that the time has now come when it will be in your best interests to seriously consider a proposal involving the exchange of the shares of your company for preferred and common shares of our company on an equitable basis.

E.P. Taylor has always been very good at laying things on the line. There was no mistake about what he was saying to Cosgrave. Taylor had celebrated his thirtieth birthday five days before signing this strong letter. Ten or twenty years later, with a cloak of more experience and maturity around him, he would have opened negotiations not by a letter but by a face-to-face meeting in the office of the man whose interests he wished to acquire. But back in 1931, the newcomer, E.P. Taylor, might have had a difficult time getting in the door.

The letter failed to move Cosgrave. He would not negotiate in spite of the implied threats. Taylor therefore arranged for the Brewing Corporation to begin buying Cosgrave's stock on the open market. It was not, however, until 1934 that Taylor was able to increase his holdings from 35 per cent at the beginning of that year to 80 per cent by the end.

When Taylor had taken his leave of absence from the McLeod, Young, Weir firm, he rented a small, unpretentious furnished office in the Trust and Guaranty Building on Bay Street and hired a secretary. From this isolated but central location he concentrated on the management and administrative problems created by the sudden bringing together of a large number of operating plants under one corporate umbrella, particularly the sorting out of people who were caught in this rapid change. There were decisions to be made about marketing and brands, transportation, new equipment, advertising, and financing. There had to be dealings with the provincial government for improved legislation and regulations concerning competition. On top of this there was constant study and research into the companies that were part of his master acquisition plan. The method and timing of the approach to each had to be precisely planned. All this Taylor did by himself, seeking advice when he thought he needed it from people he knew and trusted and who were experts in their particular fields–lawyers, such as Henry Borden; chartered accountants in the ubiquitous Clarkson, Gordon, Dilworth, Guilfoyle, and Nash firm, as it then was called; advertising and marketing people from McKim Advertising, and others.

While Jennison was chairman of the Brewing Corporation and participated in much of the decision-making, the initiatives in all aspects of the operation of the new company were clearly Taylor's, and had been from the beginning. Jennison had brought cash and the London connection to the new enterprise, while Taylor had brought Brading, Kuntz, the master plan, a compulsion to work and to achieve, and his financial expertise which included a now legendary ability to read and interpret a financial statement. But while he brought both Brading and Kuntz to the Brewing Corporation organization, Taylor had no personal ownership or control in either one.

When he and Winnie left Ottawa in 1928, they had only the money Edward had been able to save during his business years in Ottawa. Neither of them had been left any family inheritance to cushion them for the future. They were on their own. Whatever wealth they accumulated in the future stemmed solely from Edward's remarkable ability to conceive of entrepreneurial ideas and then put them into practice by convincing others of their soundness and practicality. Contrary to myth, Edward Plunket Taylor was not born with a silver spoon in his mouth. Rather it was a silver tongue.

By the beginning of 1931, Taylor's principal asset was his shareholdings in Brewing Corporation of Canada, earned under the key agreement between him and Jennison on the one hand and the Brewing Corporation on the other, under which they were paid in shares for their work in bringing in new acquisitions. This was paper wealth only, highly vulnerable to total collapse if the company could not pay its bills or if some monetary crisis occurred that Taylor could not overcome.

Taylor had the proceeds from the sale of his Douglas Drive house. He had cash and was comfortable with a reasonable income flowing in from the Brewing Corporation. But his whole world would collapse if the Brewing Corporation of Canada, which was still not making money, were to fail. On the other hand, if it succeeded in the long run and the value of its common shares (which had dipped to a low of 12½ cents) were to rise, Taylor's fortunes would go up with them.

Late in 1931, Clark Jennison died suddenly in Montreal. Now Taylor was strictly on his own. As part of the package of agreements between Jennison and Taylor which had been prepared by the Fraser and Beatty firm, there was a contract that provided that, on the death of one of the two, the survivor would purchase the shares of Brewing Corporation from the estate of the deceased. Taylor acted on this obligation and took over Jennison's holdings in the company. E.P. Taylor now effectively owned the controlling shares of Brewing Corporation of Canada Limited, which in the short space of a year and a half had become one of the largest brewing firms in Ontario.

The problems confronting Taylor as he struggled to keep the Brewing Corporation afloat from his tiny Bay Street headquarters were almost overwhelming. One of his major concerns was a lack of competent managers for his breweries. He had already talked his cousin, Allen Snowdon, into the move from Ottawa to Toronto to manage Dominion Brewery. From the McKim Advertising Agency he hired a young man by the name of James Smith-Ross to handle the sales manager's job. Smith-Ross's only experience in the beer industry was a study he had made of taste preference for beer in Ontario, a contract Taylor had given to the agency. He approached his new job unencumbered by the old-style methods of selling beer. Those included rebates to retailers, extensive price cutting, high sales promotion expenditures, and lavish "entertainment." There were many old-time salesmen still associated with the breweries in the Brewing Corporation organization. It was difficult to break their traditional way of dealing with hotel owners and other purchasers. But under Taylor, Smith-Ross and his assistant, Ian R. Dowie, restructured the entire sales approach and organization but not without causing a lot of resentment and resistance from the old hands, many of whom were let go in the process.

The ruthless competition practices in the industry were so intense and destructive that many of the larger breweries came together for discussions during 1931 to try to work out arrangements among themselves concerning practices which they would or would not engage in. Taylor reported to the London Committee in October saying, "We have succeeded in bringing together the majority of the responsible breweries into an agreement regarding undesirable and expensive sales practices, which should be of great value to the industry in general. . . . Not only is the average volume per company ridiculously small, but the very keen competition has resulted in extraordinarily high sales promotion expenses; and furthermore, with so many companies engaged in the business, there is always bound to be a considerable number that have no respect for the law, or else have to cheat in order to remain in existence." Of course, at that time, there was no Combines Law in existence in Canada. That situation would change in later years, and Taylor would find himself squarely in the middle of a Combines prosecution against Canadian Breweries Limited.

In 1932, Taylor conserved his meagre financial resources. Although he purchased twenty acres of farmland in the Bayview Avenue and York Mills Road area of the Township of North York that year, he only put $1,000 down "and the balance when they could catch me," and it was not until 1936 that he could afford to build on the land. The financial status of E.P. Taylor was slim, indeed. He had all his eggs in one basket and needed all his limited capital and resources to sustain both his family and his precarious non-profit invention, the Brewing Corporation of Canada.

During 1932, Taylor undertook no acquisitions or mergers in the Brewing Corporation. The death of Jennison, the shocking depth of the Depression, the continuing loss being made by the Brewing Corporation, and a reduction in its sales volume, caused Taylor to mark time. Furthermore, the London Committee had indicated its preference that with the depressed economic conditions as they existed in the United States and in Europe, it would be best to hold the line and consolidate. E.P. Taylor had no choice but to agree. "The very tough time was between 1930 and 1935. We had three very formidable big companies against us. They regarded us as upstarts. Naturally they did everything they could–it was good business on their part–to try to keep us from succeeding. By one method or another we managed to survive those years. Any chartered accountant or security analyst would probably say that we were insolvent and wouldn't have given us any hope for survival.

The shares of the company dropped to almost a dime each at one point. Nobody wanted them. And we had very limited sources of credit." "Limited" is an understatement.

Taylor had been dealing with a bank, which shall remain nameless, since the formation of the Brewing Corporation. Taylor needed a line of credit of $800,000 to carry the company over the winter of 1932/33. "In the brewing business, you do about 40 per cent of your business in the winter months and 60 per cent in the summer months. And we had yet to go through the winter." He had had a similar line of credit with the bank during the previous winter but he had brought Brewing Corporation's loan down to $200,000 when he approached them for the renewed position. The bank was well secured. On the other hand, the Brewing Corporation and its subsidiaries were continuing to make a loss.

The bank decided against Taylor and the Brewing Corporation. Not only was the requested line of credit refused, the bank also demanded payment of the entire indebtedness up to that point. To make that kind of call was an extremely important decision for any Canadian bank to make against a brewery with such an important part and place in the crippled economy. It was the kind of banking decision which would have to be taken by head office.

But Taylor was prepared. Having recognized at the beginning of the renegotiation of the needed line of credit a difficult attitude on the part of the bank, Taylor sensed that he was in trouble. He made a quick trip to London to talk with the London Committee and to seek assistance from the Industrial and General Trust, one of the biggest investment trusts in England. "I got to know the managing director very well and we became very friendly. He was a strange character called Major MacDonald who had a financial firm and an office in Canada House. One of his bankers was Lord Queenborough." Lord Queenborough, with the London Committee, agreed to put up the money Taylor so desperately needed in order to meet the bank's call if it was to be made. "They made a lot of money out of what they had invested, so I was pleased."

Taylor was entitled to be more than pleased when the unwitting bank, totally underestimating the ingenuity and shrewdness of this young upstart, pulled what they thought was the rug out from under him. This tactic produced not a pratfall but a horselaugh from a confident E.P. Taylor, who with great relish paid off the bank and moved the Brewing Corporation's accounts, and his own, to another bank which received him and his business with open arms.

That was the only time any bank has ever made a call on E.P. Taylor, or on any of the corporations in which he has had an interest.

In 1933, with Canada's economy staggering under the weight of the continuing Depression, and unemployment at 19 per cent, the brewing industry slipped from its 1930 production of 25 per cent of its capacity to only 16 per cent. By 1934, economic conditions were the worst ever, with beer sales lower than in any year since the Brewing Corporation of Canada was organized. No profit was made in either 1933 or 1934, making it four years in a row that a loss was suffered. At one point, payday for the company's staff was shifted from the 1st and 15th of the month to the 3rd and 18th in order to allow time for the receipts from the sole public retailer of beer in Ontario, the Brewers' Warehousing Company, to arrive and be deposited in the bank before the pay cheques were handed out. The treasurer, J. Davidson, was frequently forced to send out large cheques in payment for supplies, knowing that only if sufficient money came in within a few days would the bank not return them marked "not sufficient funds."

In the middle of the desperation of 1933, E.P. Taylor received a telephone call from a man who identified himself as James A. Bohannon of Cleveland. He told Taylor that he represented a financial group planning to enter the brewing field as soon as prohibition ended in the United States. He wanted to visit Taylor in Toronto to discuss the possibility of securing the right to brew and sell Carling beer in the United States. He had tasted this Canadian beer and knew it to be a quality product. The interests represented by Bohannon were his own and that of the firm he headed at that time, Peerless automobile company, which Taylor later discovered was in a healthy financial position. There was the scent of a windfall which Taylor, hard pressed for funds, decided to exploit to the fullest. He agreed to meet Bohannon.

Thus began a fifteen year association between the two men which, from Taylor's point of view, would have to be called disastrous in the end result.

The Peerless firm had been manufacturing luxury cars since the First World War. With the stock market crash of 1929, and the competition of low-priced production line cars, however, Bohannon decided to take his company out of automobile production. Prohibition in the United States, having lasted for a generation, was coming to an end, and Bohannon believed there would soon be a vast new market for beer.

At the outset Taylor wanted to impress Bohannon. He secured an impressive suite of rooms at Toronto's new Royal York Hotel. Bohannon came in from Cleveland with an entourage of colleagues and advisers. Taylor quickly sized him up as a big man in every sense of the word.

The negotiations at the Royal York between Taylor and this much older, overbearing man became very difficult for Taylor. Several times he was tempted to tell Bohannon to take his proposition elsewhere. But that wasn't Taylor's nature then, nor is it now. He saw the possibility of expansion for his floundering Brewing Corporation, so he quietly swallowed his resentment, gave his chuckling deep laugh, and went on with the negotiations. George Black, Jr., later said of E.P. Taylor, "He would negotiate with anybody. Not that I mean this in a demeaning sense or a pejorative sense, but it was just that he takes people as he finds them and if he's negotiating, he sort of feels his way through until some agreement or disagreement is arrived at. But Eddie doesn't give a damn what a fellow is like, what his character is like, what his appearance is like, what his manner is like. He's negotiated with so many people–many were quite repulsive, but none in my opinion was as repulsive as Bohannon."

The negotiations, difficult as they were, ended with an agreement. The Peerless Motorcar Corporation became Peerless Corporation and issued 25,000 shares of its stock to Taylor's Brewing Corporation in exchange for the right to use the brand name, trademarks, and formula of Carling in the United States. The agreement also provided for the conversion of Bohannon's Cleveland plant into a brewery. Taylor assigned his top people to advise Peerless: T.G. Ferguson on engineering problems, F.N. Ward on the brewing process, and W.C. Butler in connection with administrative, secretarial, and insurance problems. Early in 1934 the first bottle came off the line bearing the Carling Red Cap label. Before the end of that year the plant was at its full capacity of 200,000 barrels.

In the early thirties one of E.P. Taylor's major objectives was to change the law that limited the sale of beer. At that time beer could not be sold by the glass or bottle in public places in Ontario. Bootlegging was still prevalent and "blind pigs" flourished in large numbers.

Taylor and his brewing colleagues set out to rectify that situation. "It was really ridiculous because in every civilized country in the world people didn't have to drink in their homes. They could drink in public places. The problem was to convince the Ontario government." An election was coming up in 1934. George S. Henry was premier of Ontario in a Tory government. But a strong leader, Mitchell Hepburn, had emerged as leader of the Liberal Party in Ontario.

Taylor read in one of the Toronto newspapers that a man called Home Smith had made a speech in which he said he had come to the conclusion that the public was ready for a modification of the law to permit drinking beer in public places. Home Smith was the organizer of the Tory Party in Ontario and was the developer of the Old Mill area of Toronto. His responsibility was to get Henry and the Tory Party re-elected. After Taylor read the speech he arranged a meeting with Home Smith. Taylor told him that it was very important for the brewing industry and, in fact, in the interest of temperance, to have a freer sale of beer. Smith replied, "Well, any election needs money and needs support. I think we should revive the Moderation League, beer being a drink of moderation." The Moderation League had been active in the old days of local option, but had been dormant during the thirties. Taylor found the charter of the Moderation League and brought the organization back to life. Colonel Richard Greer, the head of an important legal firm in Toronto, was made the president, and Harry Pritchard, the former sales manager of the Ford Motorcar Company, became the organizer. The League sent speakers to meetings, preaching the message that it was better for the people to have access to a drink of moderation–beer–than to be in the position of only being able to buy liquor publicly. The message was "beer for moderation."

Home Smith convinced George Henry that liberalization of liquor laws would be in the interest of the people of Ontario and would appeal to the voters. Henry reluctantly accepted Smith's advice and the program became part of the Conservative platform. Taylor thought that there was some possibility that he could persuade Hepburn, the newly elected leader of the Liberal Party in Ontario, to make amendment of the liquor control act a non-political issue by promising the electorate that if his party were elected he would do the same thing. Home Smith encouraged Taylor to meet with Hepburn, which he did.

Taylor then approached Percy Parker, the Liberal organizer for the province, who arranged a meeting with Hepburn. Hepburn, a slim, round-faced man of thirty-seven, and a former onion farmer, was an able speaker on the hustings. He was given to wearing a stiff high collar and high laced boots. "Mr. Hepburn impressed me as being a very bright young man. He listened to me and then he said, 'Well, if they think they're going to inject this question into the campaign, my answer will be that we agree with the proposed amendment.' I went back and told Mr. Home Smith that I had seen Mr. Hepburn, but Home Smith was very sceptical of the Liberal Party rescinding their traditional attitude regarding the sale of alcoholic beverages."

His scepticism was soon put to the test. Just before the Ontario Legislature was dissolved for the June 1934 election, the Conservative government introduced an amendment to the Liquor Control Act which, among other things, would allow beer to be sold by the glass in public places on a local option basis. Premier Henry said, however, that the implementation of the amendment, that is the passing of regulations by the lieutenant governor-in-council (the Cabinet), would not take place until after the election itself. The debate in the Legislature raged for some time. Several prominent Liberal members, all staunch, anti-liquor people, opposed the amendment, notwithstanding their party leader's support for it. When the vote was taken it was apparent that Home Smith's scepticism had been wrongly founded and that the pervasive propaganda of the Moderation League had persuaded the people of the province and their elected representatives in the Ontario Legislative Assembly. The Conservative proposal for beer sales by the glass was passed with a great majority, with only nine Liberals opposing it. Beer was no longer an election issue.

At the polls, the Henry government was given a crushing defeat with the Liberals taking 66 seats to the Conservatives' 16.

After being elected, Hepburn lived up to his commitment to implement the amendments to the Liquor Control Act by preparing and having passed by Order in Council the regulations governing the issuance of licences to hotels and other places where beer could be sold. These regulations were approved by the Cabinet just before the completion of the brief first session of the Legislature under Hepburn. That done, Hepburn and some cronies took off for Florida for an out-of-Ontario vacation even though it was summer.

It was soon discovered, however, that there were defects in the regulations: they had not been promulgated by being printed in the *Ontario Gazette*, the official weekly publication of the Ontario government. Before beverage room and other licences could be issued, this defect had to be cured, but the only man who could give the instruction was the new premier, and he was in Florida on vacation. Furthermore, the temperance prohibitionists, under the leadership of Dr. Mutchmor, were hard at work organizing petitions to the government asking Premier Hepburn to rescind the regulations.

For Taylor, this was a crisis. He went back to Percy Parker. Mr. Parker suggested that the two of them should go down and see Mr. Hepburn and point out the problem to him. "Mr. Parker asked if the Moderation League would pay his expenses and I said yes. But as far as a fee was concerned, I said it was a case of no cure, no pay." They took the train down and were welcomed by the new premier and his friends who were having a fine time and did not want to discuss business on a holiday. All he wanted the new arrivals to do was to attend the various parties. This went on for about a week. Finally, a copy of the old Toronto *Globe* appeared and on the front page there was one paragraph that set out succinctly the flaw in the regulations. Taylor found Hepburn on the beach, surrounded by some friends. "I said, 'This is our last chance, Percy. Take this front page of the *Globe* down, underline in crayon, and ask him, please, as we have to go back to Toronto, just to read this one paragraph.' And so Mr. Parker pushed it under his nose and Mr. Hepburn read it. He said, 'Is that all you want me to do? Of course I'll do it. The minute I get home, I'll do it.' Which he did. The result was that the new conditions of the sale of beer came into operation in Ontario shortly thereafter."

The O'Keefe Brewing Company Limited was one of Taylor's last major targets in the 1930s, although other acquisitions were made, such as Welland Brewery, which he shut down after its purchase, and Cosgrave's, which was to come under his control before the end of 1934.

O'Keefe was the main objective, with its big Toronto plant,

capacity, and market. Knowing that he was making good progress in lobbying for changes in Ontario legislation, Taylor decided to move before new legislation drove up the asking price for the O'Keefe shares. He had to act quickly. His first approach in 1931 to a group of private investors who then controlled O'Keefe had been rejected. By 1934 the scene had changed. Gordon F. Perry, in his capacity as trustee for certain estates, controlled a holding company which, in turn, had effective control of the O'Keefe Brewing Company. Perry was prepared to negotiate, but made it clear that he could not accept shares in the Brewing Corporation. Taylor calculated that if he could obtain Perry's shares for cash, he would gain actual control of the company. As negotiations proceeded, the minority shareholders advised E.P. Taylor that if he was going to buy the Perry shares for cash, he would have to buy theirs for cash as well.

To buy out the shares that Perry represented would cost about $800,000, which Taylor thought he could probably get from Stride and Whitmee, the London Committee. But to buy out the entire stock of O'Keefe would require a total of $2,074,000 on the barrel head. Where could Taylor find this kind of money? Brewing Corporation, even though it had been in operation for three years, had not yet produced a profit and was living from hand to mouth. And he was certain he could not get that kind of funding from the London Committee. Where to turn? "In the course of my travels, I had met a chap called John Paul, a stockbroker in Glasgow. He was approximately my age. His business was W.J. Paul and Company, which he had inherited from his father. He controlled a lot of money and had a lot of very rich clients in Scotland." Paul and Taylor had struck it off very well. The Scotsman was fully up to date on the status of the Brewing Corporation and had a great confidence in his Canadian contemporary. Taylor had nothing to lose. He put in a long-distance telephone call to John Paul in Glasgow and told him the story from top to bottom. When Taylor had laid out his proposition, Paul's response was, "We'll do it." He then proceeded to raise a substantial part of the required money in Scotland. Paul's contribution, which came through Stride and Whitmee, and a further amount from Brewing Corporation's Canadian bankers were enough to make up the required purchase price. On May 1, 1934, the deal was completed, just in advance of the passing of the Liquor Control Act amendments allowing beer

71

to be sold in glasses and bottles in public places.

E.P. Taylor, the thirty-three-year-old "boy wonder," as he was being described in those days, had done it again—in the nick of time. The enormity of his purchase of O'Keefe Brewery was concrete evidence to everyone—Bay Street, the brewing industry, the government, and the people at large throughout Canada—that E.P.'s empire was now a strong force in the national community. He was truly one of Canada's most successful entrepreneurs, youthful and self-made. By any measure he was a success.

Many of the brewing companies acquired by Taylor in the early thirties operated soft drink bottling plants which had served to provide the breweries with revenue during the prohibition days. O'Keefe and Kuntz were typical of these. "The soft drink companies were miserable firms. I bought a whole string of them and put them in a company called Consolidated Beverages. The idea was to get the soft drink plants out of the breweries." However, during 1934, Taylor heard that the Canadian Orange Crush company was in difficulty. The company itself was not in trouble, but the shares had gone to nothing and the controlling people in the business had pledged their shares to their bank and the bank wanted to sell them. "So I bought these shares through Consolidated Beverages, which at one stage was called O'Keefe Beverages and later Orange Crush."

The two men who owned Canadian Orange Crush who had pledged their shares to the bank were the Lindsay brothers. "It was their stock I bought and I gave them jobs." The Canadian Orange Crush had the franchise for all of Canada and had many franchised bottlers. The Orange Crush shares Taylor bought for $40,000 had sold in the bull market of 1929 for several million dollars.

When he bought the Orange Crush company, Taylor wasn't interested in getting into the restaurant business, but as it happened, Orange Crush controlled the Honey Dew restaurants. "I wasn't interested in the Honey Dew Company at all. I knew that the Honey Dew Company had been very successful but was not in good order at that time." Its shares stood on the books of Orange Crush at one dollar, so Taylor wasn't very interested in what that one dollar was worth. All he wanted to be sure of from the lawyers and accountants who were advising him was that there weren't any undisclosed guarantees or liabilities. "Well, the first thing I knew, just shortly after buying the Honey Dew company, I was served with a writ by Mr. Kaufman of the Kaufman Rubber Company of Kitchener who was a substantial preferred shareholder in Honey Dew. Kaufman said that the common shares of Honey Dew were worthless, that they had been issued illegally. Kaufman had the view that no par value shares were the work of the devil. So we went to court and we won." When Taylor was served with the Kaufman writ, he knew there was a directors' meeting of Honey Dew to be held at about the same time in the broker, Jim Gardiner's office in the next building. "So I just walked over and I opened the door and said, 'Gentlemen, I am here. One of your shareholders is suing me!' " At that meeting, the board, which immediately elected Taylor to be a director, said, " 'Well now, you are the largest shareholder, you control the company. You'd better be president.' So when I left the room, I was president and had a restaurant chain on my hands. We eventually expanded the Honey Dew Company and did very well on it."

In fact, Taylor became so involved in the Honey Dew business that he wound up being one of only three people privy to the original Honey Dew formula. "Only three people were to know the secret formula to make Honey Dew; apart from the basic ingredients of orange juice and water there were certain other ingredients. So this thing was kept in a vault and only three of us, two before that and three with me, knew the formula. Once a month I had to go to a secret place and I physically mixed, with Howard Walker, the general manager of Honey Dew, and one of the Lindsay brothers, the secret ingredients for Honey Dew. That was the concentrated part of it."

Somehow the image of a tall, well-built, thirty-three-year-old Taylor in a locked, secret room, meticulously measuring, pouring, and mixing the magical, mysterious orange liquids, as required by the precious Honey Dew formula, defies imagination. But then, so do many of the things that Edward Plunket Taylor has done in his lifetime.

As a student of brewing operations, Taylor had gained full knowledge of the "tied house" system which is an ancient and integral part of the brewing industry in the United Kingdom where some brewers own hundreds of hotels which are "tied" by their ownership. Ownership gives the brewer a monopoly for his products. This was an attractive idea to Taylor, but there was some question as to whether it could be done under the liquor laws of Ontario. Taylor therefore caused the formation of a company called Mohawk Investments Limited, which was separate and apart from Brewing Corporation Limited. Mohawk acquired some Ontario hotels and operated them. There was, however, a major visible difficulty: Henry Borden, the lawyer who headed up Mohawk Investments Limited, was himself tied to Brewing Corporation as its lawyer. It was government policy that there should be no tied houses in Ontario. It was apparent to Premier Hepburn that the Taylor-Borden connection "tied" the Mohawk hotels to the Brewing Corporation. The Hepburn word went out through the Liquor Control Board, and the licences of the Mohawk hotels were suspended. The message was received loud and clear. The hotels were sold, and their licences restored. If nothing else, the exercise confirmed that what was morally and legally acceptable in the United Kingdom was not necessarily so in puritanical Ontario.

Through the purchases of securities and collateral, all held as collateral by a bank, Taylor bought control of the Riverside Brewing Corporation Limited and its plant near Windsor, promptly disposed of the assets, and wound up the company. As Taylor expected, nearly all the business that company did was picked up by Brewing Corporation's British American Company which was located in Windsor. The results shown in the following figures are a remarkable example of what Taylor was able to do by getting rid of a price-cutting, ruthless competitor in a local market. The operating results for British American Brewery are:

	Six months ending April 30, 1935	Six months ending April 30, 1936
Sales	$18,233.41	$254,164.30
Profit before Management fees	$12,725.86 (loss)	$ 28,450.74 (profit)

Not only was the Windsor operation turning around by the end of 1935, so was the overall performance of Brewing Corporation of Canada. At the annual meeting of the company in October, Taylor announced that, for the first time since its 1930 inception, the company had made a profit. While, at $168,000, it was not large, it was significant. It was a *profit* and not a loss. It meant that Taylor's brain-child could meet all its operating costs, including the cost of servicing the massive amounts of money he had borrowed, repay the principal when due, and have a surplus as well. "We had trouble with bankers having little confidence in us between 1930 and 1935, but as the record shows at that time, we turned the corner."

There were many other corners to be turned by Edward Taylor and the Brewing Corporation of Canada whose name he would change in two years to Canadian Breweries Limited.

Chapter V

The Grand Design – Part Two 1935-1938

Edward Plunket Taylor and the Brewing Corporation of Canada had indeed turned the first and most important corporate corner. They were now solvent and making a profit. Taylor could get on with the delayed consolidation and plant closing part of his grand design. In 1936 the Budweiser Brewing Company of Canada Limited, which he had acquired in 1931, was closed. The assets of the one remaining western plant, Kiewel Brewing of Winnipeg, were sold.

Taylor's next step was to bring together some of the major units operated by the company in order to concentrate production in low-cost, efficient plants in the most strategic market locations, and to reduce the number of brands produced. Consolidation plans got under way in September 1936. By the beginning of October, four plants had been merged into two. The Cosgrave's and Dominion Breweries were consolidated into one company under the name Cosgrave's Dominion Brewery Limited, the Dominion Brewery at Toronto being closed. The Taylor & Bate brewery and the Regal Brewery, both of which had been operating at a loss for some time, were merged under the name Taylor & Bate Limited at the Hamilton plant of Regal, and the Taylor & Bate plant at St. Catharines was closed. The operations of the Carling Brewery at London were transferred to the Kuntz plant at Waterloo, and the two companies were formed into a single organization known as Carling-Kuntz Breweries Limited. Taylor believed that these moves would result in improvement in the profit position of the company, a most desirable result since profit on invested capital was still far from satisfactory, despite an increased sales volume after the celebrated amendment to the Liquor Control Act in the summer of 1934.

On E.P. Taylor's major objective list, which he wrote at the opening of 1936, was the acquisition of the last of the three major breweries that had been on his initial grand design plan: Canada Bud Breweries Limited. Duncan McLaren, who had been the president of the company when Taylor made his initial approach in 1930, and who had introduced Taylor to Jennison, had sold out most of his shares in May 1934. Taylor had made a direct offer to the shareholders of Canada Bud, but this had failed because of McLaren's intervention as well as the unfavourable price comparison of the Brewing Corporation of Canada stock to the Bud shares on the date of the offer. So Taylor's 1936 tactic was different. He planned an end-run around McLaren. With its much-improved financial base, Brewing Corporation began to purchase 5,000 shares on the open market each month, Taylor calculating that by the end of the year he would have control. "Virtual control" was achieved by the end of 1936, but actual control was not in hand until December 1937.*

Now that his financial situation was more secure, Taylor was able to give his attention to the other things that were of importance to him. He and Winnie decided it was time to build a house on their twenty acres on Bayview Avenue. They had lived in a rented house long enough. Mind you, no one could say that the large, red stone Sifton residence they had used for some years was not adequately elegant. But it was time. Winnie and Edward Taylor's last child and only son, Charles, had been born in 1935.†

---

*In May of 1943, an offer was made to the minority shareholders and then the remaining shares in Canada Bud were bought, completing a deal that had taken E.P. Taylor more than a dozen years to complete. At that time the Canada Bud label and the label of its subsidiary, City Club Brewery, were discontinued. They were replaced by O'Keefe brands and the plant became part of O'Keefe.

†Charles, in his own time, was to become a man of quite an independent mind from that of his father and an outstanding Canadian journalist moving to various parts of the world as a foreign correspondent for the Toronto *Globe and Mail*. The editor of that distinguished publication maintains that "of all the assets of E.P. Taylor, the one which has been most productive and of which he can be most proud is his son, Charles." Now turned from journalism to the writing of important Canadian books, Charles lives in Toronto and participates, with his father, as an executive of Windfields Farm Limited in its horse breeding operations at Oshawa and in Maryland. The horse breeding enterprise of Windfields Farm, the most successful in the world, is the common interest of these two men who are not only father and son but, more important, close friends.

They could now afford to build the kind of house the two of them wanted: a large mansion, befitting both the rolling farm country setting and the position of prominence the Taylors had achieved, both in the Toronto and in the national community. It would be no ordinary house. It would be of cut grey stone, with conservative, traditional lines, long and of one piece rather than with wings. There would be a long, circular driveway arching back from Bayview Avenue to the house, which would be set perhaps 300 feet from the street line. There would be stables for four horses beside the garage, and just inside the north gate there would eventually (in 1945) be a small gatehouse, with a large living room with a fireplace, and a picture window looking east out across the farmlands. Edward planned to use the gatehouse as an office, a place where he could get away from the house to work or to meet with people, to do his research and study, to write his letters. He would still have his corporate office downtown.

Winnie and Edward gave their instructions to an architect, and in due course the plans were prepared to their satisfaction. Before the end of 1936 the building was emerging from the ground, and the following year the Taylor family, excited and pleased with the result, moved in.

The Taylors had to give a name to their new residence and the lands surrounding it. Edward himself couldn't come up with one, so he offered a prize of $100 to any of his friends who could come up with an appealing name. The contest had many entries, but none of them was acceptable to Taylor. Finally, on a bright, gusty fall day when the young couple were walking across their land, talking about it and the new buildings and the possibility of acquiring more land to the east and north, Winnie complained that in the fields it was rather windy. It was then that she came up with the name–Windfields. Edward agreed, and from that moment the land was known as Windfields, a name that has now become a legend in horseracing and horse breeding throughout the world. But Winnie Taylor claims she was never given her $100 prize.

In 1936 Taylor became involved in the first of what was to become a long series of charitable and fund-raising campaigns. "I was approached by the chairman of the Community Chest, the

Honourable R.C. Matthews, who had been a Cabinet minister in the Conservative government in the early thirties. He was a brother of the Honourable Albert Matthews, who was lieutenant governor, and he was the uncle of Major General Bruce Matthews. The money that had to be raised was a very small budget compared to what it is today. This was before the days of the United Fund." Taylor was asked to be chairman to succeed Matthews and he accepted. "I think that anybody who has any aptitude for raising money or serving on boards of directors of worthy institutions–no one is paid for that–should do it. My contribution has been mostly on the money-raising side rather than on the administrative. I was a very busy young man, doing more things than I wanted to do or had to do, and I'm still busy. But I was in the administrative side of business in the thirties. I had saved Canadian Breweries from bankruptcy, but it was a long, hard fight. In fact, I think that's the reason I was approached–that I had succeeded." And succeed again he did, conducting an over-the-top campaign for the Community Chest.

Also in 1936 E.P. Taylor bought his first racehorse. This was another turning point for him. He had been a patron of the racetracks in Montreal and in Toronto. So he decided to investigate the possibility of starting a small stable. "I went to my friend, Palmer Wright, who was the secretary of the Ontario Jockey Club, and I asked him if he knew of any trainer who could train for me. He said it so happened that a very good trainer had just severed his relationship with his former employer. His name was Bert Alexandra. I arranged a meeting with Bert Alexandra who said he'd train for me provided I would buy a few horses. In those days horses sold for a fraction of what they do today, and the quality of racing was at a pretty low ebb in Ontario. I told Alexandra I had $6,000. And he said, 'Well, I own one horse myself and I think there would be a conflict of interests unless you were to buy my horse.' " The name of the horse was Madfast, a Canadian-bred colt, and Alexandra's price was $1,500. "So I bought Madfast, my first racehorse."

Alexandra then went down to Pimlico Race Course in Maryland with $6,000–Canadian racing hadn't opened at that time–and bought an eight-year-old horse named Annimessic for $500.

Alexandra started Annimessic in his first claiming race on May

1 with a claiming price of $1,300.* No one claimed him and he won it. Taylor thus won his first race, and his first money–about $1,000. Alexandra now had $7,000 to spend. Before the next ten days had gone by, he had added about seven other horses, including one called Jack Patches, which he had claimed for $1,500, and a filly called Nandi, claimed for the same price. He brought the horses up to Toronto to the Woodbine meeting which was opening on May 24. "All of the horses that Alexandra bought for me won in the seven-day meeting at Woodbine–three of them won twice. I don't think I lost a race in the first ten that I started in so I had my money back and I had the ownership of eight horses at the end of a week of racing. And I said to myself, 'This is wonderful!' "

---

*The rule in racing is that you must start a horse at any meeting before you are eligible to claim. Say you set your claiming price at $1,500 or $2,000. When you enter a horse in that kind of race, anyone who has also started a horse at that race meet can claim the horse. At least fifteen minutes before the race, any person who claims puts his money in cash in the office and he enters a claim against your horse. If there is more than one person, then they draw lots. But if he is claimed, you've sold your horse, dead or alive.

Approximately 75 per cent of thoroughbred races are run under claiming conditions. These are at the lower end of the racing hierarchy. At the top are the stakes and allowance races, which account for the rest of the races run. *Stakes races* are for the elite and total only a little more than 2 per cent. Horses entered in them are of proven performance and quality. Owners must nominate horses and pay an entry fee well in advance. In the case of "futurities" this can be several years. In some, subsequent fees must be paid to maintain eligibility and in all a starting fee is required. Therefore, owners have a financial stake in these races and their money cannot be reclaimed. These fees, plus the added money, as much as $150,000 or more now put up by the racetrack operators, comprise a total purse which is divided among the first four finishers. *Allowance races* are for the next lower class of horse, although often stake horses also compete. There is no fee to enter or start. The animals eligible to start are determined by the conditions set by the track's racing secretary. *Claiming races* are established to classify the great bulk of horses whose ability is not sufficient to enable them to compete in stakes and allowance events. Instead of track officials arbitrarily making the classification of a horse, the onus is placed on the owner. It is his responsibility to place a value on his horse. The racing secretary of the track writes the conditions of the races for horses at the various claiming levels, from a few thousand dollars to as much as a hundred thousand or more. The owner then enters his horse at the value he thinks it is worth. Since any other registered owner can claim the horse at this price, the owner is faced with the possibility of losing his horse if he undervalues it. There are no fees for entering horses in claiming races and the purses usually are related to the claiming value. The higher the claiming price, the bigger the purse. There are many other costs, from training to stabling for thoroughbred owners, but only the stakes races have entrance fees, and any owner or trainer or breeder acquires much of his reputation by the number of stakes race winners he has. Broad as they are, these definitions apply only to thoroughbred racing in North America.

A final definition: a policeman is a horse bought for the purpose of running it in a meeting in order to qualify the owner as being eligible to claim. Annimessic was a policeman.

On September 26, 1936, Jack Patches won the Autumn Handicap for a delighted E.P. Taylor. This was his first stakes race win. Nandi was bred in the stables of Mrs. H.C. Phipps, a well-known breeder of stakes winners. Instead of racing her, Taylor decided to keep her as a brood mare. Her fourth foal, Windfields, was to be the first Taylor-bred horse to win a stakes race. Taylor's horses raced under the name of Cosgrave Stable. He had just acquired Cosgrave's Brewery in Toronto. Its president, Jimmy Cosgrave, had joined Taylor's Brewing Corporation as an executive. Needing someone to manage the new racing operation, and at the same time wanting to capitalize on the Cosgrave name, Taylor asked Cosgrave to take on the task. Cosgrave, a horseracing buff, agreed and so Cosgrave Stable began. Jim Cosgrave had no financial interest in the stable. Taylor's purpose in calling it Cosgrave Stable was simply to promote Cosgrave's Beer, the advertising of beer being forbidden in those days.

Taylor was to continue to race in the name and under the colours of Cosgrave for about ten years, during which time Cosgrave Stable horses were first 355 times and took second and third place in close to 500 races.

There is no indication that the former lieutenant in the Princess Louise Dragoon Guards who had such embarrassing difficulty in controlling his mounts had any horseracing grand design when he decided to take the plunge into owning and racing horses. It was the luck of being put in touch with a reliable, trustworthy expert, Bert Alexandra, and the exciting good fortune of running a string of winners starting with Annimessic in Taylor's very first race. It is said that success breeds success. The story of E.P. Taylor and his racehorses is such a breeding tale.

Expanding his stable, Taylor bought a yearling, Mona Bell, in 1936. She became his second stakes winner when, the next year, she took the Maple Leaf Stakes at Woodbine.

In the spring of 1938 Taylor entered the filly in the premier thoroughbred racing event in Canada, the King's Plate, which took place on May 21 at the Woodbine Racetrack. It is the oldest continuously run stakes race in North America. This was the first of many King's and Queen's Plate races a Taylor horse was to run in, although at the time it was still under the Cosgrave Stable colours.

For this seventy-ninth running of the Plate, the length of the race was 1 1/8 miles. It was the first year that the race was open only to three-year-olds. The field was impressive, the favourites were George Hendrie's Grande Dame and Willy Morrisey's great horse, Bunty Lawless. As the horses broke from the gate, Mona Bell took the lead and held it until the beginning of the final quarter mile when Bunty Lawless overtook her. At the finish, Grande Dame was moving up on her, but Mona Bell held and came in second.

It was a disappointment as much for Winnie as it was for Edward–horses were a common interest for the two of them and one which they shared with equal enthusiasm. It would have been marvellous to have won the first time out. On the other hand, Mona Bell had run a splendid race and the future looked good for her. But that future was short. A little over a year later, at Stamford Park in Niagara Falls, she fell and broke her leg and had to be destroyed. Taylor was shocked by this mishap, the kind of accident that he would see countless times over the years, but he has never become hardened to the anguish that comes with the injury or death of any of his horses.

"Every large stable I have has had to deal with this sort of problem. Some injuries are minor, but a break of the kind Mona Bell had–she was out of business. That means you put her away, you destroy her immediately. In fact, they buried her right in the grass at the racetrack off the centre field. We try to keep accidents and injuries down as low as we can. But at a forty-day race meeting at almost any track, you'll probably have a dozen horses break down so badly that they'll have to be immediately and humanely destroyed. Horseracing is a delicate business in which gentle animals must be treated gently. And fragile as they are, they must be handled humanely. When they suffer, those who care for them suffer with them."

Nevertheless, 1938 brought a tie to Taylor's first Plate win. He bought a yearling named Fairy Imp in the United States for $1,000. She joined Nandi as a brood mare and some years later was to be bred to Bunty Lawless who, through her, sired a colt which Taylor named Epic. It was Epic who, eleven years later, was to win Taylor his first Queen's Plate.

The first of two E.P. Taylor flirtations with the airline business took place in 1937. The Toronto financier, Harry Gundy, of the Wood, Gundy firm, believed that he had received favourable reaction from C.D. Howe, then the federal Minister of Transport, when Gundy approached him about the acceptability of establishing a privately owned transcontinental airline. Gundy and a group of people were prepared to put up money for research into the feasibility of the project. If the research was positive, they were prepared to go ahead. They had in mind using the advanced new transport which had just been put in production by Douglas Aircraft in California, the DC-1. This sleek, low wing, all metal, twin engine aircraft was revolutionizing the American airline industry. Later to become the DC-3, it was and still is the most durable aircraft ever produced.

The Gundy group approached Taylor to take a leading role in the formation of this project. As president, he would supervise the organization of the company once approval from the government had been received. With his growing reputation as one of Canada's leading entrepreneurs, Taylor would be just the man to attract public confidence and present an acceptable face to the federal government when application was made for an operating licence. Taylor was ready, willing, and more than able, but the deal collapsed when, without notice to Gundy, the Liberal Cabinet decided that a national airline serving Canada from coast to coast should be government owned and immediately certified its decision by presenting to Parliament the act that created Trans-Canada Airlines, now known as Air Canada. The Taylor/Gundy airline never got off the ground.

In 1937 Taylor decided it was time to change the name of his now huge Brewing Corporation of Canada Limited. He had acquired Canadian Brewing Corporation Limited from Dick Barnes in 1930, so its name in a varied form was available. The shortened version, Canadian Breweries Limited, appealed to him and would help to promote what E.P. Taylor liked to call "a national institution." The result was that Taylor directed the change to be made, and on April 21, 1937, the Letters Patent was issued by the Government of Ontario changing the name of the corporation to Canadian Breweries Limited.

At the next annual meeting of Canadian Breweries shareholders in October 1938, E.P. Taylor had even more startling news. The company had made a profit of a half a million dollars! It was a tremendous achievement by his firm and underscored the validity of E.P. Taylor's fundamental principles of mergers, consolidations, and closings. His company now held a dominant position in the brewing industry of Canada. Its share of the market in Ontario was 30 per cent, up from 11 per cent in 1931.

In 1938 the process of concentrating production into fewer plants continued, with the closing of the Taylor & Bate brewery in Hamilton, which was in poor physical condition, and the transfer of its business to the O'Keefe plant in Toronto. The fifteen brewing plants the company had acquired since its incorporation in 1930 were now reduced to six. Whereas the total number of labels in the early years had been fifty, by 1938 the six subsidiaries were producing only twenty-seven different labels.* Taylor's plan was to eliminate the multiplicity of labels and concentrate on the leading ones, making possible economies in production, improvements in distribution, and more effective use of sales expenditures. The 1938 profit picture was proof that his policies were succeeding. It was an exciting, satisfying time for the thirty-seven-year-old Taylor.

By the time the war began in 1939, Canadian Breweries' share of the Ontario market had increased to 34.9 per cent. The total annual production of beer in Ontario was more than twice what it had been at the low point in 1933. Canadian Breweries Limited products accounted for close to 40 per cent of this expanded production.

In the period 1930 to 1939, Taylor had acquired Ontario breweries with an annual production capacity of 940,000 barrels, but during the same period he had shut down almost half, namely 430,000 barrels. Even so, Canadian Breweries Limited entered the wartime period with considerable excess capacity, supplying only approximately 35 per cent of the Ontario market while it had 60 per cent of the total Ontario brewing capacity.

---

*The reduction process was to go on until by 1954 there were four companies concentrating on eight labels.

Chapter VI

The War Begins

The Second World War began on September 10, 1939. It was to have a considerable impact on E.P. Taylor and on his family as well. At thirty-eight Taylor was well beyond acceptable age for military service, but he was still young to be handling the enormous wartime responsibilities which later were given to him by the governments of the United Kingdom and Canada.

The life-style of Canadians was not all that much dislocated by the war in the closing months of 1939. Business went on as usual as the nation groped to get itself mobilized and men into uniform and trained. Industry geared up for orders for munitions and supplies. The government took stock of its national capability to produce men, munitions, weapons, and food.

But there was no great wrenching away from the normal, day-to-day business routine, no panic, no galvanizing thrust into dramatic action. For E.P. Taylor it was a matter of getting on with his plans for the growth and development of Canadian Breweries Limited, an objective he was never to let falter during the wartime years, even though in some periods he was totally committed to his government service to the exclusion of his business interests.

One of the sideline businesses E.P. Taylor ventured into was the publication of a monthly magazine. The first issue of *New World*, as it was called, appeared in March 1940. The whole purpose of the magazine was to circumvent the absolute ban on advertising beer in Ontario. It served its purpose. Well laced with advertising, most of it for liquor and beer, the magazine was edited in Toronto but printed and published in Quebec where beer and liquor advertising was permitted. From there, Taylor the publisher could distribute it right across Canada, which he did. The magazine used photographs liberally throughout and had a substantial amount of copy. The features were Art, Biography, Book of the Month, Canada at War; the Canadian Scene, Canadian Spotlight, European Scene, Fashion, Historical, Movies, New York Scene, Picture of the Month, Photo Credits, Science, and an article under Sports by Morley Callaghan, the sports editorial associate of the magazine. Circulation was approximately 80,000.

It was March 1940–the time of what was later to be called the "phony war." There were occasional battles in the air and encounters at sea, but there was a strange quiet across the lands of Western Europe. The British, still looking to their own resources to manufacture their war materials, did not consider Canada as much more than a place to make munitions and use as a training field, although in February, a deal worth $54 million had been concluded for Canadian production of corvettes and Bangor minesweepers. In the spring, an order was placed with General Motors for light transport vehicles. Canadians attempted to persuade the British to make their tanks in Canada but were turned down. The John Inglis Company was in full production on the Bren gun, having survived a Royal Commission that investigated charges that Inglis was profiteering. But the contract with Inglis was arranged by the British without the participation of the Canadian government.

The newspapers reported that Hitler was meeting secretly with Mussolini in the Brenner Pass. The 85,000-ton *Queen Elizabeth*, the largest ship in the world, left its Liverpool moorings under sealed orders and zig-zagged its way through U-boat-infested waters across the Atlantic to New York on what was described as "the most thrilling and dangerous maiden voyage in maritime history." The Liberal Party and Mackenzie King had triumphed in a federal election. At the moving picture theatres across the country, *Gone with the Wind* was the feature attraction.

One day in April 1940, E.P. Taylor was sitting in the Rideau Club in Ottawa having a drink with his father. "I didn't hear anything, but I sensed that I was being talked about. I turned around and I saw Mr. C.D. Howe, whom I'd never met before. He was the Minister of Munitions and Supply and the Minister of Transport before that. My old friend, Henry Borden, was with him, and Gordon Scott, of what was then P.S. Ross and Sons in Montreal, and also Watson Seller. Both Scott and Henry were working for the government as, to use the American expression, 'dollar-a-year men,' although the Canadian government never produced a dollar for any of those people. Anyway, Henry came over and touched me on the shoulder and said, 'My minister would like to speak with you. Will you come over and join us?' So I went over and we shook hands."

Henry Borden recalls that they were desperate for help at the time. When he saw Taylor at the club that day they were discussing the personnel they could get to come to Ottawa. Borden suggested that Taylor might be the answer to their problem. "I asked Howe, if he would like me to introduce him to Taylor. He said yes. So I went and brought Eddie over and introduced him to Howe, who, in his usual manner, said to him, 'We could certainly use your help down here, Mr. Taylor.' " After two later meetings with Borden, Taylor made his decision.

On June 4, 1940, a press statement was sent out from the office of the director of Public Information for release in the afternoon papers announcing E.P. Taylor's appointment to Howe's department, to serve without remuneration.

At thirty-nine, Taylor was reputed to be the youngest dollar-a-year man in government service, but, as he is always quick to point out, that distinction went to his friend Henry Borden. It was Taylor, however, who had the high public profile, and the announcement of his appointment brought responses from many places. One letter came from an unexpected quarter of the community: the Toronto Building Trades Council, who congratulated him on his appointment:

> We feel that you will be able at this critical period, to bring to the service of your country and your people, not only your vast business experience, but in addition something else, that is very often not understood by big business men (i.e.) a knowledge of and a sympathy to the human element in industry. Therefore we wish you the best of health, strength, and every requisite required to give the best that is in your power, which we know is your desire.

It was his reputation, his gregarious personality and his unchallenged success as an industrialist and entrepreneur that quickly put Taylor in a favourable position with Howe, who was himself a successful businessman as well as a politician. The minister needed a generalist at his right hand, a man who could comprehend the sweep of problems as well as the engineering and mechanical niceties that the burgeoning Ministry of Munitions and Supply had to contend with. Taylor's professional training as a mechanical engineer combined with the skills he had learned that summer long ago as a toolmaker's apprentice at the Ottawa Car and Foundry and his comprehensive understanding of business and finance were to make him a formidable presence on the Howe team.

C.D. Howe and his group were located in a temporary wartime building on Wellington Street, close to the Brading brewery. Taylor's office was slightly bigger than his small Bay Street one. "I had a rug, though. I tell you, you had to have a rug or you were nobody."

During the year E.P. Taylor was to spend in Ottawa, he was much too busy to play golf or do any riding. He took a room at the Chateau Laurier as did most of his colleagues. Like them, he was an early riser. "We would start work somewhere between 8:00 or 9:00, and we would work late. We would go either to the Rideau Club or somewhere else for lunch. Since we were all paying our own expenses it was our own choice. The government wasn't paying us anything."

Shortly after his arrival in Ottawa, Taylor became a member of Howe's newly formed executive committee which had in its membership R.A.C. Henry, Gordon Scott, W.A. Harrison, the deputy minister, E.K. Shiels, Henry Borden, and Colonel Eric Phillips, who was to become Taylor's business associate in Argus Corporation. Howe had brought together this tight little group of highly qualified dollar-a-year men (except for Shiels, who was a civil servant), for the purpose of using their vast expertise to cut across red tape. He also wanted to bring the businessman's viewpoint and knowledge into government for the gearing-up of the war effort by Canadian industry.

Some of the other dollar-a-year men in Ottawa to whom E.P. Taylor was exposed for the first time, and with whom he would have post-war relationships, were H.R. MacMillan of the H.R. MacMillan Lumber Company of British Columbia, who was in the Ministry of Munitions and Supply and responsible for timber and shipbuilding; and J.S. Duncan, who was Deputy Defence Minister for Air and who later, as president of Massey-Harris, would invite Taylor and Phillips to become directors of that firm.

As a member of Howe's executive committee, Taylor was responsible for procurement of all forms of munitions and armaments for the Canadian army, navy, and air force and for the British armed forces, should orders ever come from the United Kingdom. The current "typically British" attitude, as it was described by Henry Borden, prevailed. "They didn't want to let anybody manufacture even a .22 calibre bullet. It had to be done in Britain. This was true until they got into real trouble." Real trouble began with the collapse of France followed by the Dunkirk evacuation at the beginning of June, and with it the stripping of the remnants of the British army of its basic armaments. The disaster was brought into focus by Churchill on June 18 when he delivered from the bowels of his wartime headquarters near the House of Commons his famous "blood, sweat, and tears" speech.

Soon after he arrived in Ottawa, Taylor discovered that the intransigent attitudes of the senior level of the military, combined with the red tape of bureaucracy, made it almost impossible even to learn what the generals needed, let alone to get the Ministry to place an order. For him the situation was almost intolerably frustrating. He had to do everything in his power to get around the generals or to get them moving.

The generals "knew they needed anti-tank guns and anti-aircraft guns and field guns and machine guns and tanks and armoured vehicles, and so on, but they had made up their minds that the Canadian army didn't have a big enough demand for them to justify requisitioning this equipment. They were very defeatist about Canada ever making a contribution to the war effort. They were relying on England. Naturally my answer was that the English factories might be bombed out. The generals wouldn't even come to our office and talk about it. Well, a salesman doesn't ask his customer to come and visit him. He goes and visits them. I simply said, 'I'm getting to know these boys and I'm going to start at the top level. If I don't succeed there, I'll go to a lower level, which I did.' "

Taylor first paid calls on the senior officers in the Defence Ministry. There were three chiefs of staff–army, navy, and air force–under Colonel J.L. Ralston, Minister of National Defence in the wartime Cabinet. "I found the generals in the army most uncooperative. They were all still money-conscious. They thought there wasn't enough business to make it worth while."

The Ministry was also having difficulty getting orders from the British army even though they had a mission in Ottawa. It was a question of money. In June 1940 Britain was beginning to sell some of her investments in the United States and in Canada in order to finance the war. With that situation, and with the June military calamity which produced Dunkirk, "we knew that eventually Britain would have to give us orders. So then I neglected the generals and started working on the colonels and majors, the fellows who had just returned from Europe from the Defence Colleges in England who were very well informed about modern weapons. I found that they too were fretting that nothing was being done about establishing Canadian sources of supply for the weapons they needed."

By the end of June, Taylor was becoming despondent about the lack of "requisitions" from the military. The Ministry was getting lots of requisitions for ammunition and clothing and for motor trucks and wheeled vehicles, but nothing for anti-aircraft guns, anti-tank guns, tanks, or the other heavy weaponry needed to fight a war. Taylor therefore wrote a letter to Howe stating that he had discussed the situation with the major manufacturers. They all said that they wanted to contribute more than they had been to the war effort, but they couldn't get any orders. Taylor had showed them the specifications, and they all said they'd be willing to set up facilities if they could get orders. Taylor's letter also pointed out that:

It is contended that all of the equipment should be produced in Canada. Every week in which a decision is not made will mean a month delay in getting into production due to the increasing scarcity of machine tools. . . . If the Department is given authority, we can organize at once to deliver all the weapons listed . . . with minimum delay. If another month is lost, it is almost certain that deliveries, in quantity, could not be promised until 1942.

To tool up for such a program would probably cost $100,000,000. The major part of this investment would be in machine tools. It is submitted that this is a relatively small sum in view of the dangers of the present situation and the money being spent in other ways. There will be more than 200,000 Canadian troops in training by fall of this year, and it would seem only proper that to eventually make them effective, they should have all the weapons and equipment necessary to fight a modern war.

Furthermore, there were 23,000 Canadian military personnel already in the United Kingdom.

That letter, which was handed to Howe one June 1940 morning, had immediate results. Late that afternoon Colonel Ralston's secretary called Taylor asking him to meet Ralston in his office at the Parliament Buildings that evening at 8:00. At the meeting were about fifty top military men and Cabinet ministers. Ralston opened the meeting by saying that his colleague, C.D. Howe, had received a letter which indicated that the country could make many important items, but that neither the British nor the Canadian governments had given the manufacturers any orders. He also went on to say that the leading manufacturers with the ability to produce such items had indicated that they would be prepared to go ahead once they received an order. Then he grilled a few of the military men. The generals were very upset when they realized that Taylor had gone underneath them to get the information. "They were very angry. I was a fly on their sides, a mosquito in the rafters." At the conclusion of the meeting, Colonel Ralston assured Howe and Taylor that the requisitions would come forward promptly from the Department of National Defence.

Within a few days after the fall of France, the call came from the British. They no longer had the steel to throw at the Germans. In a telegram addressed to C.D. Howe, the Minister of Production in Great Britain, Sir Andrew Duncan, asked how many artillery guns, tanks, anti-tank guns, and other pieces of equipment could be made, how long it would take them to get into production, and what would be the capital expenditure needed. The telegram failed to mention quantities, times of delivery, or financing. But Howe's attitude was that his own people could sort out the projections themselves. "The main thing was to get on with it. Howe still could not get the army to move, so finally he just said, 'Go ahead. Get the manufacturers in. Make recommendations to me as to who should make what and we'll give them a letter of intent. Get in touch with your manufacturers and tell them to go ahead and prepare to manufacture. I'll take the responsibility.' "

Taylor brought the manufacturers in, drafted the letters of intent with Borden's advice, signed them, and got the deputy minister to initial them. The manufacturing started immediately although it was five or six months before the requisitions came in. The manufacturers financed all the orders on their own in the belief that they would later be reimbursed, which indeed they were. Taylor considers that Howe's authorizing the letters of intent was one of his great contributions to the war effort.

Dollar-a-year man E.P. Taylor was now in full stride negotiating with the manufacturers, supervising the carrying out of contracts, wheeling and dealing and cutting red tape as if it did not exist. Henry Borden said, "He'd make deals and then just tell you about them or send you a copy of the letter that he'd written, and then you had to work it all out. You had to tie all the loose ends up. He was an awfully hard man to keep in order." Indeed he was, but he performed so well that in August, when C.D. Howe decided to abolish the executive committee because it was becoming too large and unwieldy in its operation, and instead make each member the head of a department, Taylor became joint director general of munitions production, continuing his special concern for mechanical equipment and light arms.

In August 1940, as C.D. Howe's right-hand man, E.P. Taylor, was confronted with two events involving skilled refugees. One was a group from France, and the other from Poland.

When France fell, a large group of military experts in the manufacturing of munitions escaped through Spain and found their way to Canada, under the auspices of the British government which had assigned a British brigadier, Eric Wallace, to escort them. He had been with the British army in France and had come out through Dunkirk.* Wallace and his charges, about twenty of them, all of whom were in civilian clothes, were passed on to the Ministry of Munitions and Supply because of their experience. Taylor was uncertain how they arrived on his doorstep, but it was up to him to find jobs for them. Some went to Sorel and were employed in the manufacture of the twenty-five pounder guns being made there. One of them was a machine tool manufacturer, a Frenchman of substance who was put into the Canadian army with rank of full colonel. Eventually, and with no little effort, Taylor had all the men placed.

---

*Wallace has since become a close friend of Taylor. Head of Pittsburgh Industries Canada, he has also been chairman of the Ontario Racing Commission. As a lifetime horseman he has been master of the hunt in Toronto.

The next challenge followed quickly. In 1940, a naturalized Canadian from Poland, Henry Harajewicz, was in Ottawa as a member of the Polish Legation which represented the Polish government-in-exile. This is Harajewicz's brief story about Taylor:

One day we received a wire from General Wladyslaw Sikorski, the head of the Polish government-in-exile in London, with a request to feel out the Canadian government, if it would be interested in issuing entrance visas to Canada to approximately 600 Polish war industry specialists stranded at that time in unoccupied/occupied France. (If Hitler occupied this section of France, they would be amalgamated into the German war industries.) As this problem would not fall under administerial level, Victor Podoski, the Minister of the Legation, asked me to handle the problem–in consultation with him. Without knowing anybody in the Department of Munitions and Supply, I went on a cold call to the Department and met first a Mr. Crown and asked him if I could see "the right hand man" of C.D. Howe, who was then the Minister. After a wait of about fifteen minutes, Mr. Crown came back and took me into the office of Mr. E.P. Taylor. Taylor, who at that time was a "dollar-a-year man" in this department, asked me to sit down and to present him my problem. After a long conversation, Taylor, a quick thinker, asked me whether I could give him a name of a Polish war industry specialist working for a Canadian firm. After some thought I gave him the name of a professional engineer working at deHavilland. Mr. Taylor immediately phoned Mr. Garratt, president of deHavilland, who apparently did not have to refer to the proper files and replied immediately that he was one of their top men. Taylor jumped out of his chair, told me about the conversation and decided to present the case to C.D. Howe and to give me a call the next day, which he did. He informed me that Mr. Howe gave him his okay and that we both would go to Mr. Blair, who was then the head of the Department of Immigration. There we settled the details and they decided to authorize the Canadian Ambassador in Lisbon to issue necessary visas to the Polish specialists. On our part, we instructed accordingly the Polish authorities in unoccupied France to direct them to Lisbon and apply there for the visas. Thanks to Messrs. Taylor, Howe and Blair, everything went smoothly (no Royal Commission was necessary). They started to arrive in Canada in groups of forty to one hundred. Mr. Taylor nominated Mr. Leslie Thompson as the representative of his department to look after the arrival while we supplied Richard Hergert, a Polish professional engineer who knew most of the arriving specialists' experience, education, etc. Thanks to the splendid co-operation of Thompson and Hergert, the newcomers were placed in about two weeks' time. Most of them are still in Canada, retired by now, or dead.

By the end of the summer the situation in Britain was at its worst. A few brave fighter pilots were battling for the survival of their country in the skies above their homeland. The Battle of Britain was on. In the United States the British Purchasing Commission, which had been set up in November 1939, was becoming increasingly effective. Its establishment in New York was a direct result of a change in the United States neutrality law and the introduction of the Roosevelt-sponsored "cash and carry" system. Originally, the British Purchasing Commission In The United States was responsible to the British Supply Board In Canada And The United States, which was established in Ottawa soon after the outbreak of war. The commission in the United States did not place contracts through the United States government, but bought munitions of war and similar stores on the open market.

In the summer of 1940 the British Supply Board In Canada And The United States ceased to exist. The British Purchasing Commission In The United States became the British supply organization in the United States, while the Canadian Department of Munitions and Supply in Ottawa, supported by certain small missions comprising United Kingdom technicians, assumed direct responsibility for U.K. orders for war stores in Canada. Public opinion in America hardened against the Axis, and by July it had become expedient to transfer the headquarters of the British Purchasing Commission from New York to Washington, that transfer taking place in September.

The British Purchasing Commission head, the Right Honourable Arthur Purvis, an Englishman who was president of Canadian Industries Limited in Montreal when the war first started, got on extremely well with U.S. Secretary of the Treasury, Henry

Morgenthau, a relationship that eased many British supply problems in America. Roosevelt was in complete sympathy with the Allied cause, and did everything in his power to assist while at the same time maintaining his country's neutrality.

When France fell, Britain took over the French orders for United States equipment. Material declared surplus to United States needs was sent across the Atlantic. In September, concerned with the heavy toll the German U-boats were taking in the Atlantic not only of merchant ships, but warships as well, Roosevelt had fifty First World War mothballed destroyers declared surplus and turned over to the British in exchange for U.S. naval rights in Newfoundland, Bermuda, and elsewhere. It was the urging and pleading of Purvis, among other high-ranking British people, that influenced both Roosevelt and Morgenthau to make the decision, questionable from the viewpoint of neutrality, to release those desperately needed destroyers. (Coincidentally, it was one of those same destroyers that participated in saving the lives of Taylor and Howe in December 1940.)

In early November, Howe decided to pay a short visit to England. By that time Taylor was receiving orders from the Canadian armed forces but he was still getting no substantial orders from the British for anything except ammunition. "We needed those orders and we had the capacity to manufacture. So the four of us decided to go over and try to get orders out of the British government."

The next decision of Howe's was to cross the Atlantic by ship rather than bomber, a choice that nearly cost him and his colleagues their lives when the *Western Prince* was torpedoed and sunk on December 14.

After their miraculous rescue by the crew of the *Baron Kinnaird*, the survivors were taken to Greenock where they were met in great style by two admirals and a barge. After a brief stop in Glasgow for a much-needed bath and new clothes, they were on the overnight train to London and a great reception. When the festivities were over, Taylor's work started immediately. He visited various ministries and chiefs of those ministries, a great many of whom had never been to Canada. "They remembered we only made shells and explosives in the First World War. We had a hard time convincing Lord Beaverbrook that Canada was different than in 1910 when he last lived there."

The remainder of the sojourn in England was a whirlwind of

activity for Howe and Taylor–the visit to the Canadian 2nd Division; a party for Princess Patricia, whom Taylor reported to be "still very good looking"; talks with Canadian Commander General Andrew McNaughton; Taylor's first meeting with Lord Beaverbrook; tours of aircraft and munitions factories; a look at battered Coventry and Birmingham; and then a summons to return to London to begin the trip back to North America.

This time Taylor and Howe were to travel across the Atlantic in remarkable style and even more remarkable company. They were instructed to catch the 11:00 A.M. train from King's Cross. When Taylor arrived at the station, he found to his amazement that on the platform was the whole British Cabinet, with no special guard. As he told the story a few weeks later in a Toronto dinner speech, "The Prime Minister was there, and Lord Halifax, and Lord Beaverbrook. Much to my surprise, I saw Winston Churchill and Mrs. Churchill get aboard the train. That was the first intimation I had that we were on a special train going to an unknown port. Later, I saw Harry Hopkins, an American admiral and general, and British generals whom I knew, and it was obvious that we had a very interesting trainload of people. No one told us where we were going. We passed through Edinburgh at eight. At about 10:00 we passed through Perth, and realized then that we were going to the north of Scotland. We arrived in Thurso the next morning. By this time we knew we were going by battleship.

"There was some question then as to whether the Prime Minister would accompany us on the battleship, as he had a cold–but he did. We were motored to the dock, where a destroyer and two minesweepers were ready to take us to the ship. We still did not know on what ship we were going.

"We arrived at Scapa Flow and saw the Home Fleet, the Rodney, Nelson, Hood aircraft carriers and destroyers. This represented only part of the fleet, of course, other ships being stationed in different parts of the world. It was a thrill when we drew up to the *King George V*.

"We boarded the *King George V* at 3:00. As soon as Churchill had finished his lunch, he went off to spend the night on the *Nelson*, which is the flagship. We weighed anchor at 5:00.

"There were fourteen of us all together. We had a comfortable wardroom and lounge, and were told that we had the run of the ship. There was no place we could not go if the door was opened.

We certainly took advantage of that during the next few days. We were everywhere.

"I had the fun of going down to see the cordite magazine with Lord Halifax. We had to enter through a small manhole in the steel deck. Lord Halifax, being very thin, clambered through like a cat, but because of my girth, I had a bit of difficulty.

"The navy did everything possible to make us comfortable. There were sixty officers on board and fifteen midshipmen. They went out of their way to entertain us. Under the regulations of the navy, they do not charge you for your passage or your food, but they do charge you for entertainment. An ambassador pays six guineas a day for six days, and on the seventh it drops to one guinea a day, but Mr. Woodward and I gave them trouble, as we were not ambassadors, ministers, or generals. We were finally classified as bishops at one guinea a day. I have never received such value in all my life.

"The arrival at Annapolis was spoiled by bad weather. There was a cold winter's rain. The President had wired that he would come out if he could, but that he would not come aboard the ship. He came out and circled the *King George V* in his yacht. The marines lined up and gave him a salute and the band played the American anthem. It was all very impressive, in spite of the rain."

On disembarking from the *King George V* at New York, Taylor went directly to Toronto by train for a happy reunion with Winnie and the children from whom he had been separated at Christmas and who thought for a time they would never see him again. After a two-day stay at Windfields, it was back to Ottawa, where everyone was still talking about the sinking of the *Western Prince*. In the first few days Taylor spent most of his time responding to calls from well-wishers, talking with the many people who dropped in to see him about various aspects of the trip, and writing to those who had sent messages such as his old friend, John Gavin, who had cabled Taylor in England, "Members of the Brewery Workers International glad of the good news that you are safe. We join with your many friends in congratulating you. Compliments of the season. Safe return."

It was a short letter Taylor wrote to the Rt. Hon. W.L. Mackenzie King, P.C., C.M.G., whom Taylor admired but did not like, and with whom he would have a bitter public argument some two years down the road.

My wife, father and mother have told me how extremely kind you were to them during the anxious period when the fate of the members of Mr. Howe's party was unknown.

I deeply appreciate your thoughtfulness in keeping them informed when the newspaper reports were so conflicting.

And to Sir James Dunn, now back in residence at the Ritz Carlton Hotel in Montreal:

After the gruelling experience of spending four days in the ship which rescued us, I certainly made good use of your very kind gift of the bottles of extremely old brandy which were delivered to the hotel with your card. It was indeed very thoughtful of you to remember me.

And to Vincent Massey, the high commissioner for Canada in London:

I was sorry that our sudden departure from London prevented me from saying good-bye to you and thanking you for the great kindness you showed us during our visit. I know quite well that our inclusion as passengers on the *King George V* was a direct result of the representations you made on our behalf. The trip back, of course, was a wonderful experience which I shall always remember.

But before he got around to writing his letters of thanks, which he did on February 4 and 5, Taylor tended to first things first, a memo to Howe about Taylor's future with him.

During the long visit to England, Howe and Taylor had many discussions about the problems of the department and the role Taylor could play in the future. On January 29, 1941, Taylor wrote a memorandum to C.D. Howe which said in part:

While we were away, we had several conversations relative to how I could most effectively serve the Department in future. It was recognized that the principal functions of the Munitions Branch in future will be to guide production rather than to create new capacity, and also that the death of Gordon Scott leaves a gap which will be hard to fill.

I believe I can be most useful in the following capacities:

(title to be settled later–possibly Director General of Programmes)

1) to take part with each Director General and the Legal Branch in the negotiation of projects requiring substantial capital assistance and/or large contracts.
2) by having a knowledge of major projects in each Branch of the Department, I could accept the responsibility for seeing that new ones do not conflict with others already in existence or contemplated.
3) to be generally available to you to investigate for you sundry situations as they arise.

If the above suggestion meets with your approval, I will arrange to clean up my work in the Munitions Branch and find quarters in the original building in the next few days.

Taylor's suggestion to C.D. Howe was indeed acceptable. On February 11 it was announced that E.P. Taylor had been appointed executive assistant to C.D. Howe, evoking this editorial comment from the Toronto *Globe and Mail*: "Mr. Taylor's imagination and driving force will be given scope in his new position."

There were two other executive assistants to the minister, Colonel Billy Woodward, who was soon to go back to British Columbia as lieutenant governor, and W.A. Harrison, who was managing director of Estabrooks Ltd. of Saint John, New Brunswick. But it was Taylor, the imaginative entrepreneur who, as the minister's top man, would cut across all activities in the department in the name of and on behalf of the man who had great faith and confidence in him, C.D. Howe.

On February 5, after getting his thank-you letters out of the way, Taylor turned his attention to an issue that had infuriated him since he first heard about it on his return from England. A prominent Ontario Conservative and decorated First World War combat veteran, Lt. Col. George Drew, had made critical comment about both the old and new contracts between the John Inglis Company and the government concerning the manufacture of guns. E.P. Taylor was upset by Drew's statements and decided to let him know in no uncertain terms what he thought. The correspondence between these two men, who were later to become good friends, speaks for itself.

Dear George,

This is a personal and confidential letter written because I have seen, in the eight months I have been down in Ottawa, plenty of evidence that the continued attacks by you and certain sections of the press on the John Inglis Company have adversely affected this country's war effort.

You may possibly have been right that the original contract was not negotiated in the best way to allay suspicion. But since then we have become engaged in a war, and it has developed that the Inglis Company has done a remarkably satisfactory job of manufacturing Bren guns in larger quantities than required of them by the new schedules agreed to after the plant went on a war basis.

The new contract was not negotiated because of anything contained in the first one. This I know because I negotiated the new contract, for other and perfectly good reasons. As a matter of fact, we had quite a job persuading the United Kingdom people to agree to the terms of the new contract, because they said that the original contract was one of the most satisfactory pre-war contracts which they had placed, and they felt that the Company had been persecuted unduly.

I have read your comments in the newspapers and particularly in the Toronto *Telegram* of, I believe, January 11th, and I can tell you in regard to the latter that your conclusions are in every respect wrong. I presume it will be Government policy to answer questions about the background for the new one in the House of Commons when it next meets, at which time you will learn the whole story.

I am sure you will agree that the present is not the time to pursue a controversy for political gain. I, therefore, sincerely urge you, in your own interests and the interests of our National war effort, to make no further statement as to why the old contracts were amalgamated with the new ones.

As you know I have no strong partisan views. I am only trying to help in a small way to win this war. I regret that the probably well intentioned efforts of the press and others are at the present time making the task much more difficult.

Drew's response was moderate, smooth and politic. He had been tempted to shoot back in a comparable tone to the letter he had received, but decided against it. He chose to be conciliatory rather than hostile.

My dear Eddie:

I delayed replying to your letter because my first inclination was to deal with each of your statements in considerable detail. I then realized that this would involve an extremely long letter and that it would be very much better to discuss this subject in a personal conversation if you care to do so.

I know how busy you have been since you returned from England and I also know what a good job you have been doing. I am sure that with all the other demands upon your time it has not been possible to go into the involved details of a transaction which was discussed at such length two and a half years ago.

First let me point out that I have made no "continued attacks" on this contract during the eight months you have been in Ottawa. I have in fact not mentioned it in public during that time except for the comment I made when I was asked for a statement by the press after its cancellation was disclosed recently under somewhat unusual circumstances.

As for further discussion of the old contract I can only say that from the outset my contention was that this contract should be cancelled. It has been cancelled. I can see no reason therefore to discuss it further.

I do not question the fact that you have seen some evidence that the Government may have been embarrassed by the publication of the details of the original contract. I would think it must have been extremely difficult to persuade others to enter into much less favourable contracts while it was still in force. But if the Government was embarrassed, then the Government alone was responsible for that embarrassment. Mr. Justice Davis made clear and specific recommendations in his Report in January 1939. If the Government had acted upon those recommendations, the causes of criticism in this case and any possible cause of embarrassment to the Government would have been removed long before the war began. I would not wonder that the War Office may have expressed surprise at being asked to negotiate a new contract after the Canadian Government had brought constant pressure on them for a year and a half to sign the other contract. I recall that the contract which they signed in July 1938 was not the form of contract they wanted, but was the form of contract which the Canadian Government insisted upon adopting. The evidence and the findings of the Judge are clear on that point.

It was Winston Churchill who said in one of his stirring speeches during the early part of this war that he would never try to stifle criticism because criticism is the strong driving power of democracy and that the only way to end criticism is to remove the cause. That is the way, as he pointed out, to assure efficiency of government. I earnestly hope that all cause for criticism has now been removed.

I will be only too glad to discuss this subject in detail at any time. I may recall that for many years I was closely associated with the Department of National Defence under different governments in the consideration of methods for arming our defence forces. With the assistance of the Canadian High Commissioner I had unusual opportunities to investigate the production of weapons in many European countries. It is possible that I may have some information which would be of assistance to you.

Later, the two men did discuss the matter "in a personal conversation," as Drew suggested. For their purposes at least, the question was put to rest.

Preoccupied as he was with his war work, Taylor nevertheless kept his hand on Canadian Breweries Limited and its subsidiary companies which were making solid progress. In his eleventh annual report to the shareholders on February 18, 1941, E.P. Taylor disclosed that for the fiscal year ended October 31, 1940, the net profit was $552,032.78 in comparison with $519,288.32 in the previous year. During the year the sale was completed of $500,000, 5 per cent Serial Debentures. Even in wartime people had money to invest in a company in whose leadership they had confidence. Taylor used the proceeds to reduce outstanding minority interests and for general corporate purposes.

At the start of the war, Canada had imposed foreign exchange controls to curtail the outflow of the currencies of other nations, especially American dollars, but it was not until war products manufacturing began to escalate in Canada that the problem became serious. The nation's industrial capacity had been mainly centred around primary manufacturing, with the result that there was need to import from the United States a host of sophisticated products, parts, tools, and equipment, as well as high-value products such as aircraft and their engines, almost all of which came from American sources. The United States' content in Canada's output of munitions was in the neighbourhood of 30 per cent. All of this had to be bought from the United States and paid for in American dollars or gold. The British themselves suffered enormously from this situation. During the war, British investments in Canadian war industries were taken over by Canada, and British-held Canadian securities were repatriated to the extent of approximately $1 billion.

In April 1941, it was apparent that the outflow of American dollars and the trade imbalance between the two nations was such that Canada would shortly have no American dollars left and would therefore be unable to purchase desperately needed supplies in the United States.

Representatives of the Canadian Department of Finance and British Treasury had been in urgent discussions with the United States Treasury to work out a solution. Roosevelt and the Congress of the United States, which was still not at war, were sympathetic. The solution for Great Britain was the Lend/Lease Act, enacted by the U.S. Congress on March 11, 1941. It gave the President the power to sell military goods and essential civilian commodities to the United Kingdom, Canada, and their allies without immediate cash. Payments could be made by barter, in kind, in property, or in whatever other way was acceptable to the United States Treasury. This action opened the floodgates of trade, commerce, and currency in a way unparalleled in the history of the world's economy. By the end of the Second World War, the United States had provided some thirty-eight countries with goods, equipment, and food to the value of $50 billion.

The Canadian government refused to participate in the Lend/Lease program, rigidly sticking to the principle that Canada had the resources and the ability to pay her own way. The vast American industrial machine would need raw materials as it geared up to produce the huge volume of war materials which could now be sold to Britain and her allies under the Lend/Lease provisions. An idea surfaced in Ottawa: why not propose to the United States that there be a barter arrangement set up whereby Canada would supply the United States with raw materials such as iron, aluminum, nickel, and other primary commodities or ships, tanks, or other finished goods surplus to Canada's requirements; in return the United States would provide to Canada finished products such as aircraft, ships, tanks or whatever?

Mackenzie King had discussed the idea with Morgenthau, who thought that it had merit and suggested that King discuss it with Roosevelt. A luncheon meeting between Roosevelt and King was arranged for Sunday, April 20, 1941, to be held at Roosevelt's home at Hyde Park not far from New York City. These arrangements were made on Thursday, April 17, and there was precious little time to translate the barter idea from a concept into a fullfledged proposal. King would rely on C.D. Howe to put it all together. And C.D. Howe decided to rely on E.P. Taylor, who would work with two other men, Clifford Clark, the Deputy Minister of Finance, and John H. Carswell, who was the purchasing representative of the Canadian government in Washington.

The three men met in Carswell's New York hotel suite and worked late into the night on Friday, all day Saturday, and again late into Saturday night. They produced a finished aide memoire which, through special secretarial arrangements, was typed and ready on schedule for King as the basis for his proposal to Roosevelt. The document outlined the basis for agreement with the United States and contained a supplementary list of possible exports.

They met King at the Harvard Club at 9:00 Sunday morning. Actually, they arrived a few minutes early so they would be the first there and not keep the Prime Minister waiting when he arrived. This was required protocol. King appeared on time, "and we went to the billiard room on the top floor. There was no airconditioning in the club and, believe it or not, New York was ninety-three degrees fahrenheit that day. We all took off our coats, even the Prime Minister. He was certainly a great statesman, and a great politician, but he hadn't much knowledge of practical things. He approved of our document. He didn't change it at all. We coached him so that if he was asked questions beyond what was set forth in the documents, he would know what it was that we could probably supply. He didn't have to use that information, he told me subsequently.

"A special train was waiting to take him up to Hyde Park, which was only about an hour's run from New York City. Before he left he told us to meet him at the Canadian Legation the next morning." (Mackenzie King had been on a "Virginia seashore" vacation which he had to cut short in order to go to New York and then Hyde Park.)

King's meeting with Roosevelt, Harry Hopkins, and Henry Morgenthau was a success, so much so that the aide memoire was adopted in its entirety as the basis of a joint statement issued by Roosevelt and King. (Hopkins' participation in the meeting was later to be of value to E.P. Taylor who was able to call upon the highly visible presidential grey eminence for assistance in implementing the Canadian side of the bargain.) A joint statement was issued to the press by the Canadian Prime Minister in the Poughkeepsie railroad station on his departure for Ottawa on the Sunday evening. On the Monday morning, on their way to meet King who was to proceed on by train to Ottawa, "We opened our *New York Times* and on the front page in a prominent article was the joint statement, which was in fact the exact replica of the agreement reached between the Prime Minister and the President, without changing a word of the aide memoire and–here is the most embarrassing thing–without even changing the spelling of certain of the words from the English way to the American, for example, 'labour.'"

The next day the Canadian team met their Prime Minister who was well pleased. "We congratulated him and he congratulated us." When Taylor reported by telephone to Howe, Howe said, "Fine, a job well done. The old man did a good job too."

The Hyde Park Declaration, as it came to be known, provided for "a virtual merging of the economies of the United States and Canada for production of war materials, for Great Britain and for hemisphere defence," according to the *New York Times* article of April 21, 1941. The joint statement made by the President and the Prime Minister of Canada set out that the United States agreed to supply Canada with "numerous defence articles which Canada was not yet able to produce. Canada in turn would make available to the United States during the following twelve months, $200 million to $300 million worth of munitions, strategic materials, aluminum and ships," which were supplies urgently required by the United States.

It was agreed that, under the Lend/Lease Act, the United States would supply, without payment by Canada, parts needed to complete war materials the Dominion was turning out for Britain. The agreement was made, it was explained, in order that "the most effective utilization" might be made of the "productive facilities of North America" for local and hemisphere defence and for aid to embattled Britain.

The next step was implementation. In Ottawa on May 13, 1941, Henry Borden completed the incorporation of a new Crown corporation, War Supplies Limited, which was to negotiate with and receive orders from departments of the United States government for war supplies and manufacturing. This done, Howe called in E.P. Taylor and said, "Eddie, we've formed a company called War Supplies Limited. You're the president. Go out and sell it." Taylor's job was to sell to the Americans every natural resource commodity and all surplus finished war supplies he could lay his hands on.

Taylor immediately went to Washington, set up offices in the Willard Hotel and began to do what he had been told–sell. He took several people to Washington with him. His financial man was V.W. "Bill" Scully of the Steel Company of Canada, and Roy Peers, who was to be the general manager of the new company. "Roy carried on splendidly. I was whisked away in September, after being there only five months. He carried on and by that time was swamped with orders." Taylor also took with him Karl Fraser, a Maritimer who was then working as a public relations man with the National Trust Company of which Taylor subsequently became a director. "He was insistent on coming to work for me but I kept putting him off. I used to come home from Washington every second Friday or Saturday night and go back on the train on the Sunday afternoon via Buffalo. He'd get on the train and talk to me as far as Buffalo, trying to convince me. So I finally took him on in Washington, and he became one of several assistants." Fraser was to stay with him after the war and took a leading role in assembling the lands and initiating Taylor's plans for what is now Don Mills. Taylor also took on Bill Finlayson. He too stayed on with E.P. Taylor after the war for a period of time, which included the formation of Argus Corporation of which he was the first secretary.

Taylor wasted no time in getting his Washington operations under way. "The morning after I arrived, I armed myself with a copy of the April 21 edition of the *New York Times* and went to call on the Secretary of the Navy, Secretary of the Army, and the Secretary of the Treasury, which was a big procurement agency in the United States. I called on the Maritimes Commission. The army and navy people referred me immediately to their generals and admirals responsible for procurement. I'd hand these people the *New York Times* report on the Hyde Park agreement. They would read it. They'd call in a legal assistant and say, 'Mr. Taylor is here and he's got a lot of things we need, but under what authority can we buy them?' All I had was a report in the newspaper about what the President and the Prime Minister had agreed. The legal people had to find out whether they had agreed to it or not. Well, they never found out. They said, 'Come back tomorrow or the next day, Mr. Taylor, and we'll look into it.' So finally I called up Harry Hopkins at the White House–he'd been at the meeting between Roosevelt and King–and I told him my predicament. Hopkins said, 'Just tell them to call me.' So I referred them all to him and I got my orders."

That was power being exercised. Taylor understood it, appreciated it, had it himself, and respected any man who could use it properly. Taylor says of Hopkins, "He was a great man, one of the three great American civilians of the war." The others were Roosevelt and Morgenthau.

The Hyde Park agreement never received the sanction of law because it never became legislation enacted by Congress. It was purely and simply a joint declaration made by the President of the United States and the Prime Minister of Canada. It took the *New York Times* and E.P. Taylor to translate it into reality.

It has been estimated that, by the time Taylor left War Supplies Limited at the end of August, 1941, over $200 million worth of orders had already been placed and that by the end of the war the total orders obtained by the firm amounted to $1,360 million.

In July 1941, Hitler decided to postpone his major assault on Britain in order to attack the Soviet Union, which had bought time two years earlier by entering into a non-aggression treaty with

Germany. The United Kingdom and the United States would now have to divert much of their attention to shoring up the resources of their new ally. In order to establish future plans, a face-to-face meeting of Churchill and Roosevelt was arranged. In late August 1941, months before the Japanese attack on Pearl Harbour, the two leaders and their staffs met secretly in Placentia Bay, Newfoundland. Roosevelt arrived with Harry Hopkins and Averell Harriman on the American cruiser, the *Augusta*. Churchill, the old seadog and "Former Naval Person," reached the rendez-vous point on the *Prince of Wales*, one of the same series of battle-ships as the *King George V*. As was then usual, Beaverbrook accompanied the Prime Minister. Also present were all the top sol-diers, sailors, and airmen from each country. The Soviets were not present. As a result of this meeting, Roosevelt decided to offer assistance to the Soviet Union and to other countries under the Lend/Lease Act, even though the United States was not yet at war.

The high secrecy of the Churchill/Roosevelt meeting was to cost the chairman of the British Supply Council in North America, Arthur Purvis, his life, an event that was to vault E.P. Taylor into a totally unexpected position.

Purvis had moved to Washington from Ottawa in mid-January when the British War Cabinet came to the conclusion that with the proliferation of the number of separate missions it had established in the United States–food, merchant ship, air, and a host of oth-ers–some co-ordination of activities was needed. As a result, regu-lar weekly meetings were held of heads and senior members of the missions to discuss common subjects. Since it was also necessary to co-ordinate the direction of the missions at the policy level, the British Supply Council of North America was constituted as of January 15, 1941. The terms of reference given the British Supply Council by the War Cabinet were:

The Council in harmony with the Ambassador should deal with issues of policies concerning supply, including, of course, all representations made to the United States administration.

The three Supply Ministries will retain separate organiza-tions in the United States for the purpose of dealing with their supply requirements. The head of each of these organizations will be a member of the British Supply Council in North America. The Supply Ministries will communicate with their representative direct and complete information about these communications and will be at the disposal of the Council.

The Right Honourable Arthur B. Purvis, P.C., was appointed chairman of the council, with Morris Wilson, president of the Royal Bank of Canada, as his deputy chairman. The members were: Sir Henry Self, director general of the British Air Commission; Sir Clive Baillieu, director general of the British Purchasing Commission; Vice-Admiral A.E. Evans, head of the British Admiralty Technical Mission; the Honourable Clarence D. Howe, M.P., Canadian Minister of Munitions and Supply; and Jean Monnet, member-at-large. In addition, although not members of the council, the following British government officials participated in the council discussions: the Ambassador, Lord Halifax; a representative of the United Kingdom Treasury; and representatives of the three United Kingdom Chiefs of Staff.

In mid-August, just at the time of the secret Churchill-Roosevelt naval rendezvous, Purvis was trying desperately to reach Lord Beaverbrook, from whom he needed instructions. As a result of the German attack on the Soviet Union, the United States government was taking the position that there would have to be a diversion to the Russians of war materials assigned to the British. Purvis, unable to learn Beaverbrook's whereabouts, decided to track him down personally and took a bomber flight to the United Kingdom. When Purvis reached England, he was informed not where Beaverbrook was–security surrounding the Newfoundland meeting was tight–but where he was going to be. Beaverbrook would accompany Roosevelt on the *Augusta* from the Newfoundland rendezvous back to New York, where the Beaver wanted to meet with Purvis and other British officials in his capacity as Minister of War Production.

When he discovered that Beaverbrook was scheduled to be in New York almost immediately, Purvis, with the high priority available to him, tried to book a seat on a bomber scheduled to depart from Prestwick. As it happened, all the seats in the aircraft were taken. One of the passengers offered to give up his seat to Purvis, who readily accepted.

On its takeoff run, the airplane never got airborne. It crashed into a railway siding at the end of the runway and exploded. Everyone on board was killed.

In his position as president of War Supplies Limited, E.P. Taylor had been in constant touch with Purvis, working closely with him and his staff. He was shocked by the news of his death.

"They did a very unusual thing. They called a memorial service for Purvis almost immediately after he was killed. It was in a cathedral in Washington. I had to decide whether to go to the memorial service or take the day in Toronto. I had been working pretty hard and had been away from my family for quite some time, so I decided to go to Toronto. I arrived by train early Sunday morning and I was sitting sunning myself by my pool at Windfields when the telephone rang. It was C.D. Howe in Washington. He said, 'Lord Beaverbrook wants to talk to you. There's a Royal Canadian Air Force plane on the way to bring you down.'" Taylor met Beaverbrook and Howe about 2:30 in the afternoon, at the Mayflower Hotel in Washington. They were just getting ready to go to the memorial service, so Taylor went with them. "After that we went back to the hotel. Then Lord Beaverbrook, in his very direct way, said, 'I've lost my man here in the United States and I have to appoint a successor. I've appealed to my friend, Mr. Howe, to make a recommendation and he tells me that you've been very successful selling all this war material to the Americans. I've come to the conclusion that probably Americans can understand a Canadian better than they do an Englishman.' Of course, Beaverbrook was a Canadian himself. 'In short, I'm offering you the position as head of the British Supply Council in North America.'" Taylor was taken aback by the abrupt offer. He knew the enormity of the responsibility being offered to him. He had attended most of the meetings of the Supply Council representing Canada on C.D. Howe's behalf and knew the size of the operation. It was large–nineteen office buildings and 12,000 people.

"I turned to Howe and asked, 'What do you think I should do?' and he replied, 'I think you should do it!' I was only forty years of age. I thought about it for a moment and then told Beaverbrook, 'There's a war on. I'll do it!' Beaverbrook said, 'Well, now that's settled. I can assure you that you are appointed, but I report to only one man, the Prime Minister. He will be very curious to take a look at you, I'm sure. So don't be surprised if within a week you get a signal from me that the Prime Minister wants to see you.'" The discussions between Beaverbrook and Taylor continued in New York and Montreal where the two of them flew together in a military aircraft. They spent several hours discussing problems, strategy, objectives, and a range of subjects. The Beaver then left for England, and E.P. Taylor went back to his work in Washington and waited for the message to go to England. It came a week later.

"I went over in an aircraft to England from Dorval–a very cold, uncomfortable trip in a Liberator bomber–leaving Montreal at noon on August 28." Taylor well remembers the assorted crew which reflected the international composition of Ferry Command. The captain was Dutch, the co-pilots and navigator Canadian, the engineer an American, and the wireless operator, English.

Taylor stayed with Beaverbrook at his Cherkley home on the first weekend in England, receiving an invitation from Churchill to have lunch with him on Monday at 10 Downing Street.* This was the moment he had been looking forward to, meeting the great man, Winston Spencer Churchill. "We had lunch at Downing Street in the garden. It was a beautiful, sunny day, the first of September. It was a very pleasant lunch. I had expected a lot of grilling, but most of the time was spent with the two of them, Churchill and Beaverbrook, telling each other risqué stories. The discussion lasted until 4:00."

One of the reasons it took so long was that there was a problem in sorting out the position of Morris Wilson, who had been the vice-chairman of the British Supply Council of North America and who was president of the Royal Bank of Canada. In Beaverbrook's first meeting with Taylor in New York, the Beaver had expressed his concern that Wilson should not be the chairman, but that Taylor should be. On the other hand, he wanted Wilson to stay, but was certain he would resign over the loss of face if he was not put in the chairman's position. On top of that, Beaverbrook and Wilson were old friends. The Royal Bank had given Beaverbrook his earlier financing, around 1910. Taylor proposed as a compromise that they adopt the American form of organization, making Wilson the chairman and Taylor the president and chief

---

*Some of the other people E.P. Taylor was to meet during that visit indicate the kind of company in which he was moving at that time: David Lloyd George; the First Lord of the Admiralty, R.V. Alexander; Harold Balfour; Anthony Eden; the Vincent Masseys; Prime Minister King; Taylor's old colleague, Stride, of the London Committee; Pamela Churchill and Mollie Harriman; General Vanier, who later was to become the Governor General of Canada; Norman Robertson; and that diminutive, delightful Canadian war correspondent, Greg Clark.

executive officer. Taylor would do the work, and Wilson would be the ceremonial head and would go to cocktail parties, dinner parties, and other social functions. Beaverbrook was pleased with the solution but Churchill couldn't understand the U.S. system. In England it was the chairman who was the absolute boss of any company and executive head. The president, if there was one, was usually the retired chairman. But in North America it is the president, not the chairman, who is usually the chief executive officer—at least in those days. Beaverbrook was in full support of Taylor's proposal because of his interest in protecting as well as retaining Morris Wilson. Churchill was most reluctant. When the meeting broke up, the matter was by no means settled, at least that's what Churchill let on because he was still grumbling about the proposal.

As Taylor's record of the trip shows, on Tuesday, September 2, "Churchill sends for me at noon. We have a half hour's chat. He is still dissatisfied about the arrangement re M.W.W." This time the meeting was with Churchill alone, and in the Cabinet Room at 10 Downing Street. "He made another attack on me and tried to dissuade me and I said no. 'Of course, if it's an order. . . . But Lord Beaverbrook has approved this arrangement and he agrees with me it will work.' So Churchill had a memorandum prepared for the Cabinet. 'So be it,' he said. And he was cross as hell, saying, 'I don't know how I'll explain this to Cabinet.' He initialled the thing and put it in his briefcase."

A few days later there was a message from Churchill that he wanted to see Taylor. This time Churchill did not attempt to fight the chairman/president battle, but gave Taylor advice and instructions as to what he expected of him in his new post, which was of such vital importance to the war effort. When they parted, as Taylor's note puts it, "He wished me luck and expressed confidence in me."

What Taylor did not realize then, and perhaps has not until this time, is that to some extent Churchill was putting him on and could have wished him luck and expressed confidence in him after the first meeting on Monday, September 1. However, the chairman/president proposal was obviously being championed by Churchill's dear friend Beaverbrook with whom he constantly played cat and mouse. In this instance, Beaverbrook wanted something, a nominal post to keep his friend Morris Wilson happy, but, apparently truculent and bulldog-like, Churchill did not want to have any part of such a scheme. Or, at least, that's what he let on. The fact was that before his long luncheon meeting with Beaverbrook, and Taylor was finished on late Monday afternoon, Churchill had decided to give in. He knew he would have to anyhow, but he would never let on. As soon as the two Canadians had left, the Prime Minister called in his secretary and dictated a memorandum approving the entire proposal in pure Churchillian form, encompassing with his enormous mind all the points that had to be covered and putting in all the conditions. The cat was placidly at work. Churchill's memorandum for the War Cabinet authorizing the appointment of E.P. Taylor as vice chairman and president of the British Supply Council was not only dictated that day but printed as well.

Printed for the War Cabinet. September 1941.
SECRET. Copy No. 49
W.P. (41) 211.
September 1, 1941.

WAR CABINET
SUPPLY FROM NORTH AMERICA
Memorandum by the Prime Minister.

I HAVE had under consideration, in consultation with some of my colleagues, the arrangements in regard to the organisation and personnel of the British Supply Council in North America. (The present arrangements, as approved by the War Cabinet on the 12th December, 1940, are set out in the Appendix to this Note.)

2. I have accepted the recommendation of Lord Halifax and Lord Beaverbrook that Mr. Morris Wilson, at present Deputy Chairman of the Council, should now be appointed Chairman, in succession to Mr. Arthur Purvis. As Chairman he will preside at the Council which will determine general policy.

3. I have also approved the proposal that, in order to provide for the increasingly heavy responsibilities falling upon the chief officers of the Council, a new officer should be appointed who will bear the title of Vice-Chairman and Presi-

113

dent, the latter title being in common use on the American continent.

The Vice-Chairman and President will be the chief executive officer of the Council, and will be responsible for the day-to-day business relating to supplies.

Mr. E.P. Taylor, who at present represents the Canadian Government in Washington in respect of the Supply Agreement between the two countries, has been appointed to the new post of Vice-Chairman and President.

4. Advantage is said to lie in appointing another Canadian to this post. Mr. Taylor, who has been most successful in his present post, is expected to be a forceful and effective representative of our interests to the United States authorities.

5. Experience has shown that, while representations to the United States authorities should continue to be made by the Council, there is need for closer co-ordination between the Council and the heads of the Joint Staff Mission. For this purpose the following arrangements will take effect:−

(i) The Council will look to the heads of the Joint Staff Mission in Washington for advice on all technical and military matters.

(ii) The heads of the Joint Staff Mission will be responsible for making such representations as may be necessary to the War Department and the Navy Department on the strategical aspects of our supply needs.

(iii) The heads of the Joint Staff Mission will not initiate representations on supply matters without prior consultation with the Council.

6. Nothing in the above will, of course, affect the position of the heads of the Joint Staff Mission as the representatives of the Chiefs of Staff. They will continue to discuss strategical questions with the War Department or the Navy Department without reference to the Supply Council.

7. Communications from Great Britain with the Supply Council will continue to be directed through the North American Supply Committee; but, in order to ensure that the instructions given to our representatives in North America are based on strategic as well as supply considerations, it will be necessary that the Service Ministers should become members

of the North American Supply Committee, which will be responsible for all requisitions submitted to the United States Government.

September 1, 1941.   W. S. C.

On Saturday, September 6, Taylor took an afternoon train to Prestwick where he had dinner with Vincent Massey, George Vanier, Norman Robertson, Greg Clark, and Taylor's fellow bomber passenger, Mackenzie King. At 6:00 the next morning, they were airborne out of Prestwick. King, who hated flying and was a standoffish person, apparently had little to discuss with Taylor on the frigid, noisy bomber. Fifteen and a half hours later, they landed at Dorval where the Prime Minister was met by C.D. Howe and Ernest Lapointe, King's Minister of Justice. There was time for a long discussion between Howe and his increasingly successful protégé, Eddie Taylor, of whom he was enormously proud. After all, it was Howe who had recommended Taylor to Beaverbrook as Purvis' successor. Before leaving for Washington at 9:30 P.M., Edward placed a telephone call to Winnie and the three children in Toronto.

Taylor's absences were difficult for the family. Winnie wanted to be with her husband in Washington, but she had the three children to take care of. Charles was at Upper Canada and the girls were at Havergal. "My wife would drive ten or twelve people to school every day in the station-wagon and go and get them in the afternoon." At Windfields, she kept chickens and cows and even took to churning butter. "My hours in Washington would be so irregular that it wouldn't have been a good idea for her to have been there. It wouldn't have been a very happy life for her. She wouldn't have had any particular friends."

Taylor was able to get up every second or third week to be with his family, and Winnie would get down to Washington from time to time. Between Taylor in Washington and his family at Windfields, there was a constant flow of letters, with each of the children faithfully writing to tell their father about the exciting events at school.

The announcement of Taylor's appointment as vice-chairman and president of the British Supply Council in North America had been made on September 3, while Taylor was still in England. Congratulations poured in from all quarters. In its October 1941 edition, *Canadian Business* published a photograph of Taylor with an eloquently descriptive caption which brought out a curious similarity between Taylor and the late Arthur Purvis whom he had succeeded. "Nothing will bring a truly great executive to the top of a heap quicker than a wartime emergency. Young Arthur Purvis was the outstanding 'prodigy' of the last war. Today we have another in the person of youthful E.P. Taylor, who, after setting records before the war, has in his brief sixteen months' dollar-a-year career, set new ones consistently."

Chapter VII

The Washington Years
Early Forties

In Washington, E.P. Taylor plunged into his responsibilities with formidable zest and drive. As vice-chairman and president of the British Supply Council, he was responsible for the procurement of the broad spectrum of critical military material, equipment, and supplies which were absolutely essential not only to the survival of a beleaguered Britain but for the Commonwealth and other allies. At this most precarious period in the Second World War Edward Taylor's duties and tasks were the highest and most responsible of any British representative in North America. He answered to Churchill through Beaverbrook. No Canadian outside the military was appointed to a more important post during the entire war, and none carried out his responsibilities any more effectively–all at no expense to the Crown either in the right of the United Kingdom or of Canada.

Taylor's duties and responsibilities involved convincing the military, civilians, American politicians, board and military tribunals, and other groups that the United States should provide Britain and the Commonwealth, for cash payment or under the lend/lease plan, with the various types and kinds of military equipment, supplies, and food.

There were regular weekly meetings of the British Supply Council, which were mainly reporting sessions of the heads of the missions. The British ambassador, Lord Halifax, always sat on the right of the chairman, Morris Wilson, and E.P. Taylor sat on his left. Taylor often chaired the meetings in Wilson's absence. Each of the missions also reported directly to a government department in England. The co-ordinating body there came under the Ministry of Production, of which Beaverbrook was the head.

Taylor had some 12,000 people working for him in Washington and New York. In both places they were scattered through various buildings. The head office of the British Supply Council was in the Willard Hotel, an old establishment in the centre of Washington close to the White House. The British Purchasing Commission, which later became the British Supply Mission, was on 18th Street and was filled with civilians and soldiers. The Air Mission was on Massachusetts Avenue. The rest were in other buildings. The New York office occupied a whole building on Broad Street.

As the vice-chairman and president of the British Supply Council, Taylor became involved in making major decisions or solving large supply problems. In working out a solution, the first group he would take his mission to was the International Supply Committee of the War Department which functioned similarly to an Appeal Court, but "it was completely an American army organization." He would go before this committee once a week on the average. If he was turned down he could then go to the Combined Chiefs of Staff, made up of the U.S. and British chiefs. Field Marshal Sir John Dill was the U.K. representative. If they would not go along with him, he could then appeal to Harry Hopkins.

Taylor remembers one case very well because it also fell under the instructions given to him by Churchill to get the Americans to help to build corvettes, small escort vessels which were very effective against submarines. The British navy had designed them and had specified their need. When Taylor made his submission to the Combined Chiefs, he was met by opposition from Admiral King, who was chief of the U.S. naval staff. "He was a very fine naval officer, no question about that. But he was completely single-minded: he was worried about the Japanese more than he was about the Germans."

King felt corvettes were useless, and that they had no way of defending themselves. Taylor's view was that corvettes were expendable because in the time it took to build one destroyer twelve corvettes could be produced. But the Combined Chiefs of Staff turned Taylor down because of Admiral King's position. "So that's a case where I went to Harry Hopkins. I brought the appropriate British admiral with me. Hopkins listened to the story and he saw the common sense of the argument. In the President's name, the decision was made that the United States would build corvettes for the British navy."

E.P. Taylor knew that the Americans were arming themselves in the realization that they would be into the war sooner or later. "They were preparing for this event. They were in competition with us. We were using up the steel and the ammunition, the tanks and the ships and the aircraft. Our problem was to prove that the British need was greater than the American need, that our need was vital, that we had to have it in order to continue fighting the war."

From all of this it is apparent that the man who was the vice-chairman, president, and chief executive officer of the British Supply Council in North America had to be a man of enormous capacity for negotiation, highly intelligent, well versed in business, and above all respected by those with whom he was dealing on the American side. In selecting E.P. Taylor, Churchill and Beaverbrook chose well, although there were some indications that E.P. Taylor's comparative youth and the fact that he was a Canadian as well as a "new boy" did not sit well with some of the British businessmen who had been moved across to New York and Washington to participate in their country's purchasing effort. "There also may have been some displeasure or surprise in some of the missions at Beaverbrook choosing a Canadian to succeed Purvis. And, of course, I became director general in January 1942 of the most important mission which was then known as the British Purchasing Commission." That appointment, in addition to his position as vice-chairman and president of the council, probably wounded more egos in the senior levels of the British purchasing structure in North America, but it certainly did not hurt Edward Taylor's.

Taylor conducted most of his business from the Willard Hotel, where he had two offices. They were "just bedrooms with the furniture taken out." In the same building was the office of Jean Monnet, an adviser to the British Supply Council in North America. An enormously influential Frenchman, he had worked hard for the repeal of the U.S. Neutrality Act and the creation of a new lend/lease scheme. He had been the chairman of the Anglo/French Purchasing Mission, which was dissolved when France fell. Monnet was such a valuable man that he was retained. He was a very wealthy brandy manufacturer in France but could not get his money out of the country. "Monnet was very shrewd and very wise. He was the father of the European Economic Community. A sort of recluse, he was nevertheless a man who could open any door, whether it was into the White House or any ministry. He could go anywhere and was highly regarded. He was completely bilingual. The only difficult thing about him was his hours. He didn't come to work until 11:00 and didn't go to bed until midnight. A lot of our finer negotiations were done over the dinner table, but Monnet never sat down to dinner until about 10:30 at night." (Much business was done in Washington at cocktail parties and over the dinner table.) "One of our problems was the difference in hours the different nations worked. The Americans were very early risers, usually getting to the office around 7:00 and quitting about 6:00. The Canadians would get to the office about 8:00 and quit about 7:00 or 8:00. The British would get to the office between 9:00 and 9:30 and quit about that time in the evening. And the French would get to the office about noon and quit about 10:30. You had to wait a long time to see the French people."

When he first arrived in Washington, Taylor took an apartment on Connecticut Avenue, from which he could walk to his Willard Hotel office. Then, realizing that the war was going to go on for some time, and that his involvement would be extensive, he decided that he needed a more permanent, comfortable and private place in which to live, and rented a house on Charleston Terrace, overlooking the Potomac River. In Washington he didn't have time for either of his favourite pastimes, golfing and riding.

Most of Taylor's dinners were at an exclusive club close to the Willard where matters could be discussed in relative privacy and in quiet. "I'd only take a senior person there, such as H.R. MacMillan or C.D. Howe." Much business was done at dinners which had to be organized for the very purpose of getting everybody together. "You had to eat somewhere, and everyone had things to do at other hours of the day, so we had to promote these dinners." One of the over-dinner objectives that Taylor had been instructed by Churchill to pursue was getting the Americans to build night bombers. Three or four top American Air Generals and Air Marshal Sir Arthur Harris of the R.A.F. and two or three of his top Air Marshals would be invited to a dinner with one or two American civilians, and perhaps the Secretary of Air from the War Department or the Under-Secretary for Air. It would be a semi-social gathering, but the talk was always business.

It was the thesis of Air Marshal Sir Arthur Harris–known as "Bomber" Harris–that if he could get a thousand bombers a night over Germany, the war would end in six months. "I think Air Marshal Harris was right. If he had been able to put a thousand bombers over Germany every night the war would have been over months earlier and the invasion would not have been necessary." The Americans developed the Norden precision bomb sight and stuck strictly to day bombing using their B-17 Flying Fortresses with great accuracy. In the end, neither could convince the other, and both went their separate, yet successful ways in destroying the German industrial capacity.

In July 1941, less than one month after the German attack on the Soviet Union, Harry Hopkins had flown to Moscow as the special emissary of the President. On September 20, 1941, just as E.P. Taylor was beginning to get fully acquainted with the realities of his new position, Beaverbrook and Harriman, as the Beaverbrook/Harriman Supply Mission, had left for Moscow with the joint instructions of Churchill and Roosevelt to ascertain what the Soviets required in terms of equipment and to work out a scheme to get it to them. Beaverbrook and Stalin became fast friends and quickly learned to respect each other. Stalin became convinced that Great Britain and the United States were really prepared to offer more than their own security justified. When it came to actually delivering the goods, Beaverbrook performed and, in fact, delivered ahead of promises. As soon as the protocol [with the Russians] was signed, Beaverbrook wired his orders back to London and the tanks, aircraft, and other equipment started moving. We all know what a touch-and-go battle that was. It is more than well within the realm of possibility that, if the British equipment had not arrived by that time, the Russians would have despaired and lost Moscow instead of holding it."*

After Harriman arrived back in Washington from the mission to

---

*This quotation is from an address by E.P. Taylor at the annual meeting of the Canadian Manufacturers Association, June 9, 1942, a copy of which he delivered to Sir Clive Baillieu with a covering memorandum dated June 15, 1942. Earlier in the year Taylor had succeeded Baillieu as director general of the British Purchasing Commission. The memo says in part: "You will probably be amused that I devoted so much of it to the Beaver, but the reason for this is that the little man is not known today in Canada and is quite generally misunderstood."

Moscow with the signed protocol, the Russians moved quickly and established a purchasing mission in Washington known as Antorg. A young Andrei Gromyko was the ambassador. Taylor saw a great deal of him.

Many of the things that Britain had promised to the Russians were being obtained on lend/lease out of the United States. And such things as aluminum they were receiving from Canada. "My job was to make sure these commodities were delivered on time, and they were. At the beginning, the American supplies were not delivered on time." American factories were so vast that it took longer to set them up. Britain therefore did better in giving aid to Russia in the early months after July 1941 than the United States did. But in a year's time, the United States caught up and they were doing more than their fair share. "Of course, half the stuff was sunk on its way. That was the tragedy."

During his term of office as vice-chairman and president of the British Supply Council in North America, E.P. Taylor made a practice of presenting a regular written report to Beaverbrook. In 1941, the Beaver was chairman of the North America Supply Committee of the War Cabinet, operating in the depths of the cramped labyrinth of below-ground, bomb-proof offices which Churchill and his War Cabinet used in Great George Street, not far from Westminster.

Taylor made the first of his reports in a letter dated October 2, 1941. This document demonstrates not only the scope and scale of Taylor's staggering responsibility, but also his total grasp of the issues and people he had to deal with.

His report covers in detail the status of the missions–Purchasing, Air, Admiralty, Technical, Joint Staff–and particularly of the following critical items: 1) Iran Railway Equipment Motor Vehicles, Pipe Line and Refinery for Aviation Spirit; 2) Small Arms Ammunition; 3) Artillery Ammunition; 4) Rifles; 5) Anti-Aircraft Artillery; 6) Anti-Tank Equipment; 7) Armoured Fighting Vehicles; 8) Heavy Bombers; 9) Bombs, Explosives; 10) 20mm Hispano Suiza Cannon and Ammunition; 11) Oerlikon Guns; 12) Bofors Naval Guns; 13) 15" A.P. Shells; 14) Torpedoes; 15) Escort Vessels; 16) Martlet Aircraft; 17) Fleet Destroyers. Taylor concludes his letter:

I am not losing sight of the fact that my principal and most immediate task is to do everything possible to accelerate deliveries from our own contracts and to obtain substantial allocations from existing American production. . . .

The Chairman has seen this letter and is in accord with its contents.

Immediately Churchill received the news of the Japanese attack on Pearl Harbour on December 7, 1941, he decided that he should pay an official, symbolic visit to the United States, now a full-fledged partner and ally. He quickly made arrangements with President Roosevelt, who was delighted with the prospect. And, as required by tradition, Churchill attended upon King George VI. "I obtained the King's permission in order to meet the President of the United States to arrange with him for all of the mapping out of our military plans and for all those intimate meetings of the high officers of the Armed Forces of both countries which are indispensable to the successful prosecution of the war."*

With Churchill came the ever-present Beaverbrook and the top British army, navy, and air force officers. Churchill stayed at Blair House opposite the White House, while Beaverbrook, who was now Minister of Supply, stayed at the Mayfair Hotel.

Taylor had words with Churchill one evening at a party at the British Embassy. "The old man was gracious enough to growl at me that he had heard good reports. But, of course, the next day was the exciting day when he went to see the President."

One of Churchill's main objectives in going to the United States was to lift the spirits of the Americans and to assist the President in getting the nation moving. He needed to know from his own experts exactly what the American capability was. He therefore had told Beaverbrook to put an aide memoire together on the matter. Beaverbrook, by this time confined to bed by a severe attack of asthma, gathered his people in his Mayfair Hotel bedroom. "He was sitting in bed, surrounded by Lord Halifax, Field Marshal Dill, Jean Monnet, me, and several other naval, army, and air people. There were about ten of us around his bed. He sat there with

---

*Churchill's address to a Joint Session of the Congress of the United States, Friday, December 26, 1941.

some kind of mask over his face, breathing something to alleviate the asthma. He had a carton of Kleenex, and he was sneezing and throwing them around and we were all dodging the things."

Beaverbrook looked to Taylor, with his broad knowledge and understanding of the American scene, to come up with the production capacity and target figures. Taylor gave him 60,000 aircraft a year, 45,000 tanks, 20,000 anti-aircraft guns, and 8 million tons of merchant shipping. Those calculations went into the aide memoire, which was delivered to Churchill. The next evening he went to dinner with the President. "And, by gosh, within a few days, out comes another statement from the White House that this was the target for the American armed forces, exactly the figures we had suggested to them through Churchill. Of course, some of the American military brass were just furious."* It was for Taylor a matter of pleasure and satisfaction that his input, just as in the Hyde Park agreement, had, on a figure for figure basis, emerged as presidential and United States government policy.

This was just one reason among many why for E.P. Taylor 1941 was a personal pinnacle. To be appointed by, and be responsible to, one of the giant men in the history of the world, Winston Spencer Churchill, and to serve with his closest colleague and friend, Lord Beaverbrook, was a privilege and responsibility granted to no other Canadian.

At the end of 1941, Taylor's all-consuming interest and the focus of his enormous drive and energy was the war effort and the successful operation of the British Supply Council and all the British missions in North America. Between the outbreak of war and the end of 1941, the United Kingdom had contracted to spend nearly $4 billion in the United States for all manner of war stores, raw materials, and food. It was E.P. Taylor who supervised and coordinated most of this massive acquisition.

At the beginning of 1942, Beaverbrook left the Ministry of Supply and was succeeded by Sir Andrew Rae Duncan, to whom E.P. Taylor would now report in his capacity as president and chief executive officer of the British Purchasing Commission.

In Washington, another shift took place just before Beaver-

---

*Taylor's reference is to a speech by President Roosevelt to a Joint Session of Congress, January 7, 1942, in which he also declared that in 1943 America would make 125,000 aircraft, of which 100,000 would be combat aircraft, 75,000 tanks, 35,000 anti-aircraft guns, and 10 million deadweight tons of merchant shipping.

brook's departure. Sir Clive Baillieu, who had been director general of the British Purchasing Commission, was assigned to form a new organization, the British Raw Materials Mission. Beaverbrook wanted the best man he could find to fill the most important of all of the commissions. Never one to resist a challenge, Taylor accepted the new post, and on January 16 became the acting director general of the British Purchasing Commission. On January 30, 1942, Lord Halifax, the British ambassador, presented E.P. Taylor with a certificate under Halifax's hand and seal which says, in part:

> I, the Viscount Halifax, His Britannic Majesty's Ambassador to the United States of America, do hereby certify that E.P. Taylor is Acting Director General of the British Purchasing Commission, Washington, D.C., and that he has and since, on and after the 16th day of January, 1942, had authority to enter into contracts in the United States of America on behalf of His Majesty's government in the United Kingdom. And without derogation from the generality from the foregoing, I further certify that in the exercise of such power, E.P. Taylor, as such Acting Director General of·the British Purchasing Commission, has and has had since said date, full authority to bind His Majesty's government in the United Kingdom.

Taylor now had in his hands the two most important British mission posts in the United States: the Supply Council and the Purchasing Mission. It was his job to keep supplies of all kinds flowing to Britain from an American nation newly involved in the Second World War. But since the first American priority was now its own forces, it was now doubly difficult for the British and Russians to secure the necessary material, equipment, guns, ships, food, raw materials, and essentials not only for fighting a war but for survival as nations. In effect, the Americans, the British, and the Russians were competing with each other for the goods and supplies that the gigantic American industrial complex and its agricultural breadbaskets could produce. It was probably the most difficult time of the war to be in this crucial, all-important British position. The pressure was enormous. Requisitions kept flowing in from the United Kingdom for guns, food, and all manner of equipment. It was up to Taylor to oversee the huge British staff and to deal directly with the top American civilians and military. Eighteen- and twenty-hour days were commonplace, and weekends or time off almost impossible. The pace was killing, even for E.P. Taylor, with his enormous energy and capacity for work.

In April 1942, Morris Wilson decided that it was time to return to his career position as president of the Royal Bank of Canada and he resigned as chairman of the British Supply Council. He was succeeded in this largely ceremonial position by the Honourable R.H. Brand who had come to Washington in March of 1941 as head of the British Food Mission, a post in which he continued after assuming the *ad interim* chairmanship of the council. Taylor was still president and chief executive officer and chaired many of its meetings.

The two-hatted E.P. Taylor made his first written report as director general of the British Purchasing Commission in May of 1942 when he wrote to his new chief, Sir Andrew Duncan, the Minister of Supply. This short letter gives a picture of a strong, confident Edward Taylor, quite prepared to dig in his heels against his military advisers, a man who had a complete overview of the broad responsibilities he was obliged to discharge on behalf of the government of the United Kingdom.

As nearly four months have elapsed since I assumed the direction of the B.P.C., it is fitting that I should make a brief report to you.

My first close examination of the affairs of the Commission convinced me that, although an excellent system of checks and control had been established in relation to our old cash contracts, no appropriate arrangements had been instituted to properly keep track of, control, or follow up Lend Lease requisitions, now constituting practically all transactions. In private business I have always relied on accurate information to give me the position from day to day and to expose weaknesses so that they can be corrected. Consequently we established a system of reports covering the four principal stages in our operations namely:–demand to requisition, requisition to contract, contract to completion, and completion to ocean shipment.

The chain of authority and the division of responsibility has been re-organized and we now have the right and competent people doing the important jobs.

When I took over I found that there was a heavy backlog of

demands which had not been turned into requisitions, and requisitions which had not reached the contract stage in the U.S. procurement agencies. Components for U.S. tank production, signal stores and vehicle spares were the most numerous examples . . .

The proposals of the Military are so unworkable and as they affect more of the Missions than the B.P.C., I am sure Mr. Oliver Lyttelton will dispose of them promptly on his arrival. At the same time I consider that you should be informed that this discussion is going on here so that you will be prepared to meet the proposal if it should be raised in London. . . .

In conclusion may I say that it is a great pleasure and satisfaction to have Sir Leonard Browett here. He very quickly acquired a good knowledge of our organization and problems and has already demonstrated to me that he is a man of energy, has most excellent judgement and administrative ability.

The last paragraph of the letter demonstrates a quality of Taylor's that has remained constant throughout his life. He is always ready to praise when he thinks praise is due. When the opportunity or necessity to criticize appears, it is rarely seized and never publicly.

Taylor's advice to the Minister of Supply concerning "the proposals of the military" was accepted.

During this hectic period, the pressures on Taylor were beginning to pile up–the combined responsibilities of his Washington duties, which went on day and night; his responsibilities as the head man of Canadian Breweries; the constant drag of attending interminable meetings; and his lack of family life in Washington. He was short of patience, not sleeping well, and generally feeling run down. Nevertheless, he pressed on.

But whether in New York or Washington or London, whether acting as the president of the British Supply Council or the director general of the British Purchasing Commission, Edward Taylor's thinking was seldom far from the corporate boardroom. In a speech in late June 1942, at the annual meeting in Toronto of the Canadian Manufacturers Association, he made several references to the billions of dollars he was spending for the British. Then he said:

Sometimes I wonder after dealing with astronomical figures, how I can ever get back to the figures of Canadian commerce. A while ago I was here for a day to preside at a directors' meeting. We were going over certain capital commitments. I came to an item which was really $70,000, but I stated it as $70 million. Several members of the board collapsed. Small wonder.

Taylor had spent a great deal of time preparing this speech, which was a wartime watershed in his thinking and planning for his own future. An important personal assessment emerged. He could see three wartime battles that had to be won: the battle of production, the battle of transportation, and the final battle of combat in the field. As he saw it, the battle of transportation was then raging, with ship construction, the building of escort vessels, and all other antidotes for the submarine and attacking aircraft. "The first phase of the battle is as good as in the bag. The anti-submarine phase of the battle of transportation is bound to be a hard, long, drawn-out affair, but we will surely wear down the enemy and progressively reduce the losses until he becomes discouraged, as in the last war. The real and final battle of combat has yet to begin, only because up until now we have not been prepared."

For Taylor, his *raison d'être* for being in both Ottawa and Washington was production and supply. His fight was already finished. "The battle of production is virtually won. The production in the United Kingdom is amazing." In Canada, "none of us ever thought that we would produce so much. While all our plants are not yet into full capacity, in the course of a few months, they will all exceed the production targets which were set when they were established." And in the United States, "the President's objectives, which very few people thought possible last January, will be exceeded."

Although he did not put it in these words in his speech, Taylor was now of the opinion that the need for his presence in Washington had diminished to the point where he might well depart the stage. Mind you, D-Day was almost two full years away, but the perceptive E.P. Taylor had cast in his own mind a clear concept of what course the war would follow. In doing so he made an assessment for himself that would assist him some sixty days later to come to a firm conclusion as to his own future.

Edward Taylor claims to be and is an internationalist, a man who believes in free trade and the down-playing of nationalism. It was in this speech of June 9, 1942, that for the first time he was able to express from his high overview position how the thrust and urgency of war had overcome the nationalist barriers which have always impeded commerce as well as peace.

The concluding section of his talk set out fundamental principles which are, at the same time, internationalist, progressive, and then as now, valid and practical. Yet in terms of the way the world has evolved, they are idealistic–the optimum. Taylor was to cling to his June 1942 views for many years.

> I suggest, therefore, that it would be a major contribution to the peace of the world if the British Commonwealth and the United States were to declare now, I repeat now, during this war, that from now on there shall be between them free movement of goods, a common currency, and free movement of people. The three stand together–none can produce the desired results without the other, and I submit Canada has nothing to fear from such an arrangement.

Home at Windfields for a holiday at the beginning of August, worn out and unwell, Edward Taylor had, at his wife's insistence, a thorough medical examination. His doctor told him in no uncertain terms that he could not go on working at the pace he had been keeping. He had to have a rest. At his age, forty-one, he was highly vulnerable to any number of serious consequences if he did not let up.

It was a difficult decision to make. His position in Washington was one of high responsibility and enormous prestige. On the other hand, he knew full well that the battle of production and supply had been won while he had been in Washington. He was tired of the incessant grind. His family needed him, and he needed them. There were new business opportunities emerging in Canada. The affairs of Canadian Breweries really required his constant rather than intermittent attention. His life ahead was full of challenges, but he could not seize them if he was in poor health. Furthermore, no one is indispensable or irreplaceable, certainly within an organization as large as the British Supply Council.

This was one situation Edward discussed with Winnie. There was no question in her mind, and furthermore, she and the children would be delighted to have him back in Ottawa, if not at Windfields.

The decision was made.

On August 5, 1942, E.P. Taylor wrote to Sir Andrew Duncan resigning from the British Purchasing Commission citing exhaustion as his reason. He was prepared, he added, "to stay on the job for another few weeks if necessary, and shall, of course, be available to familiarize my successor with the way the mission works. . . ."

A few days later, Taylor sent his letter of resignation as vice-chairman and president of the British Supply Council. He had informed C.D. Howe of the action he had taken, and the reason. Howe immediately asked to see him in Ottawa where, after a lengthy discussion, Taylor agreed to rejoin Howe in the Ministry of Munitions and Supply, again as president of War Supplies Limited based in Ottawa. He also agreed to be Howe's representative on the U.S.-Canada Government Committee.

In addition, Howe, who was planning to resign from his post as Canada's representative on the British Supply Council, suggested that Taylor should take his place. In a letter, written August 15 to the Honourable R.H. Brand, the interim chairman of the British Supply Council, with whom Taylor had been working for the past few months, Howe raised the possibility of Taylor's replacing him.

The letter was personally taken to Washington by Taylor and presented to Brand, who was concerned that the other Commonwealth ministerial members of the council would be upset if Howe resigned in favour of Taylor, a non-minister. (Taylor's meeting with Brand did not produce a resolution to this situation. It was, however, ultimately resolved as Howe retained his seat on the British Supply Council.)

The acceptance of Taylor's resignation finally came in a letter from Sir Andrew Duncan, dated September 17, 1942. His conciliatory and sympathetic letter summed up in a very British way the esteem and regard with which Taylor was held and the real regret felt at his departure.

The plan was that Taylor would leave his Washington post in mid-October and then be re-appointed to War Supplies Limited. Indeed, that was the intent as late as the last week in September, with the question of Howe's representation on the British Supply Council still being up in the air. But Taylor wanted a brief holiday and decided to go to the Pacific coast for the first week in October before returning to Washington. (His interest in the forest products potential in British Columbia was beginning and this would be a good time to combine a much-needed vacation with a look around.)

With Taylor's successor, General Sir Walter Venning, arriving in Washington during the week of October 19, Taylor felt sure he could take on the presidency of War Supplies Limited on or before October 26. His old friend King Shiels, the Deputy Minister of Munitions and Supply, and his other colleagues in the ministry, were delighted to know that he was returning and were ready to give him a hand in getting back into the driver's seat at War Supplies Limited.

On October 12, Taylor's resignation from the British organizations in Washington became effective, and on October 15, the formality of his re-appointment as president of War Supplies Limited took place in Ottawa in his absence. But he never did take over War Supplies Limited. While Taylor was in Washington assisting General Sir Walter Venning in taking over the British Supply Mission, C.D. Howe had negotiated a position for Canada on the Combined Production and Resources Board (which had been set up in June 1942), and relying on Taylor's vast Washington experience, Howe made the immediate decision that Taylor should become his acting deputy on that board. This was acceptable to Nelson and the British. On November 13, 1942, Canada became a member of the Combined Board with Howe as its representative and E.P. Taylor as his deputy. Howe remained a member of the British Supply Council, but rarely attended a meeting.

A new organization chart of the Department of Munitions and Supply dated November 10, 1942, just three days before Canada joined the Combined Production and Resources Board, shows E.P. Taylor reporting directly to the minister as Howe's representative on the Combined Board, and the presidency of War Supplies Limited in the hands of V.W. Scully. The official history of the British Supply Council of North America states that "the position of vice-chairman and president of a council, which Mr. Taylor had held, was eliminated" on his departure and resignation. The post of president had been a very special one made by Churchill himself to suit the talents of a special man.

A description of the importance of the work of the Combined

Board and its importance appears in a *Business Week* report of January 1944. "Until recently, their chief job was that of sharing the scarcity–of raw materials, of plant facilities, of production, and of manpower. But today, as the united nations swing into the victory stretch, they are getting ready to work as a mechanism for tapering war production, to co-ordinate the reconversion of·a half dozen national economies from war to peace."

E.P. Taylor saw this conversion to peace time as the major function of the Combined Board. "The war production requirements were pretty well met, and we got very quickly into making studies of storages and surplusses and how each nation could help the other. I didn't have very much to do and I was sort of moonlighting on my own private affairs toward the end of 1943 and 1944."

Taylor's Combined Board responsibilities would not be nearly as onerous or demanding as what he had been handling for the British since the fall of 1941. It suited his talents as well as his physical need for easing up the pace. Moreover, E.P. Taylor wanted to continue his work with Howe whom he admired and respected.

And so for E.P. Taylor it was time to be back in Ottawa and Toronto where his much-neglected business affairs needed the attention only he could give them. There would be the occasional foray to Washington to attend a Combined Board meeting but that fascinating episode in his life was now behind him. His prior time in Washington had brought him a broad new expanse of experience, taught him much about personal diplomacy and the handling of people, particularly in the format of a conference or meeting, and it had given him an insight into internationalism and its practicality in the presence of an emergency and, in his view, in times of peace as well as war. He had also gained a wealth of new friends and acquaintances, many of whom he would remain in touch with during the following decades.

Chapter VIII

Other Battles

With the enormous burden of his Washington responsibilities off his shoulders, Taylor was able to give an increasing amount of time to his own business matters. Even when he had been immersed in the demanding affairs of the British Supply Council and the British Purchasing Commission, he had managed to keep a close eye on the operations of Canadian Breweries Limited–each day Taylor would receive a brief communication from the executive vice-president, D.C. Betts, indicating the company's progress and some of the problems it was encountering. During 1942 Taylor had watched, with growing concern, the escalating attacks of the Canadian Temperance Federation and its Ontario branch on the federal government, on him personally, on Canadian Breweries, and against the consumption of alcohol and beer on a national basis. He could see that the press was giving the Temperance people more and more space, and with it increased credibility.

What Taylor saw developing had begun in February 1942, when Finance Minister Ilsley stated in the House of Commons that the federal government had no intention of entering the field of alcoholic beverage regulation and would treat this matter as a provincial concern. The same issue appeared again in Parliament in June, when E.P. Taylor was specifically accused by the Opposition of interfering with the war effort by shipping beer overseas. The government was also under attack for failing to ration beer when other commodities were being rationed, and for shipping beer overseas. The government's position was that the shipments of beer were not displacing other cargoes, that the ingredients for making beer were not in short supply, and, consequently, there was no need to ration beer.

Nevertheless, this type of criticism, together with increasing pressure from the Canadian Temperance Federation, caused the federal Cabinet to begin placing restrictions on the supply of beer during wartime. In August 1942, the federal government increased the excise duty on malt, the main ingredient of beer, and as a result the price of beer was increased. However, there was no expectation that the production of beer would be affected or that there would be a shortage.

On September 12, an avidly anti-alcohol Mackenzie King received a pro-Temperance delegation from the United Church. Impressed by their arguments, King agreed with them that the sale of beer and liquor should be prohibited.

On September 14, the Prime Minister told his Cabinet that he thought "we should press on in the matter of curtailing the liquor traffic."* The Cabinet showed very little enthusiasm for this policy, and although King directed that orders be drafted to put such a policy into effect, their preparation, much to his chagrin, proceeded very slowly.

Finally, after months of furtive preparation, Mackenzie King moved. In a speech made in the House on December 16, 1942, he outlined the regulatory steps the federal government was taking and the reasons for them. Regulations were passed under the War Measures Act–which meant that they did not have to have the approval of Parliament–limiting the amount of alcoholic beverages available for sale and eliminating all advertising of alcoholic beverages. For the year beginning November 1, 1942, the quantity of beer produced was expected to be cut back by 10 per cent, wine by 20 per cent, and spirits by 30 per cent, with additional restrictions on the alcoholic content of wine and spirits. King also asked the provinces to restrict the hours of sale of alcoholic beverages.

With incredulity, astonishment, and anger, Taylor read the reports on the speech and the arguments that King used to justify his measures. King's main point was that the substantial increase in the consumption of alcoholic beverages was harming the war effort. He argued that unless the consumption of alcoholic beverages could be shown to strengthen the war effort, they should be

---

*J.W. Pickersgill, *The Mackenzie King Record*, vol. 1 (Toronto, 1960), p. 460.

rationed. Furthermore, since other commodities, some considered as necessities, were being rationed, alcoholic beverages should also be rationed. Aside from these considerations, King argued that the increased consumption of alcoholic beverages in wartime meant a "loss of efficiency to the fighting and working forces of the country"; that industrial accidents as well as the "absence from work and inefficient work are frequently due to intemperance"; and that the "use of alcoholic beverages is certain to slow down the process of the recruit in training." On a broader scope, King argued that "failure to be temperate helps to establish habits which later may lead to the breakdown of morals."

King's justification of the regulations was a reflection of the arguments used by the Canadian Temperance Federation, most of which had been laid out in full-page ads as early as July 3, 1942, when the federation had published a public "appeal of urgency to the Right Honourable W.L. Mackenzie King, C.M.G., and the members of the Dominion Government" asking them to "face the facts!" In that advertisement, under the heading of "Facts," a clear shot was taken at Canadian Breweries, although Taylor's name was not mentioned.

WHILE THE NATION FACES A CRISIS, THE LIQUOR TRAFFIC THRIVES AND ITS PROMOTERS ARE ENRICHED.
Canadian Breweries Limited, one of Canada's largest brewing mergers, published in Canadian newspaper advertisements boasting of the success of its enterprises. It announced substantial additions to capital reserves, improved plant, increased dividends and put forth proposals for eliminating all arrears and dividends on preferred stock.

The ten points listed under the "Facts" column appeared in King's speech but in different wording.

The immediate reaction to the Prime Minister's action was subdued. The brewers generally resigned themselves to the regulations, but warned of bootlegging. Some provincial premiers hailed the regulations, while others remained quiet. And, of course, the Temperance people applauded the speech, but nevertheless criticized the regulations because they thought they were too lax.

While his colleagues in the brewing business were prepared to take the Prime Minister's personal onslaught on the industry and the beer-drinking people of Canada lying down, E.P. Taylor was not. So far as he was concerned, King was using the public pressure of the Temperance people and the wartime emergency to attempt to destroy the brewers and distillers across the country for personal reasons and without any justification whatsoever. The fact that, in order to fight this battle, he would have to take on the Prime Minister was of no concern to Taylor.

On December 30, 1942, E.P. Taylor sent a letter to the Prime Minister criticizing the regulations on alcoholic beverages and, in particular, beer. He stated that he was prepared to make any sacrifice for the war effort. He pointed out to King that the regulations would have no effect on the profits of Canadian Breweries–this only meant that less excess profits tax would be paid. Taylor was especially critical of King's broadcast, "insofar as it suggested to the mass of the Canadian people that they were drinking too much and thus adversely affecting the efforts of the armed services and munitions workers," and he directly accused King of trying to placate the prohibitionist element. Finally, Taylor was highly critical of King's attitude toward the brewing and distilling industries in Canada, telling King that his action had "in effect told the public that you consider that the brewers and distillers are engaged in an undesirable business and therefore you are not going to accord them the same treatment which other commodities receive, and which they are accorded in all other English-speaking democracies." At the close of this strong letter, Taylor asked for a meeting with King to discuss the issue.

King had welcomed the prohibitionists. Would he now be prepared to receive E.P. Taylor?

Taylor received a swift reply, dated January 4, 1943, from a truculent and haughty King, who said that he was not willing to see Taylor, pointing out instead that the matter would be placed before the House of Commons when Parliament reconvened. However, the Prime Minister did condescend to attempt to justify the regulations pointing out that Britain had reduced both the supply and the strength of beer, an irrelevant position because of the vastly different situations in Britain and Canada. (Britain had to import its raw materials to produce beer, whereas in Canada the beer ingredients were domestically grown and there was no shortage.) Finally, King denied that the regulations were his personal decree asserting that they were passed by the Cabinet.

Taylor wrote back to King on January 9, pointing out the fallacy of using the example of Britain and underlining the fact that the per capita consumption of beer in Canada was less than that of Britain or the United States. He recommended that King set up a fact-finding body to learn the true facts. He closed his letter by reasserting that the Prime Minister had given in to the prohibitionist factions, stating, "the professional prohibitionists are insatiable and will be back to you again and again, urging more and more restrictions which cannot help but create discord and disunity in our country."

On February 11, 1943, an exasperated E.P. Taylor decided to go public. He wrote a lengthy letter to the editor, not of the *Globe and Mail* or Toronto *Star*, but to the Ottawa *Journal*, in the heart of King's tender domain. In his letter, which the editor of the *Journal* was more than happy to publish, he recited his criticisms of the government regulations and in particular of the Prime Minister. His letter said in part:

> So the Prime Minister took it upon himself to decide what should be done. . . . With all due respect to the many outstanding accomplishments of our Prime Minister, it should be obvious to all that he was about the most poorly qualified member of the government to make a recommendation to the Cabinet as to the amount of beer the hardworking people of Canada should be given under wartime conditions. . . . Many people in this country must be wondering if the Prime Minister is going to take over from his responsible ministers most of their duties.

Besides causing an enormous uproar, Taylor's letter to the Ottawa *Journal* established him in King's mind as a lifetime enemy upon whom he would wreak a personal act of vengeance at the end of 1943. All caution to the winds, the battle was on between the petulant, prohibitionist Prime Minister and an aggressive, angered E.P. Taylor.

Confronted by Taylor's public letter and by a hostile Opposition, King finally tabled in the House of Commons all of his correspondence with Taylor. At that time it was learned, that for reasons politic or whatever, Hartland Molson, president of Molson's Brewery, and N.J. Dawes, president of National Breweries, had discreetly disassociated themselves from the Ottawa *Journal* letter. The premier of Quebec, Adélard Godbout, objected to the ban on the advertising of alcoholic beverages because of its effect on Quebec publications depending on beer and liquor advertising for revenue. The premier of Ontario protested the loss of provincial revenues resulting from the restriction of alcoholic beverages and wanted to be compensated for their losses.

The first chink appeared in King's stone wall when on February 19, the Alcoholic Beverages order was amended to permit public relations advertising by the brewers and distillers. Working men across the nation started wearing buttons stating, "No beer–no bonds." Under continuing pressure from his Cabinet colleagues to allow an increase in the quantity of beer available for sale, King was adamant, stating, "I came out with the announcement of my intention, if there was any trouble, to advocate the nationalizing of the whole brewing business."* King dug in his heels. Except for one slight increase of 5 per cent in the amount of beer permitted to be manufactured during the period June 1 to October 31, 1943, no further changes were made by the federal Cabinet, but the outcry mounted across the country.

Notwithstanding his public confrontation with King, Taylor stuck with his dollar-a-year man work for the government as C.D. Howe's deputy on the Combined Production and Resources Board. At the beginning of the year he went so far as to take on another task for Canada, namely that of co-chairman of the new Joint War Aid Committee, U.S. and Canada, in which both countries would work toward the allocation of military supplies, civilian machinery and equipment, food, and other commodities to such countries as China, Aden, Ceylon, Cyprus, Syria, India, French North and West Africa, and a host of other nations. The first meeting was held in Washington in the spring of 1943, with Taylor as the Canadian chairman and Major General J.H. Burns as the American chairman. Lester B. Pearson was a member of this group. There were only two other meetings of the Joint War Aid Committee which Taylor attended, one in February 1944 and the last in September of that year. Conveniently for Taylor, this committee had its infrequent meetings in Washington at the Combined Chiefs of Staff building, and so he was able to combine his Joint War Aid work with his activities and meetings in Washington as

---

*Pickersgill, *Mackenzie King Record*, p. 486.

Howe's representative and deputy on the Combined Production and Resources Board.

He was also now able to concentrate on his business and entrepreneurial affairs, making plans for the expansion of Canadian Breweries to meet the demand that he knew would come as soon as the war was over, possibly in 1944, and likely in 1945. E.P. Taylor wanted to be ready.

During his time in Washington, Taylor had master-minded several corporate moves of Canadian Breweries Limited. He now gave instructions to the head of Canadian Breweries' engineering department, T.G. Ferguson, to prepare expansion plans for Waterloo, Toronto, and Ottawa, and to be ready to go as soon as building permits and materials were available after the cessation of hostilities. This was done. In addition, Taylor was laying plans to acquire further breweries as part of his grand design. This he would do in 1944, but he completed the necessary research and preparation in 1943. In 1942, Taylor had incorporated Industrial Food Services, which provided catering to war plants and industry generally. In 1943, he incorporated a holding company, Canadian Food Products Limited, which took over the catering operation of Industrial Food, and Honey Dew also became a division. Continuing the expansion of Canadian Food Products, Taylor acquired complete ownership of Woman's Bakery and a majority interest in Muirheads Cafeterias. In the following years, Taylor went on to acquire Picardy Limited, a chocolate maker with a chain of candy stores in the west which went into the holding company, as well as Willards Chocolates and a number of bakeries. With his escalating interest in British Columbia, he began to plan for expansion of both Honey Dew and Picardy in that province, saying, "As soon as the war restrictions are sufficiently relaxed, we plan additional Honey Dew shops throughout Vancouver, and there will be a chain of Picardy candy stores in main British Columbia centres with a central factory in Vancouver." Nor did E.P. Taylor allow Orange Crush to sit idle during 1943. There was an opportunity to acquire a substantial interest in Charles Gurd and Company of Montreal, soft drink bottlers, and Taylor seized it under his Orange Crush operation.

Even though he kept plugging away at Orange Crush, Honey Dew, and Canadian Food Products, Taylor was not happy about being in the soft drink bottling business or the food operations. The bottling plants had come as part and parcel of the breweries he had acquired in the early thirties. He couldn't sell them so he had to make them go, expand their operations, and carry them until he could find a market for them. The same thing occurred with Honey Dew, which was part of the Orange Crush operation he had bought in the same period. "You know, there are more failures in the restaurant business than in any other business in the world. People who are not informed say, 'The public has to eat, therefore I'll open a restaurant and get into the food business.' A great many men who retire go into the food business and lose their capital." As to Orange Crush and Canadian Food Products, "when we formed Argus Corporation, I put those two companies into it and we nursed them along. Then in the early 1950s we sold both to Bill Horsey and his associates, and he was pleased and we were pleased."

While he was reluctant about further involvement in soft drink companies, Taylor was more willing to take on a challenge offered him by the Controller of Fats and Oils. The post was held by Phyllis Turner, the mother of the former Minister of Finance, John Turner. She later married Frank Ross who became lieutenant governor of British Columbia, and she, in turn, became the chancellor of the University of British Columbia. In Taylor's opinion, she was a very able and attractive woman. She asked to see Taylor and told him about the critical shortage of vegetable oil. Mrs. Turner had tried to get the major packing and milling companies, such as Canada Packers and Maple Leaf Mills, to co-operate with her, but with no success. Maple Leaf Mills did have a small soya bean processing plant–it was the only one in Canada. And to make matters worse at that time, there were so few soya beans grown in Canada, they had to be imported from the United States.

"Then she thought of me and asked me to see her. She said, 'You're used to handling grain in your breweries. We're in desperate need of vegetable oil. Will you consider putting in a plant?' I said, 'Yes, we will. We're anxious to do some war work. We would like to think that the munition workers are producing more steel and more munitions and working overtime by consuming our beer, but we would like to do something more closely identified with the war.' She pointed out to me that I could not have quick depreciation,* which I understood.

"I told the board of Canadian Breweries that I thought we should investigate this proposition. I did a lot of the research myself. I visited some of the large firms in the United States. I went to Decatur, Illinois, which is about in the centre of the soya bean crop region in the United States, and saw the plants in operation."

Taylor then put T.G. Ferguson into the project, asking him to carry out a detailed study and to come up with a proposal which would embrace construction and costs of building as well as operation. Taylor could see that soya bean oil would relieve a shortage of shortening, margarine, and soap. In addition, it would provide a new crop for Canadian farmers. E.P. Taylor was no stranger to the soya bean. In 1938 he had decided that Canadian Breweries Limited should invest in a subsidiary company known as Sunsoy Products Limited, which processed soya beans on a small scale in Toronto. From that experience, he knew that a large unit, including elevators and a processing plant, could produce oil in substantial quantities, and he believed that soya bean oil would have a good economic future when the war was finished.

While Ferguson was carrying out his research, Taylor obtained an option on several acres of land on the lakefront at the eastern end of the Toronto Harbour.

By the beginning of December 1943, he had made the decision to proceed with the building of the plant and made a public announcement that a new $25 million project for the extraction and processing of vegetable oils would be built by Canadian Breweries.

In addition to planning the Victory Mills Soya Bean Plant in 1943, E.P. Taylor was busy researching and investigating the potential of the forest products industry in British Columbia. He was intrigued.

One of his outstanding dollar-a-year colleagues was Harvey MacMillan. They had become friends during Taylor's original Ottawa stint. Later, when Taylor was in Washington, MacMillan would often go to the American capital in his capacity as president of Wartime Merchant Shipping Limited, one of the many Canadian Crown corporations which had been set up. In Washington,

---

*Wartime depreciation provided for a rapid writeoff of capital investment against profits.

141

MacMillan would deal with the Maritime Commission, a division of the U.S. government which bought ships for lend/lease to Great Britain. "During his spare time, MacMillan would talk to me a lot about the forest products industry. That's when he told me about the Victoria Lumber and Manufacturing Company at Chemainus on Vancouver Island. MacMillan wanted to buy that company, but John Humbird, the owner, refused. Apparently Humbird disliked MacMillan and refused to sell it to him. Well, MacMillan said that if I bought the Victoria Lumber and Manufacturing Company, he would be prepared to buy it from me."

Taylor had taken a good look at the Victoria Lumber property in October 1942, when he went out to have his "short vacation" at the time of his departure from the British Supply Council. Early in 1943 he had gone back again. This time he employed a timber cruiser, an experienced estimator of the volume and value of timberland, and the two of them had a look at the property in order to make an assessment of its worth. "It looked good."

The Royal Bank of Canada, Taylor's bankers, introduced him to John Humbird and guaranteed any commitment that he might make. "At my original meeting with Humbird he wanted to know what was behind my interest in the property. I told him that at no time would I tell him who my associates were, if any, until the deal had been closed. In the autumn of 1943 I took out various people, business friends of mine, to look over the property of Victoria Lumber. All of these gentlemen, except George Drew, who was not the premier of Ontario at that time, were actively engaged in corporation financing. The company had miles of railway, and we'd go around in rough trains. There were no passenger vehicles. You just sat on a flat car and saw the country. I became very interested. I made up my mind if I did the Victoria Lumber deal, and if MacMillan didn't take it off my hands, I would be perfectly content to keep it. Late in 1943 I conveyed the news to Humbird that I was prepared to make him a firm offer for the company as a going concern and I made an appointment to go out to B.C. in January to see whether we could come to terms."

Taylor had no sooner arrived in Vancouver than he received a telegram from Ottawa saying that his father had died of a heart attack. "I had to get back. As a matter of fact, I called Humbird over at Chemainus and told him not to bother to come over, I'd be back a month later."

The sudden death of his father whom he loved and admired, and with whom he was very close, was a difficult experience for Edward. Colonel Taylor had never hesitated to place all his confidence and faith in his son. They had been business partners, working closely together in the early days of the McLeod, Young, Weir Ottawa operation. He had placed in Edward's hands the family's control of Brading Breweries at the crucial point when E.P. Taylor and Jennison put together Brewing Corporation of Ontario during one of the worst economic periods in the history of Canada. He had remained closely tied with all of Edward's activities during the thirties, giving advice and counsel and fatherly assurance during the many crises and difficulties of that marginal time. The Colonel was immensely proud of Edward's accomplishments, especially so during the war when the old soldier saw his son reach the highly influential and important positions in the Canadian government and the pinnacle of responsibility given to him by Churchill and Beaverbrook for the British interests in Washington and the United States. With the passing of his father, Edward Taylor lost the second of the two men who had most shaped his life, the first being his grandfather, Charles Magee. When E.P. Taylor returned to Vancouver he brought with him his friend, Dick Barnes, the Montreal investment dealer who was chairman of the executive committee of the Canadian Breweries board and one of his most valued associates. They had another look at the property, just to be sure.

"I'd made up my mind. I'd consulted MacMillan and other associates about the price. Humbird came to my suite in the Vancouver Hotel and I made him an offer of, I think it was, $9 million in debentures and $6 million in cash. I remember saying, 'This is my final offer. It is the best offer I can make. Take it or leave it.' And then the staring business started and lasted for forty-five minutes. Forty-five minutes is a long time to look somebody in the eye. I said, 'What about it Mr. Humbird?' and he said, 'Oh, Taylor, are you waiting for me? I was waiting for you!' I told him that it was my last offer, and my only offer, as I had to go back to Washington the next day after lunch. Humbird said he was going home and would think about it overnight.

"The next day, after lunch, he called and said, 'Taylor, that'll be all right.' I said, 'It's a deal. I'll be back on April 15 with the money.' There were two months when I just had his word to rely on."

In turn, all Humbird had to rely on was Taylor's word. In April, Taylor returned to Vancouver with Dick Barnes. After extensive meetings with the legal representatives, the parties met in the offices of Taylor's lawyers to close the transaction. At the meeting Humbird raised the point that a trustee would be required for the bonds being issued. Taylor suggested the National Trust Company, but that was not satisfactory to Humbird, who complained that there wasn't a branch of the firm in Vancouver. Taylor then picked up the telephone book and started looking through the Yellow Pages, his eyes landing on London and Western Trust Company. When Taylor suggested this name, Humbird immediately exploded. A big man, considerably heftier than Taylor, Humbird flew into a rage, slammed his fist on the table, shouting that the deal was off, that London and Western belonged to Mac-Millan, and accusing Taylor of representing him. Taylor had forgotten that Harvey MacMillan was a director of London and Western. It almost cost him the deal. Talking quickly and persuasively during the moments of crisis, Taylor was able to calm Humbird down and convince him that there was truly no commitment or tie to MacMillan. Again, Taylor's remarkable power of persuasion and force of personality overcame. The deal was closed and E.P. Taylor was well and truly launched into the ups and downs of the forest products industry. As with the brewing industry, he would later begin a chain of acquisitions and mergers which would lead to the creation of a giant in the industry, British Columbia Forest Products.

During 1943, Taylor's revitalized interest in entrepreneurial activities had produced plans for Canadian Breweries' expansion, his entry into the forest products industry, the beginning of Victory Mills and its soya bean operation, the creation of Canadian Food Products Limited, and an interest in acquiring Standard Chemical Company and other firms. Even so, E.P. Taylor's commitment to the war effort and his work as Howe's representative on the Combined Production and Resources Board continued as a significant factor in his life.

In the spring of 1943, no longer on official business of the British government but as Churchill's confidant, Lord Beaverbrook visited Washington to discuss with President Roosevelt and other important Americans certain questions that Churchill had in his mind about the future. Edward Taylor was with the Beaver as much as possible, making arrangements for him and generally assisting the elder statesman to see the people he wanted to and to accomplish all his objectives during his brief stay.

Taylor admired Beaverbrook enormously and delighted in the way the "little man" handled events and people and got things done. "Of course, he was a most troublesome man to a great many people, and most Englishmen. He was detested by many British civil servants and politicians because his methods were completely unorthodox. He started off as Minister of Aircraft Production. The production of aircraft in Britain in the early stages of the war was very, very poor and disorganized. The Royal Air Force didn't have the required number of aircraft. Beaverbrook performed miracles there. He did that by any trick he could possibly devise. First of all, he asked the person involved to do the impossible, which is a good way to get things going. He'd say, 'I want this in a week.' He knew himself it would take a month, but he'd get it perhaps in two weeks. He stole from the army and the navy. He got things made for the aircraft industry that the other departments of government wanted. This was common knowledge. He was a thief and he got priorities on things that the air force needed, and of course, we would have lost the Battle of Britain if he hadn't done it."

In his Washington home, Taylor entertained Beaverbrook at a black tie dinner party, with the most important and powerful of Beaverbrook's British and American friends in attendance. The next day the two of them were off to New York where Taylor again took charge of getting him from meeting to meeting and was with him the entire time.

When he returned to England, the Beaver wrote a note of thanks to his protégé, Taylor, which reveals his preoccupation, even in those days, with the socialist movement in the United Kingdom and the power of the Trade Union movement which today has become a pervasive force. If he could see the situation today, Beaverbrook the optimist would have to agree that the Labour Party in the United Kingdom has never become "a party of Conservatives," although they are certainly the party of "expediency."

I am so grateful to you for the help you gave me while I was in Washington, and for all your companionship there and in New York.

It is pleasant indeed to me to know that I may count on the benefits of your friendship.

Here the political situation develops at present to the detriment of the Socialists. Under the domination of the Trade Union element in their ranks they are becoming a party of conservatives. They have thrown aside their ideals and are worshipping at the shrine of expediency.

Such development is, of course, to the advantage of the Tories. They will profit from the divisions in the Socialist ranks. For the younger Socialist politicians are now violently opposing the conservatism of their leaders. And the Party is threatened with a measure of disintegration which would give the Tories power for many years.

During the summer of 1943, Taylor carried on with his wartime work in Washington and in Ottawa, while escalating his "moonlighting." His public confrontation with Mackenzie King over the beer and temperance issue had done little for his enthusiasm for his government work. Taylor had come to the conclusion that at the right time–and it would not be too far away–he would get out completely.

In September, Howe asked him to go to the United Kingdom to attend a meeting of the Combined Production and Resources Board. W.D. Batt was to accompany him. Immediately the decision was made that he should go, Taylor made application to the American State Department to travel by air to the United Kingdom by Pan American Clipper flying boat. Permission was granted to Taylor and Batt, and they were given a top priority.

However, when Taylor arrived in London, he found that he had been given a lower priority for his return trip and that he might have to return by military rather than commercial civilian aircraft. This lowering of his status prompted Taylor to seek the assistance, not only of Canadian High Commissioner Vincent Massey, but also of Lord Beaverbrook. It was the Beaver's assistance that turned the trick. The real reason Taylor reacted so forcefully to the change of priority is explained in the addendum to his letter of October 18, 1943, to Massey, thanking him for his efforts in attempting to solve the transportation problem.

Just a word about the "personal considerations" referred to in the attached letter. You should know that with certain business associates I have taken some very large financial commitments involving heavy bank borrowings. As additional security for those loans I pledged my personal life insurance, in excess of one million dollars, and promised my partners and the bankers that I would not subject myself to any uninsured risk unless it was vitally urgent in the interests of the war effort for me to do so.

Standard insurance policies provide full coverage when travelling on commercial air lines but on military ships or even Trans-Canada Oceanic, as it is now constituted, the insurance would pay nothing in the event of an accident.

In those days, and for many years to come, Taylor borrowed heavily from the banks for his own account in order to acquire shares and interests in the businesses which he controlled or in which he wished to invest. The war had brought little change to his pattern of business growth, expansion, and development involving substantial bank borrowing, not only personally, but by the companies he controlled as well. Taylor has never regarded borrowing from banks as something one does at the last minute to bail out, but rather as a normal commercial activity to enable one to make acquisitions with growth potential. When growth has been achieved, sufficient of the acquired holdings are sold to pay off the bank, leaving the investor with a substantial net gain, including control of the firm originally acquired by the use of the bank loan.

In any event, it had been his good friend the Beaver who understood Taylor's position and had used the levers of his influential power to arrange E.P. Taylor's passage on Pan-American.

Taylor's treatment by the Canadian government who had failed to back him up on the matter of his priority for his return trip from the United Kingdom was a major factor in his decision to submit his resignation. Within a few days after his return from England, he sat down in the Victoria Street office of Canadian Breweries in Toronto and prepared a letter of resignation to C.D. Howe. It was dated November 8. In the letter he reviewed his own service throughout the war, then put the point to Howe, saying:

I have come to the conclusion that the Canadian deputy on the Combined Production and Resources Board should now be someone who is prepared to carry on not only until the defeat of Japan, but also for some considerable time thereafter. It is quite conceivable that before long the members of the board will no longer appropriately be the war production chiefs of the countries. Therefore it seems to me that a new Canadian deputy should be chosen of such qualifications and of such stature that he could later become a full member in the event of your retirement.

In the last paragraph of the letter, Taylor concluded with this: "Needless to say, as long as the war emergency lasts, I shall hold myself available to do any suitable job for the country if the need should arise."

In a letter dated November 13, C.D. Howe replied to Taylor's, accepting his resignation and concluding with these words:

I am well aware of your splendid service to this Department, commencing in April, 1940 and to the British Government during your tenure of office with them. You will have the satisfaction of knowing that during the war period you rendered a fine public service and one which has meant much to Canada's war effort.

I thank you for your assurance that as long as the war emergency lasts, you will be available to do any suitable job for Canada. Personally, I will feel your departure greatly. We have been through some strenuous times together. I hope that our association and friendship during the war years will continue as long as we both live.

It did.

In his responding letter, Taylor made a statement that could have offended Howe, but Taylor knew his man very well. "It is my earnest hope that we will see much of each other in the future, and that you may, in the not too distant future, be permitted to return to private business also. It seems to me that after the immense contribution you have made to Canada, you should be entitled to let someone else carry along after the government's present term expires." Howe's reaction to this point emerged in the final letter of that series of correspondence, which was written on December 13.

Personally, I am not greatly worried about the C.C.F. My greatest worry at the moment is that I am becoming convinced that the present Government will succeed itself in office, which would be good for the country, but bad for my desire to get back to private life. I presume George McCullagh* would not agree.

At about the time that Howe wrote that letter to E.P. Taylor, he acted upon the opportunity given to the government of Canada to nominate five people for appointment to the high honour of Companion of the Order of St. Michael and St. George. Taylor's name was at the top of the list submitted by Howe to Prime Minister Mackenzie King who would make the final selection of those whose names would be put forward to King George VI. Of course, Taylor had no knowledge of this nomination by Howe.

E.P. Taylor's resignation became public on November 25, with his confirmation to the press in Washington that his resignation had indeed been submitted, accepted, and would take effect on January 1.

On December 17, E.P. Taylor attended his final meeting of the Combined Production and Resources Board in Washington. Appropriate departure speeches were made by all concerned acknowledging Taylor's contribution. Even C.D. Howe was present to join with the chairman, Donald Nelson, and Sir Henry Self, in recognizing that he had "at all times discharged his duties with skill and diplomacy and had been a most energetic and capable official."

---

*George McCullagh, the outspoken, dynamic Conservative publisher of the *Globe and Mail* at that time.

Chapter IX

Business Prospects at War's End

The years at the close of the Second World War saw the emergence of a new E.P. Taylor. Now he was ready to use his solid Canadian Breweries base as a secure financial platform from which he could expand and diversify.

Canada's people, resources, and industrial might were fully committed to the war effort. D-Day, June 6, 1944, was the turning point in the European theatre where the full thrust of the years of preparation was brought to bear on the Nazi fortress, Europe. The massive build-up of equipment and weapons of war in which Taylor had played such a significant role in the critical months during 1941 and 1942 was turned loose in the name of liberation, freedom, and victory.

Victory in Europe was accomplished by May of 1945, when the Germans surrendered unconditionally. In the Pacific the devastating, horrifying force of the first atomic bombs compelled the surrender of the Japanese in August of the same year.

The Second World War was over. There was no longer any need for huge armies, no requirement to manufacture guns, ammunition, tanks, ships, or aircraft. It was time to take apart the incredibly powerful and large allied war machine. What would happen to all the men and women in the armed forces? Would there be jobs for them in "civvy-street?" There were many politicians and businessmen who believed that Canada would be faced with an immediate and long recession, that there would be few jobs because the huge wartime demand for goods and services had been turned off. They could not envisage a turn-around to a buoyant peace-time economy. Furthermore, few industrial leaders had had the foresight to prepare plans for the transition that would inevitably arrive.

E.P. Taylor was one of those who not only could see a bright future ahead, but was prepared to do something about it. The early months of 1944 had brought a conclusion to the brewing industry's Taylor-led battle with Mackenzie King and with it a decision by Taylor to expand Canadian Breweries as soon as government controls would permit.

The skirmish with King had had its better moments. On the first day of January 1944, a sour note was struck against Taylor by his peevish enemy, the Prime Minister of Canada, whom he had had the temerity to criticize publicly. King George's honours list had appeared on that day, awarding the high recognition of Companionship in the Order of St. Michael and St. George (C.M.G.) to three of C.D. Howe's dollar-a-year men, but not to Taylor, whose record of service and accomplishment was second to none. On January 3, a disappointed, somewhat bitter Taylor wrote a personal letter to C.D. Howe. Taylor's letter is not available, but C.D. Howe's reply says it all. There would be no recognition of Taylor's work for his country. A petulant Mackenzie King had struck Taylor's name off the top of the list and had stubbornly held to his new position that there would be no more civilian honours of any kind until the end of the war. Howe said:

> No one regrets the King's honours list situation any more than I do, particularly as it represents a failure on my part to do justice to one of my oldest and most valuable associates. I had expected to have five C.M.G.s on this list, which was longer than the last one, and accordingly I put in five names, including yours and Joe Pigott's. A most acrimonious discussion developed over who should be included, not only on that list but on the others, with the result that the Prime Minister finally cut out all civilian O.B.E.s and announced that there would be no more civilian honours of any kind until the end of the war. That is about all that I can tell you at this time. I may say that you are not the only one who is up in the air about being omitted.

> When the new list comes out, you will be at the top and if any come to this Department, yours will be among the num-

ber, provided I am here to fight the battle.*

While King may have had his way in stopping Taylor's C.M.G., it was Taylor who won the war against King's prohibitionist restrictions on the sale and distribution of beer. On March 13, 1944, the eccentric Prime Minister struggled to his feet in the House of Commons to announce that his restrictions on the sale and distribution of beer were forthwith lifted. Inundated by criticism across the nation, hit by an unparalleled unpopularity in Quebec because of the liquor regulations, and put in an untenable position when it was disclosed in the press that exports of beer to the United States in 1943 had amounted to over two million gallons, King had no choice but to give in.

The Prime Minister had opened his address to the House reiterating his reasons for putting on the restrictions in the first place, reasons that, in Taylor's view, had no foundation in fact whatsoever. King said, "Restrictions upon the quantity of alcoholic beverages to be released for sale were in accordance with the government's policy to effect, if possible, a total war effort. They were in response to an informed public opinion, and to a widespread public demand for some measure of restriction." This was rather a broad definition of one single organization, the Canadian Temperance Federation, who undoubtedly were pleased to be recognized as speaking for the whole nation.

True to form, King laid the reasons for his reversal at the feet of others: the provincial governments of Alberta and Ontario, who were blaming the federal government for the restrictions on the quantity of alcoholic beverages available for sale. Since, as King said in his speech in the House, "a first duty of the federal government is to see that no differences which can be prevented are allowed to interfere with the co-operation and understanding so necessary between the federal and provincial governments" then,

---

*The King's honours list of July 1946 finally brought the royal recognition of the magnificent work Taylor had done for Great Britain during the war. Howe had finally overcome a reluctant Mackenzie King by threatening to resign if the Prime Minister refused to support Howe's nomination of Taylor for appointment as a Companion of the Order of St. Michael and St. George. This time, the reluctant Mackenzie King gave in. Taylor's appointment to the Order, which enabled him to use the letters C.M.G. after his name, was small compensation for the high responsibility which Taylor had carried not only for the British government and Churchill and Beaverbrook, but for Canada as well. If he had been a British citizen, he probably would have been knighted.

"in the interests of the war effort, sources of public misunderstanding and friction, where they exist, should be removed insofar as that may be possible." And, "where it is clear that causes other than federal action are restricting the supply of beer, maintenance by the federal authorities of the 10 per cent reduction upon the 1942 output of this single commodity is not sufficiently important to the war effort to justify the risk of continuous misunderstanding and frictions between the federal and provincial governments and of antagonisms between the provinces. In these circumstances, it is obviously preferable that the distribution and sale of such supply of beer as there may be should be left to the exclusive control of the provinces themselves."

So ended E.P. Taylor's and the Canadian brewing industry's last major battle against the prohibitionists, whose loss of credibility during the last two years of the Second World War was such that they were never able again to attract the support of the Canadian news media, a condition that was and is absolutely necessary if any propaganda campaign is to succeed.

The government shackles removed, Taylor the optimist entrepreneur was ready to begin a remarkable chain of expansionist moves using his broadened experience as a guide. Looking back at this period in his life, he later said: "a lot of people don't understand why I spread myself among eight or ten different businesses. It's because I always felt I could find somebody who could run a business on a day-to-day basis better than I could run it myself. So I would keep my finger on him and at the same time guide the policy of the company with the board of directors. But I got tired of being on one thing continuously and that gave a false impression of my importance and my influence. I quickly found out that as far as entrepreneurs and industrialists are concerned, you can take two courses of action. The first is you can stick to one thing. If I had stuck to one thing, and kept absolute control of it, I undoubtedly would have done better financially. But I like the other course of action, which gives me variety, and I like the game of negotiation in the second course of action, which is to diversify and get into several businesses. I very rarely start anything from scratch, that is, start something from nothing. I usually acquire something that could form a useful part of something bigger, or that could become something bigger, or I could see a situation where something was very badly managed. All through my life I have had great satisfaction in holding something together and improving it in bad times. Then I lose interest when the times are good."

The one business he had started from "scratch" acquisitions was Canadian Breweries. In 1944, spurred on by the impetus of the federal government's release of beer from its clutches, Taylor took steps to strengthen his corporate base. He moved to chairman of the board of Canadian Breweries and made his executive vice-president, D. C. Betts, president.

Counter to Taylor's original grand design of the early 1930s, he acquired Capital Brewing Company Limited of Ottawa for $1.5 million and consolidated it with Brading. In his original plan, the Copeland Brewery in Toronto was to have been acquired, but Labatt's beat Taylor to the wire. The Bixel Brewery and Malting Company was acquired for $150,000 and closed down. And in the Windsor area, the Walkerville Brewery was bought. For some time Taylor had been causing Canadian Breweries to buy Walkerville shares on the open market; finally, in 1944, for a total outlay of $1.5 million, control was obtained.

In April 1944, Taylor set in motion a new underwriting for Canadian Breweries Limited with 20,000 no par value preference shares and 20,000 common shares being offered to the public at $52 per unit of one preference and one common share through W.C. Pitfield and Company, and Burns Bros. & Denton. This underwriting was completed in mid-summer and produced over $1 million of expansion capital for the firm which included the new soya bean processing vegetable oil plant of Victory Mills Limited, a Canadian Breweries subsidiary.

Down on the Toronto waterfront, Canadian Breweries' new Victory Mills plant was rising out of the ground. It was an experiment with equipment not used before in Canada, with a mechanical screw press system coupled with the solvent extraction. Taylor had decided that the plant should be capable of handling about 3 million bushels of soya beans annually, even though the Ontario production in 1943 was only 874,200. The vegetable oil and the protein feed to be produced by the plant were urgently needed commodities and Taylor was sure that the Canadian farmers would respond by increasing their crop production. By November 25, 1944, three of the five mechanical screw presses were in operation, producing vegetable oil to meet the acute shortage and using imported soya beans to augment the meagre Canadian crop.* The remainder of the presses came into service in 1945, on schedule.

In his expansionist planning process, E.P. Taylor came to the conclusion that in the post-war period Canadian Breweries should move into the vast potential market in the United States. C.B.L. could build and operate its own plants or it could buy out an existing operation. Taylor chose the latter. He knew the operations of Brewing Corporation of America and its track record. And he knew its president, the tough James Bohannon, who had bought the Carling name and rights back in 1933. A follow-up now, eleven years later, appeared to be the way to go. If he could recapture the Carling name, he could then combine the Canadian Carling operation with the American plant, thus using the integrated operations and labels of the two to supply that part of the enormous American market which had not yet been touched. The Carling brand in Canada would supply the export market in the United States as part of the Cleveland-based operation and the surplus Canadian Carling capacity would be used up. Even if there was no surplus in the Canadian Carling operation, any expansion to meet the burgeoning U.S. demand could be undertaken in Canada. Taylor decided to move.

Bohannon owned sufficient shares of Brewing Corporation of America to give him effective control of the company. Curiously enough, although he could have approached Bohannon directly to work out a deal, Taylor chose another route. He caused Canadian Breweries Limited to begin buying Brewing Corporation of America shares on the open market. This meant only one thing to Bohannon, that E.P. Taylor was after control through "the back door." The big, garish American was incensed, and said so publicly. But the matter was quickly resolved when the offended Bohannon agreed to sell out to Canadian Breweries for $5 million, to be paid in two instalments, together with a ten-year personal service contract under which he was to act as president and general manager of the Brewing Corporation of America.

Both the corporate purchase and the retention of a belligerent Bohannon turned out to be a long-term problem for the brewing

---

*By 1953, the annual Canadian crop of soya beans passed the 4 million bushel mark, and was increasing rapidly.

empire Taylor had built. If Taylor claimed credit for mistakes or errors in judgement, the move into the United States market in itself ranks as a major one. The way he attempted to gain control of the Brewing Corporation of America in the open market was another, as was the managerial contract with Bohannon who, in the next few years, independently took some decisions that brought the American company to the point of collapse. And there are those who believe that Taylor's stubborn refusal later to wind up the Brewing Corporation of America, to take his losses and get out, was a major error which was to cost C.B.L. tens of millions of dollars over the years ahead.

Another major purchase was decided upon by E.P. Taylor for Canadian Breweries Limited at the end of 1944 when an outside malting company, from which Canadian Breweries purchased the bulk of its malt, advised the company that after April 30, 1945, it could no longer deliver supplies. Barley malt is an essential ingredient in the brewing process. In the early days of brewing in Canada, each brewery prepared its own malt from barley. However, over the passage of time, this had become a specialized operation, with breweries purchasing their supplies from malting companies. At the end of 1944, every brewery in Canada was operating at capacity, but the supply of beer still fell short of demand. Taylor had laid plans for a $4 million malting plant to be operated by Victory Mills Limited for its parent, Canadian Breweries, but that did not solve the immediate problem. Not only would this unit provide only a part of the company's malt requirements, it would be at least two years before the new plant was in place.

The situation called for quick action. Within twenty-four hours Taylor had completed arrangements for the purchase of 86.4 per cent of the common stock of a Manitoba malting company, Dominion Malting Company Limited, at a cost of $1,949,128. Dominion Malting had an annual production capacity of 2.5 million bushels. While this was by no means enough to supply all the plants of Canadian Breweries Limited, it was sufficient to tide the company over until the Victory Mills plant was completed and other sources of supply could be developed. With the acquisition of Dominion Malting, Taylor immediately produced a $1.2 million debenture issue for its refinancing, which was successfully sold.

The Taylor optimism and his belief that the market for beer was ready for a major expansion were well founded as were his growth plans for Canadian Breweries to meet the new demand.

At the beginning of 1945 Taylor announced that the net profit of the firm for the fiscal year ended October 31, 1944, had been over $1.2 million. The company was healthy, had a good cash flow, and was expanding. Even so, there were more companies out there to acquire and money to be raised for expansion purposes. With the war in Europe finished in May, and the Japanese disposed of in August, the expansion plan Taylor had been working up in 1943 and 1944 was put in motion. He knew that within the period of one to two years after the war there would be a severe production shortage throughout the industry. Therefore, he could see a tremendous advantage to Canadian Breweries Limited if it was able to increase quickly as well as to update its production facilities at a time when other companies were just beginning to get around to planning. In late 1944, tankage, brewing equipment, and bottling units, which were produced only in the United States, had been placed on order for delivery as soon as the war ended for expansion of the company's plants in Waterloo, Toronto, and Ottawa.

Work began during the summer of 1945. At the Brading Brewery in Ottawa, its Capital Brewery plant had a capacity of only 50,000 barrels. Within sixteen months, and without halting production for a single day, the plant was renovated and expanded to the point that production was placed on a 500,000-barrel-a-year basis, a tenfold increase. The Simcoe Street plant of O'Keefe in Toronto was completely reconstructed during a period of two and a half years, and gave Canadian Breweries' engineering department, an in-house organization that master-minded the entire expansion program, its first opportunity to construct a new brewhouse. The final result was a series of modern brewing buildings occupying an entire city block with a brewing capacity of 550,000 barrels, five times that of the plant it replaced.*

At the same time Taylor was expanding and strengthening his C.B.L. base, and that of its Victory Mills subsidiary, he was working on a similar program for Orange Crush and Canadian Food Products.

---

*Despite this enormous revitalization, two decades later both the office flagship of Canadian Breweries on Victoria Street and the Simcoe Street plant of O'Keefe literally disappeared, levelled to the ground, as in the 1960s E.P. Taylor was to rationalize production and build a new, more efficient and better located single plant near the Toronto International Airport.

In 1943, through its wholly-owned subsidiary, Associated Bottlers Limited, Orange Crush had purchased a substantial share interest in Charles Gurd and Co. of Montreal and acquired the business and assets of a firm called King's Old Country Limited of Winnipeg. When Associated Bottlers had been formed by Taylor in 1942, he had also caused it to acquire O'Keefe's Beverages Limited (the soft drink division of Canadian Breweries Limited), Evangeline Beverages (Ontario), and the right to bottle and distribute Hires Root Beer in Canada. The year 1944 saw the acquisition of control of the Gurd organization at a cost of $250,000. On December 1st, 1944, it was announced that E.P. Taylor had relinquished the office of president of Orange Crush Limited to become chairman of the board.

Taylor decided that Orange Crush should continue to expand and acquired the business of KIK Company, which operated soft drink plants in Montreal and Toronto. He immediately took the step which was part and parcel of his acquisition formula. The Orange Crush acquisition of KIK had been announced on February 14, 1945. By March 16, Taylor had organized a new issue of $750,000 of first mortgage bonds of Orange Crush which had been immediately sold, bearing interest rates ranging between 4 per cent and 4.62 per cent. Borrow from the public or from the banks, it didn't matter, so long as you had access to their funds for growth. The then small cost of money, which was also deductible as a business expense, was a major factor in the expansionist Taylor's continuing use of his public credibility and reputation to keep borrowing and building.

Although Taylor had diversification as a major goal through acquisitions and mergers, he adhered to another of his basic principles which is that mergers should be done only with companies in the same or similar or compatible line of product. "There are several kinds of mergers. One is that stupid kind of conglomerate where a lot of businesses that have no relation to each other are put together. Well, I've never done that. I've always stayed in one industry. For instance, lumber and pulp and paper go together. The chemical industry goes into many other fields of endeavour, such as salt. I would never think of putting my land development companies into a merger situation with an industrial company. There are a lot of conglomerates that have done very badly because they have put a lot of completely different things together."

In addition to the Orange Crush acquisitions, another example of Taylor's adherence to this principle was the purchase by Canadian Food Products Limited of the business and undertakings of Barkers Bakeries Limited for $500,000 cash, a deal which was completed in mid-1945. Also, it was time to raise some debt money for Canadian Food Products Limited. A $550,000, 5-per-cent convertible series debenture issue of Canadian Food Products Limited was sold, putting the total debenture indebtedness of the company at $2.5 million.

In the same period Taylor was also expanding into another area with a fortuitous purchase. The controlling shares of Dominion Stores Limited were owned by a Frenchman, François Dupré, an entrepreneur who also owned the Ritz Carlton Hotel in Montreal. After the collapse of France, Dupré's foreign assets had been frozen and could not be sold. His man in Canada was J. William Horsey, operating as president of Dominion Stores. Horsey was the prime moving force in building the company's operations into a multi-store food chain. J.A. McDougald, then a senior partner in Dominion Securities Limited and already a highly successful man at putting deals together, knew about the Dupré shares and had told Horsey that he was interested in putting together a group who would buy the Frenchman's block of shares if it ever became available.

At the close of the Second World War, Dupré's shares were released and his North American agents, Greenshields and Company, received instructions to sell. The famous American brokerage firm of Merrill, Lynch had been instructed to buy by the owners of the Safeway chain of grocery stores, a major food retailer in the United States. When flying down to New York from Toronto with some Greenshields people, Horsey accidently found out about the deal. As president of the company he was extremely annoyed at not having been informed that the shares of Dupré were for sale. Furthermore, if the firm was sold to Safeway, it would become an American-controlled firm, and he would be working for strangers or thrown out. In New York, Horsey, a large, imposing, highly intelligent and tough man, raised absolute hell with the Greenshields people. After all, Dupré owed him a great debt for his wartime stewardship of this major asset. His justified anger paid off. Horsey was told that if he could match the Merrill, Lynch offer by 2:00 that afternoon, he could have the Dupré shares.

Horsey immediately telephoned McDougald, who later recalled telling Horsey, "Well, Bill, you just take up the option and buy it. We'll find the money." There was about $700,000 involved, which does not seem like very much money now, but "sounded like a lot of money at the time. I had dinner that night with Eric Phillips and I told him, jokingly really, that I was in the grocery business in a big way. He said, 'I'd like a piece of that,' which I was very happy to give him. He also suggested that Eddie Taylor would probably like a piece, which was also very welcome."*

The Dominion Stores purchase was quickly completed. Victory Day in Europe was May 7, 1945. On May 10, the *Globe and Mail* carried pictures of Taylor, Phillips, and McDougald with an announcement by Horsey that the three had been elected to the company's board of directors. A *Financial Post* story of May 11 carried the story saying that the Dupré block "consisted of 48,975 common shares, sale of which was 'put through' the Montreal Stock Exchange recently. This represents one of the first movements of a block of stock out of Europe since its liberation. The sale was arranged by the Bank of France."

Capitalization of Dominion Stores at that time consisted of 80,014 shares of no par value common stock, so while the acquisition of the Canadian group represented a controlling interest, it did not by any means represent a majority of the issued shares which were held on a widespread basis. It did, however, represent sufficient power to enable Taylor, McDougald, and Phillips to go on the board and soon to command it through decades of substantial growth and superiority in the highly competitive food chain business.

Another 1944 Taylor move to diversify eventually led through a series of mergers of product-compatible firms which produced Domtar. The beginning was the purchase of control of Standard Chemical by E.P. Taylor and Colonel Phillips. "Standard Chemical was a relatively small company which had stayed stagnant for many, many years. It made more money in the First World War

---

*Toronto *Star*, August 9, 1975.

than it made in the second, and made very little money in between. The business of the company was the destructive distillation of hardwood, out of which they made wood alcohol, methyl alcohol and formaldehyde, and some other derivatives, and also charcoal, which is the residual product. This process is obsolete today. Methyl alcohol can be made from several materials other than wood. Standard Chemical operated four hardwood distillation plants and two sawmills in Ontario and a Montreal refinery for its product.

"The same people who had backed me in Canadian Breweries, the London Committee, had the largest block of stock in this company. It represented practical control. They saw the breweries pull through, and they got a good profit on their investment. They had confidence in me. I was really their only link with Canada except for an old chartered accountant here. Before the war they asked me if I would be interested in going into the company, taking a look at it, buying an interest, and trying to make it into a money-making concern. Well, I looked at the balance sheet and found that they had relatively a lot of cash, but no earnings of any consequence. In any event, I kept putting them off. I said I was too busy because of the war. In 1944 I was getting free from the war responsibilities and they reminded me about Standard Chemical. So I looked at it again."

Taylor inspected the plants and sawmills, but what he really found most interesting was the financial statement of the company. It showed a cash surplus which the shareholders could not get out without paying most of it in taxes. If he bought their shares for a comparable amount, it would be a capital gain for them and tax free. "I made them an offer because there was more money in the treasury per share than the amount I offered them per share. They weren't getting any dividends. I've done that several times. It's a great way of getting money. And in the back of my mind was the fact that there was a great future for the chemical industry in Canada. It was the fastest-growing industry in the world. I thought it would be like starting Canadian Breweries from a little company like Brading Brewery. I wanted to repeat the process in the chemical industry."

Once he and Phillips had control of Standard Chemical, typically, E.P. Taylor began to look ahead to see what mergers could be brought about and what money could be raised from the public.

Expansion was the driving motivation and goal, and the way to achieve it was to utilize assets against which to raise money by way of debenture or the issuance of redeemable preference shares, tied with common shares if necessary. But whatever opportunities to merge presented themselves, they had to meet the Taylor requirement of compatibility of product. Salt met that test as a member of Standard Chemical's commodity lines.

In a December 1944 news report dealing with his and Phillips' acquisition of control of Standard Chemical, this note was added: "It is also reported that the Taylor interests have purchased the Goderich Salt Co., Canada's third ranking producer of common salt, for a reputed million dollars."

The report was correct. Using Standard Chemical Company, Taylor bought Goderich Salt Company, which had few assets but had big earnings. It was a family concern that made salt in Goderich, using the distillation method. "Their assets had been written off. So now I had some earnings in Standard Chemical. Goderich Salt turned out to be a principal ancestor of the large Sifto Salt firm, one of the few major consumer product operations still remaining in the Standard Chemical, now Domtar, portfolio."

The transaction was completed in July 1944. At the annual meeting of the stockholders of Standard Chemical, held in late August, Taylor was elected a director and the president of the company, while Phillips went on the board.

By the end of the year, in a move that was in keeping with his control and management principles, Taylor had become chairman of the board and brought in K.S. MacLachlan to manage and operate the company and "run it on a day-to-day basis." MacLachlan was not only a qualified chemical engineer, but had been Deputy Minister of National Defence and had broad corporate experience. Taylor was the entrepreneur, the expansionist, the man who had the concepts and put together the financing and the transactions. He was the policy-maker. He did not have time and did not want to manage his acquisitions.

In October 1944, E.P. Taylor bought an advertising agency, but not for the purpose of getting into the advertising business. As an industrialist he believed that there would be a conflict between an agency and the many companies he controlled if they were forced to use an "in-house" advertising firm.

A. McKim Limited was the principal advertising agency for

Canadian Breweries. James Baxter, who was the number two man in the agency, wanted to buy it, and C.T. Pearce, who had been the president and general manager since 1922, wanted to sell and retire. But the company had so much cash that Baxter could not meet the purchasing price. He approached Taylor to ask whether Canadian Breweries might be interested in participating in the company. When he met with Taylor, Baxter had a copy of the company's most recent balance sheet. There was no way Taylor would get into the advertising business, but when he saw the financial statement and the substantial amount of cash on hand, he knew that a profitable arrangement could be made for everyone. It was a repeat of the original Standard Chemical situation. There was enough money in the firm to pay Pearce off, more than Pearce could get by winding up the firm, because he would have to pay heavy taxes. If his shares were bought, there would be no tax because the money would be a capital gain in his hands. E.P. Taylor bought the shares in the company from Pearce, borrowed the money from the company to pay Pearce for the shares, changed the name and purposes into an investment company, Canadian Investment Company Limited (Caninvesco), and sold the advertising assets and goodwill to Baxter, who, as part of the deal, had been able to form McKim Advertising Company Limited, which was the purchaser, rather than Baxter personally.

Caninvesco became one of E.P. Taylor's major corporate vehicles. Through it he continued to increase his personal holdings of Massey-Harris. "I accumulated a great deal of stock when I thought it was cheap, and it turned out to be cheap."

Taylor borrowed heavily from the banks in order to finance his personal acquisition of shares through holding companies he had incorporated, Caninvesco and Invesco Limited. He was prepared to take heavy personal risks when a good entrepreneurial opportunity came to his attention. He personally borrowed over half a million dollars to finance the purchase of his share of the stock of Standard Chemical. And his continuing purchase of Massey-Harris shares when he "thought it was cheap" was also bank financed.

However, it was the public and bank financing of the corporations over which he had gained control that demonstrates two things. First, Taylor had enormous credibility with the public who rushed to invest in the redeemable preferred stock and the debentures which his various new acquisitions offered usually within a few weeks or months after he had gained control. The pattern was to use the borrowed-from-the-public money to pay off the bank from which the purchase money had been borrowed. Second, it was a Taylor practice to raise money in debt or redeemable stock, and never by the sale of equity shares unless a "sweetener" of common stock was mandatory in order to make the redeemable shares more saleable. It was his objective eventually to pay off the corporate debt and redeem all outstanding redeemable shares, thereby escalating the value of the common or equity shares which he and his colleagues held. This was his master corporate financing plan and it worked.

In 1944 the remarkable entrepreneurial efforts of E.P. Taylor produced a list that he wrote out at the end of that wartime year.

		Amount Involved
1.	Purchased Victoria Lumber Company	$9,200,000
2.	Purchased Capital Brewing Company	1,500,000
3.	Purchased Walkerville Brewery Company	1,500,000
4.	Purchased Bixel Brewing Company	150,000
5.	Sold Canadian Breweries Debenture Issue	1,200,000
6.	Sold Canadian Breweries Preferred & Common Issue	1,000,000
7.	Brewing Corporation of America – Purchased Control	3,500,000
8.	Built Victory Mills	2,000,000
9.	Purchased Picardy Companies	400,000
10.	Sold Canadian Food Products – Debenture Issue	550,000
11.	Purchased Control Standard Chemical Company	600,000
12.	Purchased Goderich Salt Company	1,000,000
13.	Purchased & Refinanced Dominion Malting Company	1,500,000
14.	Sold Canadian Breweries – Debenture Issue	800,000
15.	Purchased A. McKim Limited & resold immediately to executives	300,000
16.	Purchased Control Charles Gurd & Company	250,000
		$25,450,000

Chapter X

The Formation of Argus Corporation 1945

The last half of the 1940s brought the massive re-introduction of tens of thousands of servicemen and women into the economic mainstream of Canada. The recession and unemployment that had been expected immediately after the Second World War did not materialize. Industry had already commenced a return to production of goods for a peace-time market sustained by a demand created by the multitude of military personnel returning to Canada and civilian life.

The skylines of the major Canadian cities were yet unmarked by the presence of high-rise apartments and skyscrapers. The Royal York Hotel and the Bank of Commerce building dominated the Toronto downtown core. There was no subway transit system in place under the still small cities of Montreal and Toronto. Television had yet to intrude into the homes and culture of the million Canadians who populated the low-profile nation astride the northern boundaries of the United States. The taps of immigration were slowly being turned on. In the vanguard of the gradual upsurge in the economy was that "necessary" luxury of which the American and Canadian people had been deprived during the war years–the automobile.

Canada was at the beginning of a three-decade period of unparalleled growth and development. E.P. Taylor and a new company he formed in 1945 were to play significant roles in those burgeoning times.

Before organizing his new corporation, Taylor had made two decisions. First, he wanted to incorporate a company that would buy and hold shares in a limited number of major operating companies. Since the number of companies was to be held to a few, it would be a "non-diversified" investment firm. A sufficient number of shares in each selected company would be acquired by the corporation to give it representation on the board of directors and, if possible, control of that board. Second, Taylor decided that as his partners in this new investment company he would select people upon whom he could rely. They had to be people who were respected in the financial community.

He approached three, two of whom accepted the invitation to participate in the formation of Argus. These were Colonel Eric Phillips and Wallace McCutcheon. The third man, John A. (Bud) McDougald, declined but agreed to participate in a new entrepreneurial, as opposed to investment, firm with the other three. This entrepreneurial company was to be named Taylor, McDougald & Company, and would serve as the vehicle for many of the activities of its principals.

Joining with others as partners was a new step for Taylor, although his purchase, with Phillips, of control of Standard Chemical had the makings of a partnership relationship. "In the period before the war, neither Colonel Phillips, Wallace McCutcheon, or Bud McDougald were in any way financially interested in any of the things I was in. Wallace McCutcheon was, however, a director of Canadian Breweries. He represented, through his legal firm at that time, the Dominion Bank. In the 1930s I had no partners. I had no partners in the 1930s in Canadian Breweries, no partners in the soft drink companies, such as Orange Crush, no partners in Honey Dew. Everything I did in the 1930s before the war, I did as an individual."

In choosing his new associates, Taylor selected men he knew well. They were good friends of his. Eric Phillips, a wartime colleague, was both wealthy and a skilled manager. A colourful man who had served in the First World War, Phillips had started in business in his father's picture framing firm. That led him into the glass business, then into safety glass. From there Phillips moved to Oshawa and started supplying the automotive industry in Canada with safety glass. In the mid-1940s, he sold his Canadian interest to Pittsburgh Glass. Suddenly he was a man of great capital.

Alex Rankin, a chartered accountant who worked with Phillips during the Argus formation period, later commented on the coming together of Taylor and Phillips. "It was terribly astute of Taylor to pull in Phillips, because Phillips had the manufacturing ability. He was an engineer and had an engineering approach. He was a damn good manager. In fact, as a manager of men, I don't think Phillips had an equal, which can't be said for any of the others. While I was connected with Phillips, he suddenly became a great entrepreneur.

"Phillips was the operator. He could run Domtar or Massey-Ferguson at the drop of a hat. He was the industrialist, with a wealth of knowledge in any field. The man read four average-length books between 8:00 and midnight. He was always reading things on horticulture and agriculture because he had a farm. He read anything to do with glass because he ran Pittsburgh Glass. He read anything to do with the universities. You can imagine the breadth of his reading. But what really shattered me is that, having read a book, six years later he could still quote its essence and refer to it as a reference point. Phillips had an unbelievable amount of energy and a terrific memory. He always had this great ability to size up people and read their minds. It was unbelievable!"

This was exactly the kind of partner E.P. Taylor needed, an engineer, a manufacturer, a man with capital, credibility, and a stature that Taylor could accept as equal to his own.

The third member of the Argus team, Wallace McCutcheon, had been on the board of Canadian Breweries Limited as a director since 1930 when as a young lawyer he represented the interests of the Dominion Bank on that board. He had been associated with Taylor and C.B.L. continually during those intervening years. Taylor admired the superior, direct intelligence of this forthright lawyer who had an amazing ability to pull transactions and deals together. As Alex Rankin saw McCutcheon in retrospect he "was the most decisive. He had a mind like a rapier. He would make up his mind quickly, and he did the tough negotiations. He was the brilliant man at working with agreements and documents. When I first met McCutcheon, I thought of him as the hatchet man in the organization. He was choosing people and moving people and getting things done. I thought he was a cold, hard-headed businessman to the point where nothing mattered. But as I grew to know him better, I was shocked to find out how wrong I had been. He truly wanted to serve his country. He had a great love for Canada. I've seen McCutcheon do things that could do nothing for him or for his image. But he would do them gladly and willingly, and with a great deal of devotion. He devoted a great deal of time to the Social Planning Council. He didn't need to do that to promote himself. He had all the money he wanted and all the business opportunities. Finally I realized that he would have loved to have been Prime Minister."

As to Taylor, Phillips, and McCutcheon, Rankin says, "they were terrific individuals, each and every one of them. To me it was fascinating, as a young whipper-snapper, to watch them bait each other. They would argue very heatedly and all in good fun. But I soon learned never to get drawn into their arguments. They would turn to me and say, 'Isn't that right, Alex? Don't you agree?' It was worth the price of admission to hear them jousting and fencing with each other with words, but if you ever got in the middle, you got killed.

"I often felt Taylor was dependent on the others. At least he gave them the feeling that he needed them. I think this is what made them a good team. He often brought in the ideas, had the vision, and they would wrestle with it and maybe change the direction slightly, or change the dimensions, but basically it was a go, go team."

It was this Taylor-led trio that formed Argus Corporation. So long as each of them lived they would be E.P. Taylor's trusted colleagues and friends, although the then unforeseen call of politics was later to draw McCutcheon away.

Taylor's inspiration for the creation of an investment company had come from an American, Floyd Odlum, and a company he had put together in the United States called Atlas Corporation. Odlum had been very successful in dealing with special situations. Atlas was a non-diversified investment firm which dealt with the shares of only a few companies.

With Odlum's advice, Taylor, Phillips, and McCutcheon decided that their investment company would not operate along standard trust lines, but would invest the greater part of its funds in a relatively few enterprises which were considered to have unusual opportunities for long-term growth. Taylor regarded income as a secondary consideration during the period of development of profitable prospects inherent in the companies in which the investment company had holdings. The investment company would be the largest individual shareholder of the companies in its investment portfolio with interests ranging from 15 to 35 per cent, the average holding in the individual companies being 25 per cent. Its dividend policy would be to pay shareholders between 60 and 65 per cent of the anticipated cash income for each year with the balance of the cash income and gains made on capital appreciation being used for further strengthening of its financial position.

By early July 1945, Taylor and his colleagues were almost ready to go with the investment company, but as yet no name had been selected, nor had an application been made for incorporation. Nevertheless, Taylor, with a view to continuing his pattern of getting as much credit from his bank as he could, and also because he was personally indebted to the bank for a very large sum of money against the security of many of his shareholdings, was obliged to advise the Royal Bank of his intentions. He discussed the plan with Burnham Mitchell, assistant general manager of the Royal Bank, who asked him to put the basics of his scheme in a letter. Taylor did so on July 6, 1945:

> You have asked me to give you an outline of my plans in connection with the investment company which it is proposed to launch early in September.
>
> This Company will be a non-diversified investment trust and it will take over the investment holdings of Canadian Industrial Investments Limited, Invesco Limited, Caninvesco Limited, approximately 27,000 shares of common stock of Canadian Breweries Limited, now owned by me and pledged to you, together with 14,000 shares of Dominion Stores stock and approximately 10,000 shares of Dominion Malting Company common stock now owned by Canadian Breweries Limited. The Company will also probably take over from certain of the directors additional shares of the various industrial companies which go to make up the main portfolio.
>
> The existing shareholders of the different investment companies and the directors who turn in any investments will all receive shares of the new Company in exchange. No shareholders will be withdrawing any cash. The new Company will sell securities to the public, in all probability common shares, to produce a minimum amount of $2,750,000 which will suffice to pay off the bank loans of Canadian Industrial Investments Limited and the obligations of Invesco Limited

and provide the funds to purchase the additional Dominion Stores and Dominion Malting stock from Canadian Breweries Limited. After this is accomplished the new Company will have a portfolio of shares having a value of about $6,000,000 and it is hoped that additional financing can be arranged which will put not less than $2,000,000 in cash in the Company's treasury.

Colonel W.E. Phillips has agreed to be Chairman of the Board of the new Company. I shall be President and Mr. M.W. McCutcheon, now Deputy Chairman of Wartime Prices and Trade Board, is to be Vice President and General Manager. The directors will also include Messrs. H.R. MacMillan, W.L. Bayer, E.W. Bickle, J.S. Duncan, K.S. MacLachlan and W.K. Fraser, K.C. I am also planning to invite S. Freeman Raymond of New York, J.S.D. Tory, K.C. and Norman C. Urquhart to be members of the Board. Mr. Raymond is an associate of Mr. Notebaert, who has indicated that his group will take a substantial position in the new Company.

From the names dropped in the letter, it was apparent that the corporation would be born swimming in financial blue blood and respectability.* Impressed by this galaxy of talent, the Royal Bank agreed to become the banker for the new firm and to extend such reasonable line of credit as might be required from time to time.

By the time the new company was incorporated under the name of Argus Corporation Limited on September 24, 1945, the port folio of shares had doubled from the $6 million suggested in Taylor's letter to the Royal Bank. As reported in the Toronto *Telegram*

---

*On the proposed board was David C. Baird of New York, then a vice-president of Marsh and McLennan Inc., as one of the nominees of the Atlas Corporation which had bought 5 per cent of the Argus stock. He was on the board with Roger Gilbert, also of New York City, a vice-president of Atlas Corporation. There was W.L. Bayer, a Montreal president of Canadian Bonds Company and Noorduyn Aviation Limited, and chairman of Amalgamated Electric Corporation; E.W. Bickle, a famous and powerful investment dealer, a partner in the firm Wills, Bickle and Co., who was chairman of Sterling Rubber Company, and president of Maple Leaf Gardens at that time; Harry J. Carmichael, C.M.G., of St. Catharines, who had been one of C.D. Howe's important dollar-a-year men, and an old respected acquaintance of Taylor's, was at that time president of the Toronto-St. Catharines Transport Limited and director of the Bank of Toronto and other organizations; James S. Duncan, the president of Massey-Harris and Company; W.K. Fraser, K.C., senior partner of the firm of Fraser and Beatty; J.W. Horsey, president of Dominion Stores Limited, who was on the board following the Argus concept of having presidents of major companies on the board, as was K.S. MacLach-

of November 22: "Argus will start with net tangible assets of $12,500,000 clear of preliminary and underwriting expenses and with no intangible assets." Argus had raised $4 million through the usual Taylor formula, a sale to the public of redeemable preference as well as common shares.

Prior to the formation of Argus, Taylor's corporate acquisitions had been escalating through Invesco Limited, which he controlled, owning 80 per cent of the shares, with the balance being held by the K.S. Barnes Estate* and by Colonel Phillips, and also through Canadian Industrial Investments Limited, in which he held about 70 per cent of the shares. The latter had been incorporated in November 1942, while Invesco came into being in May 1943. A third firm, Caninvesco, which Taylor owned outright, also held substantial securities.

At the opening and organization of Argus at the beginning of November, Taylor, his colleague, Phillips, and the Estate of K.S. Barnes, caused Invesco Limited to sell its holdings to Argus for just under $4.5 million. And Canadian Industrial Investments Limited put in its assets for $2.3 million. Twenty-seven thousand common shares of the Canadian Breweries Limited owned by Taylor personally were also acquired by Argus, as were Caninvesco's securities. Shortly afterwards, Taylor wound up Invesco and Canadian Industrial Investments but retained Caninvesco, which was later to become a wholly-owned subsidiary of Windfields Farm Limited, when it was formed in 1950.

In exchange for the holdings he put into Argus Taylor received 50 per cent of the issued shares of the company. He put in the big-

---

lan of Toronto, president of Standard Chemical Company. Then there was the strong man of the far west, Harvey MacMillan; Allan Miller of London, England, chairman of Broadcast Relay Services Limited; Felix Notebaert, director of Asbestos Corporation of Canada, a Montrealer, and an associate of S. Freeman Raymond of New York, and a director of International Utilities Corporation. As Taylor had advised Mitchell of the Royal Bank of Canada in the letter of July 6, Raymond was an associate of Notebaert, whose group did in fact take a substantial position in Argus. And the last in the alphabetical listing of the directors was J.S.D. Tory, K.C., who, with the Fraser and Beatty firm, had been advising the Taylor group in various of its corporate activities, Fraser and Tory, each in his own right being among the top corporate lawyers in Canada of the day. The secretary of Argus was William Finlayson, who had come back from Washington to work for Taylor, and the treasurer was R.G. MacMullen.

---

*K.S. "Dick" Barnes, Taylor's good friend, financial associate, and adviser from Montreal, died at the end of 1944.

gest part of the Canadian Breweries shares, all of the common, and the majority of the Class 'A' shares of Canadian Food Products, more than half of both Dominion Stores common and Standard Chemical common, and a substantial part of the Massey-Harris holdings. Phillips had sold his Standard Chemical stock to Argus for shares, while McCutcheon bought Argus stock with cash. At the outset, Argus, through Taylor, also became a large holder in Dominion Bottling Co. and Orange Crush Ltd. The total value at cost of all the preference and common shares first held by Argus was $10.9 million, with the substantial cash to be raised by the opening underwriting yet to come in, making the total portfolio worth closer to $15 million than the $12.5 million that had been publicly reported.

A mere two years later, in January 1947, Taylor was to tell the annual meeting of Argus that cash and investments were worth approximately $20 million against a funded debt of $3.8 million and preference stock of $5 million. By 1972, the year after E.P. Taylor did not stand for re-election as chairman and was succeeded by John A. McDougald, the assets of Argus had increased to $209 million, and the companies in which Argus had its major investments totalled in assets approximately $2.1 billion, with annual sales of approximately $2.5 billion. In 1972, the company's holdings were still divided among only six companies: Massey-Ferguson Limited, 28.6 per cent; Hollinger Mines Limited, 20.4 per cent; Standard Broadcasting Corp. Ltd., 19.6 per cent; Domtar Limited, 18.2 per cent; Dominion Stores Limited, 15.0 per cent; British Columbia Forest Products Ltd., 5.3 per cent; and the balance in cash and short-term investments. Despite the quantum leap in the value of the Argus portfolio of assets in 1972, there was no variation whatsoever from the original concept, which was to concentrate investments in a limited number of enterprises showing probability of future growth and expansion.

In retrospect, the success of Argus Corporation was directly related to the enormous intellectual capability and high degree of experience of Taylor, Phillips, and McCutcheon, and later of McDougald. Their individual talents complemented each others' and there was mutual confidence and respect among them. They were aggressive men who did not just sit in their offices waiting for things to happen. They went out and made them happen. They sought major investments in public companies with special qualities. A basic requirement was that the voting shares of the company be widely held, with no large block of stock in any one individual's hands. Thus, if they could acquire a sufficiently large percentage of the voting shares, they themselves could move in and take over control of the board and therefore the direction of the company, even though they had far less than a majority of the shares. Once in command, they could bring to bear on policy-making the weight of their combined financial power and superlative talents, which in most instances caused the company to follow an upward curve of expansion. The life-blood of Argus was an increase in the market value of its portfolio combined with a steady and increasing flow of dividends. One thing that Taylor and his colleagues could not accept was the inability or refusal of any of the major companies in the Argus portfolio to make that essential yearly return on investment.

The Argus Corporation was not, however, a manager or operator of companies. By itself, the company was a straightforward limited portfolio investment firm with a staff at its head office of only a handful of people who bought and sold stock, handled the company's money in investments, the accounting, and the keeping of corporate records.

Furthermore, the three principals–and as of 1955, the fourth, with Bud McDougald–were not employees of Argus, but rather men with their own various outside involvements and interests. They took part in Argus activities only as events required and time permitted. They liked each other, enjoyed one another's company, and kidded each other a great deal. But when it got down to business they were shrewd and hard, sometimes with each other and often with outsiders. They never had to vote on any matter, either at a board meeting or at their informal meetings because, as Taylor points out, all their decisions were unanimous, with the minority objector acceding to the decision of the majority.

"I think it was a very equal partnership. The fact that I owned more shares of Argus than the others had no bearing. We were equals. We never had any vote in Argus that we weren't unanimous in, although I did have the biggest equity. We never had a falling out on anything important. Never, never. We had differences, but we talked them over and resolved them quietly. And then we agreed. We were an inactive company in the sense that we never ran any of the companies in which we had a big interest. We

173

kept right out of it. People would come to Argus and say, 'You have a big interest in this company. Would you please do that and please do this?' We always replied, 'Go to the president of the company with your ideas.' We never managed anything. We never directed anything on a day-to-day basis. We had some interest in policy, but Argus is a very interesting company in that we didn't try to exert pressure on the chief executive officer of any company. We didn't try to direct it or manage it. We tried to be helpful and constructive."

The helpful and constructive Argus Corporation, which was to become a legendary organization, a true power in the mainstream of Canadian business, was well and truly launched and firmly established from the moment of its imaginative formation.

Similarly, the embryo firm of Taylor, McDougald & Company was created as the deal-making, entrepreneurial arm of the same group that had put Argus together. The difference was John A. McDougald, who had initially refused to take part in Argus. In Taylor, McDougald, Bud McDougald was on an equal footing with Taylor and there were deals to be done. Phillips and McCutcheon were also shareholders, but the firm was dominated by the other two men.

The main purpose of the new company was to provide a contact between people with businesses or business ideas to sell and those with capital who might be interested in purchasing. The firm would develop industrial and commercial enterprises throughout Canada. Neither Taylor nor McDougald intended that it would engage in the brokerage business or in the sale of securities to the public. McDougald, who was an executive officer of Dominion Securities Corp. Ltd., resigned to devote the greater part of his time to the new partnership, while retaining his post as chairman of the board of Commonwealth Electric Corp., and vice-president of Trusts and Guarantee Co. Ltd.

Bud McDougald later recounted the fundamental difference in the operation of the two linked firms. "In those days, we'd promote a lot of things. Argus was not a promotional company; it was an investment company. Taylor, McDougald & Company was the entrepreneurial part of it. It had nothing to do with Argus–I wasn't a director of Argus or anything at that time. This was deliberately kept separate."

McDougald also spoke of his ongoing business-partnership relationship with E.P. Taylor, which began with the creation of Taylor, McDougald & Company and ten years later expanded when McDougald joined the Argus board. "The firm of Taylor, McDougald & Company has been going almost thirty years, and I couldn't even begin to tell you the number of deals they've been in over the years. But never in the history of it did Mr. Taylor and I have a partnership agreement–nor an argument over money, or anything else. That's quite a remarkable thing."*

That relationship was not only remarkable in its surface smoothness but also in its productivity over the thirty years to follow. McDougald's and Taylor's association was to survive the life and times of both Phillips and McCutcheon and was to culminate in the younger man, McDougald, succeeding the older as the chairman of Canada's prestigious Argus Corporation. To the Argus team of three, Taylor, Phillips, and McCutcheon, Bud McDougald in his own way and in his own time was to add his special qualities and talents as a financier and a perfectionist. But that time was still many years away from 1945.

---

*British Columbia Forest Products Ltd., *First Growth: The Story of British Columbia Forest Products Limited* (Vancouver, 1975), p. 30.

Chapter XI

Years of Growth
1945-1951

The solidly established Argus Corporation provided E.P. Taylor with precisely the type of vehicle he needed to pursue his fundamental objectives of diversification and expansion. Aided and abetted by the specialized entrepreneurial activity of Taylor, McDougald & Company, Argus would use its growing financial leverage and control of boards of directors to broaden the corporate holdings of the various companies in its portfolio. This would be done through mergers and acquisitions, accomplished where possible by an exchange of shares, the device Taylor had used in the 1930s in putting together his flagship, Canadian Breweries. But when cash had to be put up in order to make a purchase, Taylor was now able to complete his deal, using bank financing, then go to the public with an offering of debentures or redeemable shares, sweetened if necessary with a small number of voting equity shares. The proceeds of the public offering would be used to pay off the bank, and the Argus-controlled company would have complete ownership of its new acquisition.

In those days any activity of Argus or of any corporation in its portfolio tended to be attributed by the press to E.P. Taylor, the acknowledged leader of the Argus enterprise. In fact, by 1947, E.P. Taylor's interests had become so broad, his accomplishments so legendary, and his prominence so pervasive, that the ultimate accolade was paid to him by the Canadian edition of *Time* magazine which gave him a four-column spread keyed to the news that "by last week he and his associates had bought up 35% of Massey-Harris common stock–and control." With the article was a photograph of a smiling, round-faced Taylor, speaking into an ever-present telephone. The caption under the picture referred to his twelve-word labour policy, "give them what they're entitled to before they ask for it." That same caption also named him "Tycoon Taylor." Whether he liked it or not, that is what Edward Plunket Taylor, "E.P." as he is universally known, had become in the public eye.

As his corporate interests broadened, so did his need for capable executives, a commodity that E.P. Taylor has always recognized as scarce in the Canadian market. In the early 1940s he had his eye on a young man, George Black, Jr., whose family was in the brewery business in Winnipeg. A chartered accountant, Black had served for four years as comptroller of the family company, Western Breweries Limited. During 1940 and 1941, he was on the staff of the Department of National Defence for Air, and from that time until he joined Canadian Breweries Limited in the fall of 1945 he had been executive vice-president of Canadian Propellers Limited at Montreal. As the war moved into its final stages after the successful invasion of Normandy in June of 1944, Black began to consider his move back to the family firm in Winnipeg. He had done an outstanding job setting up Canadian Propellers from scratch. C.D. Howe thought highly of the young man and recommended him to Taylor, who talked Black out of returning to the family brewery and into joining the Canadian Breweries organization. On October 1, 1945, Black became the executive assistant to the president of Canadian Breweries, the beginning of a long association with E.P. Taylor and his corporate interests, including the Argus Corporation, into which Black bought heavily in the early days. In addition to later becoming president of C.B.L., he was also to become an important member of the Argus board of directors and the fifth man on its main team.

From the moment he set foot in the Canadian Breweries head office in Toronto Black was caught up in Taylor's expansionist plans to increase Canadian Breweries' plants and production by increasing the Canadian output by 25 per cent each year from 1946 through 1950 (a goal which was achieved). In the United States Taylor was in the process of doubling the capacity of the Brewing Corporation of America. Thus, on all fronts, optimistic expansion was Taylor's keynote. While he was concerned that the shareholders of Canadian Breweries might consider his programs to be overly ambitious, he was determined to proceed. The risks were high. A great deal of capital would be needed if Taylor's objectives were to be accomplished, but there was still much uncertainty abroad about the way the immediate post-war economy would go. What would happen to the beer market? If Taylor guessed wrong, his entire corporate structure would collapse.

The performance of Canadian Breweries Limited was remarkable. In 1947, the company showed a "pre-income and excess profits tax" profit of $10,855,518 against $2.5 million the previous year, a far cry from 1935, when the fledgling company made its first profit of $168,000. There were now 10,684 shareholders, with Argus holding 303,000 out of the issued and outstanding two million common shares.

Important additions were under construction at O'Keefe in Toronto, Carling in Waterloo, and Brading's plant in Ottawa. The company was in excellent financial health, showing an increase in its assets over the year of almost $7 million. Nevertheless, the annual meeting in January 1947 approved a new debenture of $10 million with interest rates at bargain-basement prices of 3 to 3½ per cent, some of them maturing as late as 1967. The proceeds would be used for the plant expansions and to keep the company comfortably liquid.

In 1948, Canadian Breweries Limited continued to grow apace with control now of 50 per cent of the Ontario market as against Labatt's 20 per cent. That year Taylor was paid $60,000 as chairman of the board and executive committee, while the president, D.C. Betts, received $50,000 and the big man in Cleveland, James Bohannon, president of Brewing Corporation of America, received a whopping $100,000.

However, there were horrendous problems in the American operation. Bohannon had decided to convert the entire Brewing Corporation production into a non-returnable bottle process, a step that drove the company to the brink of bankruptcy. The bottles were defective and prone to breaking when opened. The cuts suffered by purchasers, and the injuries caused by cartons that fell apart, resulted in a series of costly lawsuits and a loss of market reputation. These factors, combined with a turn-around in the American beer market, which saw the premium Carling brand losing its market in the presence of abundant domestic beer, had turned C.B.L.'s American subsidiary into a disaster area. Steps had to be taken to get Bohannon out.

Taylor personally moved into the American operation, taking McCutcheon and Black with him to Cleveland. In the beginning of June 1948, Taylor made Bohannon chairman of the board of Brewing Corporation of America and moved in himself as president on an interim basis. By the beginning of July 1949, Bohannon was out completely.

Despite the continuing and mounting losses in the United States, which were absorbed, the C.B.L. profit for the year ending October 31, 1948, was strong, being close to $7 million against net sales of $92.5 million. Another debenture issue of $5 million at 4 per cent was the opening financial activity for the beginning of 1949 with the funds earmarked for the retirement of a bank loan.

In February 1950, Taylor invited Bud McDougald to join the board of directors of Canadian Breweries, of which George Black had just become president on the retirement of D.C. Betts. C.B.L. was expanding the O'Keefe plant at Gould and Bond in Toronto and moving back into Manitoba to buy out Drewry's which operated the second largest brewery in the province. About the same time, the acquisition of Western Canada Breweries established C.B.L. firmly in the British Columbia market. During the summer, Taylor and Black negotiated with the Cross family of Calgary, attempting to buy from them the Calgary Brewing and Malting Company, but the patriarch, James Cross, who was also president of the Calgary Stampede that year, would have none of it, at least not at that time.*

In the fall of 1950, C.B.L. and Taylor were on the receiving end of a beer boycott by the hotel keepers who wrongly blamed Canadian Breweries for a substantial price hike for beer. The Liquor Control Board of Ontario had allowed a price increase to the breweries which reflected a new federal government tax on malt. The L.C.B.O. upped the price of beer per bottle to 26¢ from 23¢. There was no price increase for the sale of draft beer by the glass. However, the price the hotelmen had to pay was raised $2 a barrel for draft beer and 40¢ a case for the bottled variety. The apparent theory behind this increase was that the 3¢ increase in the bottled beer sale price would make up the 15 per cent increase in the price hotelmen had to pay for draft beer. Unfortunately, the public didn't react according to the theory, which presupposed they

---

*Calgary Brewing and Malting was acquired by C.B.L. in 1961.

would buy draft and bottled beer on a 50/50 ratio. Instead, draft beer sales soared, and bottled beer sales dropped to a new low, anywhere from 50 per cent to 60 per cent down from normal.

The blame for the price increase was falsely laid at the feet of E.P. Taylor and Canadian Breweries. The story, which was later proved completely untrue, alleged that Canadian Breweries had railroaded a motion for wholesale price increases through the Ontario Brewers Association without sufficient warning to the hotelmen. What really happened was that the motion was made by another brewery, not Canadian Breweries, and this motion was passed unanimously by all the members of the O.B.A. Despite the fact that Canadian Breweries controlled four companies, it had only one vote at O.B.A. meetings, not four, as was generally believed. The motion was not in the form of a price increase but was a submission on the part of the breweries for price changes to be made by the government, which was the final authority in making any changes in prices. But the Hotel Proprietors Association placed full blame for the recent 3¢-per-bottle increase in beer on Canadian Breweries and charged the firm with taking the lead in raising the price. John G. Cochrane, president of the association, "denied any boycott of the three brands, but perhaps by coincidence there was a noticeable scarcity of O'Keefe, Carling, and Brading brands in some Toronto beverage rooms Friday nights." The *Hush Freepress,* a scandal sheet of the day, castigated E.P. Taylor:

[and] Canadian Breweries Limited, part of the E.P. Taylor business empire–a near-monopoly which has already gobbled all but two of the major independent breweries in the province, and probably plans to bring them all under its wing, with the exception of Labatt's. It dominates the industry. It is making the public pay through the nose to build up a Beer Baron's millions. . . . Multi-millionaire E.P. Taylor and his associates wield a lot of influence among the Mighty. Not long ago, he and his wife and George Drew and his wife journeyed together to British Columbia. . . . E.P. Taylor is engineering the deal. It may boomerang; for how many sensible people will pay 15¢ for a glass of suds which should sell for five cents?

In fact, E.P. Taylor had nothing to do with it. Not only was the

E.P.'s parents, the Colonel and Florence Taylor, Arizona, 1940.

After difficult negotiations, E.P. and James Bohannon celebrate the brewing deal, 1933.

After the Atlantic rescue, in London, England, December 1940: E.P., Billy Woodward (centre), and C.D. Howe with Canadian Generals A.G.L. MacNaughton (far left) and George Pearkes, V.C. (far right). Photo by Audrain.

Winnie and Eddie in Washington, D.C., December 1942.

November 1943. A meeting of the Combined Production and Resources Board, in Washington. (Left to right) Chairman Donald Nelson, C.D. Howe, Sir Henry Self.

Inspecting John Inglis Company's automatic weapons production, 1943. (Left to right) E.P., Donald Nelson, Major J.E. Hahn, Inglis' President, and C.D. Howe (turned).

New Year's Eve 1949, in Nassau; Eric Phillips (seated) and J.A. "Bud" MacDougald.

E.P.'s cousin, Allen Snowdon, at the hunt. Virginia, 1949.

Queen Elizabeth, accompanied by Prince Philip (right), attends the Queen's Plate, June 30, 1959.

E.P. Taylor leads Northern Dancer and jockey Bill Hartack to the winner's circle. The Preakness, May 16, 1964. Courtesy of The Maryland Jockey Club.

1953. E.P. discussing the model of the new town he proposed to build–Don Mills. Photograph by Eric Cole.

February 1970. E.P., Bahamian Prime Minister Pindling, and wife Marguerite, about to cut symbolic gauze bandage to officially open the new medical centre which Taylor's Bahamas Foundation had built in New Providence.

Ontario Brewers Association's motion for price changes not initiated by Canadian Breweries, but Taylor was out of the country and not in touch at the time. The boycott lasted for six weeks. It was settled by George Black, who later said, "I solved it in a very subtle way. Since I was dealing with Machiavellian opponents, I felt obliged to adopt Machiavellian tactics. We knew that Labatt's were going to decrease their prices. I don't remember how we knew, but these big things always leak out somehow. They had their spies and we had ours, too. We knew they were going to do it on the first Saturday in November, so I arranged with my executive vice-president to meet on that particular Saturday at 9:00. He knew they were going to send out telegrams to 2,200 hotel keepers in Ontario announcing the decrease in price on draft of 25¢, I think it was. And my idea was to beat them to the draw with a bigger price decrease. So about 10:00 in the morning, we sent about 2,200 telegrams announcing a decrease of 50¢ a keg. And sure enough, about 11:00 in the morning, Labatt's sent out 2,200 telegrams announcing a decrease of 25¢. Well, the hotel keepers were so confused they didn't know whether they were on foot or on horseback because our telegrams got there first." With that kind of an offer, the hotel keepers had to go back to buying the Canadian Breweries brands. At the time Black had sent his telegrams, Taylor was very much in the picture. On November 1, four days before the telegrams went out, E.P. Taylor made the following statement: "I told the Prime Minister [of Ontario] that if the matter was not settled this week, our company would have to engage in a price war to regain our position and put our competitors either out of business or make them so groggy that they would have to behave." The principal competitor was Labatt's. Black's telegrams gave effect to Taylor's ultimatum. The boycott was at an end.

The consolidation of Taylor's principal holdings within the single corporate framework of Argus Corporation gave the new investment company a powerful image in the minds of the nation's financial community. This factor would be of enormous assistance to Taylor, Phillips, and McCutcheon as they took steps to expand and diversify.

However, the expansion and diversification was not of the basic Argus portfolio of six major companies. On the contrary, the number of firms in which Argus held a substantial interest would remain static while the Argus team used its talents for entrepreneurial expansion *inside* each of the major companies in its holdings, guiding them along the path of mergers, acquisitions, new financings and growth. As each of the Argus firms increased in value and earnings, so would the value and earnings of Argus itself. Taylor and his colleagues, therefore, concentrated primarily on the affairs of Massey-Harris, Standard Chemical, Dominion Stores, Orange Crush, Canadian Breweries, and Canadian Food Products.

There was another industrial area that intrigued E.P. Taylor but was not yet in the Argus net of holdings. This was the forest products industry in British Columbia.

When E.P. Taylor had gone back to British Columbia at the beginning of December 1944, it was reported in the Vancouver *Sun*, that "E.P. Taylor, president of Victoria Lumber Company Limited, who is in Vancouver this week following an inspection of the company's operations on Vancouver Island, reports that 'since the purchase of the holdings of Victoria Lumber and Manufacturing Co. Ltd., early this year, production has almost doubled and approximately 250 workers have been added to the staff. There are almost 800 men employed in the mill and in the woods.' "

What had happened was that, notwithstanding the adamant position of John Humbird, who had vowed that under no circumstances would he sell to H.R. MacMillan, MacMillan had in fact emerged in June of 1944 with a deal with Taylor under which the H.R. MacMillan Company would manage the Victoria Lumber Company operation on Vancouver Island, putting MacMillan in a position of being the world's biggest forest products operator. It is not recorded what Humbird's reaction to that deal was. However, for E.P. Taylor and his colleagues in the investment–Dick Barnes, Colonel Eric Phillips, and E.W. Bickle, among others–the result of handing the operation over to tough old Harvey MacMillan was both gratifying and profitable. Within a few months, MacMillan had bought Victoria Lumber from the eastern group. As Taylor put it, "he took it off my hands in a matter of six months to a year."

This successful venture whetted Taylor's forest products appetite. He had also established a beach-head in British Columbia through Canadian Food Products and its Picardy Candy subsidiary which controlled Canadian Window Bakeries, operating nineteen stores in Vancouver and New Westminster. In addition, Orange Crush (B.C.) operated bottling and syrup plants in the province.

Immediately after Labour Day 1945, E.P. Taylor, with Winnie and the children, travelled by train to the west coast. For Taylor it would be a business-as-usual trip. He wanted to get back into the forest products business and the only way he could do it was to be on the ground. Having disposed of the Victoria Lumber firm to his friend, MacMillan, Taylor kept asking him what else there was in the province. "I am naturally an entrepreneur and a promoter. I made a thorough study of the other companies in the industry which might be acquired. I wasn't going to waste any time. By that time we were out of war planning. I had my own planning for the peace. I immediately went to work, but I couldn't really attack a monster company. I had to look for the little fellows. That was when I met all these characters–I met old Matt Sutton first, from Sitka Spruce, then the people from Industrial Timber Mills and the Camerons from Victoria. I had to look at their financial statements and employed a timber cruiser.*

"In doing the deal with Humbird and H.R. MacMillan, I really went to school insofar as learning about the pulp and paper business, the lumber business, and the plywood business in British Columbia is concerned. I came to the conclusion that the same trends would develop there as had been developing all over the world, namely that the number of companies engaged in any line of manufacture or commerce would become smaller because the big ones tend to get bigger and the small ones usually find it in their interest to sell out to the big ones. MacMillan was very helpful in informing me of any companies that might be for sale. I met the owners of these companies, the chairman or the president, as the case might be. They were nearly all Americans who had come up from Oregon and invested their money in British Columbia because the same forests go down through Oregon. I found they were quite receptive, especially since some of them were getting older. Once there was a willingness to receive an offer on the part of the person who controlled the situation, they would give me financial statements which I would study. I would study all the

*First Growth, p. 24.

183

facts about the timber limits and the record of profits and so on and then go back to my Argus board of directors for approval and then make the offers."

When asked why he thought the sellers of the B.C. lumber companies were so ready to do business with him at the time, Taylor's response was, "Price is usually the reason that people sell. The price has to be right. It has to be satisfactory. The second reason is that they wanted to sell. There were no capital gains taxes in Canada in those days. Undoubtedly they were going to get higher prices than their original investment, and we paid good prices which were subsequently justified. The first thing you do if you're going into any business is to survey the whole industry. It's an easy matter to find out how many firms are in an industry. There were several hundred companies in British Columbia in the lumbering industry–not in pulp and paper. I put together all the information I got from various sources, and I reduced the number to a short list, using ordinary common sense and the advice of people in the business. Is this thing worth bothering about? Has it a future? The main thing is, has it got timber limits? Is the timber acceptable? Can you get it to the saw mills? Then I started to ring door bells and make appointments to see people. That was my merchandise–putting things together and giving the sellers either shares or money. Some people won't take money. They want to take part in the bigger show and they want shares rather than money."

Taylor's plan was to acquire the lumber companies he had chosen, consolidate them in one company, and then go to the public for financing. Taylor engaged R.O. Denman from Hamilton to assist him in negotiating options to purchase shares of the lumber companies he wanted to buy (Cameron Lumber, Industrial Timber Mills, Sitka Spruce, Hammond Cedar). Once acquired, these options were then exercised through Taylor, McDougald & Company. Then, as the sole shareholder of those firms, Taylor, McDougald caused all of their assets to be transferred to Vancouver Cedar and Spruce Limited, a company Taylor had incorporated. That step took place on May 31, 1946, the same day that Vancouver Cedar was renamed British Columbia Forest Products Limited.

On the same day British Columbia Forest Products, following the typical Taylor pattern, went to the public, offering 1.5 million common shares at $5.00 a share and $6 million in first mortgage bonds, $2.5 million of which were at the incredibly low interest rate of 2¾ per cent. The total amount raised by the public offering was $14 million, with the proceeds to be used mainly for the acquisitions. In addition to the shares offered to the public, Taylor and some friends* bought 500,000 common shares at one dollar per share. Of the half million shares, 200,000 went into Argus.

British Columbia Forest Products, the company E.P. Taylor put together, was both large and strong right from its birth, with 1,700 employees, four saw mills, and a total capacity of 225 million board feet a year against a total holdings of timber of 3 billion board feet. To complete the package, Taylor knew that he had to find an expert to run the company. By June 1946, he had worked out an agreement with his old friend, Harvey MacMillan, to supply management for British Columbia Forest Products through his H.R. MacMillan Export Company Limited. As Bud McDougald put it, the MacMillan management "got it off the ground, but after 1953, B.C.F.P. became an independent operation. The relationship between Argus and H.R. MacMillan had always been right at the top–bearing in mind that MacMillan looked after MacMillan; that's human nature. There was a tremendous amount to do in the first few years by way of capital expenditure. We were very much involved with B.C.F.P. at that time, and most of these things were discussed with the whole group. Taylor gets full marks for putting it together, but then he was on the move. He more or less turned it over to McCutcheon to clear things. McCutcheon was very much in the picture all the time."† Indeed, Wallace McCutcheon had been with Taylor during all of the negotiations and in on the planning of the corporate structure and financing of B.C.F.P.

By the end of 1946, the company employed approximately 2,000 people. More timber companies had been acquired, and B.C.F.P. was well and truly launched as a major Canadian forest products firm. E.P. Taylor, the merger master, had done it again and with complete success. In the first year of operation, the after tax profits of B.C.F.P. were in excess of $400,000.

British Columbia Forest Products had another excellent year in 1947, netting over $2.5 million, a remarkable accomplishment for

---

*Austin Taylor, Don Lauder, and Hugh Mackay.

† *First Growth*, p. 32.

a company that had been in operation for only two years. It was now an important holding in the limited Argus portfolio.

While Taylor was putting together British Columbia Forest Products, he was also expanding Standard Chemical, beginning with a five-for-one share split early in 1945.

On June 25, 1945, there was a new issue offered of $1 million of 5 per cent non-voting redeemable preferred shares with a par value of $100 each, and 71,115 common shares. What would the money be used for? The construction of new buildings; the paying off of debts resulting from the acquisition of Goderich Salt Company and the purchase of Schofield-Donald, Ltd., wholesale importers and exporters of industrial chemicals; and also for the new purchase of the subsidiary Taylor had organized, Maritime Industries Limited, which would build a plant near Amherst, Nova Scotia, to make high-grade salt for meat packing, fish packing, and other uses, with a capacity of 120 tons each day.

On August 31, 1945, the *Financial Times* reported:

> There is a rumour on the "Street," which has been cropping up for the past several weeks, to the effect that a deal is cooking that may result in control of Dominion Tar and Chemical Co. Ltd. being acquired by Standard Chemical Co. Ltd.
>
> The report seems far fetched in view of the relative size of the two organizations–Dominion Tar at the end of 1944 had total assets of $11.8 million, while assets of Standard Chemical as at March 31st last, amounted to only $3.75 million–no confirmation can be obtained from interests close to either company that negotiations for any such deal have been underway.
>
> The one angle to the situation that would justify any credence being placed in the reports is the association with Standard Chemical of E.P. Taylor, prominent financier and industrialist, who has been actively engaged during the past year or so in establishment or merging of companies operating in other industries.

In those freewheeling days, "Bay Street," measured in terms of the numbers of stockbrokers and investment dealers, was a very small and closed shop, so that it was extremely difficult to keep security or secrecy in any transaction in which it was necessary to have arm's length negotiations and dealings. Rumours were constantly flying. They still make up much of the information on which speculative decisions are made in the marketplace on the question of whether to buy or sell.

At that point the report was of a rumour, but it was in fact correct. Taylor was indeed at work on such a merger, but it would not come to fruition for a few months.

At the beginning of 1946, Taylor had seen an opportunity for the merger of Standard Chemical and Dominion Tar and Chemical Co. Ltd. Dominion Tar and Chemical had originally been controlled by English capital, but since 1929 had been under Canadian control. It was the dominant operator in tar distillation and the creosoting industry in Canada and produced some fifty different chemical products. As Taylor saw it, although Standard was much smaller, with assets of $3.75 million as against $11.8 of Dominion Tar, the two companies would fit well together, being of the same industrial base. His colleagues agreed, and Argus Corporation began to acquire Dominion Tar shares through Standard.

This accumulation of Dominion Tar stock became apparent to its board of directors, who could see a takeover bid coming from the Taylor group. In response they quickly entered into a voting trust agreement for a two-year period. This agreement consolidated their shareholdings in a single voting block which would bind them together to prevent the takeover bid and any change of control. Taylor was not ready for a flat-out, large-scale fight. "We asked for representation on the board. First of all they refused, but then they gave in." They did so on the condition that Taylor and his associates join with them in their newly created voting trust agreement. This was done by agreement in February 1946, but it was not until July of 1948, after the voting trust agreement had expired, that E.P. Taylor and Eric Phillips went on the board of Dominion Tar. And it was not until 1951 that the much-sought-after merger was managed by the Taylor group with Dominion Tar buying the assets of Standard Chemical.

At Standard Chemical, Taylor had become chairman of the executive committee in 1947 and Phillips chairman of the board. The planned merger with Dominion Tar was still being held up by the voting trust. Under Taylor's guidance, expansion was the key word for Standard. In mid-summer a new $2.5 million plant was announced by Commercial Alcohols Limited in which Standard had 25 per cent of the common shares and *de facto* control. The installation would be designed to produce about two million imperial gallons of ethyl alcohol from the waste sulphide liquor of Canadian International Paper Company's Gatineau Mill. In November of that year, with Taylor and Phillips setting policy, Standard Chemical went to the public for $2 million in 5 per cent cumulative redeemable preference shares. By this time, Standard Chemical owned 40 per cent of the common shares of Dominion Tar and Chemical Company. It would take another three years, the expiry of the voting trust agreement, and considerable negotiating. Finally it was done.

At the beginning of April 1951, Taylor became chairman of the board of Dominion Tar and J.A. McDougald was elected a director. Then, on April 17, at a board meeting of Dominion Tar and Chemical Company, chaired by E.P. Taylor, the decision was made to approve the acquisition by Dominion Tar of the assets and business of Standard Chemical Company Limited with the exception of Standard's holdings in Dominion Tar common shares. The price would be $5,850,000. Standard had already sold its two salt plants at Goderich and Napan, Nova Scotia, to Dominion Tar.

Standard Chemical held slightly over 52 per cent of the common shares of Dominion Tar. With Argus in control of Standard Chemical, the scene had been set for Taylor's long-sought merger. What he had engineered in putting together Dominion Tar and Standard was a firm approximately three times as large in assets as Standard had been in the mid-forties, making profits which were several hundred per cent larger. Once again, Taylor had created a major industrial force in the Canadian industrial community.

While the organization of British Columbia Forest Products was taking place and Dominion Tar was being pursued, Taylor and Phillips were giving much of their time and attention to the affairs of one of the main Argus investments, Massey-Harris.

At the Massey-Harris annual meeting on February 12, 1947, Taylor and Phillips were joined on the board of directors by three other Argus nominees, Joseph Simard, J.S.D. Tory, Q.C., and

Harry J. Carmichael. With five seats, the Argus group had moved into a commanding, although not a majority position on the board of directors. This had happened even though Argus Corporation owned only 150,000 voting shares out of the total of 1,104,008 then issued and outstanding.

Early in 1948, a sixth Argus nominee went on the Massey-Harris board. He was the brilliant legal mind of the Argus trio, Wallace McCutcheon. The next move was the creation of an executive committee of the board, a J.S. Duncan decision which was supported by Taylor. This powerful committee was formed in 1948. With Taylor's people making up the majority of its members, the Argus group had gained control of the company, something that no group of shareholders had done since the Massey family sold their interest in the 1920s.

Taylor used the device of an executive committee of the board of directors in most of his major companies. "It is common practice to have an executive committee that relieves the board of many minor decisions. In the case of Massey-Harris, the board normally met only every quarter. That's common in many companies. The executive committee, on the other hand, meets every month, and it goes into the affairs of the company in greater detail than is possible at a big board meeting. Certain limitations are placed on what it can do, but the executive committee is the one place where management, or any member of the committee, can bring up a subject for discussion."

The period 1947 through 1949 was one of tremendous growth for Massey-Harris. As of November 30, 1947, the company's total assets were $63 million. By the same date two years later, they had risen to $113 million. In the same period, net sales went from $84 million to $164 million, and net profits from a 1947 figure of $4 million to $16 million, representing a healthy profit of $9.71 per common share.

In January 1949, another Argus nominee, although not a member of its board of directors, John A. McDougald, was elected to the Massey-Harris board—by this time very much under the pervasive policy influence of the Taylor group and under the operating and management direction of the man who had invited in Taylor and Phillips in the first place, James S. Duncan.

Early in 1947 the Taylor group had made the first skirmishes for a takeover of St. Lawrence Corporation. The Toronto *Star* reported on February 28:

> A battle of the financial titans for control of St. Lawrence Corp. Ltd., one of Canada's leading pulp and paper companies, which carries with it control of three other companies, is shaping up with the annual meeting in April as the probable D-Day. A group headed by Taylor, with whom is said to be associated Arthur White, recently resigned chairman of the board and director of St. Lawrence Corp., and reportedly backed by U.S. capital, is believed behind recent buying activities.

The report was accurate. The pulp and paper industry is very much tied in with the chemical processing industry, and therefore St. Lawrence Corporation and its subsidiary, Donnacona Paper, met Taylor's merger requirement of compatibility with the activities of Standard Chemical (later Dominion Tar), which would be the takeover vehicle.

The U.S. interests opposing the Taylor and White group control bid were Van Alstyne, Noel and Co., a large New York investment house which had earlier made an unsuccessful attempt to gain majority representation on the St. Lawrence Corporation's board of directors. However, the advertised confrontation between the "titans" did not occur because they resolved their differences before the annual meeting of St. Lawrence held on April 28, 1947. It was announced that they had reached an agreement in respect to the composition of the board of directors of the firm with J.A. McDougald, Hugh Mackay, and Robert Fennell going on the St. Lawrence board representing the Taylor, McDougald and the Arthur White group. Even so, the fight for control was a long way from being resolved. By 1951, representing Argus and Dominion Tar, E.P. Taylor and Wallace McCutcheon joined the board of St. Lawrence and its subsidiaries. In January 1952, the old executive group was moved out. Wallace McCutcheon was elected chairman of the board and the takeover was complete.

––––––––––

Dominion Stores, with Taylor and the Argus group firmly in control, and William Horsey as president, continued to expand in the

190

post-war years. New modern supermarket stores were opened, and the smaller stores closed out. When Horsey had taken over the presidency of Dominion Stores in 1938, there were 475 stores and the profit had been $46,700. By 1949, the number was down to 210 groceterias and master markets, now called supermarkets, but the net profit was over $800,000. In November 1948 another member of the Argus team, Wallace McCutcheon, joined the board to participate with Taylor, McDougald, and Phillips in directing the solid growth and expansion policies of this outstanding food retailing organization and significant Argus Corporation holding.

Keeping an eye on the American market, Taylor saw an opportunity for Orange Crush Limited, of which he was chairman, to pick up control of Orange Crush Company of Chicago. Seventy-six per cent of the outstanding share capital of that company, then in private hands, could be bought, putting the Canadian company, another Argus investment, in effective control of the Orange Crush business throughout the world. This was Taylor's goal. So, reversing the usual procedure of U.S. interests buying out Canadians, the Canadian Orange Crush company bought 76 per cent of the outstanding share capital of the American company for just a little over $5 million through financing which "had to be accomplished privately." With worldwide control of Orange Crush, economics of scale in production and in international advertising could be achieved, both of them being major plus factors in the Taylor formula.

In 1947, Bill Horsey became the chairman and president of Orange Crush while maintaining his positions as president of Dominion Stores and a director of Argus. Taylor continued as a director and chairman of the executive committee of the board. The move to put Horsey in as chief executive officer was part of a plan that Taylor had devised to take some of the pressure off himself and to spread the work load among the various board members of Argus Corporation. His first move in this direction was his retirement in 1947 as chairman of the board of Standard Chemical, although he continued as chairman of the executive committee. J.A. McDougald of Taylor, McDougald & Company, but not yet of Argus, also went on the Orange Crush board in early 1947. Orange Crush lost $500,000 in 1948, but returned to good health with a net profit of over $400,000 in 1949. The making of a profit was a cardinal requirement of any Argus holding.

During this period of expansion of the Argus investments and concentration on the growth of the companies in its portfolio, Taylor still found time to pursue other business interests in keeping with his belief in diversification.

At the time he formed Argus Corporation, his career as a publisher was still alive through his Anglo-Canadian Publishers Limited, and its only home-grown picture magazine, *New World,* the first issue of which had appeared back in March 1940. At the beginning, its advertising made it appear somewhat like a house organ for the Taylor brewing interests. But by 1946, no one would mistake the magazine for a company organ. Under Taylor's control, *New World* had risen from a circulation of 70,000 newsstand copies to what was described as a total guaranteed circulation of 200,000, of which about 145,000 were subscriptions. Furthermore, Taylor, always ahead of his time, was also publishing a French-language edition, *Nouveau Monde,* which carried identical advertising and editorial matter, had a circulation of some 16,000 copies, and hit the newsstands two days after *New World.* But notwithstanding the circulation success of *New World* and *Nouveau Monde,* they were losing money. Taylor would sell them if he could find a buyer.

Early in 1948 Taylor received a visitor at his Windfields gatehouse office. It was the so-called (by *Time* magazine of the day) "cocky, fast-talking, Jack Kent Cooke, boy wonder of Canadian magazine publishing." In December 1946, Cooke and his partner, Roy Thomson, later to become Lord Thomson of Fleet, had paid $500,000 for the ailing Canadian edition of the U.S.-published *Liberty* magazine. By the time he paid his visit to Taylor at the beginning of March 1948, Cooke had become involved in a publicity-making libel suit in Alberta for a story on the province's baby-adoption mill. As a result, *Liberty* had lost $137,000. Cooke and Thomson had, however, started to issue the magazine on a monthly basis, and things were looking better, the latest edition having sold 233,000 copies. Cooke wanted to up his circulation and had heard that *New World* might be for sale.

As Taylor recalls the meeting, "Cooke said, 'I hear you might sell *New World.'* And I said, 'Yes, I think it has accomplished its purpose.' He said, 'What do you want for it?' I said, 'Virtually nothing.' We had a circulation of 200,000 and I practically gave it to him–sold it to him for $100,000. He went out with his objective accomplished. He put the two circulations together and that made him bigger than *Maclean's,* but he realized he would have to take terrible losses for a year or so because he couldn't get the advertising revenue increased based on the circulation since there were contracts for a year with all the advertisers. Eventually he got rid of both of them." Cooke sold all his Canadian holdings, such as the Toronto radio station, CKEY, in 1961, when he decided the United States fields were greener, and moved to California where he has flourished. For Taylor, the selling of *New World* was a good deal. While the magazine had lost some $400,000 over the years, it had accomplished Taylor's purpose of carrying the brewery message across Ontario during a time when advertising was prohibited in that province.

On another publishing front, Taylor, McDougald & Company acquired controlling interest in the Stovel Company Limited of Winnipeg, publishers of the *National Home Monthly* and a group of trade papers. It was an old family firm which had been formed in 1889. "I purchased it with the idea of doing what I could to improve it and then selling it at a profit. I'd had the experience with *New World."* Taylor asked Floyd Chalmers to become president of the Stovel operation but he declined, rightly believing that he had a future with Maclean Hunter. Taylor, McDougald then asked Lloyd Stovel to stay on as president. And, of course, they went to the public for funds in debt form, namely $600,000 in 4¼ per cent, twenty-year bonds, and 52,000 in 5 per cent, $10 par preference shares, issued by Stovel Press Limited which Taylor, McDougald had incorporated in July 1947 to purchase the undertaking, property, and assets of the Stovel Company. Of the 300,000 authorized common shares of the new company, 125,000 shares were outstanding and in the hands of the Taylor, McDougald company. This was another classic example of the Taylor formula of acquisition followed by public debt financing which could later be paid off. The entire transaction required little or no capital outlay on the part of the acquiring entrepreneur.

An even more curious Taylor fling was another attempted venture into the air through the formation, in 1946, of a short-lived airline called Peruvian International Airways. Evidently Harry Gundy, of the Canadian investment banking firm of Wood, Gundy, wanted to start an airline. A man by the name of Clement Melville Keys, then seventy, who had at one time been the top executive of Trans World Airlines and North American Navigation Incorporated, and other American aviation firms, proposed to Gundy that a Montreal-to-Lima run was needed and would be an economic success. Gundy bought the suggestion. Keys obtained a charter from the Peruvian government and Gundy raised some $4 million from Americans, Canadians, and Peruvians. The company finally did get into operation, using four-engined Douglas airliners with a carrying capacity of forty-four passengers each. The board of directors of the firm, which began its operations the next year, included three Canadians, four Americans, and four Peruvians, the Canadians being J.E. Savard of Montreal, J.H. Gundy of Toronto, and, of course, E.P. Taylor. What happened to the Peruvian International Airline? For lack of traffic, it collapsed shortly after it started.

Diversification, expansion, growth, development, financing, planning, calculating, risk-taking and corporate building–these were the consuming involvements of the energetic E.P. Taylor who had emerged from his remarkable wartime experience with new goals and the confident belief that he could use his considerable resources to create a broad spectrum of holdings. In a brief period he had transformed his entrepreneurial and investment goals into realities, all the while looking ahead for new opportunities.

There would be many new challenges for the dynamic, creative mind of Eddie Taylor, and they would not be confined to the world of business, finance, and industry.

During the war years, the number of horses in Eddie Taylor's Cosgrave racing stable had dwindled. Bert Alexandra, left much to his own devices, had run the horses principally in the United States. In 1945, E.P. Taylor began again to find the time to become involved in his favourite pastime. The 1936 agreement with Jimmy Cosgrave terminated in 1945 and from that time on E.P. Taylor's horses would run under the name of his own stable and the Windfields turquoise and gold colours.

One of the original horses Alexandra had picked up for the Cosgrave Stable at Pimlico back in 1936 was the mare, Nandi. The second of her offspring by Bunty Lawless was a brown colt that Taylor decided to name Windfields. In 1945 the two-year-old won his first start by six lengths. He was then entered in the Victoria Stakes which, to Taylor's great delight, he won while setting a new track record, which he later broke again in the Rosedale Purse. The future for Windfields looked bright.

Spurred on by the first stakes winner under his own name, Eddie Taylor turned his attention to the conditions of horseracing in Ontario. There were seven tracks in the province, most of which were in poor shape. Each had a federal charter which permitted operation for only fourteen days a year, a period no longer sufficient to accrue enough earnings to run and maintain an expensive track. Even those, such as Old Woodbine, that had two federal charters, and therefore operated for twenty-eight days, were having difficulty. A racetrack needs a large tract of land and costly buildings, not only for the public but for stables and for the many activities that are part of racing. The grandstands and restaurants were neglected and rundown. There were no changeroom or washroom facilities for the grooms. Furthermore, most of the tracks were far too close to each other, cutting into each other's markets. There were four tracks operating in and around Toronto competing with each other in the 1920s. There was another at Hamilton, and Stamford Park and Fort Erie were not far away. Woodbine, the principal track owned by the Ontario Jockey Club, was located near the waterfront at the east end of Toronto. It had not been renovated since 1928, and showed it.

The result of the extremely limited operating periods and the high competition was that the tracks were rundown and shoddy. The reputation of some of them tended to be unsavoury, and the purses were small and unattractive. Even though the federal and provincial governments collected between them a cut of 12 per cent of all money wagered at the tracks, they provided next to no regulatory supervision.

With purses averaging under $500, and few stake races for superior horses, there was no incentive to develop better breeds. (Many stable owners today, even those with first-class horses and top-line money winners, find racing is a losing proposition. In 1976, while Taylor-owned horses earned half a million dollars, the racing operation ran up a net loss of over $300,000.)

In 1947, when Taylor accepted the invitation to become a director of the Ontario Jockey Club, he started to think about the future of racing in central Ontario. This process was ultimately to lead him to a plan for consolidation and merger, using the techniques that had become his trademark in business. Taylor's plan was to purchase the tracks, close some of them, and expand and refurbish those that were kept. A new track would be established as the linchpin of the entire operation.

Before he could put such a scheme into operation, Taylor first had to acquire a substantial block of the shares of the Ontario Jockey Club. His fellow directors were well-known and wealthy men, representing such families as the Seagrams and the Hendries, and including Colonel "Sam" McLaughlin, who was then the chairman of General Motors of Canada and one of the first great motor magnates. The Seagram family had the largest holding of shares, although not control. Jockey Club shares were trading on the market at around $600, but Taylor knew that if he was to acquire the largest single holding he would have to pay a premium. His negotiations with sportsman J.E. Frowde Seagram resulted in Taylor's purchasing his family's shares at $1,500 each, thereby becoming the largest shareholder in the Ontario Jockey Club Limited. He could proceed with making plans, now from a position of strength, but he knew it would take time.

The Taylor plan developed into maturity over the next five years and was finally made public just before the 1952 Queen's Plate. In the intervening years, he thoroughly researched the operations and holdings of all the tracks operating in southern Ontario. Which of them should be bought? Which could be shut down? Could all of them be acquired, then the whole group merged into a prosperous, profitable enterprise?

Another thing of concern to Taylor, by that time thoroughly immersed in horseracing and breeding and the betterment of the industry in Ontario, was the Ontario tax bite out of each dollar bet. He considered it to be excessive. "The Ontario tax was 12 per cent on the betting, and then the track got about 8 per cent. And it was killing the tracks. If you know when you put in a dollar bet that 20¢ is taken out of it immediately, so only 80¢ is working for you, you are discouraged. I had to get that problem out of the way before I could do anything about improving the situation at the tracks. So I went to Leslie Frost (Conservative Premier of Ontario) and I told him about the situation."

At the time, Taylor was also negotiating with Frost on easing the restrictions on the sale of beer. It was therefore possible for him to approach the Premier with a suggestion that the racing tax be cut from 12 per cent to 5 per cent. Taylor explained to Frost that the province would gain in the end because the racetracks and the quality of the horses would improve and the flow of revenue would therefore increase. Taylor's point was that taxation on racing should not be onerous, and not go beyond the point of diminishing returns. Eventually Frost was convinced that he should reduce the tax, but he would do it only on the basis of one per cent a year for six years. "He did everything that way, on a compromise basis. That's why he was in office so long. He was a man of great character who liked to be thought of as a country boy. There was never any finger of suspicion about him, but he was slow. I got him to reduce it by one per cent a year, but I couldn't get him below 6 per cent."

With the Ontario tax being reduced in an orderly way, Taylor could now proceed with his plan for the redevelopment of the Ontario Jockey Club and the rationalization of the racetracks in southern Ontario.

In his discussions with Frost, Taylor also promoted the need for an Ontario government agency to co-ordinate thoroughbred horse-racing in the province. There had to be a resolution of the continuing confrontation between the Incorporated Racing Association, a group of track owners led by James Heffering, and the Canadian branch of the Horsemen's Benevolent and Protective Association, which had been formed in 1947 to protect the rights and positions of horsemen. This latter organization was led by the formidable Willie Morrissey. The fight between the two groups escalated to such an extent that Frost was finally convinced that a governing organization ought to be created by legislation. He named it the Ontario Racing Commission, a body that greatly diminished the power of track owners and brought order out of chaos. With power to govern, direct, control, and regulate all types of horseracing in Ontario, it could make and enforce rules, license or refuse to license anyone carrying on business in horseracing, hold hearings, impose fines, approve all track officials as well as inspect books.

In 1949, Taylor first had the thrill of watching one of his horses win the King's Plate. His mare, Fairy Imp, had been bred to the great Canadian horse, Bunty Lawless, producing a foal in 1946 which Taylor named Epic. As he watched the young horse develop, he decided that Epic should be entered in the King's Plate. Epic was, however, unraced as a two-year-old because of bad ankles. But with the expert care and attention of Bert Alexandra and his assistant Johnny Collins, Epic came back to full form with excellent times.

The first start of Epic's career was on Saturday, May 21, 1949, the opening day at Woodbine Park, in the first division of the Plate trials. With jockey Chris Rogers up, Epic won handily and was ready for the big race, one where a last-minute decision by Alexandra almost cost Epic the opportunity to run. There were seventeen horses in the King's Plate, so the Jockey Club decided to start the remainder of the field outside the barrier. When Alexandra found out that Epic had drawn the post position outside the twelve-stall starting gate, he complained loudly that all horses should have an equal chance and should start from the old open barrier. The stewards refused, whereupon Alexandra announced that Epic would be scratched from the race. When he found Taylor, he also found that the owner was not in agreement with the scratch. While they were arguing the point, four other owners removed their horses from the race, with the result that Epic went into the last stall at the starting gate. Only one horse would start from outside.

Epic ran well, overtaking the pace setter at the eastern turn coming out of the back stretch just as Speedy Irish, a last-minute-drive specialist owned by George McCullagh, began to move up. In the home stretch, Speedy Irish made a final effort to catch Epic but failed. Taylor had won his first King's Plate, the most prestigious horseracing event in Canada. It was a moment of sweet victory and celebration, one that Taylor would savour many times again.

Winnie proudly accompanied her husband to the winner's circle, where photographs were taken. Viscount Alexander congratulated Taylor and made the presentation of the King's guineas. It is recorded that Bert Alexandra had a pertinent comment to make when the Governor General said to Taylor, "My congratulations on your first winning of the King's Plate. It was a magnificent effort. First win for you, first win for the jockey, and first win for the trainer." Alexandra, keyed up and ecstatic, interjected, "And the first win for the horse!"

But it was the last for Alexandra, who decided that he had had enough. Not yet fifty, he had sufficient income from family investments to retire in Florida. But for E.P. Taylor, it was just the beginning.

In 1950, the King's Plate winner was the Taylor-bred McGill, a colt he had named after his alma mater. McGill, which he had sold to Frank Daugherty, an American who subsequently sold him to Vince Sheridan (a foreign-owned horse could not then run in the Plate), won for Sheridan. In years to come a host of Taylor-bred horses would win the royal race, many carrying the Taylor turquoise and gold colours.

After the war Taylor expanded his breeding business, producing so many horses that he was unable to race all of them under the Windfields colours. In the late 1940s he enlarged Windfields from the twenty-acre parcel, on which he had built the family residence, to a farm of almost 1,000 acres. Taylor ploughed an enormous sum of money into Windfields, building three large red brick stables and a series of barns to house and serve the stable, which by 1950 comprised thirty-eight brood mares, a number of foals and yearlings, and the stallions, Windfields and Illuminable, a horse bred in the United States.

At that time there was no international market for horses bred in Canada. Furthermore, the Canadian tracks offered such low purses that there was little possibility of earning more money than was spent. The future of the breeding of thoroughbred racehorses in Canada appeared black indeed. But not to Eddie Taylor, who had been studying the economic potential of the breeding business in the United States and the United Kingdom. It was obvious that, with the average Canadian-bred yearling going for about $1,500, neither he nor any other horse breeder in Canada would be able to operate. A market had to be created and the quality of the breeding had to be upgraded enormously. His studies and observations brought him to one irrevocable conclusion: in the breeding of thoroughbreds, the mare plays a 75 per cent part. "You can have the greatest stallion in the world and a poor mare and you'll get a poor horse. With an ordinary stallion and a great mare, your chances are much better. But with a great stallion and a great mare, your chances are excellent."

If Taylor was going to succeed at horse breeding, he would have to be prepared to spend large sums of money to buy the very best stallions and mares. Eventually they would produce horses that would gain international reputations and fetch prices that would allow his operation to pay its own way.

It took Colonel R.S. (Sam) McLaughlin to change E.P. Taylor's horse breeding plans. In 1950, Colonel Sam, who was approaching his eightieth birthday, decided that he could no longer handle his 450-acre Parkwood Stables horse farm, located just north of Oshawa, the seat of his automobile empire. Colonel Sam decided it was time to sell Parkwood, which had some 200 acres of paddocks, a half-mile training track, five horse barns, a dispensary, houses for staff, and a number of cattle barns. Populating Parkwood were stallions, brood mares, foals, yearlings, horses in training, and cattle.

If anyone would be interested in buying Parkwood, it would be Eddie Taylor. McLaughlin could easily have sold to real estate developers, but he wanted the place to be kept for horse breeding, if he could possibly arrange it. Taylor's first response was that he had his own operation going and the last thing he needed was another horse breeding farm. However, he suggested to McLaughlin that François Dupré might be interested. It was Dupré's block of Dominion Stores stock that Taylor, McDougald, and Phillips had bought in 1945. Dupré had a large, first-class stud farm in France. The Colonel agreed to wait until Dupré's next visit to Toronto.

When Dupré eventually did appear, he toured Parkwood with Taylor and was exceedingly interested but, it is said, his wife talked him out of it. By this time Taylor himself had become excited about the possibilities of Parkwood. He could also see that Toronto was expanding rapidly. Within a decade Windfields would probably be in the path of high development, and he would be forced by economic circumstances and high taxes to give up his magnificent farm to urbanization. When Dupré gave his negative decision, Taylor asked Colonel Sam for forty-eight hours in which to put something together. What Taylor had in mind was to convert Parkwood into a breeding farm similar to the National Stud in the United Kingdom, to be operated for the purpose of improving the stock of Canadian-bred horses.

In the time granted by Colonel Sam, Taylor approached nine other affluent and interested horsemen. Each agreed to come in for a 10 per cent share of the purchase price as a partner in the proposed operation. With these people behind him, Eddie Taylor made his offer to Colonel Sam, who accepted. Before closing the deal, however, Taylor went back to the nine saying that his analysis of the situation showed that there could be a substantial loss in the operation and that he was prepared to go it alone, which he did.

As soon as the deal was completed, Taylor held a sale disposing of all the horses and other livestock on the place. He put Gil Darlington in charge as general manager, and Harry Green as a stallion manager. Two other members of the original group were Peter Poole, who was brought in by Darlington, and Gordon (Pete) McCann, who was to replace Bert Alexandra. The new horse breeding enterprise was to offer to all thoroughbred horsemen in Canada an across-the-board facility for breeding, foaling, raising, and training. These services would be offered at what Taylor considered to be a reasonable cost, and as further incentive to other breeders, he lowered the stud fees on the five well-bred stallions he placed on the farm, which would no longer be called Parkwood Stables. For the time being, it would bear the name of its English counterpart–The National Stud Farm.

Chapter XII

Land Development and
Don Mills
1951-1954

Eddie Taylor will always remember his fiftieth birthday and the party Winnie had for him. About eighty people were invited, all good friends, including Eric Phillips, Harry Ratcliffe, Jim Baxter, of McKim's Advertising, and George Black, and their wives. As George Black recalled it some years later, "It was a buffet dinner. There was drinking and lots of conversation. There were no awkward silences, I promise you that. After dinner we were invited to go downstairs where Eddie had a little theatre he used for motion picture projecting. But it also had a stage. We all trooped below to the theatre and sat down. Then Jim Baxter and Colonel Phillips put on a show which was a total surprise to Eddie." Jim Baxter was the master of ceremonies, along with Phillips.

After appropriate fun-poking opening remarks, Baxter introduced the real surprise of the evening, some scantily-clad chorus girls who had been hidden in the basement, ready to burst onto the stage. George Black didn't think much of their looks, however: "I had seen probably ten thousand chorines and I have seldom seen any more facially ill-favoured than those. However, they did their little jigs." Baxter had put them through one rehearsal, both dance and song. He had equipped each of them with canes with little wooden horses on the top, an appropriate touch. As Black put it, they did their jigs and sang two songs, one extolling the virtues of Canadian Breweries beer, and knocking its competitors, and the other extolling the birthday man himself.

There was great hooting, laughter, and applause from the audience, with Eddie Taylor the loudest and most vocal. Not only had he been surprised, but absolutely delighted. When the show was over, Phillips and Baxter called Taylor up to the stage and presented him with a gift from the assembled group, a large silver tray which had been engraved with the signatures of everyone present. To cap it all off, Baxter had recorded the entire event and later had records pressed and copies sent to the guests as souvenirs of the great occasion.

The fifty-year-old Taylor had long wanted to get Canadian Breweries into the Quebec market, which at that time was shared mainly by Molson's and National which, between them, had 85 per cent of the market with C.B.L. at 12 per cent and Labatt's at next to nothing. He considered the possibility of building a plant there but if he could get control of an existing Quebec firm with an established market, that would be the best possible course of action. With this in mind, he had been keeping a close eye on the fortunes of the Montreal-based National Breweries Limited. Its published figures indicated that sales were dropping regularly. Even though the company was financially sound, it would not be long before it was in serious difficulty.

National was a holding company formed in 1909 with Dow Brewery as part of the organization. National had enjoyed great success over a number of decades but the management group that had maintained control for many years had failed to train key executives to replace the originals when they retired. The company's operations began to suffer. In the post-war period the company was faced with high costs, an inconsistent quality of production, and deteriorating management, which led to an inevitable drop in sales. In sizing up the situation, E.P. Taylor recognized that no other major brewery in Quebec would be able to move in to take over because it might be accused of attempting to establish a monopoly in the province. If another Canadian brewery did not attempt to acquire National, however, then the company would undoubtedly fall into U.S. hands.

E.P. Taylor decided to attempt to obtain control of National Breweries. He, Wally McCutcheon, and George Black carefully organized the tactics of their approach and the details of an offer to purchase. The next step was to open the negotiating door with the Dawes family, which had the largest block of shares in National and, in effect, controlled the company. The president was Norman

Dawes, a courtly, aloof man, who carried himself with dignity and was well into his seventies.

Taylor wrote to Dawes and asked if he might come to Montreal to present a proposal. Dawes agreed, and in April 1951, accompanied by Wally McCutcheon and George Black, Taylor met with the board of directors of National. At some length he explained the advantages that would flow to the shareholders if they agreed to join Canadian Breweries. But when he finished his talk, there was a stony silence. Not one question was asked. Finally Norman Dawes said, "We will consider your proposals, Mr. Taylor, and we will let you know." The meeting was over. Later in the day Dawes informed Taylor that the National board considered that the time was not appropriate for a merger. With that, Taylor and his team retreated to Toronto to regroup.

Characteristically, Taylor did not give up. Once he has decided on an objective he explores every avenue in order to achieve it. But there had to be a different approach to the Dawes problem.

After lengthy discussions and conferences with his Argus colleagues and financial and legal advisers, the decision was made to make an offer to all the shareholders of National Breweries with a cash price of $35 for each preferred share and an exchange of common shares of the two companies on a share-per-share basis. This new Canadian Breweries proposal was received with considerable resistance by the Dawes group. Then a breakthrough came through an idea of Bud McDougald's. He had noted that each preferred share carried four votes. George Black later recalled, "Bud knows his way around the intricacies of corporate finance better than most people. He came up with the idea that we should make a bid of $50 a share to preference shareholders, thereby getting four times the number of votes." The cash offer did bring in most of the preferred shares, but the exchange of common shares was not as successful a move. By late fall, Canadian Breweries had over 40 per cent of the voting shares in National, but still did not own enough stock for actual control.

The next skirmish came when Dawes advised Taylor that National Breweries had received a cash offer for one of its plants, the Frontenac Brewery in Montreal. Dawes refused to disclose either the amount of the offer or the name of the firm making it, but told Taylor if he wished to make a counter-offer, he could do so within forty-eight hours. Taylor considered it essential that

National Breweries should not be broken up piece by piece before control was acquired. The shrewd Norman Dawes knew he had Taylor over a barrel and Taylor knew he knew. Taylor, McCutcheon, and Black immediately went to Montreal, talked further with Dawes, and then put together an offer for the Frontenac Brewery. It was, according to George Black, "a unique offer in my experience." Canadian Breweries offered to buy the Frontenac Brewery for 10 per cent more than any other offer, the amount not to exceed $4,250,000. The proposal was delivered to National Breweries just before the forty-eight-hour time limit expired. As Black said, it was a unique offer and it worked. Dawes subsequently disclosed that the original bidder had been Labatt's, who had offered $3,400,000, almost a million dollars less than the limit to which Taylor was prepared to go.

In March 1952, Taylor and his C.B.L. associates attended the annual meeting of National Breweries held in Montreal with 47 per cent of the voting stock of National in hand. When the meeting was called to order and the preliminaries out of the way, the president of National Breweries proposed a slate of directors for the coming year, at which point E.P. Taylor stood up and nominated his own group. The vote settled the issue decisively. Many of the shareholders at the meeting supported the C.B.L. group, with the result that the Canadian Breweries nominees were elected, and effective control of National Breweries Limited went to Taylor's firm. Within the next year Canadian Breweries acquired virtually 100 per cent of the shares of National Breweries and control was total.

Taylor made another major move with Canadian Breweries in 1951, but it was internal and shook up his establishment considerably. He decided that it was time to decentralize the C.B.L. operation for reasons which he briefly set out in a letter to C.B.L.'s advertising agency, McKim's: "We have found that our company has grown so much, and as is so often true in cases of this kind, too many policies and decisions were being made at head office. We have accordingly dispersed most of our senior men to the subsidiaries, and these subsidiaries will have a high degree of autonomy in the future." What he wanted to do was to simplify the head office operations to the greatest degree possible, consistent with retaining control of policy. The result was a complete decentralization with the exception of the departments of the comptroller, treasurer, and secretary. Phillips and McCutcheon were in on the decision. But they would leave it to the new president, George Black, to do the dirty work of carrying it off.

Shifting large numbers of management people around, moving them to new cities and different jobs causes problems. Black said Taylor, Phillips, and McCutcheon "were all for doing it at once. It was in the summer, and it was a very complicated operation. I am opposed philosophically and every other way to doing complicated things in a large company in a hurry without proper consideration. So I fended them off for a few months. Finally I had my memoranda composed and I was ready. We decentralized in November and that created a hell of a convulsion. I called a meeting of all the important people in the Canadian operation, I guess there would have been about fifty of them. There was no discussion. I simply distributed copies of my memoranda and stood up and read it. That was that and that was final. I subsequently learned that there were all kinds of meetings of people who thought of resigning, but they got over it and it turned out to be a great success."

The decision to decentralize C.B.L. brought with it the end of the Taylor concept to consolidate the company's brewing operations in the Toronto area into one large plant with a new town built around it for its workers. Plans for the new town had begun in 1947 when Taylor had decided that O'Keefe Brewery should buy 628 acres of land in the area of Don Mills Road and Lawrence Avenue, east of the east branch of the Don Valley, where he would build the new brewery. But with the plans for the new plant scrapped, what should be done with the property? It was good farmland. Should it be sold or should it be developed along with other lands around it?

Taylor discussed the situation with Karl Fraser, whom he had engaged to assemble the lands for a new C.B.L. subsidiary, O'Keefe Realty Limited. Taylor had put Fraser in the O'Keefe Realty operation for the specific purpose of having him assemble the land and hire a small staff to prepare land-use plans for the area that had been acquired. Fraser had spent a great deal of time gathering ideas.

After considerable thought, Taylor opted to keep the land and develop a new town. The financing would, he knew, have to be considerable. Eventually, the lands would have to be removed from the C.B.L. O'Keefe portfolio because neither of them was in the land development business.*

Taylor's Argus partners were not keen about a long-term commitment to a fledgling industry they knew nothing about. High finance, manufacturing, and the retailing of food and drink products they understood. Land development they did not.

This attitude, together with the obvious need for much capital, prompted E.P. Taylor to attempt to find a partner. Through New York contacts he met the most colourful and, at that moment, most successful land developer in the United States, William Zeckendorf, but, "He used my first name right away and he said, 'Eddie, I'm in as your partner.' " Zeckendorf did not come in as a partner, although keen to do so, because Taylor sensed that he was "a little too high pressure." As a result of this experience, Taylor decided that partners in his land development business were not needed. On the other hand, the enthusiastic Zeckendorf later became a principal partner in the original development of a high-density residential and office complex, Flemingdon Park, just to the south of Don Mills.

By the beginning of 1952, although Taylor was reluctant to admit that he had any knowledge of a newspaper report about a possible $50 million housing development in the southeastern section of North York, he was, in fact, well advanced with the assembly of more land and the design of the new town which he would name Don Mills. He wanted as little publicity about it as possible until he had made all the necessary zoning and servicing arrangements with the Township of North York within which all the land for the development was located. Of particular concern were sanitary sewers and water, the latter being a major problem. Water was in short supply because of lack of co-operation between North York and the municipalities lying between it and the prime source, Lake Ontario. There was no metropolitan form of govern-

---

*Nor was E.P. Taylor, for that matter, although in 1947 he and two neighbours, Major General Bruce Matthews and James S. Duncan (under a company Taylor had formed, Wrentham Estates Limited), had bought land at the southwest corner of Bayview and York Mills and built on it one of the first shopping centres in the Toronto area with Dominion Stores conveniently coming in as their main tenant. They had bought the property which was open for development in forty-foot residential lots in order to protect their own Bayview properties. In the process, they were also able to make a profit, a not unusual happening for these three successful men.

ment in those days. In fact, it was this same lack of co-operation, which was also impeding the growth of North York, Scarborough, York, and Etobicoke, that forced the creation of the metropolitan form of government in Toronto in 1954.

By the spring of 1952, Karl Fraser had acquired a little over 1,000 acres, in addition to the original 620 for a new firm, Canadian Equity and Development Company Limited, which Taylor had incorporated as the parent organization for all of the Argus land development interests and companies. The time had arrived to complete the removal of the C.B.L./O'Keefe lands from their brewing portfolio and put them into the hands of Canadian Equity. This was done in early 1952 by a trade of the original 620 acres of O'Keefe Realty lands for 1,675,000 shares of Canadian Equity.

But there was a key, central parcel of land which was yet to be acquired and without which the Don Mills project would be in jeopardy. It would be E.P. Taylor who successfully negotiated its purchase. In August 1952, Taylor made a deal with D. Moffat Dunlap to purchase Dunlap's 600-acre Donalda farm property which lay to the east of Don Mills Road between York Mills Road and Lawrence Avenue, astride the east branch of the Don River. (The huge Dunlap residence on the edge of the valley, about 200 yards south of York Mills Road, Taylor later converted into the Donalda Club with a golf course in the valley, and with curling, and other facilities.) The Dunlap purchase brought the total area of land owned by Don Mills Developments Limited, the operating subsidiary of Canadian Equity, up to 2,200 acres.

With the Dunlap lands in hand, Taylor could now turn into reality his concept of a new town. And he could let the press know about his plans. When the key 600 Donalda acres were secured in August, Taylor and Fraser were ready to finish off processing the general plan through North York Planning Board and Council and to get on with servicing the first quadrant, which lay in the area to the northwest of the intersection of Don Mills Road and Lawrence Avenue, on the Watson farm, the first piece of land Fraser had acquired. Its servicing was to begin in 1952, and the first houses would be under construction in 1953.

Don Mills Developments Limited did not build any single-family houses on its own, but sold off lots to builders. "I wanted it to be developed appropriately and nicely so people would be comfortable and in reasonably good, but not expensive, housing. Mind you, in those days, we sold a house lot there for $3,500. The houses that were built sold from $12,000 to $15,000, including the land. Today those houses would be worth $50,000 or $60,000. We always used building contractors, but they couldn't put up a whole row or a whole street of houses that looked alike. I got involved in major policy decisions about how Don Mills should be developed."

One of the general policies was that there would be severe building restrictions to ensure that each building erected would be approved by the development company. "I decided that Don Mills must not look like a lot of places I had seen around the world where you see 500 or 1,000 houses that all look alike close together. The contractor therefore had to submit to us the plans for each house on each lot that they bought. I also had a policy of no blue roofs. That was the only thing I imposed. No blue roofs. I don't like blue roofs because blue fades. Blue is also a bad colour in the sun. I don't like blue roofs! They could have red roofs, green roofs, yellow roofs, any roofs they liked, but they couldn't have blue roofs." If there are any blue roofs in Don Mills today, it is only because E.P. Taylor's restrictions have expired. All Don Mills blue lovers no longer have to bow to the firm opinions of the world's most devoted anti-blue-roof man.

Although at least one other person has claimed authorship of the idea for Don Mills, it was E.P. Taylor alone who put it together, hired the people to acquire the land, to prepare the plans, and to get on with negotiations with the Township of North York in which the land was located. He put Karl Fraser in charge of the project from the beginning of the assembly of the land. Fraser was president of Don Mills Developments Limited and Taylor chairman of the board. Fraser had a town planning crew. "They came up with the basic land-use plan for the Don Mills acreage of which I approved. Karl had done a very good job of assembling the land. He did about three-quarters of it and I got the Donalda farms. We should also have bought the priests' farm [Christian Brothers' land, east of the Donalda farm, lying north of Lawrence]. There was only a difference of about $1,000 an acre between what I wanted to pay and what my associates wanted to pay. I wanted to pay $5,000 an acre and my advisers said $4,000 an acre. I should have overruled them but I didn't." In a few short years, the Chris-

209

tian Brothers' land would be worth more than ten times the amount Taylor could have bought it for.

With the Don Mills project under way, the services going in, and houses and factories being built, E.P. Taylor's enthusiasm for land development was on the increase. He decided to expand his involvement. Through his Canadian Equity and Development Company Limited, he bought the lands of the former Hamilton racing club from the Ontario Jockey Club. News of this Taylor move came in mid-February 1953 as part of an announcement by Simpsons-Sears' president, E.G. Burton, of a major expansion program, both at Burnaby, British Columbia, and Hamilton, Ontario, where a new commercial complex would be built on the lands of the former Hamilton Jockey Club and would be known as the Greater Hamilton Shopping Centre. Simpsons-Sears would build a large department store there, while the balance of the land, another fifty acres, would be developed by the Greater Hamilton Shopping Centre Limited. The announcement stated that the development company was "controlled by a group in which is included the Argus Corporation Limited. The president of the Greater Hamilton Shopping Centre will be Karl C. Fraser, who is also president of Don Mills Development Limited." Unfortunately, Taylor was to lose his long-time friend and associate, Fraser, when he died of a heart attack a few months later, just as industry was moving into Don Mills in strength and people were moving into the first houses. Taylor appointed Angus McClaskey, who had joined Canadian Equity from a senior position with Central Mortgage and Housing, to be president of the growing firm.

Expansion and diversification continued to be major personal objectives for E.P. Taylor, and the middle 1950s saw no abatement of his desire.

Chapter XIII

New Horizons
1955-1960

In the late fifties Canada was in the second decade of tremendous economic, industrial, financial, and population growth that had begun after the war. There was to be a new government in Ottawa, as the Conservatives under the rousing leadership of John Diefenbaker took the reins of power from St. Laurent and his Liberal Party. The new Prime Minister was to make many controversial decisions that would shake and dislocate industry. One such was his order to terminate the development of the promising Avro Arrow all-weather jet fighter, an aircraft a decade ahead of its time which the Royal Canadian Air Force and the Canadian aircraft complex both needed desperately. With that decision came the virtual dismemberment of advanced aerospace know-how in Canada, and the abandonment of skills and jobs.

It was a time of "Visions of the North" and "Roads to Resources." But the federal bureaucracy had not yet grown to the point where it would begin to impose such onerous legislation and tax burdens on private enterprise that Canadian entrepreneurs, builders, manufacturers, and professional people would be forced to look elsewhere for a climate where economic growth and individual productivity were encouraged.

Argus Corporation and E.P. Taylor and his colleagues were flourishing. They were also keeping as far away from the clutches of government as they could. Even so, the government was after E.P. Taylor.

When Taylor had made his first moves toward the takeover of National Breweries in 1951, the commissioner of the Combines Investigation Act opened an enquiry on the proposed merger and

211

monitored it through to its completion. Taylor believes, and probably rightfully so, that one of his powerful competitors, who was listened to in Ottawa, was able, through political means, to attract the interest of the commissioner. In February 1954, the Director of Investigation and Research had completed his mission and emerged with a charge that C.B.L.'s acquisition constituted a breach of the Combines Investigation Act, Section 32 (i), "being a merger, trust or monopoly which had operated or was likely to operate to the detriment or against the interest of the public." The director also alleged that the national scalawag, Mr. E.P. Taylor, by reason of his activities, was a party to the offence. In effect, the director's charges ranged over the whole history of the development of Canadian Breweries, claiming that the pattern Taylor had created of acquisition and shutting down of plants by C.B.L. "had been to establish [C.B.L.] as a dominant factor in Ontario which would give it the power to regulate and control the policies and practices of the industry." And that, "by acquiring National Breweries, Canadian Breweries had reduced the principal competing suppliers of beer from three to two, a situation one step removed from a monopoly." And "the elimination of many firms has created a quasi-monopoly situation in which the likelihood of maintaining active competition . . . is lessened."

There was no doubt that the allegations made by the director shook E.P. Taylor, his senior Canadian Breweries staff, and his Argus colleagues. Nevertheless, there was no ignoring the fact that the federal government was intent on prosecuting both C.B.L. and Taylor himself. A reply had to be prepared. After countless meetings between Taylor and his lawyers and after the collection and consolidation of evidence that would support Canadian Breweries' response, the C.B.L. reply was prepared and delivered. It stated, among other things, that:

> No monopoly or quasi-monopoly situation could exist because provincial government control was so extensive in terms of price, advertising, alcoholic content, etc., that it is "a regulated industry" and that within the bounds of regulation competition was keen, primarily in terms of quality. . . . The effects of the merger on the public interest must be judged at the present time. All that was said in letters and memoranda of past years was irrelevant. No public detriment arose. In

fact, Canadian Breweries performed a public service by eliminating excess capacity and putting an end to bootlegging and other illegalities. Business is done on a clean, decent basis. All mergers were approved by the Ontario Liquor Control Board. E.P. Taylor is only one officer of the company. He should not be singled out. He acted only as a company official.

The next stage in the proceedings involved hearings before the Restrictive Trade Practices Commission which began in Ottawa that fall. These were both extensive and time consuming. From those hearings would come a recommendation to the Minister of Justice as to whether or not charges should in fact be laid in the courts against the company and Taylor.

The wheels of justice turn slowly. As 1955 ended there was still no final decision on whether to prosecute. The Restrictive Trade Practices Commission's report to the minister for the year ended March 31, 1956, stated that the matter had been referred by the minister to Norman L. Matthews, Q.C., of Toronto for his opinion as to whether any court proceedings were warranted by the evidence disclosed in the report. On the last day of that fiscal year, Mr. Matthews was still reviewing the situation. By coincidence, the second matter referred to in the report of the Director of Investigation and Research was on asphalt roofing, "being a report concerning an alleged combine in the manufacture, distribution, and sale of asphalt and tar roofings and related products in Canada." The manufacturers were ten in number. Prominent among them was another Argus jewel, Dominion Tar and Chemical Company Limited. That report was referred by the minister to Walter B. Williston, Q.C., of Toronto for opinion as to whether the evidence warranted prosecution. He subsequently advised that it did.

It was now clear to E.P. Taylor that one of the prices of big business in small, parochial Canada was prosecution, government style.

Norman Matthews eventually gave his opinion, and in due course formal charges were laid against Canadian Breweries Limited but not against E.P. Taylor. Nevertheless, he would be a central figure in the thirty-eight-day trial which began in late 1959 before the then chief justice of the trial division of the Supreme Court of Ontario, the Honourable J.C. McRuer. Taylor was to sit through most of the long, tedious trial. His most vivid recollection of his first day in the courtroom is that the judge caught him sitting sucking a lozenge but thought he was chewing gum. Whereupon his Lordship sent the bailiff to tick off Taylor publicly for chewing gum in court.

It was not until the end of March 1960, nine years after the initial enquiry, that the trial ended and McRuer delivered his judgement–not guilty.

In 1955 Argus Corporation was alive, well, growing phenomenally, and exerting through its three leaders a more powerful influence on industrial, corporate, and general business activities than any had ever done before in the history of Canada. Argus was becoming a legend in its own time, as was its creator, Edward Plunket Taylor.

With its close relationship with Taylor, McDougald & Company on the entrepreneurial side, Argus had been an outstanding success. Its opening assets of under $14 million were now valued at $78 million. On a per-common-share basis, the value went from $12.64 in 1946 to $38.56 in 1955.

It was now time for Bud McDougald, who was on most of the boards of the companies in which Argus had a substantial interest, to become a partner in Argus and a member of the board.

Taylor wanted McDougald in. He therefore agreed to a reorganization which saw his own voting share holding reduced to 10 per cent although his equity position remained intact. This was accomplished by converting a percentage of Taylor's voting shares into non-voting Class 'C' shares which were created for this purpose. McDougald joined the board of Argus.

"The subject who is truly loyal to the Chief Magistrate will neither advise nor submit to arbitrary measures–JUNIUS."
Imagine the furore of that day if the Argus quadrumvirate and their colleagues had bought the *Globe and Mail*, the Canadian newspaper that carries that lofty principle at the top of its editorial page each day or, for that matter, if that multi-faceted, high-powered group had bought the influential Toronto *Star*. Even today either prospect would be almost as controversial as the status of Confederation.

214

But, in 1955, the purchase of the *Globe and Mail* was high in the Argus corporate mind, although Taylor had his reservations. A friend of all of the Argus leaders, George McCullagh, the publisher and owner of 51 per cent of the shares of Globe Printing Company, had died, and the 111-year-old newspaper enterprise had to be sold. The executors set 3:00 P.M. on Thursday, February 10, 1955, as the cut-off time for bids to be submitted.

As the deadline approached, speculation was rampant. On February 9, the now-defunct *Telegram* began its front-page story:

> Who is going to get the *Globe and Mail*? Some pretty impressive names are being tossed about on Rumour Street–names like Steel's Cyrus Eaton, Beer's E.P. Taylor, Oil's Clint Murchison, Baseball's Dan Topping, in addition to men already identified with the publishing business, such as Roy Thomson, the Southams, the Knights, Lords Rothermere, Beaverbrook and Kemsley, Jack Kent Cooke, Max Bell and some less well known U.S. publishers. Within a week–maybe as soon as tomorrow afternoon–the successful bidder in Toronto's intriguing newspaper auction will be announced, if there is one.

Taylor recounts that at Argus "consideration was given as to whether we would be interested. We had talked about it, and three of my associates felt that the paper should fall into the hands of constructive people who had a big stake in the country, because it certainly was Canada's leading morning paper, and that it should grow with the country. We always looked for companies that would grow. But I was never keen on the idea of becoming a publisher or the proprietor of a newspaper."

Taylor reasoned that the proprietor of a newspaper was a target. Newspapers have to criticize editorially and, as he saw it, the owner would be criticized for whatever the editor said. He also believed that an owner should be uninfluenced by any other investments he might have, on the one hand, and on the other, what the editorial policy of the newspaper should be. His partners, however, were of the opinion that the paper should be owned by constructive people like them who could be an influence for the good of the country.

"When the day of reckoning came, I said I preferred that we should not bid for it. The other three said they would like to do it.

As we have always made things unanimous, I said, with reluctance, I would go along with it." On the Monday before the closing of the bids, "I was at a meeting of the directors of the board of Dominion Tar. After the meeting, my friend and fellow board member, Colin Webster, said to me, 'I hear a rumour that your group are going to be bidders for the *Globe and Mail* on Thursday when the tenders close.' I said, 'I'm afraid we may, Colin, but I hope we don't get it.' And, being a friend, I told him the background of my feelings about it.

"Then I went back to Toronto and on Wednesday Colin called me on the telephone and said he was very embarrassed about our conversation on Monday with reference to the *Globe and Mail* and I asked him why. He said, 'Well, I had no knowledge at that time that a member of my family, one of my brothers, Howard, was planning to make a bid through a trust company in which the family is interested but of which he has control. The rest of the family isn't too pleased about going into the newspaper business for, I suspect, the same reasons you expressed to me about you and your group. But I want to assure you I knew nothing about this on Monday. If you do make a bid, I hope you get it and not us!' In jest, he added, 'Please bid as much as you possibly can.' I went back to my partners and told them about the conversation, and, if memory serves me right, our bid was raised by $1 million, to somewhere in the vicinity of $11 million. When the bids were opened, I think we were $100,000 less than the highest bidder," who was no other than Howard Webster and his family, dark horses in the field who were not even considered in the speculative reports of that week.

A note E.P. Taylor had made on his "Major Objectives for 1955" sheet of foolscap, which listed "*Globe and Mail* or Toronto *Star*," meant exactly what it said. Both newspapers were acquisition targets, notwithstanding his reservations and reluctance. The Argus group had lost out to the Websters on the *Globe and Mail* bidding, but now the Toronto *Star* was also up for sale. In 1949, on the death of the *Star*'s founder and owner, Joseph E. (Holy Joe) Atkinson, the Ontario Conservative government reacted strongly to the way Atkinson had set up his estate. He had left the paper to the Atkinson Foundation, a charitable trust. Alleging that by so doing he had deprived the province of "millions" in inheritance taxes, the Legislature passed a retroactive act preventing any charitable foundation from owning more than 10 per cent of a business and setting a time limit of three years for the disposition of holdings which contravened the new act. The Atkinson trustees protested violently, but all they could squeeze out of the adamant government was an extra four years before divestiture was required. That date was now coming up. *Newsweek* carried a story, complete with a picture of a smiling Taylor wearing his famous pearl-grey top hat, reporting:

> With the deadline now in sight, Toronto has been filled with rumours. At least six offers, reports run, have been made for the paper. The most eager buyer seems to be Edward Plunket Taylor, 55, a Canadian millionaire, and owner of O'Keefe's "Old Vienna Beer." Taylor is said to have offered a splashy $20 million plus for the paper. The *Star* last week quickly moved to plug the story leaks.

Taylor, Phillips, McCutcheon, and McDougald went through the same process again as they had with the *Globe and Mail*. "Will we bid or will we not bid? I expressed my unhappiness about it, but said I'd go along if the other three wanted to. Our negotiator was Mr. McDougald, who knew Mr. Hindmarsh, who was Joseph Atkinson's son-in-law and headed up the *Star*." McDougald had begun to discuss a possible deal with Hindmarsh in late 1954. As a result of the preliminary discussions and the positive reaction from Hindmarsh, who was only one of five trustees of the Atkinson Foundation, the Argus group incorporated Fleet Street Properties Limited, which would acquire the *Star* shares. In the fall of 1955, McDougald submitted Fleet Street's bid to Hindmarsh, who put it before the board of directors. The offer was $20 million. Of the five directors, only Hindmarsh and his wife voted in favour. Two others joined Joseph S. Atkinson, son of the founder. He, like his father, was against any support of or alliance with a brewery interest, and voted against the proposal. Even in the face of this setback, the determined McDougald refused to give up. He obtained the concurrence of his Argus colleagues to up the bid to $23 million, then continued his discussions with Hindmarsh, who usually took an early lunch in the Stoodleigh Restaurant, located in the basement of the old Toronto *Star* building on King Street. McDougald would sit down with him and talk about things in general and about the sale of the *Star* in particular. But even the substantial upping of the bid price would not help. However, on

December 20, 1955, Hindmarsh had good news for McDougald. There had just been two resignations from the board of trustees. Argus and its Fleet Street properties would be the new owners. The two men shook hands on the deal. It was then simply a matter of getting the final approval of the new board, having the legal documents prepared, and the deal would be completed.

But it never came off. That same day, Hindmarsh suffered a heart attack and died within a few hours. Without him, the Argus group did not stand a chance. Atkinson now dominated the group of trustees, and there would be no way that he would look on Hindmarsh's verbal agreement with McDougald as binding. Furthermore, it was perfectly clear that he was dead set against the Argus acquisition. In the end, the editor-in-chief, Beland Honderich, with five other *Star* senior executives, made a successful bid.

The Argus group never did own or control a newspaper, although much later Taylor himself was to make a bid for one in another country.

High on the priority list of the holdings of the Argus Corporation was Massey-Harris, in which the firm had a huge investment. After a five-for-one split of Massey-Harris common stock in 1951, Argus held 775,000 shares, or just a little over 10 per cent of the equity. On the other hand, of the sixteen seats on the board of directors nine either belonged to the Taylor group or appointments to fill them were influenced by them. The Argus group was clearly the dominant force in the company.

Earnings were good at a dollar per share for 1949 and $1.70 for 1951 after the share split. The Argus people relied heavily on the dividends of the reliable Massey-Harris and the other companies in the Argus portfolio to keep their corporate ship afloat and to meet their repayments to the banks of loans which had been arranged for the purpose of buying stock of the dividend paying company.

Massey-Harris appeared to be in good condition, and expansion by merger and acquisition was the policy of the day. In 1953, the chairman and president of the firm, James S. Duncan, with a late assist from Phillips, McCutcheon, and McDougald, had negotiated a deal with the eccentric Irish inventor, Harry Ferguson, under which his tractor-manufacturing company in the United Kingdom and its North American operations were merged with the Canadian corporation under the new name of Massey-Harris-Ferguson. This move expanded and strengthened the company by giving it access to Ferguson's line of products and inventions and its market overseas. As part of the original deal, Ferguson had become chairman of the board while Duncan remained as president. However, Ferguson, unable to accept that he was not the chief executive officer, tried to run the whole show. In 1954, he finally announced that he would resign if Argus would buy his shares. "I think he needed the money, Taylor says." The Argus group made arrangements for the disposition of his shares, taking 725,000 themselves. By November 1954, Ferguson was gone but his patents and his name remained.

The next two years brought a rapid breakdown in the relationship between the Taylor group and Duncan. Taylor and Phillips became concerned with the trends they saw developing in the company's performance. Duncan, on the other hand, was optimistic and of the opinion that his executive direction of the company was taking it to new levels of sales and profits.

Profits were, in fact, falling rapidly, dramatically so in the United States. The 1954 profits of the newly merged Massey-Harris-Ferguson organization were $8.9 million, but this masked a sharp decline in the profits of the United States operations, which went down to $700,000 from $2.4 million. If defence contracts had been excluded there would have been a loss of $1.5 million in the American operation. The 1955 loss in that country, excluding defence contracts, was $900,000, but the overall profit of the company was $12.2 million.

Taylor and Phillips had always made sure that Massey-Harris-Ferguson got the expansion money it needed. In March 1955, Duncan and his management group, arguing that they wanted to expand and modernize their plants in order to reduce costs and make the firm more competitive, asked for more money. Phillips and Taylor went along with them, authorizing a preferred issue of 500,000 shares, which sold easily for $24 million. However, by the year end, October 31, the profit ratio of the company had fallen drastically to 3.3 per cent. At this point, and with Duncan ill, the two Argus men decided it was time to make some shifts in management. They brought in Albert Thornbrough, then vice-president in charge of procurement for the Ferguson division in Racine, Wisconsin. He would fill the new position of executive vice-president and give them a hand in sorting out what they believed had to be done to turn the company around.

As 1956 began, the United States losses were accelerating and it was apparent that the Canadian operation's profits, which declined on a steady scale from $7.7 million in 1951 to $1.1 million in 1955, would suffer a further loss in 1956. The losses could not be attributed to the recent merger, which had created a more balanced product mix and had permanently increased the overall size of the organization and the relative importance of the sales of the company outside North America. One area of harm did come from the merger and that was the perpetuation and extension of the two lines of machinery tractors, and combines, each under a different name, and the continuation of the two separate distribution systems inherited from the merger. Having two competitive lines and two competitive distribution systems had created chaos. The cost of sales in North America was climbing toward the impossible figure of 90 per cent (which was reached in 1957). And to cap it all off, inventory was growing rapidly and was already well beyond an acceptable level. By 1955 it had reached an alarming 48 per cent of net sales and was heading for its 1956 high of 55 per cent. (By 1966 it was to be down to less than 30 per cent.)

In 1956 it became clear that the company urgently needed more money to build up working capital in both the United States and Canada. The big U.S. market was in bad shape, although sales were on the slight increase in Canada. The major problem was that the company's inventory had risen sharply, and cash balances were going in the opposite direction just as quickly. Deeply concerned, Taylor and Phillips told Duncan they believed the Massey firm was headed for trouble. In their view, either sales would have to go up or plants would have to be shut. Taylor and Phillips authorized the sale of $21 million in new debentures, which was completed in March 1956. By May the company's inventory had increased $53 million in six months to the staggering figure of $182 million.

Always the optimist, Duncan held firm to his opinion that sales in the United States would improve quickly and that the inventory would be reduced. But during May and early June sales remained low, the factories were still churning out products, inventory continued to climb, and Taylor and Phillips agonized through the worst cash squeeze they had ever experienced. It was estimated that between Argus' corporate holdings and their own personal shares in the company holdings, the Argus partners controlled close to 30 per cent of Massey-Harris-Ferguson, a multi-million dollar investment. Their losses would be disastrous should the company fail.

By the middle of June, Taylor, Phillips, McCutcheon, and McDougald had decided that unless they took drastic measures to turn the company around, Massey-Harris-Ferguson would not be able to meet its short-term commitments and the firm would be facing bankruptcy in a matter of weeks. Since Duncan still refused to agree to their plans, Taylor and Phillips took the steps themselves. They proposed that the ailing Duncan become chairman with Phillips as president and chief executive officer, but this was unacceptable to the proud Duncan, the man who had invited these two on the Massey-Harris board in the first place. He resented the Argus interference in the management of the company. At a July board meeting, Taylor and Phillips accepted Duncan's resignation and gave him a generous pension. The official explanation for Duncan's retirement was ill health.

Phillips immediately became chairman and chief executive officer of the company. E.P. Taylor became chairman of the executive committee of the board, and Albert Thornbrough became president. One of the first decisions they made was to establish a policy that there would be only one line, one distribution system, and only one sales outlet in each market. The excessive inventories of 1956 were written off and prices reduced.

Finally in 1957, the losses in Canada and the United States bottomed out at a staggering $15.5 million, although overall worldwide loss was $4.7 million. The company returned to a profitable position by the end of 1958. Taylor and Phillips were convinced that if they had not taken the decisions that the circumstances dictated, Massey-Ferguson* would have collapsed.

For Taylor, the episode with Duncan was, for personal reasons, one of the most difficult in his career. It is still a matter of great regret to him. Duncan was a good friend and a neighbour. On the other hand, as he saw it then and sees it now, there was absolutely no alternative.

Through their involvement in the management of Massey-Ferguson, Taylor and Phillips learned that Standard Motors, a

---

*The shortened name was adopted in 1957.

major motor vehicle manufacturer in England, which had a long-term contract to make Ferguson tractors for what was now the merged Massey-Ferguson firm, was making a good profit, whereas Massey-Ferguson was making nothing on the units but had to bear all the selling expenses. They had to get Massey-Ferguson out of that situation. Tractors were by far the largest part of their world-wide market, so the production and sales had to be integrated. It was mandatory. In 1957, on behalf of Massey-Ferguson, they made an offer to buy Standard Motors who were producing the machines in a modern, high-production factory. It was only the tractor factory of Standard Motors that they wanted but they went after control of the entire operation. When the Standard Motors people refused to sell, Taylor and Phillips decided to go on a different track. Their research showed that the shareholdings in the company were widely held. If they could obtain a large block Standard would be vulnerable. The decision was made to buy Standard stock on the open market. Eventually they had obtained 24 per cent of the voting shares. At that point the two Canadians confronted the officers and directors of Standard saying, "We're the largest shareholders and we will go to the shareholders on this matter." This "matter" was the purchase of the tractor works, which was all they wanted. And they got it, in exchange for all the Standard shares they had bought, plus $32 million, for a total of $45 million–rather an expensive way to do business, but the only way if the down-the-line operation from production through to sales was to be profitable. For Massey-Ferguson it now was.

The time spent in England on Massey-Ferguson business revived Eddie Taylor's long-time love affair with that country. Within a few months of completing the Standard Motors deal, Taylor would be signing a Canadian Breweries agreement which would lead him toward a long and productive involvement in the brewing industry of the United Kingdom.

Taylor's interest in British breweries had begun as a result of the 1951 visit to Canada by Thomas Carter, managing director of Hope & Anchor Brewery Limited of Sheffield. Hoping to find a Canadian brewing company willing to produce his company's Jubilee Stout, Carter made contact with E.P. Taylor, who was keenly interested, particularly so if he could interest Carter in a reciprocal deal, whereby Carling's Black Label beer would be brewed and bottled by Hope & Anchor in the United Kingdom.

Tom Carter and Eddie Taylor worked out a deal. Canadian Breweries (International) Limited was incorporated in England on April 9, 1952, its name being changed to Carling Brewery of Canada Limited in 1954. The English company would market Carling's Black Label in Great Britain, the product being brewed and bottled by Carter's Hope & Anchor firm. At the same time, Jubilee Brewery Limited was incorporated in Canada by Hope & Anchor for the purpose of marketing Jubilee Stout throughout Canada, the product being brewed and bottled by one of the Canadian Breweries group.

But by 1958 Thomas Carter became decidedly unhappy about the reciprocal deal he had made with Canadian Breweries in Canada. The English subsidiary of Canadian Breweries, for whom he was making and marketing Carling beer in the United Kingdom, was producing far better results than Canadian Breweries was in Canada, making Jubilee Stout and selling it in Canada for Hope & Anchor. Carter, a big, beefy, former national water-polo player, felt that he was being had by Taylor and company in the deal they had originally made in 1952. In Britain, Hope & Anchor gave Carling's access to their own 200 licensed houses, thereby guaranteeing the Carling product good sales. On the other hand, no such marketing advantage existed in Canada, because "tied houses" were not permitted. Jubilee Stout had to compete on the open market, and sales were not going well at all.

Rightly or wrongly, Carter, who increasingly felt that he and his people were putting far more effort into the marketing of Carling's Black Label in England than Canadian Breweries was putting into the marketing of the Jubilee Stout, decided he'd had enough. Without saying anything to Taylor, he purchased twenty acres of land in Metro Toronto and quietly managed to obtain from the Ontario government a licence to brew and sell his stout in Ontario. Taylor knew nothing about this until the two men met to discuss the future, and when he was informed of what was going on, Taylor was quite cross about it. Nevertheless, and typically, he was prepared to bargain and negotiate. The result was that Canadian Breweries agreed to take over Jubilee Brewery Company of Canada Limited with all its liabilities, which by this time were considerable, while Hope & Anchor would take the Carling Brewing

Company of Canada Limited in England without its liabilities. There would be exchange licences to both companies with undertakings that each would do the best to promote the respective brands. Carter and Arthur Elliott, an intelligent, even-mannered Sheffield solicitor, went on the board of Canadian Breweries and Taylor and Ian Dowie, president of the Brewing Corporation of America, were appointed directors of Hope & Anchor.

Taylor and Carter then signed a joint declaration of intent which was to have far-reaching consequences for Taylor personally, for Canadian Breweries, and for the whole structure of the brewing industry in the United Kingdom. That declaration stated that both parties would make their best efforts to promote the creation of a national brewery group in Great Britain. Taylor thereby committed himself to do in England what he had done in Canada when he established Canadian Breweries. By acquisitions, mergers, consolidations, and shutdowns, he would attempt to put together a new national brewery in the United Kingdom.

In 1959, beginning steps were being taken to build a national group of breweries as called for in the agreement between Hope & Anchor and Canadian Breweries. Thomas Carter and Arthur Elliott, by then chairman of the board of Hope & Anchor, were making their opening moves. Their first merger prospect was Hammonds United, controlled by the seventy-three-year-old H.L. Bradfer-Lawrence and his son, Colonel Philip Bradfer-Lawrence, with whom Carter and Elliott got on well. Also in the first merger net they wanted to capture Leeds and Wakefield Breweries Limited, controlled by John and Edward Ford. The men all knew each other, and it was not difficult to get a discussion started. A committee of directors was established to report to a steering committee comprised of Arthur Elliott, John French of Yorkshire Trust Limited, who was consultant to the group, Tom Carter, and the senior Bradfer-Lawrence. But in mid-summer 1959, negotiations broke down due to a clash of personalities between Tom Carter and the difficult H.L. Bradfer-Lawrence.

Edward Taylor had been to Spain on a purchasing trip. On his way back through London, he was invited to dinner by Arthur Elliott to meet the two Bradfer-Lawrences. At that meeting, and at others that were held, they discussed the merger difficulties. Taylor could see that they were getting nowhere, but he was not yet ready to become actively involved; he just had too much on his plate and could not get back to England until October. When he returned that month, he did two things. He negotiated for and acquired the small Scottish brewery of John Jeffery and Company and had Northern Breweries Limited incorporated as of October 8, 1959. As a holding company it would complete the Jeffery purchase as a Canadian Breweries subsidiary. Second, he got involved in the merger negotiations. His attitude, as Arthur Elliott described it, was to say to the parties, " 'Would you mind? You're not succeeding. Could I possibly take a run at it, because that's been my business?' Mr. Taylor came and endeavoured to cope with the negotiations which were extremely difficult, owing, I think, almost entirely to personalities."

Taylor turned to the merchant bankers, Philip Hill, Higginson, Erlangers Limited, rather than to the Yorkshire Trust for assistance in the complex arrangements. Leeds and Wakefield withdrew from the negotiations. Finally, Taylor got the Bradfer-Lawrences, Elliott, and Carter to the brink of an agreement to bring together Hammonds and Hope & Anchor, but the senior Bradfer-Lawrence became extremely difficult about the question of who should be chairman of the board and almost scuttled the whole transaction. The younger Bradfer-Lawrence discussed the crisis some years later. "Eddie, Arthur Elliott, Father, and I all had dinner together about three weeks before we finally got the thing down on paper. The whole issue then was who was going to be chairman of this damn company. I remember Father saying, 'Why the hell should this good old-fashioned Canadian tycoon stride in here and become chairman of a group of British breweries? I ought to be!' So we had a long discussion. Father was quite a nice chap, but he was extremely difficult on occasions. About halfway through that dinner, I said, 'Father, I think it's futile to go on now. We'll go home.' So he stomped out to the lift and I went with him. We went back to his flat and I didn't know what to do. So I said to Father, 'They said you could be chairman for two years. By then you'll be seventy-five.' I thought he was going to retire when he was seventy anyway. He said, 'All right. What will we do?' I said, 'Well, I think the best thing you can do is to ring Eddie up at Claridge's and say the thing's still on.' That's what he did," and the merger was agreed.

Meanwhile in Canada, as a result of certain unfavourable occurrences, the departure of Taylor's protégé, George Black, Jr., from the presidency of Canadian Breweries, was becoming imminent. As soon as Taylor arrived back in Canada in October, a confrontation took place between the two men.

There had been a seven-week, industry-wide brewery strike during the summer which was ultimately settled with the breweries standing together, largely as a result of Black's efforts. Taylor would have made a settlement with the union because a shutdown of C.B.L.'s plants would cost at least $100,000 a day. But in his absence, Black, the president and chief executive officer, fought against the union and the costly strike was on.

This had been one point of contention between the two men. The other was a decision made by Taylor to recentralize the management of the company, a step with which Black disagreed. As George Black recalled, "when Taylor got home in October, he expressed dissatisfaction with the way I handled the strike. That did it. I said, 'Well, I did the best I could, Eddie.' He said, 'I think perhaps it's time we had a new president of Canadian Breweries Limited.' I said, 'Well, that's fine with me.'" And as to the recentralization, "I said, 'Eddie, I think your policy is nuts and I'm not going to have anything to do with it.'" Black then suggested to Taylor who the next president should be. "Well, he was so bloody mad by this time that if I'd suggested the Archangel Gabriel, and had he been available for the office, Eddie would have turned him down, too. I just got up, shook hands with him and walked out." Despite this episode, the two men remained good friends and business colleagues, Black being a substantial shareholder in Argus and a member of the board, and a wealthy man in his own right.

The Hammonds and Hope & Anchor merger that E.P. Taylor had negotiated in October 1959 was completed on March 30, 1960, with Taylor putting the Canadian Breweries holding of John Jeffery and Company of Edinburgh into Northern Breweries Limited, the name of which was at the same time changed to Northern Breweries of Great Britain Limited, with the senior Bradfer-Lawrence as chairman, E.P. Taylor as deputy chairman, Arthur Elliott as vice-chairman, and the younger Bradfer-Lawrence as managing director. Thomas Carter and Ian Dowie were on the board, pursuant to the original agreement.

By moving in and completing this first merger, E.P. Taylor had shaken the owners of the British brewing industry who balked at the intrusion of this outsider. The first thing that bothered them was that as soon as he had formed Northern Breweries in October of 1959, Taylor had instructed his broker to buy £25 of equity in every publicly quoted brewing company. Philip Bradfer-Lawrence recalled that "this created an absolute uproar in the brewers' society. Nobody ever thought of buying each other's shares. It just wasn't done. And everyone was saying, 'Who the hell are these people?' It caused absolute chaos. What Taylor wanted to do was to get every bit of information sent to him about every company and he got it. I suppose there were other ways of doing it, but people just didn't think it was the British thing to do."

Arthur Elliott also describes the reaction: "Here was this chap, Taylor, who had come to buy up the English breweries as he had done in Canada. I don't think he was ever described as dishonest or a sharp operator, but rather as a steamroller, or as a harvesting machine who will just gather you in. You'll be part of the flock, whether you like it or not and you will be crushed whether you like it or not."

Like it or not, E.P. Taylor had arrived in England, and the brewing industry would never be the same. After completion of the initial merger on March 30, 1960, there developed a typical Taylor whirlwind of negotiating and dealing activity. "Beer's Mr. Big," as Taylor was already being referred to in London's Fleet Street financial pages, was off and running, seeking the takeover of the companies which he had studied in detail and were on his master plan list.

His bringing together the three medium-to-small North Country firms had made Northern Breweries roughly an £18 million brewing group to start off with. Canadian Breweries, which had a 30 per cent stake in Hope & Anchor, wound up with a 10.7 per cent equity in Northern.

Jack Campbell, then president of Canadian Breweries, recalls that having established Northern Breweries, Taylor "then set out on a spate of activity of travelling around breweries in England and Scotland, the intention at this juncture being to start with companies in that part of the United Kingdom where Hammonds, Hope & Anchor, and John Jeffery were already located. His method was to telephone the chairman or managing director of a company he wanted to approach, seeking permission to be seen. Between March of 1960 and the end of the year he succeeded, in this way, in acquiring eight breweries, which was a pretty fair do in nine months. He did this, nobody else. He was helped by Philip Bradfer-Lawrence largely and occasionally by me. Derek Palmar of the Philip Hill firm was in the background and always came along and concluded the negotiations with an official point of view and did the necessary merchant banking. Mr. Taylor used to take all sorts of lists from the *Brewers' Manual* and the stock exchange gazettes and all the other data that one could get. Then he just got in his car and went around to their offices, after telephoning them perhaps a few hours before, saying, 'I would like to see you.'

"C.B.L. put up the money to get a piece of each of these twenty or twenty-five brewing companies so that we would have a stake. It was really a one-man effort. I used to be of some help to Mr. Taylor in arranging the financing. When we had negotiated a fair share of the outstanding ordinary shares in a brewery, quite often Mr. Taylor would go and see the executives and explain who he was and what he was doing. He's a very personable fellow and he's a tremendous salesman. I used to go with him and they'd say, 'Mr. E.P. Taylor is coming. Mr. E.P. Taylor is coming.' Then they'd almost line up to have a look at him. I remember one day we went to a little brewery in Scotland and this fellow was so flattered that E.P. Taylor had come to see this little brewery, he went in and introduced himself. They knew he was coming. He made a great hit. I mean, these people were just overjoyed that this fellow was their new leader. He would shake hands with the top people. He'd make a few jokes, and if he had time, he'd have a drink with them and stay for lunch. He's a very likable fellow with a tremendous personality, this great big Canadian. He was called 'Big Eddie.' "

Taylor moved from the Northern Breweries merger of Hope & Anchor and Hammonds to an offer for all the issued ordinary and preference capitals of George Younger and Son, of Alloa, John Fowler and Co. of Prestonpans, and William Murray and Company of Edinburgh. Those offers were delivered on April 8, 1960, and by April 25, the boards of all three companies had recommended acceptance. By May 10, all three deals were in hand, setting the Fleet Street financial pundits and the brewers agog. They now recognized that "the whole weight and financial strength of the Canadian giant [C.B.L.] is behind Northern Breweries, and the experience of Mr. E.P. Taylor, who is the prime mover behind the development of Canadian Breweries out of a large number of small units, should be enough to enable him to expand Northern into one of the major groups in the U.K. brewing industry. . . . On the medium to long-term point of view, there seems little to prevent Mr. E.P. Taylor from obtaining ultimate success."*

On through the countryside Taylor went, probing, negotiating, and always selling the desirability and profitability of a small brewery becoming part of his growing firm which would become a national group. In mid-July he announced that Northern Breweries was about to make its first acquisition in the southern part of Great Britain, with an agreement having been reached for Webbs (Aberbeeg), the Monmouthshire brewer, to join the group under a share exchange. The company was to retain its identity following the merger and would continue to trade under its own name. The offer was accepted, and B.M. Lindsay-Fynn, who had been chairman of Webbs for eighteen years, became a vice-chairman of Northern Breweries.

In September, Taylor picked up the last acquisition for that year, Calder and Company of Edinburgh, which had fifty-two pubs. This acquisition was described in the press as a "brewery bid shock" for many shareholders because Taylor's successful bid was at 4s.3d. for the Calder ordinary shares, compared with 7s.6d. in the market.

Shades of the early 1930s. By the end of 1960, this "very sociable, bulky man of 59, with a keen brain and a no-nonsense direct manner, who positively enjoys building up large undertakings,"† E.P. Taylor had put together a British brewery group of more than 1,500 houses in Yorkshire and Scotland. His expressed intent was to search for companies to form another six similar groups in the other main consumer areas. "We didn't expect to become the predominant brewers, but to rank with the biggest and the best."

Why was he doing it? What was driving him? "Quite frankly, I felt I had a duty to my stockholders to do as well as I could. Everyone in business has competitors, and you must at least keep pace with them—you owe that to your company. Canadian Breweries was as big as it could get in Canada. We also had our share of the U.S. market. Britain was only a logical step, especially since beer sales there had risen considerably. As a Canadian, I could see

---

*The Stock Exchange Gazette (London, England: 20 May, 1960).

†The Sunday Times (London, England: 19 June, 1960).

nothing wrong in expanding into the British market. In fact, I think it should be pointed out that although we've heard much criticism in recent years of American capital in Canada, some of the largest firms that have moved into this country are from the United Kingdom. Surely the Commonwealth should be a two-way street." If it wasn't a two-way street, E.P. Taylor would do his best to make it one.

By the end of 1960, the name Northern Breweries was obsolete for a company that was becoming a national force. On October 31, Northern Breweries of Great Britain Limited became United Breweries Limited. However, that name would last for only two years.

Chapter XIV

Other Interests
1950s

Throughout his life Eddie Taylor has continuously devoted much of his time and his money to worthy causes and to his community. Not even his many business activities during the post-war years detracted from contributions. He approached fund-raising in support of community needs with the same energy and imagination as he did his business enterprises.

There is a saying: "If you want a job done, give it to a busy man." That is exactly what the chairman of the board of trustees of the Toronto General Hospital, Norman Urquhart, did in 1951 when the decision was finally made to go ahead with a campaign to raise money for new hospital buildings and the renovation of antiquated ones. To head the campaign he chose a fellow trustee, a man whose track record showed he was keenly interested in the betterment of his community, E.P. Taylor.

As an involved trustee of the hospital, Taylor was fully aware of the problems and their urgency. The main building had been completed in 1921, in the days when doctors could take no training in Toronto and had to go to other cities to learn. Now the Toronto General was a training hospital, overcrowded with patients and doctors, almost bursting at the seams. It was old and urgently required modernization. It needed new equipment of all sorts, twice as many operating rooms, more specialized labs, and many more rooms to accommodate patients. Brain surgery was, at the time, being performed in a converted basement storeroom. The emergency operating room was ventilated by two circulating fans,

231

a totally unsatisfactory technique. There had been some 700 births at the hospital in 1950, and the nursery was some distance away from the maternity ward. The needs were critical, urgent, and readily understood by the public.

At the mid-summer meeting with Urquhart, at which Taylor agreed to be chairman of the fund-raising campaign, the two discussed the target at length. The building committee had advised that they would need $14 million, but Urquhart felt that the most they could hope for was $11 million. The Hospital for Sick Children had raised $8 million a few years before and had needed two stages to their campaign in order to reach their objective. It had been a terrible struggle. Urquhart was therefore of the view that $14 million could not be achieved. Colonel Phillips had been on the building committee that had recommended the $14 million figure. That would be Taylor's objective. Urquhart did not argue the point.

Taylor organized a smashing public campaign which was scheduled to last less than a month, from January 9 to February 2, 1952, but with major solicitations of governments, corporations, and wealthy persons starting much earlier than that. Taylor built a massive organization, all volunteers. There were some sixty section chairmen, and all committees worked through a management committee on a business-like basis.* For the next six months, and throughout the campaign, Taylor put in the equivalent of a full working day each day, chairing innumerable meetings, conferring with all the committees, making himself available for the press and photographers and providing drive, enthusiasm, and confidence for the hundreds of volunteer workers. In addition, he personally solicited people and corporations on a grand scale, the estimate was that he was responsible for over 40 per cent of the corporate contributions. The companies he controlled made major donations, and the executives from them were free to work on the cam-

---

*Some of the division heads and other officials taking part in the Toronto General Hospital Fund drive were Edgar G. Burton, president of Robert Simpson Co. Ltd.; J.C. Hungerford, executive vice-president of National Trust; W.P. Scott, vice-president of Wood Gundy & Co.; Kenneth M. Sedgewick, assistant general manager, Royal Bank of Canada; Mrs. A.G. Walwyn, chairman of the Women's Division of the Hospital Fund; Mrs. C.F. McEachren, honorary chairman of the Women's Division; Brigadier W. Preston Gilbride; J.S.D. Tory, Q.C.; George L. Jennison, a partner in Wills, Bickle & Co.; Harold M. Turner, vice-chairman of the Toronto General Hospital board of trustees; George McCullagh, publisher of the *Globe and Mail*.

paign, setting an example for other firms to offer their executives the same opportunity.

A healthy leg up came from the provincial government and the city of Toronto, each of which promised $3 million before the formal campaign started. The County of York came in with $500,000. With these donations added to those obtained by the Taylor team, the amount pledged and given by the opening of the campaign on January 9, 1952, was already over $11 million. A saturation propaganda program through the newspapers, magazines, and radio media started immediately after the New Year, with many commercial advertisers including references to the campaign in their advertisements, some even taking full pages in support.

As the Toronto General Hospital campaign entered its last week, Taylor and his fund-raisers were still $850,000 short of their goal. He pushed his team and the public hard. The result of this final effort was amazing. The T. Eaton Company came in for $250,000 and its employees contributed another $40,000. The Atkinson Foundation put in $200,000. After the official closing date of February 12, money kept pouring in. The final tally was $16,128,134, well over $2 million above the target. The Toronto General Hospital campaign was one of the most successful, best-organized, highest-dollar-figure, single-purpose, fund-raising efforts ever staged in Canada. As a result of this enormous success, six new buildings were erected, including 400 new beds, many labs and operating theatres, and the modernization of the old buildings was completed.

In a letter to Edward Taylor, the president of the University of Toronto, Sidney Smith, himself an active participant in the campaign with a special interest in the Toronto General Hospital because it was the main teaching hospital of his university, said it all: "Dear Eddie–What a man! What a citizen! What a leader you are!!!"

Taylor's Toronto General involvement and the dramatic success his team achieved received nation-wide attention, and in particular, that of his old friend, Governor General Vincent Massey, who had become increasingly concerned about the affairs of an organization with which he had close ties, the Victorian Order of Nurses for Canada. If anyone could get the V.O.N. on its feet, it was Eddie Taylor. Massey asked Taylor to join the order.

Without fanfare, Edward Taylor was elected president of the

233

executive council of the Victorian Order of Nurses for Canada at its 54th annual meeting, in May of 1952. At the next annual meeting, held the following year on May 5, at Rideau Hall in Ottawa, Taylor announced that the order would shortly launch a campaign for funds to provide for the needs of its national office for the next five years.

When he first became president, Taylor took a look at the V.O.N.'s finances.

"Miss Christine Livingston, the chief superintendent, was the senior person and a very able nurse. She managed the organization. I went into it with some reluctance because I had expected to find the affairs in a terrible mess. I didn't believe that women could be as capable as men in matters pertaining to operations and money. I had a pleasant surprise. I found that operationally it was just about as efficient as anything I had encountered before. It was a great relief to me."

There were about 100 branches throughout Canada and some 600 nurses. The services of the order were in great demand since there was a shortage of hospital beds everywhere in the country and the cost of being hospitalized was going up all the time. Many of the people who went into the hospital could be well looked after in their own houses at much less expense by the Victorian Order of Nurses. However, the financial requirements were increasing. "Everything was costing more–salaries and rent, and that sort of thing. Most of the nurses had to have a motor-car. I had to find money."

Taylor decided he would raise money to establish an endowment fund which would produce income sufficient to make up the deficit and provide a working income for the V.O.N.–the fund would have to contain a million dollars! "I suggested to the national board that they have an appeal every five years, rather than one capital appeal. This would produce more money per annum in interest than capital would have produced if we had gone on a capital appeal. People are more critical about the capital appeals. The big givers fall into two classes. Some people want to give a lot of money and say, 'Now don't come near me again,' but most people with money to give away are supporting scores and scores of things on an annual basis. They contribute more than they would if you came to them for a capital sum." The national board accepted Taylor's proposal and the campaign was launched.

So the dynamic E.P. Taylor, having been general chairman of the highly successful Toronto General Hospital fund-raising campaign, now brought his considerable experience, talents, and influence to bear on shoring up the finances of the Victorian Order of Nurses with a program that would last for at least fifteen years. And, of course, he was successful once more.

In the fifties, the federal government began to respond to calls for support for the arts and culture in Canada, and in 1957 decided to create an umbrella body that would dispense money to worthy persons and groups across the nation. It would be named the Canada Council, and E.P. Taylor would be invited to be one of its charter members. He agreed, but with reservations because he had little interest in doling out the taxpayers' money. There was no challenge for him. He participated in the first few meetings then submitted his resignation.

There was, however, a challenge in Toronto. In 1958, E.P. Taylor became president of the Art Gallery of Toronto, which, as always, needed money badly. At that time it had a current operating budget of about $200,000 and very little money with which to acquire paintings or other works of art. With his customary vigour and his remarkable capacity for raising money, whether for business or charitable purposes, Taylor immediately set about collecting a substantial sustaining fund for the Art Gallery. He even went so far as to address the Empire Club in Toronto as part of his campaign to raise funds, outlining to the august members of that organization the valuable contribution the Art Gallery of Toronto was making to the community, pointing out that in the spring of 1958, for four hours on a Sunday afternoon, more than 1,100 people per hour had entered the gallery to see paintings by the most famous amateur artist in the world, his hero, Sir Winston Churchill.

Taylor knew how to twist arms. In a superb mailing piece sent out by the Art Gallery, in which his entire Empire Club speech was printed, the financial statement showed an accumulated operating deficit as of June 30, 1958, of $337,175, and this Taylor plea:

The Art Gallery of Toronto can only continue to perform its important service to this great metropolis if it is supported by the corporate citizens of the area. In 1959, it is our hope to acquire a great painting of international importance–the kind which will unquestionably bring art lovers to the city–but to buy this picture, we must go out and raise additional funds because our Sustaining and Picture and other endowment funds cannot meet the price. Your generosity in giving to this appeal will help us in this and future purchases. Donations, of course, entitle you to income tax deductions.

Even though he was immersed in getting the Art Gallery of Toronto on its financial feet, Taylor by no means claimed to be an art buff or to understand much about it. During his presidency and with new money in hand as a result of his effort, the Art Gallery acquired its first Henry Moore sculpture. It was a typical production by the brilliant British sculptor, much more a smoothly rounded theme piece than an attempt at literal representation. It was unveiled with great ceremony at a special affair over which Taylor presided. He surveyed the massive metal object for a moment as he struggled to sort out his impression of it. His face expressionless, he commented, "Too bad some of the parts fell off. I hope it's insured." It was.

While he may have had difficulty with a Moore sculpture, he had no problem recognizing architectural excellence. Taylor, John A. McDougald, Colonel Eric Phillips, and Wallace McCutcheon were roundly applauded when, as the *Telegram* reported on December 5, 1958, "four Toronto financiers [gave] Toronto a Christmas present for which every citizen can be grateful. They have saved for the city its finest piece of architecture–the Bank of Canada building on Toronto Street, which faced demolition next year."

The magnificent old building at 10 Toronto Street was to become and remains the head office of Argus Corporation. Considered one of the best examples of Greek revival design in Canada, it was built as a post office in 1852 when there were two postmen in Toronto–one for the east side of the city and one for the west–and delivery was a penny a letter. Canada's first postage stamps were sold at No. 10 and the country's first postal money orders written there. The structure, which cost £3,500 when it was built, is described in Robertson's *Landmarks*: "The building is in the Ionic style of architecture. . . . It has a frontage of 48 feet, with a depth of 90 feet. The front is of cut stone. The large public hall with enriched oak and plate-glass-letter blocks has three compartments, intersected by Doric columns with delivery windows and a separate entrance for ladies."

The crisis came in 1957. The Bank of Canada, which had occupied 10 Toronto Street for many decades after the post office had outgrown the building, was to move to new premises on University Avenue. The federal government announced it would tear down the building when the move was made. The outcry was enormous, much of it led by John W.H. Bassett of the *Telegram*, who started a crusade to save the building. The then finance minister, Donald Fleming, was not moved by pleas by the Toronto Board of Control, architectural groups, or the *Telegram*. He infuriated a host of people when he reiterated that when the bank left the property the building would be sold. His position was that "regardless of the worth of the building, the property on which it is located is valuable." Among the people who joined the struggle to save the structure were columnist Judith Robinson, Paul Duval, the *Telegram*'s art critic, and a visiting architectural expert from Smith College, Professor Henry Russell Hitchcock, who said that the old Bank of Canada was one of three buildings worth preserving in Toronto. (The other two were Osgoode Hall and the Dundas Street Grange.)

Martin Baldwin, director of the Art Gallery of Toronto, also got into the fight, saying, "There is a special responsibility to the people involved in the case of public buildings, such as the old Bank of Canada. To destroy it would be little short of criminal. It seems we need a clamour or nothing is going to get done. Some sort of citizens' committee should be immediately formed, composed of persons from many walks of life." The citizens' committee that Baldwin wanted emerged in the form of E.P. Taylor as the president of the Art Gallery of which he, Baldwin, was director. Taylor and his colleagues bought the building for Argus' offices. The cost was $500,000. In praising the Argus quadrumvirate, a *Telegram* editorial of December 6, 1957, stated, "Purchase of the Bank of Canada Building by these public-spirited business leaders earns them the gratitude of all those who love beauty and respect history."

Not only did they buy 10 Toronto Street, they also renovated it at a cost exceeding $700,000. None of the ancient building's dignity or granite grace was altered by the face-lift. The mood of the place was accurately caught by a Toronto *Star* reporter who said:

> You get the feeling of opulence when you push against the heavy, solid black doors and enter the reception room. It's like stepping into an 18th century French villa. The boardroom for Argus directors off the entrance hall looks like a baronial dining room. It has ivory painted walls, a chandelier like the one in the entrance foyer, a highly polished table twelve feet long, silk curtains, brocade drapes and broadloom. The private offices of E.P. Taylor (about fourteen feet square), Eric Phillips, M.W. McCutcheon, J.A. McDougald, Argus directors and junior executives of the company are upstairs. The upstairs offices drip with chandeliers. The floors are hidden under the deepest of wall-to-wall carpeting. The back stairs are also broadloomed. All very tasteful and posh.

Taylor denies that he is oriented to the arts, although he has contributed in many ways to their advancement in Canada. The birth of the O'Keefe Centre is one such contribution.

The idea for a new major theatre for Toronto can be traced back to Floyd S. Chalmers, who, in the late forties, was on the board of the Royal Conservatory of Music and most anxious to have a new building constructed for it. Taking the initiative, he brought together E.P. Taylor and J.S. McLean, the president of Canada Packers, who was then chairman of the venerable concert centre, Massey Hall. The broad-thinking Chalmers envisioned a new building on Bloor Street near the University of Toronto. It would house not only the Royal Conservatory of Music and a new Massey Hall, but would also provide a central studio location for the operations of the Canadian Broadcasting Corporation, which had yet to get into television.

Taylor liked the concept and said he was willing to head up a fund-raising campaign. Chalmers already had a commitment from Vincent Massey for the first $1 million, which would be provided by the Massey Foundation. But McLean had reservations about the venture, with the result that the project never came to fruition.

In 1954, when Taylor was searching for a visible and ongoing contribution that Canadian Breweries could make to Toronto, its largest market, his mind went back to Chalmers' idea. Once again he was struck by the need for a major community theatre which would present opera, ballet, musicals, and theatrical productions and, at the same time, be a centre for many other cultural activities in the Toronto community. Taylor settled on this concept, although he was not yet sure how big it would be or where it would go. At the beginning of 1955, he made public his proposal that O'Keefe Brewing Company Limited would build a new cultural centre and theatre to be called O'Keefe Civic Centre. "Our competitors, Molson's, had bought the Canadiens hockey team in Montreal and Labatt's had a sports stadium in London which they had financed. And I recognized that Toronto, like other cities of its size, had no large theatre. This wasn't all charity or philanthropy. To be perfectly honest, one of the reasons behind building the O'Keefe Centre was to sell beer. But we also wanted to do something for all Ontario. We thought it was a goodwill gesture. We had the funds to build it and it was badly needed. In big American cities, city councils had helped substantially with financing of this nature. But here they wouldn't do it. In money it represented about $12 million, which was not an insignificant sum."

The City Council quickly accepted the proposal in principle but immediately had to fend off attacks of the prohibitionists, led by United Church spokesmen who could not tolerate the thought of money earned from the sale of demon beer being used for a worthwhile community development.

It was to be an extended struggle to obtain final approval. By 1958, all the negotiations and agreements had been completed with the city, a building permit had been issued, and construction of the Earle Morgan-designed structure finally got under way.

On Saturday, October 1, 1960, the O'Keefe Centre was officially opened, a glittering, gala event with the world premier of a dazzling musical production. It was *Camelot*.

Camelot! That fantastic dreamland of fictional fantasy where dwelled King Arthur, his lovely queen, and the noblest of his knights, Lancelot, was brought to life in a Broadway-bound musical production. What a remarkable and fortuitous opportunity–the combination of the opening night of a star-studded musical in its first-ever performance and the unveiling of the magnificent O'Keefe Centre, a multi-million-dollar contribution to the cultural life of Metropolitan Toronto created by the civic-minded chairman of the sponsoring Canadian Breweries, E.P. Taylor.

Opening night was a celebrity-filled, gala event. The musical cast Richard Burton as King Arthur, a role that he was described as having performed "with some grandeur and strength"; Julie Andrews as a delightful, beautiful Queen Guinevere; and the then new arrival to the heights of stardom, a young man who had been around Toronto a long time playing in such shows as *Spring Thaw*, a tall, handsome fellow with a large voice, Robert Goulet, as Lancelot. The *Globe and Mail* drama critic, Herbert Whittaker, wrote, "Every luxury has been lavished on *Camelot*, the successor to *My Fair Lady*, which opened at the O'Keefe Centre Saturday night. The colour, the music, the movement, the bright new fabrics and the procession of splendid scenes filled out an almost endless evening of expensive entertainment." The show was a great success that night and went on to a long run on Broadway.

On opening night, the 3,200-seat O'Keefe Centre, a modernistic structure of granite, glass, and limestone, located at the corner of Front and Yonge Streets in the centre of Toronto, was filled to overflowing from its chartreuse-carpeted orchestra to its last balcony row. The seats had been sold for $25 each for the benefit opening which was attended by formally attired first-nighters, among whom were Lieutenant Governor Keiller MacKay and such celebrities as Giselle MacKenzie, television personality Joyce Davidson, American dancing stars, Gower and Marge Champion, the musical comedy star, Carol Channing, John David Eaton and his wife, conductor André Kostelanetz, singer Jane Morgan, and, of course, the man who had made it all happen, E.P. Taylor, with Winnie at his side. It was a memorable event not only for them but for *Camelot* authors Allan J. Lerner and Frederick Loewe and their director, Moss Hart, who were delighted with the reception their new production received, even though Moss Hart himself warned from the stage before it began that the show was "woefully long." It was. It finished at 12:30 A.M., but more than three hours later some 500 guests at a Royal York Hotel party thrown by the centre's "angel," industrialist-brewer E.P. Taylor, was still going strong.

In the 1950s, at the same time as he was overseeing the creation of the O'Keefe Centre, E.P. Taylor was becoming enmeshed in a Caribbean island on which he would begin a development project which would be his own Camelot. The island was New Providence in the Bahamas. The project would be Lyford Cay.

In December 1945, Edward and Winnie Taylor had accepted the invitation of a colourful American Argus board member, Allan Miller, to be his house guests in Nassau in the Bahamas. This was their first visit to the islands. As many Americans had done in the First World War, Miller had gone to Canada to train as a pilot. Eventually he wound up in Billy Bishop's squadron overseas. He used to refer to himself as the worst airman in the Bishop's unit. At the conclusion of the First World War, he volunteered as part of a group joining Kerensky's forces in Russia. Coincidentally, Eric Phillips was also a member of that group. As part of his Russian adventures, Miller got possession of a cargo of metal scrap which he managed to get out of Vladivostok into England where he sold it for a large sum. With this money as seed, he developed cable radio in Great Britain and made a fortune. He made even more money in the stock market in the United States in the twenties and survived the 1929 crash, but almost went broke in the process. During the Second World War, he manufactured small motors in Canada and, through his contact with Phillips, met E.P. Taylor, with whom he hit it off right from the beginning.

Miller had been invited by both Taylor and Phillips to go on the Argus board and to invest in the company. Part of the consideration for his doing so was that the Taylors would have to come to his home in Nassau for a winter vacation. Phillips also had a house in Nassau, which made Miller's invitation even more attractive as the three could then get together. Miller's house was at Lyford Cay, at the west end of New Providence Island, twenty miles from Nassau, and at the time of the Taylor's first visit there were very few houses and much of the land was swamp. To Winnie and Eddie it was an enormously attractive place, with beautiful beaches, the Atlantic Ocean on the north side and Clifton Bay to the south. It was a spot which would be transformed dramatically, almost magically, by Taylor in the years to come.

"Miller wanted to get away from the more heavily populated district. He built a beautiful house. We stayed with him there. That's how I got to know Lyford Cay and Harold Christie. I went every year. Never missed a year. Sometimes we stayed for only two or three weeks. After the first ten years, I said, 'This is the place I want to retire to. I like the climate.' I get very chesty in the winter in Canada. I used to get bronchitis and the dry cold weather doesn't help me. Harold Christie had a lot of land owned with some partners in the Lyford Cay area. He wanted to develop it and he didn't know how to go about it. Since I was then working on Don Mills and the Hamilton Shopping Centre, he had me in his mind as a prospect for his land. He wanted me to go in as a partner. I said, 'No, Harold, this is a long process and I wouldn't go into it as a partner because I rarely enter partnerships, not even in racehorses. It doesn't make for a good friendship because there are too many disappointments.' But then in 1954, I had a riding accident and the doctor told me I should take things easier."

The accident to which Taylor referred occurred at Windfields. One morning he was riding a grey mare whose name has been forgotten. "She dumped me on a hard road and I was in Toronto General Hospital for six weeks with a stretched pelvis. It took that length of time to pull the pelvis together." When the hospital session was over, he was off to the Bahamas with Winnie.

It was during this recuperative period with little to do that he took a long, hard look at his own future and at the potential of Lyford Cay. He could see that Lyford Cay was close to Windsor Field, which was to be the site for the new international airport. The cay was largely swamp, but on each side there were clean beautiful beaches. On the Atlantic side, the surf rolled in continuously, but on the Clifton Bay shoreline the waters were usually calm. In Taylor's inventive mind's eye, he could see ways to drain the swamps, clear out the mangroves, build a yacht harbour, a golf course, and clubhouse and hotel and, all in all, create an island paradise which would be attractive to well-to-do people from all over the world. Taylor could easily envision it. He was enthusiastic. It was something he could do.

"One day I simply said to Harold Christie, 'I won't go in with you, but if all the land is for sale, and if the price is right, I'll buy it. But the price must be right because it's going to be a long, long wait before I ever get anything out of it.' I never have got anything out of it, actually."

Why did Taylor develop Lyford Cay? "I've always found it difficult to refrain from embarking on a business venture which appeared to be constructive, which would fill a need, and which, in a reasonable period of time, could be successful in an economic sense. Lyford Cay afforded the opportunity to lay out a perfectly

242

planned community that would stand out for generations as a pleasant place in which to live."

In 1954 Taylor formed the Lyford Cay Development Company to buy the land, about 2,800 acres, and begin his heavy investments. "I have sent down maybe $35 million altogether and I've had only 25 per cent of it back by way of a return of capital on the sale of land. I didn't raise it from anybody else. I found it myself. Actually, the amount for the Lyford Cay Development Company was $16 million. My total net investment there is now about $30 million and I'm getting no return on it. But the background of it simply was that I never liked the winters in Canada and I love the Bahamas. I felt I could do something constructive. I knew that so many people are lost when they retire. I could see years of work ahead down there that would keep me interested and busy. I nearly go crazy when I haven't anything to do. I knew I would have to turn over everything to younger people in Canada, which I've pretty nearly completely done now. So it was all part of a preconceived plan. The thing that worries the public is they think it was a tax saving plan, but it hasn't saved me any taxes of any consequence whatsoever. The way my affairs are ordered, any taxes that I might have saved would be minuscule. I went there for reasons of my happiness and my health and to make a contribution. Everything I leave when I die, irrespective of where it is, is willed to my Ontario foundation, the E.P. Taylor Foundation Inc. Everything I leave goes to it, my boots, my shoes, including my house in the Bahamas, which is the only thing I own personally. The companies such as Windfields are controlled by my family who invested their own money in them years ago."

Don Prowse, who joined E.P. Taylor in 1954, the year Prowse became a chartered accountant, spent a great deal of time in Nassau with his new employer. "I remember going down to Nassau shortly after he bought that land. He was terribly enthusiastic about it. We'd drive out to Lyford Cay with the jeep we'd bought with the land. He'd drive across the fields and trails up to a height of land. He'd stand there looking toward the sea to the north. All I could see down there was mango swamp. He'd say, 'We'll put the golf course over there, the beach club will go there, and we'll have the first residential development over there.' He could see it. The place was transformed by his visions because he could see what most of us can't see. That's the nature of the man. At that stage of the game there was no development on paper at all. Ultimately, of course, it was done by professionals, but the concept and the basic ideas were his."

By 1956, Taylor was beginning to spend a great deal of time in Nassau, concentrating on the enormous amount of planning that would be necessary to create the facilities and development he envisaged. The Lyford Cay Development Company was formed, and a Toronto engineer, Bev Zavits, was installed to oversee the development.

Of the 2,800 acres of land he had bought, 1,000 acres were set aside for development by the Lyford Cay Development Company. The balance of the land Taylor reserved for the moment. In addition to Zavits, he retained golf course architect Dick Wilson to design a first-class, eighteen-hole course. And his old friend, architect Earle Morgan–who was just finishing off the New Woodbine Racetrack, had overseen the refurbishing of the Fort Erie track buildings, and was designing the O'Keefe Centre–was brought in to create a lavish clubhouse inside a $2 million budget. As Taylor puts it, "I formed a company, as I always do. Then I got an organization together and I appointed advisers and employees and we worked out a plan of development." In order to provide a base, now that he was spending so much time in Nassau, he bought a house in town from Sir Francis Peek. This attractive older building and property on East Street is known as Tamarind. At the same time, Taylor had already picked out his own choice location at Lyford Cay where he would eventually build his residence, a guest house, and two beach houses. The parcel he had in mind had a broad frontage on the excellent Atlantic beach and stretched right across the cay to the shore of Clifton Bay, a distance of 200 yards.

Before he could begin construction Taylor had to get permission from the Bahamian government. What he proposed to do was beyond the experience of anyone in that government. No development of this kind had ever been undertaken in the Bahamas. So he had to tread cautiously, gain the confidence of the government as to his long-term intentions, and to make it perfectly clear to them that he was there to stay and was in no way a fly-by-night operator. Without the co-operation of the chief minister and his colleagues there would be no development. As a result, Taylor spent a great deal of time with government officials as the plans and proposals emerged. Permission to build was granted, and before the end of 1956, construction had started with the building of the roads and the filling of the golf course area. Taylor was doing what he liked best. He was building, developing, looking into the future, changing the landscape.

The formal announcement of the development was finally made in the Nassau *Guardian* newspaper in the February 13, 1956, edition. It would be a luxury project with an eighteen-hole golf course on 1,000 acres owned by the Lyford Cay company. Development would take place in several phases over a period of ten years or more and the community would be of the highest calibre. The land in phase one comprised about 700 acres and was to be serviced by December 31, 1958. In addition to the golf course, the company would build ten and a half miles of road. In phase one there would be 365 lots, including forty-four on the beachfront. Purchases of lots would have to conform with company building restrictions which would ensure maintenance of high standards in the area. To be sure, there were to be no blue roofs. All services would be installed and provided. The company would not sell lots until early in 1958. There was a huge earth and rock moving job ahead, a big swamp to fill, a golf course to build, roads to be constructed, waterworks and sewers to be installed, a clubhouse to be built, a marina to be put together, and a channel and turning basin dredged. Taylor even had to buy a small freighter to bring much of the building materials, equipment, and supplies from Florida. On one of her voyages, she brought in eight acres of sod so the golf course could be opened in time.

The superb new golf course was ready for use by mid-year 1958. What was to be the magnificent Lyford Cay Club, designed by Earle Morgan, was under construction. Purchasers had started picking up many of the beach lots which are an acre to an acre and a half in size, with a then bottom price of $40,000 and top of $75,000. Three hundred half- to one-acre lots were available by the end of the year for residential development.

The $2.8 million Lyford Cay clubhouse which emerged out of a mixture of block, steel, and mortar, was finished and open on December 15, 1959. It had fifty guest rooms, three large dining areas, bars, ballroom, and 1,200 feet of private beach. By then virtually all the waterfront lots had been taken up. Houses were being built in many locations throughout the development. The Lyford Cay Club had more than 500 members. Taylor headed the Lyford

Cay company, his development firm, but he was simply one member with one vote in the Lyford Cay Club itself. At the 1960 annual April meeting of the members, Sir Francis Peek was reaffirmed as chairman of the general committee of the club. In May of 1960, E.P. Taylor said, "Up until the winter season just now completed, the Lyford Cay residential project had been all work and no play." From that time on there would be time for some, although not much, play for Eddie Taylor at Lyford Cay.

If there was little time for play at Lyford Cay there was none at all in Canada, where Argus Corporation and its holdings and their myriad subsidiaries were making progress under the nurturing care of Taylor, Phillips, McCutcheon, and McDougald. In addition to the heavy demands of the corporate world, the expansionist Taylor was pushing the growth of his horseracing and breeding enterprise and, at the same time, re-organizing the Ontario Jockey Club.

By the early fifties, Taylor the horseman knew what he wanted to do with the Ontario Jockey Club. His plan had the same ingredients he had used in putting together Canadian Breweries–acquisitions, shutdowns, and mergers, all leading to fewer, but much more attractive, facilities. But if Taylor had not already been successful in convincing Leslie Frost that the government tax should be reduced, there would have been no money in the coffers to make Taylor's or anybody else's revitalization plan work. The taxation problem in hand, Taylor could now move. He secured the approval of the board of directors of the Ontario Jockey Club.

Then with a touch of drama and excellent timing, he hinted at his expansionist proposals publicly at an opportune moment–the first Horse of the Year award dinner. The award was made and the dinner hosted by the owners of the *Daily Racing Form*. The place was the Royal York Hotel on the eve of the running of the 1952 royal race. As the owner of the winner for the 1951 season, Bull Page,* Taylor was also the principal speaker. For his purposes the

---

*Taylor's Bull Page, which he had bought as a yearling at the Kentucky sales in 1948 for $38,000, had six wins, was second five times and had three thirds, all in sixteen starts. When the 1951 racing season was finished, the *Daily Racing Form* polled its own turf writers and others from newspapers which covered thoroughbred racing in Ontario in order to determine their choice of Canada's best racehorse. Bull Page was unanimously chosen and Taylor was the winner of Canada's first Horse of the Year award. Bull Page

audience was ideal because not only were the top people in thoroughbred horseracing present, but many provincial government and municipal politicians were as well. Taylor was careful not to go into the details of his plan but chose to lay out the principles that were going to be followed. Because acquisitions were part of his master plan, it would be bad tactics to let the world know exactly what he had in mind. He said in part:

> All our tracks are outmoded and inadequate for present day racing. We need improvement in racing itself, better conditions for horsemen, and more facilities for the public. This can only be accomplished with modern racing plants.
>
> There has been some progress made to reduce taxation, but the present structure is still excessive. It should be lowered so that racetracks will have a higher percentage in order to provide higher purse distribution. [This was a light thrust at Premier Frost to remind him that the commitment was to continue to reduce the Ontario tax by one per cent a year.]
>
> The establishment of the Ontario Racing Commission is the best thing that could have happened to our racing. [A pat on the back for Premier Frost.]

With the accession of Queen Elizabeth to the throne, the Canadian race of 1952 was again called the Queen's Plate. The race was run in the rain on a track that was a sea of mud. The start was delayed at least thirty-five minutes. First, an eight-stall gate had to be set up next to the fourteen-stall gate to accommodate the large number of horses. But the larger gate became stuck in the muddy infield while the crew were trying to get it into position. When they finally did get the gates into place, Acadian, Taylor's entry in the race, reared up in his stall, caught one of his hooves in the front of it and fell over backwards into the mud beneath the gate, throwing his rider. Acadian was put back on his feet, checked by the veterinarian, and pronounced fit to race. The jockey remounted and everything was ready. The moment was tense throughout the track when the starter bell rang–but the gates didn't open. The gate

---

would later sire New Providence, a Canadian Triple Crown winner and a Queen's Plate winner, Flamingo Page, who was the dam of Nijinsky H, a winner of the English Triple Crown. In addition to these prestigious wins, E.P. Taylor was honoured by being elected president of the Canadian Thoroughbred Horse Society, a position he held until 1957; and in 1951, his Major Factor brought him his second King's Plate win.

mechanism had broken down, so the gates had to be opened by hand. When the race finally did get under way, a soaking wet E.P. Taylor, drenched in his pearl-grey top hat and morning suit, watched as his Acadian was beaten by Epigram, a horse he had bred, but which he considers one of the worst horses ever to win the Queen's Plate.

With the backing and approval of the Ontario Jockey Club board, Taylor began to move on its behalf to implement his plan to re-organize thoroughbred racing in Ontario. His first move was to call John Cella of St. Louis, the principal owner of the Niagara Racing Association, which owned the Fort Erie track. The track was run down and losing money, but Taylor was prepared to pay a million dollars for Cella's shares if necessary. Cella gave him a pleasant surprise by asking only $780,000. There was no haggling. Taylor accepted immediately.

Taylor wanted to refurbish the Fort Erie track as soon as possible, but a survey team discovered that one end of the track was twenty feet higher than the other. It had to be rebuilt before anything else was done. Fort Erie would serve racing fans in the Niagara Peninsula and across the border in Buffalo and Niagara Falls and beyond.

Old Woodbine, already owned by the Ontario Jockey Club, would also be renovated and retained, but all other tracks which Taylor could acquire under his plan would be purchased and then shut down. In September, Taylor completed the purchase of the Hamilton Jockey Club and with it its fourteen-day charter. The track was shut down and eventually the land was redeveloped (by an E.P. Taylor company) as a shopping centre. In October 1953, the Belleville Driving and Athletic Club, which owned the facilities at Stamford Park, was acquired. The racing facilities were eventually moved and the land developed for housing. And in December of 1952, Taylor bought the Thorncliffe Park Racing and Breeding Association from its Baltimore owners. It, too, had been losing money. Subsequently, this valuable piece of real estate, lying about a mile and a half south of Don Mills, was sold for a major mixed high-rise and commercial development, still known as Thorncliffe Park.

The linchpin in Taylor's master plan for the Ontario Jockey Club was the building and development of a huge new racetrack which would serve both the Hamilton and Toronto regions. Putting this new facility together would be a major undertaking which Taylor had no intention of doing by himself. So an executive committee of the board of the Ontario Jockey Club was created with Taylor as chairman. On the board were the president of the club, Colonel K.R. Marshall; George C. Hendrie, its managing director; and J.E. Frowde Seagram.

The committee first turned its mind to the matter of a location for the new track. It looked at many sites, ranging between Hamilton and Toronto, and finally decided on a location on Highway 27 to the east of the Toronto International Airport. It was easy to get to by road, close to Toronto, and not too far from Hamilton. To the committee the location appeared to be ideal, and it was, although some of the early critics wondered what the Jockey Club was doing setting up a track so far away from the city.

By the end of 1952, the committee had settled on the location and negotiations had started. The land was acquired early in the new year, but shortly after the deal had been closed, Taylor and George Hendrie took an inspection trip to Hollywood Park in Los Angeles, then one of North America's most modern racetracks. One of the things they saw from the air was that the track's parking lot was jammed full and there was no room to expand. Hollywood Park had about 400 acres, the same as that which Taylor and his colleagues had just bought. Obviously that amount was not enough. More land was immediately acquired.

One of the first things Taylor had done in 1952, once the executive committee was formed, was to retain the distinguished Toronto architect, Earle C. Morgan. He had worked on several developments for Taylor who had complete confidence in him, even though Morgan had no prior experience in designing or building racetracks. Morgan was to spend the next two years researching tracks all over North America and consulting with Arthur Froelich, a Los Angeles architect who had been retained by the Ontario Jockey Club to act as an adviser to Morgan. Both Hollywood Park and Garden State Park in New Jersey had been designed by him. By the time Morgan had prepared his preliminary drawings, he was expert in all aspects of the facilities which had to go into a supertrack which Taylor and his colleagues wanted to be the best, most modern and attractive in the world.

The acquisition of racetracks and charters launched by E.P. Taylor and the executive committee of the Ontario Jockey Club stretched the financial resources of the organization to the limit. The purchase of the land for the new super racetrack had cost a million dollars. Furthermore, there was refurbishing to be done at Woodbine and at Fort Erie. Canada's most renowned industrialist knew what to do. The Jockey Club had a good reputation in the community. It would borrow the money from the public by means of debentures. In 1953, the first issue was made in the amount of $2 million and was quickly taken up. The much-needed renovations, started in 1952, proceeded as planned at both the Fort Erie track and at Old Woodbine, later to be renamed Greenwood. Construction was in progress and on schedule for the new supertrack, which was to be called New Woodbine, and on December 1, 1955, a deal with Fred Orpen was closed for the purchase of both the Long Branch and Dufferin charters. The price was $4.1 million, racing legend crediting the delivery of that amount to Orpen in cash, crammed into a suitcase which the deliverer dumped on Orpen's pool table. Another version says that the deal was closed in the usual conservative way with the delivery of a certified cheque against the appropriate documents. However it was done, this was another Taylor transaction which "was done with the full knowledge of the Ontario Jockey Club," but the Jockey Club was not the direct buyer. "The outfit dealing for the purchase of Mr. Orpen's tracks and charters was the Toronto Racing Securities Limited. Naturally, I hoped the charters ended up with the Jockey Club."

The fundamental problem was that the Ontario Jockey Club was still struggling to get its financing organized. Taylor stepped into the breach and bought the Orpen charters when he could. He would turn them over to the Jockey Club–he was chairman of the executive committee–as soon as it was in funds and, of course, he would do so without any profit. Among other things, the Orpen purchase allowed the Jockey Club to extend its permitted racing days, which had started out at eighty-four before its first new acquisitions in 1952 to 196 days, giving it an economic operating period.

By 1956 the fruits of Taylor's initiative, imagination, drive, and know-how were coming into final shape in the form of a racetrack which was named New Woodbine. It was his supertrack. By this time the Ontario Jockey Club had gone public with its shareholdings and had embarked on a series of debenture issues to finance the heavy capital spending that was necessary not only for the construction of New Woodbine but as well the other track acquisitions that it made and the refurbishings that had been done at Fort Erie and the old Woodbine track, now to be called Greenwood.

For New Woodbine, Earle Morgan produced a grandstand that is high rather than long, his intent being that the patrons should be as close to the finish line as possible. Verandahs overlook the walking ring where the horses are viewed before each race. The stands can easily hold 40,000 people, and there is parking space to accommodate even the largest crowd. There are three race courses and two training tracks. The modern stables can accommodate over 1,000 horses, and facilities are in place for approximately 700 employees. In the grandstand area there are several small restaurants and cafeterias. There is even a small hospital for emergencies. The infield is beautifully landscaped with trees and shrubs and four small ponds.

Fourteen million dollars had been poured into the "posh" new supertrack, as the *New York Times* described it. The usual band of hecklers and detractors, who had tagged the new track "Taylor's White Elephant," were soon to discover that, once in operation, it was anything but a white elephant. It was a huge, functional, comfortable and highly attractive track. And it was enormously successful.

On a bright, sunny afternoon, June 12, 1956, the man who had encouraged Taylor and the rebuilding of horseracing in Ontario by a much-needed reduction in Ontario taxes, the Honourable Leslie Frost, the premier of Ontario, officially opened New Woodbine in the presence of thousands of racing fans. The first race ever held at New Woodbine was to run that afternoon. The winner against fourteen other horses was Georgian Bay. The owner was E.P. Taylor.

The winning of that first New Woodbine race was appropriate and coincidental. It was also a mark of Taylor's ascendancy in both thoroughbred horseracing and breeding. A breeder of racehorses can be god-like in that his selection of the right sires and mares can, with good engineering, planning, and judgement, produce a superior line of horses. As the years have proven, Taylor the engineer is also a master planner whose genetic successes have made him the world's top breeder of thoroughbred racehorses.

The laying of many of the foundation blocks for that exalted status in the horse world occurred in the 1950s.

Taylor made a most fortuitous buy in the December 1952 sales in Newmarket, England. One of the horses recommended for purchase by his English consultant, George Blackwell, was a mare called Lady Angela who was descended from the great stallion, Hyperion. Lady Angela was in foal to the famous Italian stallion, Nearco, which had recently arrived in England. Blackwell was instructed to buy on the condition that the owner agreed that Lady Angela, as part of the deal, would be mated again with Nearco after she dropped the foal she was carrying. The price Taylor offered was over $30,000, a substantial amount and enough to seal the deal.

In 1953, Lady Angela was again mated with Nearco and when she was certified as being in foal, she was shipped by boat to Canada with her most recent offspring. In the spring of 1954, she produced a colt which E.P. Taylor named Nearctic. He later became a champion racehorse and was the sire of many of the best horses bred by Taylor.

On April 16, 1953, writing in the Toronto *Star*, Joe Perlove, the knowledgeable journalist who had quite a clout in the horseracing world, acclaimed E.P. Taylor as Canada's leading breeder.

After being runner-up for the past two years in the leading breeder for Canada department, E.P. Taylor made the top rung in 1952, thus ousting, for the first time in six years, R. James Speers. This is revealed in the latest edition of the *Yearbook of Canadian Thoroughbreds*, which is put out by the Canadian Thoroughbred Horse Society. Taylor's brood, 22 winners, has knocked off a total of 69 races for purse earnings of $150,756. Speers had 56 assorted beetles going for him and they piled up in their careers a total of $121,274. At the clip Taylor is breeding and with a flock of young horses scooting about the various tracks, it's going to take two or three packs of wild horses to knock him off that perch.

E.P. Taylor has not been knocked off to this day.

The man's growing stature in the world of horseracing and breeding was now being widely and appropriately recognized. There would be many honours to come in the years ahead, but for his own personal satisfaction, there were few privileges bestowed upon him that he cherished more than his 1953 election as an honorary member of the Jockey Club of New York, the only Canadian to have been so recognized up to that time.

The Taylor entry in the Queen's Plate for 1953 was a horse he had bred that he once described this way: "Canadiana's conformation is very unusual in that she has a very long barrel set between her fore and aft moving parts." In other words, she was somewhat sway-back. As a two-year-old filly, Canadiana had racked up an excellent record, particularly in the United States. So good was her performance that she was unanimously selected as Canada's Horse of the Year for 1952, an unusual honour for a two-year-old. Even after she finished fourth in the Plate trial on May 23, Taylor was confident that Canadiana could win the Queen's Plate, and he got the best jockey he could find for the big ride: American Eddie Arcaro, who rode Canadiana to Eddie Taylor's third Plate victory. He was now the only person other than Joseph Seagram in the early 1900s to win both the King's Plate and the Queen's Plate. By the time Canadiana was retired to the Windfields Farm as a brood mare in 1955, she had finished in the money in forty out of sixty-two races she had run.

The year 1953 closed with Taylor purchasing the three-year-old chestnut filly, Fair Colleen, at the sales in Newmarket, England, in his bid to upgrade Canadian blood lines. Fair Colleen had won five races and placed third in October of that year in the Cambridgeshire, one of Britain's big races. Racing writer, Clive Graham, of the London *Daily Express*, said the purchase of Fair Colleen "underlines the point that Canada will shortly become one of the great racing centres of the world." Graham was right.

The breeding operations at Windfields Farm and at National Stud were highly productive, so much so that in the spring of 1954, E.P. Taylor had a harvest of almost forty yearlings on his hands, too many to dispose of through the Canadian Thoroughbred Horse Society's annual summer sale. He began to look for an alternative and came upon a scheme that he used successfully for many years. He would offer his entire crop of yearlings at pre-designated prices. The sale would be held at Windfields Farm with a catalogue comparable to those used at public auctions. The sale would be terminated when half the colts and half the fillies were sold. The horses left he would keep and race under his own colours. Under this scheme people could not say that he was culling. They had an opportunity to buy his best and his worst. Furthermore, he wanted to spread the ownership of excellent horses around in order to help upgrade thoroughbred racing in Canada.

To ensure that his first sale would not fail, Taylor sat down and drew up a list of select people in the sport of thoroughbred horseracing whom he believed would be interested in acquiring horses of superior blood lines. His first sale was a success, although only five colts and three fillies were sold out of thirty-five yearlings offered. At Taylor's sale the following summer fifteen out of the thirty-five yearlings offered were sold. For the next few years it was not surprising to have a stake race in Canada with six or eight entries, with most or all of them being E.P. Taylor-bred horses, each running for a different owner. The price spread per horse between the first Taylor sale and the Society sale that year averaged $3,200. It climbed to $4,400 in the second year, a public recognition of the superiority of the Taylor-bred horses.

In 1956 Taylor had fifty-seven horses in training. They won seventy-five races and earned $234,000. In addition, Taylor-bred horses ran first in 149 races and earned $436,000, with the Queen's Plate being won by Canadian Champ, a horse Taylor had sold as a yearling to Bill Beasley in 1954 for $7,500.

Taylor was back in the winner's circle again when the Queen's Plate was run in 1957, proudly accepting the Queen's guineas as a result of the win of one of the horses he had bred himself, Lyford Cay. The horse had been sold as a yearling at Taylor's annual sale, but M.J. Boylen, the buyer, later came back unhappy because of the look of one of Lyford Cay's knees. When he returned the horse, Taylor offered him another (later called Chopadette), or his money back. Boylen took the money. The post-1957 Queen's Plate chagrin of Boylen is not recorded. In that same plate race, Winnie Taylor's horse, Chopadette, came in second. This prompted the witty Eric Phillips, in England at the time, to cable his close friend Eddie Taylor. "Congratulations on winning the Queen's Plate. Aren't you ashamed of beating your wife?" The Taylor cable response was immediate. "Thanks so much for your cable. At least I do it in public."

In 1958, Nearctic, the offspring of Lady Angela, the mare Taylor had purchased, was unanimously elected Horse of the Year. Taylor entered the horse as a two-year-old in 1956 in the Saratoga Special which he won, demonstrating his considerable prowess. He was to win seven of his races before a quarter crack in a hoof pulled him up short for the rest of that year. As a four-year-old, Nearctic lost the Dominion Day Handicap but set a new track record at the Michigan Mile at Detroit. He later took the Greenwood Handicap.

Joe Thomas, who joined Taylor that year as general manager of the Windfields operations and is still with him, says of Taylor, "He had a desire not only to breed top Canadian horses, but to breed horses that could go anywhere and win and would be a credit not only to himself, but to Canada and to Canadian breeding. One of his basic ambitions was to breed the winner of the Kentucky Derby, the top race in North America. I think most of his friends, particularly those in Kentucky, thought that there was no question he could raise better Canadian breeds than had ever been raised before, but they doubted that he would ever, or that anybody could ever, raise a Kentucky Derby winner up there in the wilds of the north." As many people had done before them, such scoffers badly underestimated the ability of Edward Plunket Taylor not only to establish virtually impossible goals but also to achieve them.

Also in 1958 Taylor bought back Canadian Champ from W.R. Beasley for his stud farm. Canadian Champ had had an excellent racing career, earning $151,705 for the pleased Beasley plus the undisclosed sum that Taylor was to pay him for the buyback. In addition, this strong stallion had been named Canada's Horse of the Year in 1956.

At the time of Taylor's annual yearling sale in the fall of 1958, Windfields Farm and National Stud combined had seventeen stallions, eighty mares, fifty-three yearlings, fifty-seven foals, forty horses in training and a hundred employees on the payroll. In a Toronto *Star Weekly Magazine* article in October 1958, Milt Dunnell asked, "What is Taylor doing to the racing game in Canada? A reasonable guess would be that he intends to make sure there are sufficient Canadian-bred horses to fill the races at the tracks in which he has a tremendous stake. And he doesn't care especially whether they run for him or someone else. At the get-away-day feature in Fort Erie, eight Taylor-bred two-year-olds went to the post. Only one carried Taylor's colours. It lost."

The 100th running of the Queen's Plate was a significant occasion for Canadian racing. Taylor wanted to mark the 1959 event by having the Queen and Prince Philip attend. Both of them are avidly interested in the racing world, the Queen, as her mother has done, racing horses under her own colours. The question was, would she come? The invitation went forward through Government House in Ottawa.

In early spring, word came back that Her Majesty and Prince Philip would be pleased to attend. Planning began immediately to ensure that this running of Canada's top race and all the surrounding social events would be absolutely first class. The man in the centre, a master at organization of this very kind, was the president of the Ontario Jockey Club, E.P. Taylor, who also happened to have a horse entered in the Plate. Although not the favourite, New Providence was a strong entry. He was the first foal of the mare, Fair Colleen. New Providence, sired by the famous Bull Page, had won the Cup and Saucer handicap, one of Canada's leading two-year-old races, and placed in three other stakes events. During the 1959 season before the Queen's Plate, he had won one race and placed second, third, and fifth in three others.

The Queen's Plate was run under an overcast sky and in a light rain. Eddie and Winnie Taylor were surprised and delighted when New Providence came on to win the centennial royal race.

In the winner's circle, a beaming Winnie and Edward Taylor, he resplendent in a grey, pin-striped morning suit and his traditional pearl-grey top hat, received from a smiling Queen Elizabeth the small purple bag containing fifty gold sovereigns, the royal donation which her great-grandmother, Queen Victoria, had authorized a century before.

With the win of New Providence, Taylor had bred eight of the last ten winners of the classic, five of which had raced to victory in his turquoise and gold, polka dot silks.

In recognition of his many and valued contributions, E.P. Taylor was made honorary president of the Canadian Thoroughbred Horse Society.

The next honour bestowed upon E.P. Taylor was one which had never before gone to a Canadian. He was made an Honorary Lifetime Member of the Thoroughbred Club of America and asked to be the special guest–with Winnie at his side–at the 28th annual testimonial dinner of the club held on October 10, 1959, in his honour at the Phoenix Hotel in Lexington, Kentucky. The program of the evening shows past guests of honour, among others,

Alfred J. Vanderbilt, James Fitzsimmons, Isabel Dodge Sloan, and William duPont, Jr. The menu started off with Crabmeat Cocktail *à la* Windfields. The main course was broiled prime Filet Mignon Major Factor with Lyford Cay String Beans, Canadian Champ Baked Potato, Hearts of Lettuce Epic, Coupes St. Jacques Nearctic, Rose Canadiana. The meal was served with Queen's Own assorted relishes and finished with New Providence coffee.

It had been a big horse year for both Edward and Winnie Taylor. Taylor's two-year-old, Victoria Park, had put in a series of excellent performances, winning seven of his ten races and earning $82,162. As Canadian sports writer, Jim Coleman, wrote in the December 19, 1959, edition of *Saturday Night*:

> Victoria Park's ability to carry his blazing speed over impressive distances has encouraged his owners to nominate him for the American "Triple-Crown" events–the Kentucky Derby, the Preakness Stakes, and the Belmont Stakes.
>
> Therein lies the story–never before has a Canadian-bred horse been considered good enough to run in The Derby, The Preakness and The Belmont. No longer is it fashionable for horsemen to utter sanctimonious platitudes on "the improvement of the breed."

The Taylors felt that Victoria Park was the first Canadian-bred horse capable of matching strides with the very best in the United States. Knowing that Conn Smythe had passed over Victoria Park at Taylor's annual fall sale in 1958, because the horse was "pigeon-toed," Coleman also made this comment: "In justice to Smythe, the other horseman who spurned this remarkable colt, Victoria Park also had a pair of front knees which were reminiscent of those of a housemaid who had spent her life scrubbing kitchen floors." In the margin, opposite this paragraph of Coleman's article, Taylor has written the letters "B.S."

Victoria Park was hailed in 1960 as the greatest Canadian-bred in history. The superb bay, a son of Chop-Chop, blazed a trail of achievement up to then unmatched by any other home-bred horse in the century-long period of thoroughbred racing and breeding in Canada. He began the 1960 season with a track-record-breaking performance at Hialeah, then finished second in an allowance race and the Blue Grass Stakes. He was third in the Kentucky Derby, and second in the Preakness. Victoria Park was the first Canadian-bred ever to start in the Kentucky Derby and the Preakness.

After the Preakness, Taylor had to decide whether to send Victoria Park to Belmont, where there was an excellent chance he could win and where the purse was much larger, or to the Queen's Plate. Both races were scheduled for the same day. Taylor finally chose the Queen's Plate, since he felt that the Canadian public was entitled to see the horse in Canada's premier classic. Returning home, Victoria Park was loudly acclaimed, and at the 101st running of the Queen's Plate, he outclassed his home-bred rivals, establishing a new mark of 2:02 for the mile-and-a-quarter classic.

At his next race he set another track record for a mile and a furlong in the Leonard Richards stakes at Delaware Park. Joe Thomas says, "When he won the Leonard Richards and set a new track record, it was probably the best race he had ever run in his life. So we decided he should go out to Hollywood Park and run in the Hollywood Derby out there. That was a $100,000 race and it didn't look like there was anything in it. It would be an easy $100,-000 to pick up. Then he'd come back east and go from there. We took him back to New York and everything seemed to be all right with the horse. We put him on the plane." Since his fifth start in 1959, Victoria Park had been trained by the astute South American horseman, Horatio Luro. Luro had been a familiar figure internationally for many years and was responsible for importing and developing many good horses, especially distance runners.

On the Sunday after Victoria Park had been flown to California, Thomas recalls that he and E.P. Taylor were sitting by the pool at Windfields going over matters "which we always do. He does all his business on the week days and then we do the horse business on days off, on the weekends and the holidays. At least that was the way it was before he retired. Beside the pool he said, 'Have you heard from Horatio lately?' And I said, 'I haven't heard from him. I don't know whether he's there or not. He's going by train but he should be there about now.' " Luro and his wife wouldn't fly. They had gone by train, and they were running about three days behind Victoria Park. Taylor and Thomas calculated that they would be able to catch Luro at his hotel about noon, California time. "So we called him on the phone and Horatio said he had just got there and he was very upset. He thought the horse had a bowed tendon and he wasn't very optimistic. That was a terrible blow to Mr. Taylor. He was really upset. It was a great disappointment because here was an opportunity to prove a point again about the quality of Canadian horses. The horse was quite fit when put aboard the plane, but jarring throughout the eleven-hour trip probably brought on the swelling."

All the hopes Taylor had pinned on Victoria Park were shattered. The horse's racing career was finished. At the end of the summer he was shipped back to Toronto and put out to stud.

Undaunted, Taylor pressed on, not realizing that just a few weeks before, immediately after the Queen's Plate, he had made a decision that would eventually put him in the winner's circle of the Kentucky Derby.

The Taylor filly, Natalma, which he had bought at Saratoga for $35,000 two years before, was in serious difficulty with a chipped bone in her knee. Joe Thomas recalls this situation: "After the Queen's Plate we always used to have a luncheon party down at Oshawa. After that luncheon Gil Darlington, Mr. Taylor, Horatio Luro, and I went over to Darlington's stone house and we sat down to decide what we should do with Natalma and what the future program should be for Victoria Park. It was almost the middle of June, which was awfully late to think about breeding a mare. If Natalma was to race again she would need some surgery on her knee and wouldn't be able to race any more that year. So there was a consensus—we'd breed her. Nearctic had just gone to stud. We brought Natalma home and bred her to Nearctic in about the middle of June." The next year she foaled, producing a bay colt, one of the smallest of all the weanlings transferred to Windfields Farm in Toronto in November of 1961. He was Northern Dancer.

Chapter XV

The Man and the Myth
1960-1965

At the opening of the 1960s, housing developments were spreading outwards from the fringes of all urban centres across the country to meet the high demand of a rapidly increasing population. High-rise apartments were mushrooming upwards, signalling a new Canadian life-style. Foreign capital was pouring into the country, welcomed by those who wanted to see expansion and development and were not concerned about the nationality of the incoming money or of the owners of businesses being established in Canada. The Conservative government of John George Diefenbaker was in power, backed by a record number of seats in the House of Commons. Even so, Canada was on the low road of high unemployment and economic problems.

In those days Edward Plunket Taylor was a prominent figure in contemporary Canadian folklore. When political cartoonist Duncan MacPherson of the Toronto *Star* needed "a capitalist," he would draw a caricature of Taylor's round face capped by the inevitable top hat. In myth Taylor was the reigning tycoon of the nation and master of all the hidden levers of power. Whenever anyone wanted to take potshots at a public target, they automatically chose E.P. Taylor, the symbolic bigshot, as synonymous with power and pomp. There was always something being said about him, some things true, some false, but all part of the myth.

In *Maclean's* magazine in 1963, there was an excellent article by Barbara Moon entitled, "The Last Chapter of the Great E.P. Taylor Myth." While coming to the conclusion that Taylor was not the tycoon that myth portrayed him but really a very human guy, the writer quoted many comments by people she had talked with in preparing the article.

A jaded business editor said recently, "I haven't found anyone who is a success in the business community who isn't prepared to be ruthless. But I must say, E.P. Taylor is better than most. He has a bigger heart. . . ." There is literally nothing personal in what the public thinks or says about him. Aside from horse-racing, the rich man's hobby, he has no tastes, crotchets or secret vices. He is simply the power and pleasure of money in a top hat: "I hear E.P. Taylor is going to be the next Governor General" . . . "That anonymous four-and-a-half million dollar gift to the Canada Council in February for scientific research; they say it's E.P. Taylor" . . . "Whattaya bet he'll be Sir E.P. inside two years?" . . . "Is it true E.P.'s buying the *Globe and Mail* for his reporter son Charles . . .?"

"There's no doubt that there's a basic resentment of him in the business community," says one financial expert. "The hired hands–the company presidents–envy him. And most of the really important men inherited their basic wealth and consider him an upstart."

On the other hand, his employees and close associates, almost to a man, like him wholeheartedly and consider him grossly misunderstood. "I'd like to see somebody write the *real* story of Eddie Taylor," says one former colleague. "I'd like to read an article that said Eddie is the country's most public spirited businessman. But nobody wants to hear *that* . . ." . . . he said recently, "there is a very big segment of the public who could never understand what motivates me. People don't understand the principal motivation is not money." He has also said, "I do something that is constructive. There are people who like to paint or garden. I like to create things." And in commenting on his personal staff he said, revealingly, "I *have* to have a number of people around to protect me . . . so I can do the things I have to do."

All Taylor himself, in a valedictory mood, will say, is "Sometimes I like myself and sometimes I don't."

He will *not* be the next governor general–"That's something I *won't* do for the Queen," he says. (He didn't give the money to the Canada Council, by the way.)

A knighthood? "No Canadian can receive an honour that takes the title without the permission of the government," he counters smoothly. "Yes, there are one or two who have, but only after they have left the country. I don't think I'd be interested though. It just isn't done."

It should be.

As to the image and myth of E.P. Taylor, the reigning tycoon of Canada, master of all the hidden levers of power, Barbara Moon's conclusion was that mythical E.P. Taylor "is not real and never was."

He was, however, tangible and real in the minds of countless Canadians, among them the redoubtable John Diefenbaker. In response to a growing concern about unemployment, the depressed state of the economy and foreign trade, Mr. Diefenbaker announced in the fall of 1960 that he was going to establish a National Productivity Council to advise the government on economic matters. Taylor, who was deeply worried about where the country was going, was strongly opposed to Diefenbaker's plan. So strongly in fact, that he wrote what he mistakenly claimed was his first-ever letter to the editor.* In a covering letter, he said to Ronald McEachren, the editor and director of the *Financial Post*:

I cannot ever remember writing a letter to the press for publication. However, I am so concerned with the economic problems facing Canada that I have broken my rule and am sending you the enclosed which you can use if you see fit.

While the Prime Minister, the Minister of Finance, and the Minister of Trade and Commerce † may be coming to realize our plight, I do not believe any of them has a clue as to what should be done about it.

The creation of a Productivity Council is about the stupidest thing that Diefenbaker has ever done. What will come out of it?

In the letter to the editor, which was indeed published by the *Financial Post*, Taylor discussed the economic problems of slackness in business, large-scale unemployment, and a continuing dim-

*His first was to the editor of the Ottawa *Journal*, February 11, 1943, when he criticized Mackenzie King on his anti-beer action.
†Donald Fleming, Finance, and George Hees, Trade and Commerce.

inished flow of desirable immigrants. The point he wanted to make was clear.

> The answers to our problems will not come as a result of the appointment of advisory bodies to the government composed of many people of largely divergent views such as a newly announced Productivity Council.
>
> What the country needs to deal with the present national emergency is a new department of government, a Ministry of Economic Affairs or Welfare, headed by a Cabinet minister drawn from the upper echelon of business and/or industry.
>
> He must be not only a strong character, but a successful, well-informed, practical man of good judgement, who is prepared to gather advice, form his own conclusions as to steps which should be taken and then obtain authority from the Cabinet to implement his recommendations, no matter how unpopular they may be in some quarters.

In the covering letter to McEachren, he had said that man should have "the best qualities of Mr. C.D. Howe or Ludwig Erhard in Germany."*

Taylor had a gratifying response to his proposal from several quarters, but nothing, of course, from the Prime Minister who was busy culling the country for the best possible members for his new organization. One of the people he was compelled to ask to sit on the new council was none other than E.P. Taylor. "Notwithstanding the fact that I told the Prime Minister and Minister of Trade and Commerce on several occasions that I did not feel that the council could possibly do very much to solve the economic problems of the country, Diefenbaker insisted that I should become a member of it." And notwithstanding his strong views, he allowed his name to stand. George DeYoung, president of Atlas Steels of Welland, was to be the chairman, and some of the other members were Taylor's colleagues: George Metcalf of Loblaws, N.R. (Buck) Crump, president of the C.P.R., Claude Jodoin of the Canadian Labour Congress, and Taylor's old friend, Harvey MacMillan.

The council held its first meeting on Monday, March 20, 1961.

---

*Taylor denies that he had himself in mind as the minister, but he could have filled the bill. Within two years, his partner Wallace McCutcheon, who also shared the described qualities, would be called upon by Diefenbaker to join the Cabinet and do a job much along the lines of Taylor's recommendation.

In spite of his reluctance and firm belief that this body would be a waste of time, E.P. Taylor was there, having flown up from the Bahamas especially for the meeting. In the afternoon session, he told his colleagues that while he believed the Productivity Council would be useful to the country over the long term, he was not too optimistic that within its terms of reference it could contribute too much towards a solution of the present emergency. "It was an advisory council. It had no power. The government wouldn't pay very much attention to our advice. I was very, very busy and I thought we were wasting our time. Even so, it was an honour to be appointed because the list was a formidable group of capable people. But I like to serve on things that are worth while, where something is being accomplished."

At the next meeting of the council on April 24, 1961, in his absence, Taylor was made a member of a committee to establish a Productivity Council in Ontario which purportedly would act within the province in co-operation and liaison with the provincial government. When Taylor discovered that without his knowledge an approach had been made to Premier Leslie Frost in an attempt to set up a meeting at which he was expected to be present, he thought he should let Frost know about his own position. He therefore wrote to Frost, asking for the opportunity to discuss the matter privately.*

The premier agreed to meet Taylor privately and the two had an encouraging discussion on racing matters, after which Taylor offered some cautionary words of advice concerning the potential

---

*In the same letter Taylor thanked Frost for the most complimentary words Frost had written to him and Winnie on May 18, sending regrets that Mrs. Frost and he could not be at the annual Canadian Horse of the Year dinner on June 9 when the Taylors once again were to be honoured, this time for Victoria Park. Frost, who was in a position to judge, said, "I know that your contribution to horseracing and the industry generally has been such as to raise the tone and standard of the operations in this province to what, I am sure, is the highest in America. In any event, I know that we are surpassed by no other jurisdiction. This is in part due to your own good selves and I am glad to acknowledge and thank you both. Quite aside from racing, may I say that you are both good citizens of our country. In business, industry, and community effort, you have both been in the forefront." The Taylors were flattered by those words and Taylor wanted to say so personally.

The final item in Taylor's letter was a request to discuss "some thoughts I have about the future of harness racing in this province. I believe that I have worked out a plan which will ensure that the guidance of it in the major centres can have the benefit of the knowledge and experience of the Jockey Club, and yet leave the majority ownership of the new tracks to be built in the hands of local responsible interests in each area."

pitfalls if Ontario was taken in by the offer of the federal government to become enmeshed in the Productivity Council net. It was not.

While Taylor didn't think much of the National Productivity Council, and said so publicly, he thought a great deal about the economic ailments of the country and the steps that he felt ought to be taken to cure them. When he was invited to address the annual dinner of the Canadian Chamber of Commerce in Halifax he decided that he would use that platform to deliver a lecture not only to the audience before him, but to all those in the country who were truly concerned about the future. He chose the title, "Restoring Canadian Economic Growth," decided what the structure of his speech would be, then retained two economists to research his chosen areas. When they had reported, he sat down to write what turned out to be a masterful analysis of the economic problems of the day. He also dealt with their solutions. His speech was what he intended it to be: a fact-filled, controversial look into the future. He wanted to influence the government of the day into taking action, but he wanted to do so without criticizing. So well did he deliver his message that Gordon McCaffery, a Toronto *Star* writer covering the conference, said, "In his forty-minute speech concluding the Canadian Chamber of Commerce annual meeting, the president of Argus Corporation got closer to the heart of Canada's ailing economy and came up with more concrete proposals than 650 delegates in three days of floundering."

Taylor proposed a four-point program. First, Canada should drive a harder trade bargain with Uncle Sam–using the considerable bargaining point that Canada buys a lot more from the U.S. than it sells. Second, Canada should jump with both feet into selling in the expanding European Common Market, which (with Britain) bought 27 per cent of Canada's exports. Third, Canada should be laying the groundwork for expanding markets in Asia and in underdeveloped countries. Fourth, Canada should get labour management and government to stop scrapping and work together as a team as they do in Europe. That last point–indeed all four–is as valid today as it was in 1961.

On top of this, Taylor was still hammering away for the formation of a new federal Cabinet post, a Ministry of Economic Affairs. In his mind, the minister would be a sort of "Big Daddy" over several departments–Finance, Trade and Commerce, National

Revenue, and Labour. He was not recommending a socialist kind of planning, but a co-ordination of Canada's efforts. "The Germans have done this, and the French, in a different way. This is one of the main reasons they're getting things done over there."

Although Taylor's speech was commented on editorially all across the country, there was no evidence that anyone in the government of the day either heard, understood, or gave a damn about what he was saying. They should have. By the fall of 1961, the council had been forced into holding a press conference because editorial writers across the country were beginning to call it a failure, fulfilling Taylor's prediction that it would be difficult to convince the press and the public that a council could possibly cure the country's economic ills. By the end of December 1961, Taylor had resigned from the council, his letter of resignation being accepted by George DeYoung "with understanding."

The federal election in the spring of 1962 brought Diefenbaker's government to its knees, returning the Conservatives with a minority in the House. Diefenbaker, frantic for ways to counter his dramatic fall in popularity, finally got the message that his Cabinet needed a businessman if it was to be credible. That summer, Wallace McCutcheon accepted the Prime Minister's offer of a position in his Cabinet* and a seat in the Senate. Diefenbaker badly needed a business leader and McCutcheon's credentials were both impeccable and impressive. However, acceptance of the post meant that McCutcheon had to give up all his directorates and his "partnership" in Argus Corporation, which by that time owned 1.5 million shares of Massey-Ferguson, about 12 per cent of its outstanding shares; 400 shares of B.C. Forest Products common; 2.4 million shares of Canadian Breweries common; 1.9 million shares of Dominion Tar and Chemical common; .5 million shares of Hollinger Consolidated Gold Mines common; 107,499 shares of Standard Radio and a substantial holding in Dominion Stores. The market value of the Argus portfolio, which had started off at under $15 million in 1945, was now close to $140 million and, in the wake of Taylor's momentum, was expanding.

---

*First as a minister without portfolio, later as Minister of Trade and Commerce.

Taylor's business interests were also expanding, and were more and more often taking him away from his home base in Toronto. He was dividing his time almost equally between Canada, Britain and Europe, and the Bahamas, where he could now play as well as work. The Lyford Cay development was moving ahead satisfactorily, not only in the building but in its merchandising. At Christmas 1961 Taylor pronounced his new harbour at Lyford Cay open for visiting yachts. He had dredged the new facility out of swamp land at the eastern end of the cay at a cost of about $3 million, making it the largest yacht harbour on the shores of New Providence outside the port of Nassau itself. The land-sheltered basin had been dredged to a depth of eleven feet at low water. Appropriately, the first three yachts berthed in the new harbour were Colonel Eric Phillips' eighty-two ton motor yacht, *Sea Breeze*, and the fourteen ton yacht, *Diana II*, and E.P. Taylor's *Scorpio*. Building Lyford Cay, willing it to emerge out of the swamp, overseeing every step of its growth and watching people move in and enjoy its superlative living facilities gave Taylor pleasure and satisfaction.

In the United Kingdom during 1961 Taylor pressed on towards his objective of creating a major national brewery.

The pace of activity and the frequency of his visits to the United Kingdom had increased to the point where he needed a home there. He talked it over with Winnie, who approved of the idea, especially since it meant she would be able to spend a great deal of time in England with him. After much searching, they found a superb Old Georgian mansion called Birch Hall, near Windlesham in Surrey.

By the end of 1961, United Breweries was firmly established in Scotland and Yorkshire and, to a certain extent, in Lancashire and Wales, but had no productive capacity in the Midlands, London, or southern England. This was a major target for Taylor, who by this time was being darkly accused in the large circulation dailies of the United Kingdom of attempting a "big takeover," a term which in Britain of that day was associated with *nouveaux-riches* North American invaders acquiring tradition-soaked village factories–and sometimes the villages with them. When Bass, Ratcliff, and Gretton merged with Mitchell's and Butler's to form a £67 million firm that year, the *Daily Telegraph* trumpeted, "the move shuts one more door for Mr. E.P. Taylor, Canadian head of the United Breweries, who had been energetically pushing his way into the British brewing industry. Earlier this year [1961] he was defeated by Courage, Barclay, and Simonds in a bid for Bristol Brewery Georges." To the allegations that he had been leading a "tycoon's invasion of the U.K.," Taylor's response was a brief "Nonsense," which, of course, did not mean he was giving up his plans for United Breweries to become a major company in the United Kingdom. The *Sunday Observer* commented that Taylor "follows Beaverbrook and Roy Thomson in newspapers, Garfield Weston in bread and Billy Butlin in the entertainment world. In the Canadianization of Britain, Taylor may be the biggest name yet."

Back in Canada, friends and admirers were becoming concerned that E.P.'s image was changing. Devon Smith, then the financial editor of the *Telegram*, a man who liked Taylor, expressed this concern. In June 1961 he wrote:

E.P. is having trouble with his shadow. He's finding that its size throws people into a panic. Not too many years ago, E.P. was known, trusted and liked by a very large number of unimportant people. He was recognized as honest, good-natured, friendly and superbly confident. A big man physically, he had a merry twinkle in his eye and a thoughtful–sometimes grim–expression, though the ability to smile or laugh heartily was always pretty well in evidence. And he had infinite patience with people who depended upon him, like lady shareholders and green reporters. Somehow or another, E.P. disappeared behind a thing known as Argus. And as he disappeared, a far less charming and likeable shadow seemed to loom in his place. . . .

E.P. seemed to disappear as his shadow grew. Once in a while, you'd hear a friendly voice say, "Hello, there!" and you'd spot the half-forgotten twinkle behind a cloud of smoke from E.P.'s ever-present pipe. But those occasions have become mighty rare. E.P. very definitely became one of those persons who are known of, but not known. And, like all such persons, he has been endowed by public opinion with the kind of personality people will imagine for a man with a big shadow. That's why he is having trouble with his shadow. The frightening thing has grown so big it has the British press writing myths about it.

But I just don't see E.P. as a greedy monster, gobbling up industry for the sake of an appetite. The thing that seems to me to distinguish this likeable man from others was this, when others said, "Why don't they" about a situation, he would say, "Why don't we." I don't think E.P. has changed much and I hope he doesn't mind my using his shadow as an illustration of something–that most of the frightening monsters we see in the world of business are distorted shadows of quite human beings.

Taylor's intensive research into the British brewing industry during 1961 showed him that in the U.K. the eight largest companies transacted about 60 per cent of the business. The next fifty largest companies did about 30 per cent of the business, and the remaining 125 were very small and, in the aggregate, did less than 10 per cent of the business. He had surveyed the fifty companies in the second category and found that about twenty-five of them were not controlled by large shareholders. Therefore, they were vulnerable. He had also observed that the technique used by most of the large brewing companies in England to build up their size was similar to that which he had used in assembling Canadian Breweries. They would acquire a substantial interest in a company which was owned largely by the general public. Then they opened negotiations with the board of directors, usually with satisfactory results. That was the course of action that he would follow over the next few years. It was his opinion that even if he failed with some of his bids, although he would end up without the companies concerned there would be substantial profit on United's investment, which he anticipated would have to be between £5 and £10 million spread over a period of about three years. At mid-December 1961, Taylor's bid for Hewitt Brothers in the Lincolnshire area, with about 346 licensed properties, was successful, bringing his merger tally for the year to five. Even so, he still did not have the major markets in England that he wanted so badly. However, he could see light ahead in his brewery tunnel.

In the early sixties Taylor was frequently contacted by Colonel William Whitbread, chairman of Whitbread's Brewery. Whitbread was not, in Taylor's opinion, interested in joining hands in a merger, rather he was "trying to find out what I was up to. Although Colonel Whitbread was friendly whenever he came to see me,

269

word came to me from many sources that he was protesting to them that I was an interloper and had no business getting mixed up in the brewery trade of Great Britain."

The Whitbread Company had formed the Whitbread Investment Trust, a company with substantial holdings, usually more than 10 per cent, in a long list of independent brewing companies. This trust was jocularly known as "The Whitbread Umbrella." "Its purpose was to acquire the companies in which Whitbread had an interest and presumably to prevent other large companies from taking them over."

As Colonel Whitbread was adding to the number of these companies from time to time, there seemed to be no end to the process. In response, the board of United Breweries decided to form an investment company to buy a substantial interest in uncommitted companies and particularly ones in which the Whitbread Trust was not already financially involved. An investment company was formed under the name of Hare Place Investments Limited with a capitalization of £16 million of which United Breweries was to invest £7 million, Canadian Breweries of Great Britain £7 million, and sundry institutional investors for the City of London the remaining £2 million. This company invested its capital in brewing companies which were uncommitted and in which the Whitbread Investment Trust was not known to be a shareholder.

Colonel Whitbread quickly became aware of the existence of Hare Place Investments and called on Taylor. After some discussion it was agreed that before either of them entered into any new situation they would consult each other. "But it was not long before Colonel Whitbread purchased breweries with which we were negotiating, and the gentleman's agreement was off."

As of September 1961, Canadian Breweries' remittances to Hare Place for the year had reached an amount just short of $5 million, clear evidence of the strength of E.P. Taylor's intent to forge by merger a major national brewery organization in the United Kingdom.

The question on the minds of all Taylor watchers was, "Could he bring it off? Could he make the big merger which would produce one of the largest breweries in the United Kingdom?"

The answer to the question came early in 1962, shortly after the second annual general meeting of United Breweries Limited, which was held on January 15 in London, and at which the chairman, H.L. Bradfer-Lawrence, retired. E.P. Taylor became chairman of the board. Profits were up 12 per cent; there had been dramatic growth in the size of the business through mergers; sales had increased, and the future looked excellent.

The new chairman had fixed his merger eye on the huge Charrington brewery. He had opened that door through his friend, Lord Fraser of Lonsdale, a bluff, hearty man originally from South Africa who had lost the sight of both eyes to a sniper in the First World War. Even so, he had become a reputable and substantial figure in the financial world. One of Lord Fraser's clients was the recluse, Sir John Ellerman, regarded as one of the richest men in the United Kingdom at the time, the owner of Ellerman Shipping Lines. As it happened, Ellerman held the largest single block of Charrington, a 20 to 25 per cent holding. He was the key. Taylor discussed the potential of a Charrington and United merger with Lord Fraser, who could see that it would certainly be profitable to Ellerman. Fraser, in turn, convinced Ellerman that a merger would be wise. That done, Fraser then discussed the matter with John Charrington, chairman of the brewing establishment which had been founded in 1757 and run by the same family for two centuries. Philip Bradfer-Lawrence recalls, "I remember having a meeting in Eddie's office on Davies Street when John Charrington and one of his directors came along. They said they thought they'd like to take us over. They would take two of us on their Charrington board. Eddie said, 'Well, that's very interesting,' and the meeting just came to a close. We were bigger in volume than they were and I think bigger in profits. Eddie said, 'Well, we'll turn this over to the merchant bankers,' which was done, with Philip Hill, Higginson, Erlangers acting for United Breweries and Lazard Brothers and Co. acting for Charrington." From that point the meetings and discussions and negotiations proceeded apace, but security surrounding the talks was loose with the result that rumours of bids and counter rumours of mergers began to fly. Everyone knew that E.P. Taylor's United Breweries was bidding for someone, and many were trying to spot in advance who the "victim" was. The victim did very well, with the price of a Charrington share rising from 100 shillings in November, to a peak of 130 on the basis of the takeover rumour.

The rumour was confirmed on January 24 by a joint announcement by the two firms that discussions were going on with a view to a merger between the two groups which, if it came off, would create a £78 million enterprise controlling over 5,250 public houses. Once again, Taylor had shocked the British brewing industry and, in the short period of two years, had spearheaded the creation of a brewing group which was now the third largest in tied public houses and in overall size. Only Watney Mann and Ind Coope were ahead of him, with 6,440 and 7,846 public houses respectively. The Charrington merger put him where he wanted to be, into the heavily populated south of England.

The announced merger was consummated in April 1962, but in the process was not without its touchy moments. Arthur Elliott, who was in the middle of the negotiations, recounts, "When it came to the question of the board, John Charrington said, 'We're going to have two more directors than you have because we must have the majority.' And Eddie said, 'Well, that's all right, John.' I think we were all appalled. I thought to myself, 'We're really going to get ground down now.' After the meeting was over, I said, 'Eddie, what are we going to do now? They're going to outvote us on every occasion.' And I remember Eddie saying, 'Look, boy, I've been one out of ten on a board and got my way.' When we did form the board, there were six of them and four of us. We never had a vote and we always got our way."

John Charrington was the chairman of the new company, Charrington United Breweries Limited, and E.P. Taylor was the deputy chairman. This happy arrangement made it clear that the Canadian did not want to have the management of the new firm. All Taylor wanted was to be the leader of the group on the board responsible for those further acquisitions and mergers which would make Charrington United the largest brewery group in the United Kingdom.

During 1963 and 1964 Taylor, accompanied by Winnie, made many long visits to England as deputy chairman of Charrington United, working with his colleagues at the brewery and the merchant bankers Philip Hill, Higginson, Erlangers in sorting out financing matters and negotiating new mergers, which in that period included Woodhead's Brewery Limited, Lyle and Kinahan Limited, and Old Bush Mills Distillery Co. Ltd. In addition, Taylor was maintaining his contacts with the chairman of the three largest brewing firms, Allied Breweries Limited, Bass Mitchell's and Butler's (Bass M and B), and Watney Mann. Since he considered it essential that Charrington United join forces with one of them when the opportunity arose, he made sure that he became well acquainted with the principals of all three firms.

With Bass M and B, the discussions had been most encouraging. Sir James Grigg, the chairman of that company, had agreed in principle that a merger with his firm would be desirable, but because his company had only recently (in 1961) acquired Mitchell's and Butler of Birmingham, he had requested of Taylor more time to consider a merger. "Sir James Grigg kept his managing director, Mr. Alan Walker, fully informed of our interest and Mr. Walker was present at several of the meetings which we had with Sir James at his flat in Albany, Picadilly." When Sir James died in 1964, Walker was named chairman of the company. He was to be the key man in the final negotiations that Taylor was to conduct with Bass M and B in the years to come.

———————

There were two other deaths in 1964, both of which shook Taylor and his wife. In the spring, Taylor had gone to visit his old friend and hero, Lord Beaverbrook, at his home in Cherkley, Surrey. The two pragmatic entrepreneurs had had a grand time together over dinner and drinks, discussing the past, rooting out the problems of the day, and revelling in each other's company. When Edward Taylor had written to thank the Beaver for his hospitality, the brief response was poignant.

> My dear Eddie, So very many thanks for your letter. No visitor to my house in a long time has been as welcome as yourself. I have deeply regretted your long absence.
> And with very good regards,
> > Yours ever,
> > Max.

On June 9, the eighty-five-year-old Lord Beaverbrook passed away. Taylor was pleased that he had had that last visit with his friend, whom the London *Times* obituary called "a paradoxical man of genius–loyal, yet mischievous, warm-hearted yet ruthless, an uncanny judge of human nature whose embrace of lost causes has become legendary. As a proprietor, he was both loved and feared; as his own best publicist, he was hugely indulged, and as a mercurial adventurer, he will be sadly missed." And Eddie Taylor was among those who missed him most.

The day after Christmas 1964, E.P. Taylor's partner, Eric Phillips, suffered a fatal heart attack while at his winter home in Palm Beach, Florida. Colonel W. Eric Phillips, D.S.O., M.C., O.B.E., was seventy-one years of age, a dear, wise, loyal friend and ally who understood Eddie Taylor perhaps better than any other man. The man who took part as an equal in virtually every aspect of Taylor's widespread business life was gone. And with him went a part of E.P. Taylor's zest and drive, and his interest in the things he and Phillips had built together. They had been the senior partners in Argus. They had put it together as equals. Together they had suffered the abuse, taken the risks, made the tough decisions, accepted the credits and the criticisms, and they had sustained each other as only close, intimate, trusting, best friends can. No one would take Eric Phillips' place in the life of Eddie Taylor, or in the boardroom of the Argus Corporation.

In the Argus stable of holdings, Canadian Breweries, Taylor's personal flagship, was experiencing difficulties. At the end of March 1965, E.P. Taylor stood on the stage of the O'Keefe Centre to face over 400 shareholders of Canadian Breweries, the company he had founded. For the first time in thirty years as chairman, he had to present an annual report that was less than satisfactory. It was a report that he did not like to give but he did it well. In one hour and five minutes, his whole board of directors had been re-elected. Taylor fielded a series of questions, some of them prickly, but did so superbly, with grace and much humour.

Ian Dowie, who had been with the company since the thirties, and latterly as president, had resigned just a few days before. Taylor emphasized that Dowie's departure was based on an honest difference of opinion on the way the company was run. Taylor said in response to a shareholder's question, "I'm not saying Mr. Dowie isn't right, either. He could well be right, but we disagreed." In such a situation, E.P. Taylor never lost. His nominee for the presidency, J.G. (Jack) Campbell, was installed. While sales for the year ended October 31, 1964, were up 3.6 per cent from the previous year, net profit was down 3.4 per cent. Taylor was unhappy with the results and for the first time had started to hold back on his normal expansionist policies. When one shareholder suggested that the company might "cut back on the program of expansion," Taylor said, "It's exactly what we are doing." Although it went against the grain, Taylor's good judgement made him recognize that, so far as C.B.L. was concerned, restraint was the order of the day.

Furthermore, with Phillips gone, Taylor was not sure that he wanted to carry the main burden of expansion for Canadian Breweries or any of the companies in the Argus portfolio. He had spread himself out broadly in all his activities in Canada and the United Kingdom and the Bahamas. There were one or two places where he would like to press on, such as in the United Kingdom with Charrington United, because his final goal there had not been reached. But by and large, the corporate game was wearing a bit thin. Life, what there was left of it, should be for enjoyment. After all, he should be doing only the things he wanted to do, and taking a lot of flack from shareholders was not necessarily one of them.

During 1965, Taylor was more visible than usual in his public statements and opinions, particularly about government. He was convinced that Canada's growth would be stymied unless governments modified the crushing load of taxation on business and individuals, encouraged more foreign investment, and pursued more liberal immigration policies. "Canada is now being run as if it were an old, decadent country. I'm a very simple fellow. I believe that Canada should be growing much more than it is." If Canada had a more liberal immigration and foreign investment policy, "more brains and capital would come here to develop our natural resources and industry. There is a tremendous shortage of skilled people in Canada today. From a long-range standpoint Canada has an obligation to populate this land because it can, according to experts, support fifty to a hundred million people with a high standard of living. You can't have punitive taxation on profits. This is why people won't come to this country." He was in favour of social security for all. "But only if we can create the wealth to support such social security." Foreign capital should be encouraged to enter Canada, "because we can't get along without it."*

---

* *Winnipeg Free Press* interview, October 6, 1965.

275

That fall, Taylor made one of his rare public speeches. He was the principal speaker at the opening of the New Centennial Ballroom at the Inn on the Park Hotel in Metropolitan Toronto, a project of Isadore Sharpe, Eddie Creed, and Murray Koffler.* Taylor donned the mantel of a major land developer, which indeed he was, to attack municipal authorities for what he called their mediocrity and land development policies: "The proper use of land is one of the major problems facing all cities. In the past, land has been wasted on a prodigious scale, not only at great economic loss, but also with failure to provide a living environment to which people are entitled." He attributed this state of affairs to municipalities which, when faced with financial problems, invariably look on land development from an assessment point of view. "The result is a lot of so-called planning that becomes merely an exercise in assessment, unrelated to proper land use or the needs of people. Unfortunately, planning has been on a piecemeal basis, and while we have zoning by-laws, it is a cliché to say that these by-laws seldom produce anything that is good and may prevent something that is bad. The result is a great deal of mediocrity."

And, as to being called a developer, Taylor said, "I am proud to be a developer. Unfortunately the word developer is in many minds synonymous with 'land speculator.' There is a vast difference. A developer creates value. A speculator creates nothing. A speculator buys land with the idea of contributing nothing but the hope of making a profit. A developer buys real estate and, besides his talent and imagination, invests capital income–sometimes millions of dollars–to create assets, and these assets are reflected in development. Developers are an integral part of our economic system and should be recognized as such." For developers, "the ideal is not always attainable and with our present government controls, even the possible often becomes difficult."

As to Taylor's qualifications to talk to his audience about land development, there was absolutely no question. He was the developer of the internationally known new town of Don Mills, an integrated community of residential, industrial, and commercial properties with a population by 1965 of some 27,500 people. Don Mills also embraced some seventy industries, two major shopping

---

*As a young druggist, Koffler had made a start at Taylor's York Mills Shopping Centre and then in the Don Mills Shopping Centre.

centres, and a complete range of educational and recreational facilities. In addition, he had used subsidiaries of his Canadian Equity and Development Company Limited to enlarge his land development interests. Wrentham Estates, which had built the shopping centre at York Mills and Bayview, was engaged in the acquisition, development, and sale of other residential and industrial property in the Bayview and Leslie Street areas near Don Mills. A new project was now under way on St. Clair Avenue, just east of Yonge Street in Toronto. It would have 185 residential units and a shopping mall on the ground floor, with a Dominion Store. The massive Erin Mills land assembly was complete and frustrating negotiations were under way with the provincial and municipal governments to commence development. The Greater Hamilton Shopping Centre on the old Hamilton Jockey Club land had been completed and was producing revenue.

Argus Corporation had a direct investment in Canadian Equity of just under $3 million, but Taylor's Argus partners really did not want to be in the real estate and land development business. The return was not good enough for them. Taylor tried to talk them into staying on but they didn't want to be known as developers. The decision was made and, as was the custom at Argus, Taylor had no choice but to make it unanimous. He did not, however, want the Argus interests to go to strangers. His own investment company held about 40 per cent of the shares of Canadian Equity, and since Taylor was not interested in having a strange, uninvited bedfellow, he offered to buy the Argus interest through the family company, Caninvesco. He asked his partners to tell him what they thought the Argus shares were worth and he would buy them. They came up with a value of almost $4.5 million. Taylor did not quibble. He paid the price, providing Argus with a substantial profit.

During the 1960s, E.P. Taylor's natural instinct and drive to become the leader in any field in which he becomes involved, was more and more apparent in his successful horseracing and breeding endeavours. His achievements, as in his brewing and financial interests, were not confined to Canada but were international, both in scope and in the recognition he was to receive.

In 1962, proud Winnie and Edward Taylor entered the Queen's Plate winner's circle to collect the gold trophy and the sovereign's guineas from the guest of honour of the Jockey Club, Queen Elizabeth, the Queen Mother. Taylor's filly, Flaming Page, and Winnie's colt, Choperion, had just finished first and second for Windfields Farm's seventh victory in Canada's premier race. Furthermore, Taylor had bred the first four horses to cross the wire. It had been another superb day. The Queen Mother enjoyed herself thoroughly in the presence of a record crowd of 32,169 which was delighted by the pageantry of her visit for the 103rd consecutive running of the Queen's Plate. Her Majesty had arrived accompanied by the Lieutenant Governor Keiller MacKay and was met in front of the grandstand by E.P. Taylor in his usual formal morning clothes and pearl-grey topper. Her landau was surrounded by the gleaming silver helmets and dark blue uniforms of the Governor General's Horseguards who escorted her, their uniforms in vivid contrast to the bright tunics of the Royal Canadian Mounted Police and the dark blue of the Ontario Provincial Police. An avid horsewoman and owner of racehorses, the Queen Mother was right at home. In making the winner's circle presentations, she gave the gold cup to Edward Taylor, but presented the coveted guineas to Winnie Taylor. It was a grand day all around.

At Taylor's 1962 sale of yearlings, he disposed of nine colts and six fillies for $196,000. The average price of a horse was the highest yet–$13,077. Jean-Louis Lévesque bought two horses, a filly which he named Ciboulette and a colt, Pierlu, a shortening of the name of his young son, Pierre-Louis. Larkin Maloney bought a colt tagged at $25,000, which he called Brockton Boy, and Frank Sherman collected one which he called Grand Garcon. Maloney had wanted a bay son out of Natalma by Nearctic, but backed off on the advice of his trainer. Joe Thomas recalls that the young horse was "a neat-looking little horse who looked as though he wouldn't go very far. We put a $25,000 price on him. At that time, Larkin Maloney was our best customer. He and Conn Smythe used to have great fun. They would come to the farm and sit down and have the yearlings paraded. They looked at this little horse, and Maloney said, 'Gee, he's a neat little horse. And he looks sound and everything, but how will he ever win a Queen's Plate?' " No one bought that neat little horse. All of the buyers, expert horsemen every one, had gone by Northern Dancer.

The favourite to win the 1963 Queen's Plate was a Canadian-bred three-year-old, Jet Traffic, owned by Russell Firestone, Jr., of

Dallas, Texas. But on May 23, the Jockey Club ruled the horse ineligible because of a technicality in the entry procedures. This moved into the favourite position Royal Maple, a Taylor-bred horse owned by Jean-Louis Lévesque of Montreal. Taylor himself had an entry, Canebora. Ontario racing fans were extremely unhappy about the removal of Jet Traffic. It was rumoured that Taylor himself had been behind the close look at the horse's nomination, or that his people were. The *Globe and Mail* demanded that Taylor re-instate Jet Traffic saying that if he did not, "sportsmanship will have a sadder meaning in the lexicon of the game." In response, Taylor pointed out that if Jet Traffic were re-instated and he won, the Jockey Club would be faced with a lawsuit from the other owners. There was nothing he could do. "It's a fiasco. Now the poor person who wins the Plate is going to get the raspberry." The man who won it was E.P. Taylor.

His Canebora, a son of Queen's Plate winner Canadian Champ, with Panamanian jockey, Manuel Ycaza, up, won in a tight finish, one length ahead of Wilf Farr's Son Blue. The Woodbine crowd started booing Canebora as he approached the winner's circle. And as the Taylors joined their horse to receive the Queen's Plate trophy and the guineas from the Honourable Earl Rowe, then lieutenant governor of Ontario, the noise increased. There were a lot of unhappy fans who were fed up with Taylor's domination of the Queen's Plate. This was the twelfth time in fifteen years that a Taylor-bred horse had won the Plate.

Outwardly, Winnie and Eddie paid no attention, but inwardly, they were hurt. Canebora went on to win the Prince of Wales Stakes and later the Breeders' Stakes, becoming the first horse since New Providence in 1959 to win the Triple Crown and the Horse of the Year award.

On August 2, 1963, Taylor's Northern Dancer ran his first race with the young New Brunswick jockey, Ron Turcotte, up. Northern Dancer had been placed in the hands of the colourful, highly regarded trainer, Horatio Luro, who trained horses for a number of owners at his public stables. Northern Dancer was a playful colt given to nipping–a habit he maintains to this day, according to Winnie Taylor, who says he still recognizes her voice and gives her a pleasant if painful nip when she visits him. At his first race, he took on Brockton Boy, the colt Larkin Maloney decided to take instead of Northern Dancer at the pre-priced sale in September

1962. He beat Brockton Boy by a good six lengths. By the end of November, he had run in six more Canadian races, three of them stakes. The Dancer won five out of the six starts and was second in the Cup and Saucer stakes to another Taylor-bred horse, Grand Garcon. The "neat little horse" was looking good.

A thoroughbred racing milestone was reached on December 4, 1963, when Indian Line, owned by Tom Hays, won the fifth race at Tropical Park. With that victory, the earnings of horses bred by E.P. Taylor exceeded the $1 million mark for the year. It was the first time that thoroughbreds bred in Canada by a Canadian had reached this amount in a single season. It put Taylor third in the amount-won category and first for the fourth year in a row in the category of races won, as well as the category of the greatest number of stakes winners in North America.

In the United States Taylor had been looking for a place where he could set up a training facility of his own rather than putting his horses with a public trainer. He wanted to find a location convenient to most of the racetracks so his horses could be trained there up to racing time. Mrs. Richard duPont heard of Taylor's search. She telephoned him and said, "I've got the ideal location where my place is in Maryland. It's within a hundred miles of New York and fifty miles of the Jersey tracks." Taylor knew the area well. He went down, looked over the situation, and liked it. The location was fine. But he was looking for about a hundred acres, and a hundred acres weren't available in the right location. But, as Joe Thomas remembers, "there was an old farm of about 700 acres that had been neglected for a number of years right across the road from Mrs. duPont. Mr. Taylor decided he would buy the whole 700 acres and then develop the 100 he wanted. In time, he would probably sell off the rest and encourage other people to come in and build similar facilities. In 1963 construction began on Taylor's new training centre, Windfields Farm, Maryland Inc.

Then came the year of the Dancer—1964.

After Northern Dancer finished his highly successful fall season in Canada, he went straight down to the New York circuit where he won an allowance race at Aqueduct and the important Remsen Stakes which had been taken by Taylor's Victoria Park in 1959. Joe Thomas recalls that "just before the Remsen, Northern Dancer popped a quarter crack. That's something like a bad break in the cuticle of your fingernail. It can be very sore, and if it starts to hurt and breaks through, the horse just can't race. You have to cut it out and then let the whole hoof grow out. It's six or eight months, sometimes even a year, before it can grow out. We were undecided what to do, but there was a blacksmith out in California by the name of W.R. Bane who had developed what he called 'the vein patch' in which the hoof is patched with a special plastic that stays until the hoof grows out. We decided we would go ahead and run Northern Dancer in the Remsen, and if everything was all right and we hadn't done too much damage to him, then we'd put the patch on him and go on. Well, he won the Remsen and did so impressively. We put the patch on him and sent him to Florida, thinking he'd be out for perhaps two months, but within a month he was ready to go back to serious training. Then he went on and won the Flamingo and the Florida Derby and then the Blue Grass Stakes." Willie Shoemaker, the excellent, experienced jockey, rode Northern Dancer at Hialeah and then in the Flamingo Stakes which the "neat little horse" won with a two-length victory over Mr. Brick. It was his first $100,000 win and he was the first Canadian horse to win a purse of that size. Winnie Taylor saw that race by herself since Eddie was fog-bound at the Orlando airport.

Taylor was nearing his target, the Kentucky Derby, but there were several races ahead. He had to get the best jockey he could, but there were problems. Since Shoemaker, who was the top rider at the time, couldn't ride Northern Dancer in an allowance race on March 28 in preparation for the Florida Derby at Gulfstream Park, Manuel Ycaza was in the saddle for the Dancer's third Florida win. A week later, the magnificent Canadian horse won the Florida Derby by a length over The Scoundrel. Shoemaker was back on him again. "We thought Shoemaker was going to ride our horse right through all the big races, but to Shoemaker, Northern Dancer wasn't as impressive in the Florida Derby as he had been in the Flamingo. He figured that maybe the little horse had come up big for the Flamingo and was now tailing off. So Shoemaker went back to California and won the Santa Anita Derby with Hill Rise." Eventually Shoemaker chose to ride Hill Rise for the Kentucky Derby. Needless to say, this made Taylor, a very loyal man who expects loyalty from others, furious, although nothing was said. Luro had to scramble for the best jockey he could find. Through Bill Hartack's agent he found that the temperamental, hard-driving young Pennsylvania jockey could be had for the

Derby. Taylor agreed and Hartack was on, harsh crop and all.

The odds went with Hill Rise and Shoemaker. When the bettors saw him on Hill Rise, they took him as the favourite. Thomas describes the race: "At the start of the race our horse broke well and then he dropped in with the pack and was about fourth or fifth. He was running very easily and was just where we wanted him. Going into the back stretch, Hill Rise was lying behind him and on the outside. About half a mile from home, an opening came and Hartack took advantage of it. He just asked our little horse to run. He could accelerate just like that. And he went through that hole and went right to the lead and opened up three or four lengths. In the meantime, Hill Rise was making his run on the outside. We ran right away from him. When we turned for home, we were two or three lengths in front and Hill Rise was coming on the outside. Every stride, he kept closing up and closing up. About seventy yards from the wire it looked like he might catch us. Then you could see our little horse react. He won by about a neck." The "little horse" had not only won the Kentucky Derby, but had run the mile and a quarter in two minutes flat for a new track record.

Now that his superb Northern Dancer had won the Kentucky Derby, E.P. Taylor and Winnie were bursting with pride. There were great celebrations in the Taylor entourage that night, just as there were later on when Northern Dancer, with Hartack riding him, again took Hill Rise in the Preakness at Pimlico. This time Northern Dancer beat his arch rival by two and a quarter lengths.

The next target was Belmont, for the Triple Crown, but in that race Northern Dancer finished third in a field he had beaten before. Thomas says, "Luro has a fetish about a horse going to the front too soon in a race. He had told Hartack to take him back, but in order to take him back Hartack had to choke him down. When he went past the stands the first time he had his mouth wide open." When the race was finished, the little horse spent two hours coughing up dirt that had been rammed into his open mouth. Of this race the extremely disappointed Taylor was to say in a letter written to a friend a few days later, "His trainer, Horatio Luro, and I are convinced that it was due to our jockey carrying out the pre-race strategy. . . . If he had not choked the horse for the first mile and realized that the pace was so slow, we believe he would have won it."

The fact was that the superlative young horse had not won, but that in no way took away from the cheering greeting the packed crowd gave him when Bill Hartack rode him past the New Woodbine grandstand in the post parade of the Queen's Plate. The ovation was emotional. This was their horse, the fans' horse, a Canadian horse, the best they had ever seen. Northern Dancer won that Queen's Plate with a seven-and-one-half-length victory, brought home by the crowd on its feet shouting, "Go Dancer, Go."

The boos of yesteryear were gone, converted now into loud cheers for this determined, hard-working Canadian who had brought glory to Canadian racing in a way that every racing fan understood. That day, with Winnie by his side, Eddie Taylor was every racing fan's hero. As he received the gold cup, lifting it high above his pearl-grey-top-hatted head, the entire crowd at Woodbine erupted with a heart-warming cheer.

A few days later Northern Dancer was shipped back to Belmont for further training before the Arlington Classic, a major race in Chicago. Joe Thomas recalls, "Luro had arranged for a workout at Belmont on the morning before the horse was to be shipped to Albany to catch a plane for Chicago. That morning it rained. Luro didn't know what to do. He didn't like the idea of working the horse in the rain, but on the other hand, if he didn't work the horse, the whole plan to run him in the Arlington would be off. Luro decided that he would give the horse an easy workout, over seven furlongs. When Northern Dancer came back and was being walked to the barn, Horatio looked down and there was a little bump on the tendon. It didn't look too serious at the time. Luro hoped that perhaps the Dancer had given himself a little rap with a hoof. But it was serious. It was a bowed tendon." Donald Prowse, who was with Taylor when Luro called with the bad news, remembers: "It was a terrible shock to him. It was a bitter disappointment, and I just remember him saying, 'Oh, God.' He had tried for so long to produce a horse of international stature, and he had finally succeeded. He was terribly fond of that horse because it was a symbol of what he had been able to do. Then, to have this happen, just when the horse was at its absolute peak, was a bitter blow to him."

By late October, Northern Dancer had made an almost complete recovery from his tendon injury. Taylor then had to decide whether to return him to racing or put him out to stud. He announced his decision in a letter to those fellow horse breeders who were interested in syndication or complete purchase of the horse. He wrote advising them that he had decided to retain complete ownership and planned to stand him in Canada at stud. "I simply wanted to keep the horse here and I am sure that his multitude of admirers in Canada would not be happy if he were to go away. Instead, he will enter stud in 1965 at my National Stud Farm, Oshawa, Ontario, at a fee of $10,000 Canadian funds, live foal."

Today, Northern Dancer, the pride and joy of the Taylors, who have raised hundreds of horses, still stands at stud—now in Maryland—and still nips at Mrs. Taylor.

It was that same Winnie Taylor who set her husband straight and won the battle of opening to women the Directors' Room at the Jockey Club tracks. She tells the story: "They had a rule against ladies being admitted to the Directors' Room. Sometimes I would sit for hours in our box waiting for the directors' meetings to break up. Finally, one hot afternoon, I said, 'To Hades with this! Those men sitting in there, eating and drinking, all air-conditioned and comfortable while their wives wait outside!' I barged right in and said, 'Mr. Taylor, this is one fight you are going to lose. I am staying right here.' From that time on, the wives have been admitted." It was another racing first for the Taylor family.

While Taylor did not win the Queen's Plate in 1965, his stature among horsemen throughout the world continued to grow. He was the first Canadian to be elected president of the Thoroughbred Racing Association, an association of fifty American and Canadian Racetracks, organized in 1942 to provide thoroughbred racing with direction, purpose, control, and unity of effort. During his tenure as president of the T.R.A., Taylor continued his crusade against excessive taxation and the overexploitation of thoroughbred racing by governments, pointing in his speeches in the United States to the lead which had been taken in Ontario in reducing the tax of 12½ per cent on wagering to 6 per cent.

On Monday evening, October 5, 1965, Taylor held his annual pre-priced sale of yearlings at Windfields Farm, at which he sold twenty-four yearlings for a gross of $442,000, topping anything that he had done before, and exceeding the sales of the Canadian Thoroughbred Horse Society, held only three weeks before, at which the C.T.H.S. grossed a record high of $345,900. At Taylor's sale, Quebec industrialist Jean-Louis Lévesque paid $100,000 for a foal sister to the champion Northern Dancer. This was the highest-priced yearling filly in the history of public sales to that time. Taylor was pleased. It was good evidence of the genetic success he was achieving and another spur toward his goal of becoming the world's top breeder.

———————

Taylor the engineer, developer, and financier was also pleased with the progress of his development at Lyford Cay. Names such as the Earl of Carnarvon; C.B.S. board chairman, William Paley; the Earl of Dudley; Henry Ford, II; and Roy E. Larsen, vice-chairman of Time, now graced and enhanced the ownership list. The Taylors had settled into their new Bahamian home which had been completed in mid-1961. An elegant and formal Bermuda-Georgian bungalo painted in muted shades of grey, it was designed by New York architect, Eldredge Snyder, and decorated by the Taylors' daughter, Louise. In front of the house there are gardens laid out with formal brick pathways furnished with white wrought iron furniture. On the ocean side of the house there is a large semi-circular terrace overlooking the lawn which sweeps smoothly down to the beach where there is a charming guest cottage with a native stone floor patio and heavy outdoor furniture. In the main house, the most striking room is the library, panelled in rich brown Canadian pine, shelves filled with books, and comfortable lounging chairs, and a chesterfield.

With the population of Lyford Cay growing rapidly, Edward Taylor, an Anglican by upbringing, still carrying the influence of the late Archdeacon Snowdon, decided that it was time to cater to the spiritual well-being of his neighbours and his own family. On Sunday, January 7, 1962, a new church, which had been donated by Winnie and Edward Taylor, was dedicated at a special ceremony conducted by the Lord Bishop of Toronto, the Right Reverend Fred Wilkinson, assisted by the vicar general of Nassau and the Bahamas, the Very Reverend F.E. Ellis. The itinerate Taylor had seen to it that the church was appropriately named Saint Christopher, after the patron saint of travellers. He had also seen to it that the right people were invited, among them His Excellency the Governor Sir Robert Stapledon and his wife, Chief Justice Sir Ralph Campbell, and the man from whom he had bought the Lyford Cay area land, the Honourable Harold Christie.

That same year, Taylor incorporated the New Providence Development Company Limited in Nassau for the purpose of developing the 2,000 acres lying to the east of Lyford Cay. He would later acquire more land for development,* develop a new fresh-water resource, purchase a dairy operation, and undertake many other projects, but these would be some years down the road.

The big event at Lyford Cay in 1962 came at the end of the year. On Wednesday, November 28, the Bahamian government announced that a summit meeting between President Kennedy and Prime Minister Harold Macmillan would be held at Lyford Cay. It would be a two-day meeting, beginning on December 19. President Kennedy would stay at the Taylor house, while Macmillan would be headquartered a hundred feet away in a house called Bali H'ai, which belonged to another Canadian, Barbara Holt, the daughter-in-law of the Canadian banker, Sir Robert Holt.

It was the ubiquitous White House press secretary, Pierre Salinger, who had picked Lyford Cay. As it turned out, all of the participants, particularly the press, were grateful to Salinger for his splendid choice, which allowed them to enjoy the sun, the luxury of the Lyford Cay Club, and the beaches and water. Salinger had visited Nassau in late November and met the Governor of the Bahamas, Sir Robert Stapledon, and his officials. He then spent a good deal of time with Eddie and Winnie Taylor sorting out the arrangements for accommodation of all the principals and the functions which were to take place. The Taylors immediately volunteered their own home for President Kennedy's use. Taylor got on the phone to Babs Holt next door, who was delighted to make her superb home available to Macmillan. Taylor would ensure that the facilities of the Lyford Cay Club would be available for press conferences, parties, and other functions. The arrangements were quickly settled. The Taylors would vacate their house, as would Babs Holt, and both leaders could move right in. Salinger left Lyford Cay with Taylor's assurance that everything would be looked after. A better, more gracious, solicitous host than Edward Taylor would be hard to find. He would be absolutely in his element looking after the requirements of these two popular world leaders and the important men who would accompany them.

In addition to the other preparations for the President's arrival,

---

*The company currently holds 5500 acres including about five miles of beach.

E.P. Taylor scurried around and found a sturdy, high-backed carved rocking chair which he was sure Kennedy would be delighted to use. The President, however, brought his own.

Also scheduled to appear on the scene was a much lesser light, the Prime Minister of Canada, John George Diefenbaker, whom Macmillan had asked to come down to Nassau to have a chat after President Kennedy left. It had become customary for a British Prime Minister who had just had a conference with the President of the United States on the North American side of the Atlantic to have a review of the events with the Canadian Prime Minister–a rather colonial touch. The Ottawa pundit, Charles Lynch, hastened to reassure Diefenbaker, saying that he "needn't worry about taking a back seat at the Macmillan/Kennedy pow-wow here this week. E.P. Taylor has things well in hand and the nation's honour is being upheld."

The Monday before the dignitaries were to arrive, Taylor was on hand to see that everything was in order. A resplendent figure when he hosted Her Majesty the Queen at his Woodbine Racetrack layout in Toronto in 1959, Mr. Taylor dressed like a beachcomber for this event. In old clothes and disguised by dark glasses, he hurried around the place getting his own belongings out and making sure everything was in shape for President Kennedy. Next door at Bali H'ai, Babs Holt was also preparing to vacate.

Charles Lynch reported: "Mr. Taylor said he didn't like publicity, though he seems to take kindly to the thought that a million dollars' worth will come to Nassau through this conference, and the fame and fortune of his Lyford Cay experiment should be assured for all time."

Late Monday evening, December 18, Prime Minister Harold Macmillan arrived in Nassau in a special R.A.F. Comet accompanied by his Foreign Secretary, Lord Home, and Duncan Sandys, the Secretary of State for Commonwealth Relations, and for the Colonies. They were later joined by Peter Thorneycroft, Minister of Defence.

The next morning the young President of the United States, John F. Kennedy, arrived in his Air Force One, accompanied by a galaxy of advisers who were to populate the Taylor house for the next three days: Robert S. McNamara, Secretary of Defence; George W. Ball, Under-Secretary of State; the ever-present W. Averell Harriman, whom Taylor knew from the Second World

287

War days when Harriman was then Assistant Secretary of State for Far Eastern Affairs; John Kenneth Galbraith, the renowned economist and Canadian expatriate, then Ambassador to India; David K.E. Bruce, Ambassador to Great Britain; William R. Tyler, Assistant Secretary of State for European Affairs; Kenneth O'Donnell, Special Assistant to the President; McGeorge Bundy, Special Assistant to the President for National Security Affairs; and the man who had brought them all there, the rotund, cigar-chomping Pierre Salinger.

After the appropriate speeches, inspection of the guard of honour, and attendance to all necessary matters of protocol, a caravan of cars took both leaders and their parties off to the seclusion and luxury of the Taylor and Holt houses where they held two days of discussions concerning the then controversial Skybolt air-to-ground nuclear missile which Kennedy wanted to scrap, giving Britain Polaris missiles for nuclear submarines instead. There would also be discussion about the situation in the Congo which Kennedy believed might develop into another Cuba.

The first session between the two men was held in the Holt house on Wednesday. On Thursday, the scene moved to the comfortable library of the Taylor home. Tuesday night, President Kennedy went to the press party which host E.P. Taylor had staged at his Lyford Cay Club. The President enjoyed himself enormously, making a circle tour of the gathering, flanked by secret service men and shepherded by the genial Taylor who told him about the Lyford Cay development and the distinguished people who were now living there. Macmillan went to a different party that night at the Emerald Beach Hotel.

By mid-day Thursday, Kennedy decided he should stay over another day, which meant that Prime Minister Diefenbaker, who was to arrive on the Friday morning, would be there when Kennedy was. As it turned out, Diefenbaker was invited to lunch with Macmillan and Kennedy but not asked to take part in the discussions.

Columnist Jean Campbell commented on the situation: "Now Taylor and Diefenbaker are not close friends, either politically or privately, but Taylor's second man in his octopus Argus Corporation, Wallace McCutcheon, is a minister without portfolio in the coalition Cabinet. Ironically enough, McCutcheon never approved of Taylor's Lyford Cay real estate ventures. He thought Taylor had spent too much money for the land and had invested too much money in its development. Today this Lyford Cay is the scene of the conference, and I suspect the ladder by which E.P. Taylor will clamber into the backrooms of big-time politics. 'He falls on his feet,' is the curt comment of Canadians about the portly Canadian brewer."

Taylor did land on his feet, as did Diefenbaker with his ninth-inning arrival which put him squarely in the middle of the picture. But instead of staying at the Taylor house, which was to have been vacated by Kennedy, he and his wife, Olive, wound up as guests of the governor, Sir Robert Stapledon, at Government House.

From the moment President Kennedy first arrived at the Taylor house, his special presidential flag, dark blue with a huge American eagle, wings extended and encircled by fifty white stars, flew from the flagpole of his Lyford Cay "White House." It was taken down when he departed, but as he was leaving and thanking Winnie and Edward Taylor for their hospitality, he called for the flag and presented it to his delighted hosts as a souvenir of his visit.

Both the treasured flag and autographed pictures of Macmillan and Kennedy are today displayed in prominent places in the Taylor's Lyford Cay residence. They serve to remind the Taylors and their many house guests of that historic summit meeting which took place there long ago.

Taylor, who knew how he was regarded by the Canadian public, was becoming more uncomfortable in the continuing glare of publicity that surrounded him. At the same time, he realized he could do nothing to change it except perhaps to stay away from it as best he could. Retreat to Lyford Cay was part of the answer. In 1963 he went on public record saying, "My main residence now is in the Bahamas. I am seeing out my business commitments in Canada, leading to my retirement."

The determined Taylor had made his decision. His main base would be at Lyford Cay, and from that vantage point, he would maintain his involvement in Argus and the brewing industry in the United Kingdom, his horseracing and horse breeding in the United States and Canada, and any other business throughout the world he might generate.

Late in 1963, Taylor was approached by a group of Lyford Cay Club members. "They came to me and said that they loved the place and were wondering about its permanence. 'Would you consider letting us into the company?' they asked. Their principal interest was in becoming directors." Taylor was amenable so they sat down and worked out an arrangement. Among the participants, all residents of Lyford Cay, were Peter B. Ruffin, who was a financial and realty development man from New York and spokesman for the group; Robert E. Blum, a vice-president of Federated Department Stores; Roy E. Larsen, then chairman of the executive committee of Time, Inc.; George B. Storer, chairman of Storer Broadcasting Company and president of Miami Beach Sun Publishing Company.

A new company was formed called Lyford Cay Investments Limited, which acquired from Taylor the club, golf course, marina, and the remaining residential land in the original 1,000 acres Taylor had set aside for the development of Lyford Cay. Taylor still retained 2,000 adjoining acres which he also planned to develop. Taylor's holding company—he owns nothing personally except some shares in one investment company which owns everything that he has through a maze of subsidiaries—was paid cash, took back a first mortgage in the amount of $8.5 million, and retained 73 per cent of the equity. Taylor remained as president and chief executive officer, with Ruffin as chairman of the board. Taylor has four seats on the eleven-man board of directors. Rather a reasonable deal for all.

Putting his roots even further into Nassau, Taylor became chairman of the board of directors of the Trust Corporation of the Bahamas Limited in 1963, succeeding Arthur Vining Davis who had died. At £4 million, the assets of the trust company were not all that large, but the board members brought with them substantial weight in the international banking circles. The two deputy chairmen were the Right Honourable Lord Rennell, O.B.E., C.B., a director of Morgan, Grenfell and Co. Ltd. of London, and Donald E. Kerlin, president of the Montreal Trust Company. Other directors were John H. Gaffney, the managing director of the Trust Corporation of the Bahamas; the Right Honourable Viscount Astor, listed as a financier of London; Sidney G. Butler, vice-president of Morgan Guaranty Trust Company of New York; Sir Harold G. Christie, realtor, Nassau; John S. Lithiby, retired, of Paris; Arthur F. Mayne, executive vice-president, the Royal Bank of Canada, Montreal; William M. Mitchell, partner in Clifford-Turner and Co., London; Albert E. Mosher, vice-president and general manager, South Eleuthera Properties Limited, Nassau; Sir Francis Peek, deputy chairman, Metropolitan and Provincial Properties Limited of London; and George O.W. Stewart, manager for Europe of the Hong Kong and Shanghai Banking Corporation. All in all, a rather dazzling group to be involved in a financial firm in a country which was destined by the mid-seventies to become a world banking centre.

But Taylor's participation in the Trust Corporation of the Bahamas did not satisfy his interest in encouraging the presence of a strong world-based financial community in the Bahamas. For some time, he had been pressing the Royal Bank of Canada, of which he had been a board member for many years, to become more involved in the Bahamas. Its banking operation there was thriving, and a new Royal Bank of Canada building had been opened at Nassau in March of 1965. But Taylor wanted the bank to establish a facility to make mortgage and development loans not only in the Bahamas, but throughout the British Caribbean Territories. He succeeded. At the end of August, the formation of Roy-West Banking Corporation Limited was announced. It would be a $30 million lending organization, headquartered in Nassau. Its major participants were the Royal Bank of Canada, the Westminster Bank of London, the Montreal Trust Company, Morgan, Grenfell and Co. Limited of London, Power Corporation of Canada, the Hong Kong and Shanghai Banking Corporation of New York, all familiar names in the Bahamas. The chairman of the new corporation was none other than E.P. Taylor.

For several years Taylor had also been thinking about a brewery for the Bahamas. All beer was imported but he believed the market was big enough to support a brewery. He decided to build one. Plans were laid for the construction of a £1 million brewery on a fifty-acre site which was acquired in Oakes Field under the name of Gold Star (Bahamas) Brewery. It was scheduled to open in the spring of 1964. Typically, Taylor the optimist was enthusiastic as the new brewery started to emerge from the ground. "The plant will be first class and I'm sure that the product will be first class, too." As events were later to prove, his assessment of the plant and the product was correct, but his judgement of the market was not.

In 1964, E.P. Taylor was awarded the Constitution Day Medal by Chief Minister Sir Roland Symonette in appreciation of services rendered to the colony in which the Taylors had been granted status of "belongers," then the closest thing one could get to citizenship. The Gold Star Brewery opened for business with appropriate ceremony.

Off in Freeport, it was announced that Taylor's good friend, Daniel K. Ludwig, the international financier who today is reputedly the richest man in the United States, and with whom Taylor was later to do business, was about to develop the first phase of a $100 million living, shopping, and leisure-time community. The first part of this new development would be open in January of 1965. As was Taylor's, Ludwig's golf course was designed by Dick Wilson, the famed U.S. golf course architect. E.P. Taylor, the Bahamian pioneer, had the satisfaction of knowing that financiers of the calibre of Ludwig were now following his lead.

Leadership has been one of Edward Plunket Taylor's greatest strengths and is one of his essential characteristics. He has used that quality throughout his life not only to his own advantage but also to the benefit of those who have followed him.

Chapter XVI

"Retirement"
1966

The news release was terse and to the point. It was dated Wednesday, January 26, 1966. "E.P. Taylor announced today that, as he will be sixty-five this week, he has resigned as chairman of the board of Canadian Breweries Limited and of Domtar Limited. Major General A.B. Matthews, who has been vice-chairman of Canadian Breweries Limited, has succeeded him as chairman of the board of that company. Mr. T.N. Beaupré has succeeded him as chairman of the board of Domtar Limited."

This was big news in the corporate world and warranted a press conference at which Taylor said, "All my business life I have said that anyone who is prominent in competitive industry in a large public company should never continue to serve as one of its principal officers after he reaches the age of sixty-five. Whenever I have departed from that principle with people in the employ of public companies, I have found that on balance it is a very bad practice. People change and lose some of their energy. It rather discourages those down the line."

Prior to the news conference there had been much speculation that E.P. Taylor would resign as president of Argus Corporation and assume its chairmanship, which had been vacant since the death in December 1964 of Colonel Phillips, but that move was not in the cards. Neither did he have any intention of giving up his directorates and other executive positions.

At a press conference, Taylor said, "I am one of the largest shareholders of Argus and when I feel I'm not performing properly, I'll retire. But I'm in very good health for a man of my age." And as he fielded questions in the splendour of the Argus Corporation's offices at 10 Toronto Street, Taylor indeed looked fit and tanned, even though he had recently undergone minor surgery.

Speculation was rife about who would eventually succeed Taylor as the head of the powerful Argus Corporation, which in its 1965 report showed assets totalling $208 million, with an effective control of close to $2 billion in corporate assets in a broad range of industry. A top Argus director, J.S.D. Tory, Q.C., had died shortly after Colonel Phillips, but still in the picture of speculation were Maxwell Meighen* and John A. McDougald, the man who had been Taylor's partner in Taylor, McDougald & Company since 1945 and in Argus for almost a decade as a director and vice-president.

But they would all have to wait. The headline of a *New York Times'* story on Taylor's birthday announcement read, "He doesn't really own Canada. Chief of Argus, 65, changes posts but keeps domain." While he didn't own the country, he was still very much the king of industry and commerce in Canada, and he was not ready to give up the helm of Argus nor was he prepared to give up his directorates in the firms in the Argus stable. Taylor's move out of the chairmanship of the company he had founded, Canadian Breweries, and also Domtar, did, however, underscore his intent to devote more time to his expanding Bahamas interests, the world of racehorses, the pursuit of new entrepreneurial ideas, and the achievement of some objectives he had set for himself, the main one being the expansion of Charrington United.

By mid-January 1967, Edward and Winnie Taylor were back in England at Birch Hall. There was Massey-Ferguson business to be attended to as well as the continuing attempts to reach the main objective for Charrington United. When he had moved into the United Kingdom brewery scene in 1959, bringing together Hope & Anchor, Hammonds United, and John Jeffery and Company, the goal Taylor shared with Arthur Elliott and Philip Bradfer-Lawrence was to create a major national brewery group. That objective had still not been reached, even though in the eight-year period since that first merger, Taylor and his British colleagues had indeed put together a significant brewery group, Charrington

---

*M.C.G. Meighen, a member of the Argus executive committee and president of two investment firms which had acquired 11.8 per cent of Argus voting shares and 12.6 per cent of its non-voting shares.

United. As chairman of the firm,* he worked closely with Philip Bradfer-Lawrence and Derek Palmar of the Philip Hill firm, both of whom were almost totally dedicated to the acquisition of other breweries. The pace of their activity during 1966 was hectic. Contacts were made with some eighteen firms but only one merger was carried off, that of Massey's Burnley.

The expansion committee membership also included Denis Ledward, the managing director of Charrington United, its chairman, John Charrington, and another valued person who had been in at the beginning, Arthur Elliott. All were in accord that the ultimate objective was a merger with one of the three large brewing firms in the country, namely Allied, Bass Mitchell and Butler's, or Watney's.

There had been some possibility of a merger with Allied, but as 1967 opened it was apparent that it would not come off. The decision was therefore made to concentrate on Bass Mitchell and Butler's. The groundwork had been laid in the early 1960s, first through discussions with the then chairman, Sir James Grigg, and the managing director, Alan Walker. Taylor always enjoyed the talks with Sir James, a tough, haughty, opinionated man who had been Secretary of War in the Churchill government when Taylor had first met him. Of him, Churchill once said, "If only Grigg would treat me as an equal, I wouldn't mind."

When Sir James died in 1964, Alan Walker became chairman and friendly contact was maintained with him, principally by

---

*Taylor's relationship with Charrington United was, to say the least, unusual. He received no remuneration for his services. He had no day-to-day administrative duties and was not normally required to attend the company's offices or routine board meetings. His special assignment was the expansion and development of the firm and, in particular, the negotiations with other brewing companies.

By formal resolution, the board of Charrington United recognized that since he did not reside in the United Kingdom, his duties were to be performed from his residence abroad, so far as that was possible. If and to the extent it was necessary for him to go to the United Kingdom to carry out his special assignment, he would be regarded as travelling on the business of the company, which would bear all expenses.

Whether he received a salary or not was of no concern to E.P. Taylor in his pursuit of a merger with one of the big three, and with it the creation of the biggest brewing firm in the United Kingdom, a feat comparable to what he had achieved in Canada in the 1930s. Taylor, however, was pursued by the tax authorities in the U.K. who claimed that the money paid to him for his travelling expenses was income. The matter was resolved some ten years later by a majority decision in the House of Lords. It was in Taylor's favour.

Arthur Elliott and Taylor. At a mid-May meeting of the expansion committee, an analysis was made of all the factors that would be involved in a Bass merger. There would be many advantages, not the least of which was that Bass had large borrowing power and attractive liquidity, whereas Charrington United was now extremely limited because it had borrowed so heavily in order to expand. Each brewery had markets that would be advantageous to the other. In preparation for the expansion committee meeting, Taylor sat down and wrote out on a sheet of his usual lined foolscap seven good reasons why there should be a merger. At the bottom of the list he wrote, "It is our last chance to become a truly national company." The committee agreed with Taylor and the decision was made to concentrate on the Bass situation. Mind you, it would not be done overnight. One had to proceed slowly and in gentlemanly British fashion about this sort of thing.

On May 19, 1967, E.P. Taylor, now back at Windfields, wrote to Alan Walker, saying, "Before leaving London this week, I had a most serious conversation regarding the future of C.U.B. with my senior colleagues, in the course of which I made certain strong recommendations. The purpose of this note is to say to you that I would like to meet you shortly after I return to England, which will be early in July, for a serious discussion relative to our mutual interests." Walker's response was that he would look forward to such a meeting. At the end of June, Taylor wrote to Walker advising that he would be arriving in London on July 7. Just before Taylor left Windfields for London, he received a call from Walker suggesting that they might meet on Sunday afternoon at Walker's house in the centre of London. Taylor agreed, realizing from that telephone call that Walker had done his homework and was ready to negotiate.

At the appointed hour, Taylor appeared at Alan Walker's home. With lunch out of the way, there was no opportunity to talk business because an unexpected family visitor had appeared, so the two men went out for a stroll around St. James' Park. By the time they had circled the park twice, the merger had been agreed upon in principle and with it most of the basic details, all subject, of course, to the approval of their respective boards. The next step would be to get their merchant bankers together, give them instructions, and let them work out the refinements. Alan Walker and Edward Taylor were two happy men when they shook hands on their deal in the bright sunlight of that July day in London.

Working at top speed in the utmost of secrecy, Walker, Taylor, and the top people in their two firms laboured hard to come up with an agreement, which was signed on July 20, 1967. It was a merger of truly complementary groups which brought together two companies on equal terms. At a press conference shortly after the stock market closed at mid-afternoon that day, John Charrington, Edward Taylor, and Alan Walker faced the shocked press and the secret bombshell was out. The new £200 million group was to be called Bass Charrington. It would be the biggest brewing company in Britain with 11,272 outlets compared with Allied Brewers' 10,220. It would have about 19 per cent of the United Kingdom market, with combined overseas sales of Bass brands and those of Charrington.

It was expected that there would be a big increase in sales of Jubilee Stout and Carling Lager. After all, it was Carling's Black Label beer that had brought E.P. Taylor to Great Britain in the first place, and it was this man, who, through his optimistic persistence, had been the main architect in building the biggest brewing group in the United Kingdom. Within the first two years of the merger, Bass Charrington closed six breweries, nine bottling stores, twenty depots, and a distillery. (Shades of the 1930s and C.B.L.)

For Edward Taylor it was another achievement of a lifetime. Now that it had been accomplished, done on behalf of the shareholders of Canadian Breweries Limited, whose interests he represented in the United Kingdom, he would begin to phase himself out so that he could further his "retirement" in the Bahamas. In September, Alan Walker agreed to Taylor's request that an alternate to Taylor be placed on the new board, "because I reside overseas." The man who succeeded him as chairman of the board of Canadian Breweries Limited, Major General A. Bruce Matthews, an Argus colleague, would be that alternate.

Taylor's association with Canadian Breweries ended in 1968 with the sale of the Argus-held shares of C.B.L. to Rothmans of Pall Mall, Canada Limited. By 1970, the new rulers of Canadian Breweries needed cash. The money tied up in the C.B.L. 5 per cent holding in Bass Charrington could be put to far better use in North America, so C.B.L. sold its shares. The same applied to C.B.L.'s 46 per cent interest in Hare Place. Alan Walker, chairman of Bass Charrington, was amenable to the suggestion that Hare Place be liquidated. From its original investment of £14 million in Hare Place, Canadian Breweries received £15.5 million on the winding up.

Even with this final Canadian Breweries severance of its U.K. connection, Alan Walker and his U.K. colleagues recognized the enormous contribution Eddie Taylor had made to their corporate existence. They looked upon him as a person quite separate from and above the company whose interests he had originally represented in the United Kingdom. Would he please remain on their board of directors? He would be delighted to stay for the time being.

His U.K. involvement and commitments had diminished to such an extent that Taylor decided the time had come to sell Birch Hall, the comfortable Georgian manor in Surrey. The Taylors had spent many delightful years in their English home-away-from-home. There was no trouble finding a buyer; their old friend, a former City of London banker, Henry Tiarks, stood ready. After thirteen years of unabashedly coveting Birch Hall, Tiarks and his wife, Joan, parents of the Marchioness of Tavistock, were fortuitously selling their own home in Jersey, and at the same time looking for a home in England. The price was quickly agreed to. The Tiarks fulfilled their long-standing wish and the Taylors severed the last of their direct ties to England.

On Wednesday, April 26, 1972, twenty gentlemen gathered at 7 Grosvenor Gardens in London, England, for a dinner to honour Mr. E.P. Taylor, C.M.G., who was retiring as a director of Bass Charrington. It was a happy, yet difficult, leave-taking from the people with whom he had worked in putting together this, the largest brewing organization in the United Kingdom. Among others, Bradfer-Lawrence was there with Arthur Elliott, D.R. Ledward, Derek Palmar, and Lord Fraser of Lonsdale. The guests, led by Eddie Taylor's good friend, Alan Walker (later Sir Alan) presented Taylor with an illuminated scroll. After all the cigars were smoked, the cognac sipped, the speeches made, and the farewells said, Eddie Taylor was no longer part of Bass Charrington.

The ease with which Taylor sold his United Kingdom real estate holdings contrasted with the difficulties he had experienced as one of Canada's largest land developers. Canadian Equity's Erin Mills

298

development had become entangled in provincial red tape and was not able to get under way. Taylor finally asked for a meeting with Ontario Premier John Robarts to plead for the basic governmental land use approvals which would allow the 6,000 acre development to get started. Erin Mills was planned to hold 85,000 people. The demand for housing was enormous, and Taylor just simply could not understand why the provincial government was standing in the way of this urgently needed development. Robarts, always sympathetic and understanding, listened to Taylor and Angus McClaskey, but was non-committal.

Frustrated to the point of exasperation, Taylor was receptive when he was approached by Cemp Investments Limited, a Bronfman Corporation, and by Eph Diamond, the bright, sure-footed head of the highly successful Toronto-based Cadillac Development Corporation Limited. They wanted to buy and Taylor wanted to sell. Furthermore, the price was right, $26.4 million for all the assets of Canadian Equity and Development Company. The deal was completed in March 1968. It was a Taylor transaction, Argus and Canadian Breweries having sold out to him the year before.

The next 1968 move was the sale of Windfields Farm's Toronto land. Municipal roads, sewer, water, and other services had long since been built past the boundaries of the property and the Borough of North York had designated the land for residential purposes, mostly single family houses. Much of the area surrounding the farm had been developed and the pressure from eager buyers was mounting. Taylor was most reluctant to give up Windfields Farm, recognized as one of the top racehorse breeding facilities in the world. But he had the National Stud Farm in Oshawa, and his Maryland operation was expanding and successful. It was time to sell and Taylor was in the selling mood. He let it be known that 330 Windfields acres would be sold. For the time being, he would retain sixty acres, which included the Taylor home on Bayview Avenue. There were twelve bidders, the top one being Morenish Land Developments Limited, a United Kingdom-financed firm, which paid $13.7 million. Taylor would have four years in which to phase out his breeding operation on the land, then possession would go to the buyer. Today, the rolling, open farmlands where Northern Dancer, Flaming Page, and other famed Taylor horses roamed, are filled with expensive houses, and the magnificent stables that housed them are gone. The Windfields Farm horse breeding operations, tops in the thoroughbred world today, were gradually transferred to the National Stud Farm, which Taylor renamed Windfields Farm when the sale to Morenish was completed.

In the fall of 1968, the Taylors made a gift to the Borough of North York worth approximately $4 million. Thirty acres of the balance of the Windfields land, including a ravine along the Wilket Creek which runs through the property, was donated as a park. The twenty acre parcel on which the Taylor home and its gatehouse building sat were also given to North York, with the proviso that Winnie and Edward Taylor would have the right of exclusive possession during their lifetimes and they would pay real estate taxes.* The Taylor's gift to the borough was well received. When the news was announced by the mayor of North York, James Service, Lotta Dempsey of the *Star* talked with E.P. Taylor. " 'I hope this doesn't mean we are going to lose you altogether, Mr. Taylor,' I asked. He smiled, and everybody's picture of the man whose name has become synonymous to Canadians everywhere with power and money flashed into view again, 'There is still a racetrack around here, you know,' was his response." Canada was indeed losing E.P. Taylor, but not "altogether."

For the legion of Taylor watchers, the next 1968 sale was an eyebrow lifter. The crown jewel among the commodity-producing firms Taylor had founded, Canadian Breweries Limited, was the keystone to all his corporate, industrial, entrepreneurial accomplishments, and his fortune. And yet Taylor and his Argus partners sold their 11 per cent interest in the firm to Rothmans of Pall Mall, Canada Limited. Taylor had not been monitoring the affairs of Canadian Breweries nearly as closely as he had in earlier years. The firm's profits, which had gone from a high of $17 million in 1963 to a low of $9 million for the year ending January 31, 1967, had been edging back up to $11 million for the last fiscal year.

The beginning of the deal with Rothmans was a chance meeting between the Canadian president of the cigarette company, John

---

*The original right was exclusive possession during the lifetime of the Taylors' children, but this was subsequently changed. Ten acres out of the original sixty had been sold off to the Board of Education.

Devlin, and E.P. Taylor in 1967.* The South African-controlled firm had arrived in the Canadian cigarette and tobacco market in 1957, and wakened up the sleeping giants, McDonalds and Imperial Tobacco, by quickly grabbing a large hunk of their market. Devlin and his South African principals wanted to expand their Canadian operation and were looking around for an opportunity to make a major acquisition and at the same time diversify.

Devlin's opening discussion with E.P. Taylor at their chance meeting had been encouraging. The Argus holdings in Canadian Breweries might be for sale. Rothmans followed up with an offer and the price was right. It was $12 a share, which put $28.8 million into the Argus till, a handsome price for the shares which had originally gone into the Argus portfolio at a fraction of that value. For Taylor the only disappointing part of the Rothmans deal was that the purchaser was later unable to carry out its unwritten commitment to make a $12 offer, half cash, half in shares, to the multitude of other shareholders in the company. Those who expected Taylor to be upset by the sale of his brainchild were astonished that he was not. He knew it was time to sell. "I'm a realist, not a sentimentalist."

To those who were not only Taylor-watchers but Argus-watchers as well, the sale of the Canadian Breweries stock meant that none of the Argus holdings were sacred in the future. Since the death of Phillips and the departure of McCutcheon, Argus' founder and president, E.P. Taylor the expansionist had not been able to maintain the interest of the Argus board of directors in doing what he considered to be absolutely essential—expanding and growing. In his opinion, the Argus board had become conservative, far too conservative for his liking. With the C.B.L. holdings disposed of by Argus, Taylor began to consider the possibility of giving up his interest in the other keystone corporation he had founded, Argus Corporation itself.

However, a decision to leave Argus did not have to be made immediately. He was still its president and involved in the affairs of the boards of the companies in which it had significant holdings, one of which was British Columbia Forest Products, another successful firm Taylor had founded. While T.N. Beaupré, for whom

*According to the *Globe and Mail*, June 7, 1968.

E.P. Taylor had the highest regard, had taken Taylor's place as chairman of the board of B.C.F.P., Taylor had nevertheless stayed on the board of directors of the massive pulp and paper company. The firm was doing very well with net earnings of over $8 million during 1968, and increasing. From the Argus point of view, which was Taylor's interest, B.C.F.P. was paying a good return on its investment.

But the status quo was about to change behind Taylor's unsuspecting back. In a 1955 agreement Taylor negotiated with the Scott Paper Company, the American firm had bought one million shares of B.C.F.P. at $15 a share, thereby holding a 29 per cent interest in B.C.F.P. At the same time Scott agreed to buy a minimum tonnage of pulp at the new Crofton mill which was to be built. However, in 1960, Scott needed some financing for its part in the ownership of the Brunswick Pulp and Paper Company Limited, which was located in the State of Maine. In order to raise its share, Scott sold one-half of its one-million-share holding in B.C.F.P. The buyer was its Brunswick partner, the Mead Corporation.

Taylor and his Argus partners had no objection to the sale, which included two of Scott's seats on the B.C.F.P. board of directors. However, there was a proviso to Argus' approval. It would have to be a condition that none of the three companies would make a major move with their holdings–sell or trade any of its B.C.F.P. shares to a third party–without giving prior notice and a first right of refusal to the others. This covenant was part of the original agreement between Argus and Scott in their 1955 deal and Mead was bound by it. It would last until 1965. However, when the tenth anniversary of the Scott/Argus deal went by, there was no continuing covenant agreed to which would bind either Scott, Mead, or Argus.

Noranda Mines Limited then came onstage in a 1969 transaction that offended Taylor's sense of honour.

Noranda had purchased a British Columbia pulp and paper firm, Northwood Pulp Limited, which was almost bankrupt. B.C.F.P. had been interested in buying it, but it was refused permission by the provincial government. The purchasers of Northwood were Noranda and the Mead Corporation, as equal partners. By this time the cross agreement covenant between B.C.F.P., Mead, and Scott had expired. Mead, a B.C.F.P. insider, and Noranda, its 50 per cent Northwood partner, decided that now they were into the forest products business, they had better go into it in a big way. They would attempt to take over control of British Columbia Forest Products. And they would do it without informing either Argus or Scott. However, by law, each of the insiders could acquire no more than 10 per cent, at which point they had to make a public disclosure. A major final acquisition of a Sun Life block took them into the region of compulsory disclosure.

When Taylor heard the news of the Mead/Noranda takeover, he was angry. Why? Mead was an insider, a partner in B.C.F.P., and even though the written agreement that none of the partners would sell its shares without informing the others had expired, so far as Taylor was concerned such agreement never had to be in writing in the first place. It just existed on a continuing basis between gentlemen. Instead of honouring its obligations, the Mead Corporation had gone behind his back, surreptitiously taking advantage of its insider position to acquire control of a company which he, Taylor, had personally put together. This was a terrible slight, an insult, and completely contrary to the high ethical standards to which E.P. Taylor adhered. On his instructions, the Argus connection with the board of directors was immediately severed. He and Beaupré, the chairman of B.C.F.P., and the other Argus nominees forthwith resigned, much to the astonishment of the perplexed Mead and Noranda people. What they could not understand was that E.P. Taylor's sense of good business morality could not tolerate an insider group moving to take over a company without informing the other principals. There was nothing wrong with it from a legal point of view, but morally and ethically such action was totally opposite to Taylor's beliefs.

Attempting to make amends, Noranda quickly moved to make an offer to Taylor whereby, with Mead's approval, Noranda would purchase from Argus 80 per cent of its holdings in B.C.F.P., namely 400,000 shares at a premium price of $22.50 per share, plus a half share in Noranda. The total would have been equivalent to $40 a share, triple what Scott Paper had paid for its shares ten years before. This offer, if accepted, would have seen Argus sell the bulk of its B.C.F.P. shares at a substantial profit.

When he becomes determined, E.P. Taylor has a set of his mouth and jaw reminiscent of the Churchillian bull-dog look. And Taylor was determined to the point of stubbornness that he would not do business with the Mead/Noranda group. Argus simply would not sell. For the partners so anxious to gain control of B.C.F.P., their first-year results must have caused them to wonder whether their covert takeover actions, which so offended Taylor, were really worth it as the B.C.F.P.'s 1969 net earnings of almost $9.4 million tumbled to less than $1.4 million.

At the same time the Mead/Noranda takeover of B.C.F.P. affair was going on, Taylor was continuing to cut back on his personal commitments, not only in business matters but in community involvements.

In keeping with his "retirement" decision, he resigned from the board of governors of McGill University, explaining that, since he had permanently settled in the Bahamas, and made infrequent visits to Montreal, he had been able to give only poor attention to the board's affairs in the last three or four years. From 1948 through 1950, he organized and was the chairman of the Alma Mater Fund and had spent at least the equivalent of six working months in a row selling his idea of the fund from coast to coast, using Canadian Breweries' aircraft. Then, as chairman of the McGill Fund Council, he headed a successful five-year fund-raising campaign beginning in 1964. Although he resigned from the board in 1969, his McGill connection would continue, but in a different way.

As the result of his sympathetic interest in a child who was suffering from a learning disability, Taylor came in contact with a McGill psychologist, Dr. Sam Rabinovitch, who was undertaking research in this underexplored field. Taylor talked with Rabinovitch about what could be done for children suffering from this impediment to learning and became keenly interested in the humane potential of the doctor's experimental work. From the old school, Taylor had been of the simple opinion that children could either learn or they couldn't, but his discussion with Dr. Rabinovitch soon convinced him that help could be given to young children impeded in this way. Rabinovitch, however, had been hampered in his research on the specialized subject by a lack of funds to train teachers to deal with children with learning disabilities. In Rabinovitch's approach, those teachers would be taught and then put back into the school system to deal with these exceptional, unfortunate children.

Taylor was convinced that something had to be done to facilitate

Rabinovitch's continued work. He would fund an institute to do the research and to carry out the program Rabinovitch had described to him. After all, he had been the financial backbone of the establishment of a chair of Canadian Studies at Harvard.* The creation of a learning centre at McGill, which would help generations of children to come, was a cause he could embrace more easily than he could the objectives of the Harvard chair. After negotiations with Dr. Rabinovitch and the appropriate McGill administrators, the McGill University Learning Centre was established, funded by the E.P. Taylor Foundation Inc., which to the end of 1975 had contributed well over a million dollars to this new and much needed institute.

---

*Taylor participated with David Rockefeller in the creation of this chair in 1965. Rockefeller was concerned about the lack of understanding in the United States about Canada, its people, historic background and relevance to the United States.

In 1977 Taylor was recognized by McGill University with an Honorary Doctor of Laws.

Chapter XVII

Two Continuing Interests

With his retirement in 1966, Edward Plunket Taylor hoped to limit his life to a two-dimension scale of activity: his Bahamian interests and the breeding and racing of thoroughbred horses.

When the Windfields Farm lands were sold in 1968, Taylor began to move that operation in stages to the National Stud Farm, which he then renamed Windfields Farm, and also to Maryland where Northern Dancer would be sent. The Dancer went there the following year to stand at stud and attracted some of the best mares in North America. Taylor was reluctant to take him out of Canada, but in Maryland he could be more readily available for service.

The Maryland operation of Windfields Farm was expanding. Some 320 acres were added in 1968 and the Maryland Stallion Station was purchased complete with land, staff houses, and barns. On the original land Taylor had acquired for the operation, two frame barns for a training centre for brood mares were completed. They were put up to house the mares while the more durable brick and mortar stables were being built. Tragically, however, the mares were brought down from Oshawa only to be destroyed on the evening of their arrival in a fire that swept through the new buildings. Those were the last wooden barns built by Eddie Taylor.

In the fall of 1968, Taylor sold his yearlings not at Windfields Farm, as he had in the recent years, but through the annual Canadian Thoroughbred Horse Society Sale. At the 1966 pre-priced sale of yearlings, only ten out of his offering of sixty-two had been purchased. It had been clear then to Eddie Taylor that his sales pattern had to change. There was great concern expressed by many of the breeders that the entry of Taylor horses in the Canadian Thoroughbred Horse Society Sale would swamp the market and Taylor would monopolize the event. But George Frostad, the president of the Horse Society, a shrewd businessman, a land developer, and successful horse breeder, thought that the Taylor horses would elevate the sale from its parochial position to an event of international stature. Frostad was right. It was to this sale that Charles Englehard, the ultra-rich American mining industrialist, sent the reputable Irish trainer, Vincent O'Brien, who was to inspect a colt sired by the great French stallion, Ribot. O'Brien rejected the Ribot offspring, but was taken by the big, superbly built colt he discovered was by Northern Dancer out of Flaming Page. O'Brien's advice to Englehard was to buy this yearling and not the Ribot colt. Englehard, then in Sarasota, could not get up for the sale himself, but instructed one of his Canadian executives, George Scott, to go to the event and bid for this choice yearling. Scott did so and bought the bay colt for $84,000.

Following the terpsichorean hint in the name of the young horse's sire, Englehard was to call him after the man who up to that time had been the world's best ballet dancer, Nijinsky.*

Immediately after acquiring Nijinsky from Taylor in 1968, Englehard had the young horse shipped over to Ireland to the man who had found him, the great trainer, Vincent O'Brien, to be trained at his Ballydoyle Stables. As a two-year-old, Nijinsky ran in five races, winning four in Ireland and the fifth in England. Nijinsky had established quite a reputation for himself, and expectations were high as the 1970 season opened. On the advice of O'Brien, Englehard's target for the year was the English Triple Crown, the first race of which was the Two Thousand Guineas, which Nijinsky won easily with England's top jockey, the tall, five-foot-seven Lester Piggott in the saddle.

Then it was on to Epsom for the Derby where, against a field of eleven horses, Nijinsky came from behind to take the second race of the Triple Crown. There was great excitement among the British racing fans since it was widely believed that this magnificent horse might now go on to take all three of the classic races. Eddie Taylor,

---

*The name of the horse was later expanded to Nijinsky II to avoid record book confusion with another horse which had carried the same name.

whose infinite patience, breeding skill, and judgement had produced the splendid horse, was as much concerned with Nijinsky's
well-being and future as was its owner, Englehard. Taylor followed his training carefully and attended every one of these
important races. After the Derby win, Taylor was pleased and
proud as Englehard and he were invited to the royal box to receive
the accolades of the Queen, Prince Philip, the Queen Mother, and
Princess Anne.

At Ascot on July 25, in the King George VI and Queen Elizabeth stakes, Nijinsky again won against a high-calibre field of
horses–with considerable ease.

There was a great controversy when Charles Englehard
announced in mid-August that Nijinsky had been syndicated. The
news was taken as an indication that the owner was not going to
enter the horse in the third race of the English Triple Crown, the
St. Leger. However, Englehard did put him into the St. Leger,
again with Piggott in the saddle. Nijinsky won it, again with no
difficulty. The much-vaunted Triple Crown was his and with it the
fame and glory accorded to the few super horses in racing annals.

The syndication of Nijinsky was at $5.4 million, making him the
most expensive stallion in the history of horseracing. Eddie Taylor
bought two shares, which cost him $340,000. Englehard had paid
him $84,000 for the horse in 1968. Taylor would make a similar
but far more costly transaction in 1977 for a horse he had bred and
sold called The Minstrel.

Nijinsky was to run two more races, both of which were losses
and, in the opinion of many, need not have been run at all. The
first was the classic, Prix de l'Arc de Triomphe, where he was
beaten out at the Championship Stakes at the Newmarket Course
in England, finishing second by a neck.

Within a few days after the syndication of Nijinsky, Taylor
decided it was an opportune moment to syndicate Nijinsky's sire,
Northern Dancer, which he did for a price of $2.4 million–a
remarkable amount for a horse already nine years old. He is still at
Maryland and earning over $1 million a year in stud fees for his
shareholders. It is reliably reported that Northern Dancer is a
happy horse.

The 1970 Canadian Horse of the Year award went to a Taylor-
bred filly, Franfreluche, a three-year-old by Northern Dancer. She
was also selected as the champion three-year-old filly in North

America by the Thoroughbred Racing Association, the first for a Canadian-bred horse. After twenty-five years of breeding thoroughbreds, E.P. Taylor had achieved the pinnacle.

In 1970, Windfields Farm-bred horses earned $1,720,535, making Taylor the world leader in thoroughbred breeding; horses sired by his magnificent stallion, Northern Dancer, won $1,506,030, making him the world's leading sire; and Northern Dancer's son, Nijinsky II, won $629,077, to top the list of the world's best racers. Never before had a breeder had such international success. With its own sire line established, Windfields Farm had also achieved a world-record syndication value of $8,890,000. Founder of the dynasty was Nearctic who had been syndicated for $1 million in 1967.

Taylor didn't enter a horse in the Queen's Plate in 1970. His domination of the event as owner or breeder or both, and the controversies over his participation in the royal race, had dulled his appetite. At the end of the first week in June 1971, Taylor issued a brief announcement to the Canadian news media. "For the second successive year, Windfields Farm will not have a starter in the Queen's Plate." The turquoise and gold polka dot silks would be seen in many other races, but not in Canada's premier classic.

Taylor was concentrating more and more on breeding and letting his buyers do the racing. As the world's leading horse breeder, he had produced a staggering record: in Canada, ten Horses of the Year, fourteen Queen's Plate winners, and 112 stakes winners. He had seven trainers employed in Canada, six in the United States, and one each in Ireland and France, looking after more than fifty horses of all ages. In 1971, he had eighty-two yearlings to sell, scores of brood mares, eleven stallions, and shares in twenty-six syndicated stallions. His highly successful Windfields Farm trainer, Pete McCann, went into semi-retirement in 1971, at which time Taylor re-organized his Canadian racing division, as he had done in the States the year before by utilizing the services of several public trainers rather than maintaining a private stable.

Out on the American west coast that year to address the California Thoroughbred Breeders Association, Taylor offered "one man's opinion" on racetracks, their physical characteristics, and the manner in which they are operated. He was concerned because the economics of the breeding industry are so dependent on the economics of the racing industry. Among other things, he proposed that racetracks should schedule the featured race of a card as the last race of the day.* He also discussed the desirability of having a forty-eight-hour closing rule for entries in a race. Later he was to be both delighted and astonished that somebody out there was paying attention. He had given his address on February 28. On March 21, the Golden Gate Fields Racetrack did exactly as he had suggested for the first time, putting the featured $25,000 Berkley Handicap as the ninth race, the last position on the program, a step that kept the fans at the track and a practice which was to spread in California. Furthermore, the California horseracing board requested all tracks in the state to institute forty-eight-hour entries.

In Canada Taylor launched a campaign to get the federal government to enact amendments to the Criminal Code of Canada that would permit legal outlets for off-track betting. More than a campaign, it turned into a personal crusade which is still going on.

In Taylor's opinion, legalized control of off-track betting would bring in "millions of dollars which are currently being wagered on horseracing through illegal bookmakers, to the benefit of organized crime and at the expense of our industry and of the government. There is no doubt in my mind that off-track betting, if implemented in a proper manner, would benefit all segments of the industry–owners, breeders, and racetracks, large and small." The Ontario Jockey Club had prepared its own projections of the volume of off-track betting in Ontario–$330 million annually, by the fifth year of operation. Assuming an equitable basis for revenue distribution, this would permit a doubling of purses from current levels.

Taylor recognized that conditions would have to be placed on off-track betting. First, it would have to be operated through a non-profit corporation comprising representatives of the provincial government and of the various segments of the horseracing industry, including racetracks, owners, and breeders. To have it in the hands of one group only, namely the government, would be disastrous. Second, industry should not support off-track betting without assurances that the proceeds would be distributed on an equitable basis between the industry and the government. "Because of legal interpretations given to certain sections of the Criminal Code, we have been living with a form of off-track bet-

*Taylor says this was a mistake. It should have been the second or third race.

ting for several years, during which the Government of Ontario and the racing industry have lost millions of dollars of revenue. In addition to such losses in revenue, the costs, financial and otherwise, to law enforcement agencies and the judicial system have been considerable."

Taylor and his racing colleagues won half the battle. On July 7, 1971, the premier of Ontario, the Honourable William Davis, issued a public policy statement in which he said that the Attorney General of Ontario had written to the Minister of Justice of Canada stating that Ontario would favour an amendment to the Criminal Code allowing any province, if it so desired, to implement off-track betting. He also announced the establishment of a task force to study all aspects of off-track betting and advise the government as to systems, methods, and procedures.*

It was the tight economic pressure, inability to pay adequate purses, and a reasonable return on investment to its shareholders that caused the Jockey Club Limited to become a non-profit organization, a step which was taken at the end of 1971. At a meeting of the Jockey Club at the Royal York Hotel in Toronto, shareholders voted overwhelmingly to approve a re-organization of the horseracing operations into a non-profit set up without share capital. Taylor told the meeting, "Return to common shareholders and the growth in the market value of the shares have both been totally inadequate. The move to a non-profit organization was primarily made to upgrade racing and provide for some tax relief." Through their companies, Taylor and his family owned two million common shares, about a third of those outstanding. In the re-organization, each shareholder received a $6 debenture bearing interest at 10 per cent annually.

The new organization would be known as The Ontario Jockey Club, administered by a board of trustees. Taylor, the eternal optimist, said that the Jockey Club would become a natural partner with the government when a suitable system of off-track betting was implemented.

In 1973 E.P. Taylor once again played host to the Queen and

---

*In 1971 the Ontario task force on off-track betting received its report from Woods, Gordon and Co., re-evaluating the economic position of the industry in the province. The study concluded that the owners and breeders of horses continued to incur large net losses estimated to total some $19.8 million in 1970. There had to be a solution to that economic squeeze.

Prince Philip at the running of the Queen's Plate, the pillar of Canadian racing and the oldest continuously run race for thoroughbreds on the North American continent. In the special Queen's Plate commemorative issue of the *Daily Racing Form*, Joe Hirsch, who had written countless pieces on Taylor and his horses, capped them all with an excellent full-page article captioned, "E.P. Taylor Has Done It All–Moulded Canadian Sport." Hirsch put the description of the 1973 status of Taylor's breeding operation this way:

> Taylor now owns 153 brood mares, 9 stallions outright, and has shares in 33 other stallions. He is raising 75 foals a year in Canada, another 30 at two farms in Maryland. He has more than 100 employees at Oshawa, at a 1,000 acre farm in Chesapeake City, Md., and at an adjacent 500-acre farm in the Chesapeake City area where his U.S. stallions are based. Overseeing his vast racing and breeding operations since 1956 is Joe Thomas.
>
> Taylor, who raises more horses than he can possibly incorporate into his stable, has been selling a portion of his homebreds since 1954, when eight head brought $51,500. Last year, he sold 75 head for $1,500,000. Many of the finest Canadianbreds of the past 20 years were bred by Taylor but campaigned for other interests.

Later that year, Hirsch was able to report, "Windfields Farm owner, E.P. Taylor, was busy buying and selling yearlings this summer when he achieved yet another milestone, that of becoming the world's leading, living breeder of stakes winners. Between purchasing five yearlings for $547,000 at Keeneland and selling thirteen for $987,000 at Saratoga (where he also bought three head for $325,000) Taylor broke a tie with C.V. Whitney at 156 each." Taylor's total of stakes winners at that moment was 160. The all time mark of 192 belonged to Harry Payne Whitney. It would only be a matter of time before E.P. Taylor, operating Windfields Farm at both Oshawa and Maryland, would overtake Whitney.

The Taylors' new white brick Georgian mansion had just been completed at the Maryland Windfields Farm. It was reminiscent of Birch Hall, the home in England they had enjoyed so much but had recently given up. From his bedroom-study windows, Taylor could look out and see the magnificent stables, barns, staff houses, and other buildings and watch his yearlings, stallions, mares, and foals in the fields. It was another home away from their home in Lyford Cay.

When Taylor wasn't selling, he was buying, always attempting to improve the bloodline. In 1973, Windfields Farm paid more than $2 million for Tentam, a four-year-old which had established a world turf record at Saratoga, New York. Tentam was bought to replace the greatest contributor of all to Taylor's stable, the nineteen-year-old Nearctic, who after many years as chief stud at Windfields Farm in Maryland, had to be put down. He was the horse that turned it around for the Canadian thoroughbred industry. As a sire he put Canada on the map internationally and gave Canadian-bred horses respect everywhere in the world. Nearctic had sired the fabulous Northern Dancer who in turn had sired 1970 English Triple Crown winner, Nijinsky. Even though Nearctic was failing during the 1973 breeding season, he left a legacy of 28 mares, all in foal.

On July 14, 1973, the formal announcement was made by E.P. Taylor that his retirement as chairman of the board of trustees of The Ontario Jockey Club would take effect the next day, immediately after the last race at Woodbine Racetrack. Lt. Col. Charles (Bud) Baker would succeed Taylor, who would continue as a member of the board and the executive committee. Henceforth he would be honorary chairman of the board and chairman of the finance committee. In a brief, unpretentious press conference in the boardroom at Woodbine when the announcement was made, Taylor said, "The only thing that has not happened that we wanted to accomplish since I have been chairman of this organization is that legalized off-track betting has not been established." There was no way he was going to give up that fight. That colourful sports columnist Dick Beddoes marked Taylor's transitional announcement with a typical salute, which concluded:

Chances are Taylor would have resigned before now, but he wanted to preside over the introduction of legal off-track gambling. When it comes in Ontario, money bet in shops away from the track will funnel directly to the tracks and therefore benefit the horsemen who make the game go. The federal Government, urged by Taylor, will probably legalize off-track shops next year.

Taylor always requested, "three cheers and a tiger" for the Queen when she attended the Plate. This morning the racing mob should respond in kind. Three cheers for E.P.

And a tiger, like Northern Dancer driving through the stretch.

Three weeks before, in an incident reminiscent of his public skirmish with Mackenzie King over his wartime beer prohibition when Taylor wrote a strongly critical letter to the editor of the Ottawa *Journal*, Taylor had unleashed a biting attack against Prime Minister Pierre Trudeau because of the federal government's failure to implement legislation to permit off-track betting. Taylor went after the Prime Minister publicly in a speech delivered at the annual meeting of the Canadian Thoroughbred Horse Society, saying "the Prime Minister is reputed to be an outdoor man, a good skier, a good canoeist, and a good swimmer. He evidences his interest in hockey and football on special occasions by dropping pucks and kicking off footballs. To the best of my knowledge, he has never accepted an invitation to attend an important racing event. Racing is honoured regularly by members of the royal family, the Governor General, the lieutenant governors, premiers of provinces, but not Canada's Prime Minister.

"Does he understand that there are between 800,000 and 900,000 horses and ponies in this country that give a great deal of pleasure and relaxation to hundreds of thousands of Canadians? Does he believe that our race courses are comparable to gambling casinos, or does he understand that the vast majority of people who wager on horseracing are backing up their considered opinion, as persons who speculate on the stock market? Does he not understand that the overall attendance at racing in any year in Canada and the United States includes more people than any other spectator sport?"

In discussions with reporters after his speech, Taylor said that if his criticism failed to shake up the government, the only course of action left to him would be "personally to knock on the Prime Minister's door or to go canoeing on the same river as Trudeau."

He has yet to get on either the same river or mainstream as Trudeau, although he is still trying to communicate to the Prime Min-

314

ister that unless off-track betting is approved and revenues from it diverted to the racing industry, purses will be cut, and the sport of kings in Canada will degenerate to the kind of shoddy operation it was before he pulled it together after the war.

Taylor's 1973 racing year was capped by a sell-out $100-a-plate testimonial dinner held at Toronto's Constellation Hotel on October 26. The committee arranging the dinner would use the proceeds to establish the E.P. Taylor Equine Research Foundation. Its purpose was to provide money for the advancement and improvement of equine medicine, surgery, and husbandry, and money for scholarships or bursaries to graduate students, and provide grants to educational institutions for equine research.

Columnist Joan Sutton was at the dinner. She had difficulty in matching her mental picture of E.P. Taylor and his image with the name:

> Eddie!!!!! Who would have the temerity to call him that? Two things resulted from the dinner. The Fund got off to a $50,000 start and E.P. Taylor, rich, powerful, and famous, emerged as a very human guy—the sort of man you just might call Eddie. He is also a man with a wife who seems to be the last word in "liberated." A "Tallulah"-voiced Queen's Counsellor, Joe Sedgwick, chaired the dinner, but it was that extraordinary man, Harry Red Foster, who gave it its focus, with his unscheduled speech about Mr. Taylor's contributions, both to horseracing and the community at large.

It was a gala evening full of fun, jokes, speeches, emotion, and above all, affection for Eddie and Winnie Taylor.

The next major presentation to Taylor was at the third annual Eclipse Awards ceremonies staged by the Thoroughbred Racing Association at Bal Harbor, Florida, on January 11, 1974. Taylor had been president of this American organization from 1964 to 1966 and a director since 1960. Cited for his personal contributions in upgrading racing in Ontario, to the point where it was "the equal of any on the continent," and as the breeder of winners of both the Kentucky and English Derbys, and for ten years breeder of winners of more races in North America than any other, E.P. Taylor was honoured as horseracing's Man of the Year for 1973. When he stepped up to the microphone after receiving his award, this time he had little to say. "My racing stable hasn't done much this year, and I think I have been given this honour probably because I'm a stayer. I have been in racing now some thirty-odd years, and I've loved every one of them."

Perhaps his racing stable hadn't "done much" in 1973, but 1974 was to see him achieve one of his major objectives. For the first time, Windfields Farm-bred horses were at the top of North American-bred horses in money won and at the same time at the top of the list of stakes winners. Taylor had arrived at the pinnacle of thoroughbred horse breeding. This had been his ambition from those long-gone days at the end of the 1940s when he tackled the business of breeding. No one could quarrel with his description of himself as a "stayer."

In 1974 he had first achieved the ultimate distinction of breeding the winners of more money than any man in the history of horseracing.

At the beginning of the year, a new racing body was formed, The Jockey Club of Canada. According to its first chairman, it would "instructively influence governing bodies and promote the best interests of thoroughbred racing and would provide Canadian thoroughbred horseracing interests with a voice at international conferences." The chairman? E.P. Taylor.

At Windfields at the end of May, Taylor received a letter informing him of yet another honour. This one, unexpected, pleased him greatly. The letter said, "Your career in the building and promotion of horseracing is one of the greatest success stories in Canadian sport. Your highly successful National Stud Farm has produced some of the greatest race-winning horses in North America and Europe. Year after year, the Stud Farm has led North America as top race-winning breeder. All these achievements have found their culmination in the familiar reference to you as 'Mr. Horse Racing' of North America." It was signed by W. Harold Rea, chairman of the board of governors of Canada's Sports Hall of Fame to which Taylor had just been elected as an honoured member.

In his continuing battle for off-track betting, Taylor had discovered who in the federal Cabinet was standing in the way. It was not the Prime Minister, who apparently could not care less about horseracing, but his erstwhile, irascible Cabinet member, the tough-talking Eugene Whelan, Trudeau's Minister of Agriculture. Whelan told a meeting of the National Association of Canadian

Race Tracks that he did not feel off-track betting was required. In his opinion, it would hurt the smaller tracks across Canada which would not have a chance to develop. It was reported that members of the horseracing fraternity thought Whelan might be living in the past. However, the minister was very much alive and in the present. He had dug in his heavy political heels and would be a difficult, if not impossible, man to turn around, even for E.P. Taylor.

At the Fasig-Tipton yearling sales at Saratoga in mid-summer 1975, Taylor broke the five-year-old filly record for the sales when a yearling, sired by Buckpasser out of Taylor's old favourite mare, Natalma, was purchased by Daniel Van Clief for $260,000. It was remembered that Natalma was the first home in the 1959 Schuylerville at Saratoga only to be disqualified when careless riding by her jockey resulted in "her number going down." E.P. Taylor, the master of Windfields, had placed a reserve bid on Natalma's filly of $150,000, a price that was bound to sort out the weak-hearted bidders.

The sale of the Buckpasser/Natalma filly was on Friday night, August 8. The night before, Taylor had watched the proceedings from his assigned front row seat, narrowly escaping serious injury when he was grazed, but not hurt, by a long-kicking yearling that was being paraded around the ring. Unruffled and with the calming presence of his son, Charles, by his side, he went on to bid on three yearlings. It was later reported that Winnie, who was not present at the incident, asked him with her sweet, sharp-edged sense of humour, "Were you kicked on the arm or the head?" With the kind of money Taylor later received from Van Clief, it was apparent that he had been touched neither on the arm nor the head.

In 1974 Taylor had bought controlling interest in Epsom Derby winner Snow Knight. He recognized that Epsom winners which had been brought to Canada and the United States have had a profound effect on the direction of breeding on this continent. In North America, for 1975, Snow Knight won the Eclipse Award for the best grass horse honours with a first-class series of wins in the Man O' War Stakes, Canadian International Championship, and Seneca, Brighton Beach and Manhattan Handicaps, becoming the first winner of the Epsom Derby to have classic wins in Canada, the United States, and England.

Taylor-bred horses won $2,366,571 in 1975, breaking the world

317

record which had been set just two years before by Elmendorf Farm. It was Taylor's second straight title in a row.

Apart from knocking off thoroughbred racehorse breeding records and becoming the world's leading breeder, Eddie Taylor continued to be honoured by the industry to which he had contributed so much. The Jockey Club, the *Daily Racing Form*, the Canadian Thoroughbred Horse Society, and the National Association of Canadian Race Tracks had banded together for the purpose of annually honouring the outstanding people in Canadian thoroughbred racing. They named their top recognition the Man of the Year Sovereign Award. The 1976 and first recipient was chosen unanimously–E.P. Taylor. At the First Annual Sovereign Award dinner at the Skyline Hotel in Toronto, E.P. Taylor collected two more presentations for breeding two outstanding horses, Victorian Queen and Momigi. Also receiving an award for the best newspaper story was the knowledgeable, witty Toronto *Star* columnist, Milt Dunnell, who couldn't resist doing a column on Taylor when the announcement of the winners had been made two weeks earlier. In his column, which was captioned, "Taylor's Always Man-of-the-Year," Dunnell had some pithy comments. "It's a good thing they didn't make the award retroactive. Taylor's trophies and trinkets would have to be delivered by truck. The last time he wasn't Man of the Year in Canadian Thoroughbred racing was the year before he came in."

Taylor had talked to Dunnell about things done–and to be done. "I get my greatest satisfaction out of what has been accomplished to improve track facilities–to upgrade the calibre of the horses–to make racing more enjoyable for everybody. These are the really important things. It has been gratifying to have successes in racing and breeding. I've made a little money out of breeding, but I've lost a lot of money in racing. We offer all our yearlings for sale, as you know. If somebody buys an outstanding one and it turns out to be a great bargain, I am pleased, because usually I have the sire or the dam or other members of that horse's family." Dunnell had come to the conclusion that "Taylor already has done enough for Canadian racing to be Man-of-the-Year until the Queen's Plate's 200th running."

But the 1976 Queen's Plate was only the 117th running of the premier Canadian classic. The turquoise and gold Taylor colours were up on Confederation, who finished third. The winner was a

Taylor-bred horse, Norcliffe, a "super horse," as his jockey, Jeff Fell, called him. His owner, Bud Baker, had purchased him from Windfields Farm, paying $80,000 for him as a yearling. Norcliffe went on to win the Prince of Wales Stakes at Fort Erie. A proud and optimistic Baker ran Norcliffe in the United States during the winter and spring season of 1977, urged on by an enthusiastic Eddie Taylor.

For the third straight year, Taylor had taken the North American Breeder title, shattering his own world record with earnings of $3,022,181, led by the Canadian Horse of the Year for 1976, the same Norcliffe. The 252 Taylor-bred starters running in 1976 included 151 winners and between them they won 356 of their 2,718 starts.*

Still chairman of The Jockey Club of Canada, and pursuing with enormous vigour the objective to which he was dedicated as the prescription for racing's financial ills, off-track betting, Taylor was preparing to make an all-out assault on Prime Minister Trudeau and his Ottawa colleagues, and in particular, the still-adamant Minister of Agriculture, Eugene Whelan. In Taylor's opinion, "In the competition for economic survival, off-track betting is racing's best hope. One shouldn't judge off-track betting by what has happened in New York. That was and is a disastrous approach so far as racing is concerned. A well-organized plan can broaden the base of patronage significantly, upgrade the class of the horses and enable racing to thrive in modern times."

Well, that wasn't the way Whelan saw it. In a letter to the editor of the *Globe and Mail*, published on August 10, 1976, rebutting a letter to the editor by J.H. Kenney, president of The Ontario Jockey Club, published a month earlier regarding off-track betting, Whelan went over the bad results of the New York scheme, a plan quite different from the one Taylor and his colleagues were proposing, and finished off his letter saying, "I am not convinced that a provincially operated system of off-track betting as has been suggested would in the long term be of benefit to the racing industry at large. In my view it would concentrate racing in major cities, and mean the failure of many of the smaller tracks that play an important role in the industry."

---

*Taylor was the breeder of two of Canada's top two-year-olds: Stafford Farms' Sound Reason ($149,843) and Jean-Louis Lévesque's Gilboulee ($131,712).

Another record-making year for horseman E.P. Taylor was 1977. On June 8, one of the horses he had bred, Right Chilly, won the Yearling Sales Stakes at Exhibition Park in Vancouver. This was the 193rd stakes win by a Taylor-bred horse, a new world record, surpassing the 192 mark set by Harry Payne Whitney in the first part of this century. By the end of 1977, Taylor had crossed the 200 mark.

He had set a new dollar record for yearlings in sales held in Kentucky, Maryland, and Canada–$4,199,000. For the fourth year in a row Taylor-bred horses topped the world in money won.

To cap it all off, Taylor syndicated the magnificent horse, The Minstrel, for a record-setting price of $9 million. (The record price in 1976 was $8 million, paid for the American horse, What A Pleasure.) During the 1977 season, The Minstrel, a son of Northern Dancer, captured the Epsom and Irish Derbys and the King George VI and Queen Elizabeth Stakes at Ascot for England's Bob Sangster.

Sangster had bought The Minstrel at Keeneland in 1975 for $200,000. The horse, regarded in Europe as one of the best horses to race there–along with his three-quarters brother, Nijinsky–in the last decade became Taylor's hope for a replacement for the sixteen-year-old Northern Dancer.

When The Minstrel won the Ascot race, Taylor decided to buy back this superb three-year-old. The horse was syndicated at 36 shares–the Sangster group retaining 18 shares and Taylor, with others, taking the balance at $250,000 each. In the summer of 1977 The Minstrel joined his illustrious father at Windfields Farm in Maryland. These two stallions will continue the remarkably successful blood line produced by the man recognized throughout thoroughbred horseracing as the world's premier breeder, Edward Plunket Taylor. Late in 1977 it was announced that Taylor would be given the prestigious Eclipse Award, for leading producer of thoroughbreds in North America, the first Canadian so honoured.

While E.P. Taylor's life from the time of his "retirement" in 1966 appears to be filled to the brim with racehorses, he also found time for his Bahamian interests, which have held not only his attention but much of his investment money.

In taking the retirement route, the sixty-five-year-old E.P. Taylor determined to play a much less active part in the management of the Argus group of companies and in fact had so declared with his resignation from the chairmanship of Canadian Breweries and Domtar. He had said he was going to retire and he meant it, although the word "retirement" from E.P. Taylor's mouth really meant scaling down to a pace of activity equal to the output of a normal high-powered executive.

The main focus of his business and leisure activities was the Bahamas. He had made a personal and investment commitment, which, to Taylor's logical mind, meant that he should become a citizen. However, in those days before the Bahamas' independence from the United Kingdom, when all the people of those islands were British subjects, citizenship status could not be obtained by a person, such as Taylor, who was already a British subject. The best he could do was to ask the Bahamian government for "belonger's" status. In the application forms he completed, he was required to declare "his intention of making his permanent home in the Bahama Islands." At the end of January 1967, the government granted his "belonger's" title and gave him a "certificate that the person belongs to the Bahama Islands." Winnie also received hers.

Still a firm believer that councils recruited by governments to advise them really cannot do a job because they have no power, Taylor nevertheless considered it prudent to accept an invitation of Premier Lynden Pindling, whose party had just won power in 1967. Pindling asked him to become one of the original members of his Economic Advisory Council to which economic and fiscal matters of general interest to the Bahamas community were to be referred for its views and advice.

To help the economy of the Bahamas, not just advise on it, E.P. Taylor created a new industry. With much fanfare, a new, $1,350,000 rock-crushing plant was built and put into commission by his New Providence Development Company for the purpose of producing a high-grade building aggregate from the cap rock that covered the island. In the building of Lyford Cay, and from his knowledge of construction throughout the island, Taylor could see that there was an urgent need for aggregates with which to make concrete and to pave roads. As with almost everything else, that commodity had to be imported. Now it could be produced on the island, using the rock in place, and would therefore create new jobs. Premier Pindling was on hand to press the button that officially started the new plant in operation. Almost all of its forty-five employees would be Bahamian.

Taylor's New Providence Development Company had also proceeded with the completion of a master plan for a new town development in the western end of the island, some twenty miles from Nassau, where he envisaged that a large community would be developed.

In November 1968 Taylor announced the first phase of the development, which would involve 350 acres out of the total of over 5,000 then owned by the company. At the same time, the company went public, selling 3.5 million common shares which were oversubscribed in the first offering and brought in just over $3.5 million. There were unfounded complaints in Nassau that the issue had been totally sold out in Canada with no shares available to Bahamians. Under an agreement with the government, Taylor's New Providence firm was required to build a 120-room hotel. The yacht harbour, beach facilities, an eighteen-hole golf course, tennis, and swimming pool, to serve the residents of the houses, condominiums, and apartments, would be built. There would also be office and commercial complexes with special industrial areas for manufacturing and bulk facilities. The operation of Golden Mile Dairy, a subsidiary, was to be expanded from a herd of about 340 cattle to 1,000 head. And underlying the company's lands was an aquafer from which quality fresh water flowed at the rate of about three million gallons a day.

In addition to these Bahamian projects, Taylor continued his heavy involvement in the RoyWest Banking Corporation as well as in the Trust Corporation of the Bahamas operations. During the mid-1960s when Taylor's involvement in the economic life and development of the Bahamas was becoming more concentrated, he and his fellow directors of the RoyWest Banking Corporation saw an opportunity to offer their banking and investment services to a small Middle East country, Abu Dhabi, where crude oil was beginning to flow from wells which promised riches to that small Persian Gulf sheikhdom which became part of the United Arab Emirates in 1971. Arrangements had been made to meet the ruler, His Highness Sheik Shakhbut. As chairman of RoyWest, Taylor wanted the corporation to be appointed the investment representative of the ruler, primarily in the Bahamas and North America, but also in the United Kingdom, and elsewhere in the sterling area. As he saw it, the Sheikh's liquid resources would multiply rapidly as a result of his increasing revenues from oil royalties. Taylor speculated that in due course he "will want to salt away some of his capital in overseas countries of stability." And who better to assist in the salting away than the Trust Corporation of the Bahamas which had "the benefit of the highest possible expertise in the investment of funds, either in the dollar area or the sterling area."

Taylor's original contact with the ruling family in Abu Dhabi came from Sir Desmond Cochrane, one of the trust company directors. He had established friendly relations with the ruler over a period of years, and was a financial man who controlled a private bank in Beirut with which one of the financial institutions in the RoyWest group had recently become associated.

Taylor went to Beirut early in April where he met Cochrane and his son, Mark, then the three of them went on to Abu Dhabi, where all were well received. While there, Taylor renewed his acquaintanceship with William Clark, the ruler's secretary, whom Taylor had met previously in England.

Taylor felt that he had made a favourable impression upon the ruler during his short stay, but it would be a period of months before he could expect a firm commitment, Arab rulers being notorious for their caution in handling their money and reluctance to put it in the hands of financial houses in the western world. Nevertheless, E.P. Taylor was satisfied with the results of his long journey and began to consider ways of keeping the pressure on the ruler. However, in August, the sheikh was removed, overthrown by another member of his family. The new ruler, Sheikh Zaid, promptly terminated Bill Clark's employment but gave him a generous financial settlement. Even so, Taylor understood that Clark was persona *grata* with the Sheikh, as were Sir Desmond Cochrane and Mark, both of whom had hurriedly gone to Abu Dhabi to pay their respects to the new ruler. Mark, fluent in Arabic, had served as a member of the former ruler's staff and was liked by all members of the royal family. Between the Cochranes and Clark, Taylor felt that he had an excellent team who could present the case of RoyWest very well and, indeed, could act on behalf of Massey-Ferguson in putting an agricultural plan before Sheikh Zaid, which, if accepted, would result in much business being done by the British arm of Massey-Ferguson. By 1968 the Royal Bank of Canada received business from Sheikh Zaid but nothing came of the Massey-Ferguson approach.

A decade later, Taylor would again be in the Middle East looking for and doing housing business, quite a different kind of enterprise than banking.

Meanwhile, Taylor's New Providence Development Company was hard at work installing roads, water, sewers, and electricity in the initial residential stages of its Bahamian land. The golf course and hotel were also under construction. Even at this early time, the company was able to report a profit of over $400,000 for 1969.

At the end of that year, the chairman of the Bahamian Economic Advisory Council resigned and Prime Minister Lynden Pindling asked E.P. Taylor to take his place. Taylor agreed– reluctantly. He had worked hard on the business of the council for the better part of two years. In accepting the chairmanship he thought he might be able to get the government more interested than it had been in the advice of the council. However, during the next few months, Taylor found that he could make no progress. Finally, he went to the Prime Minister in November 1970 and said, " 'We've run out of ideas. You've had all the reports on six or more subjects. We don't think they've been taken seriously. You've only referred one thing to us which we concurred with, and that was to collect taxation on real estate,' which they weren't doing. People weren't paying real estate taxes and we told them they should collect them."* When, in 1971, Taylor resigned as chairman and a member, no appointment was made to replace him. The council has been dormant ever since.

While Taylor's involvement in business and entrepreneurial activities in North America and the United Kingdom had become markedly reduced, his ever-present philanthropic interests in Canada continued undiminished. Parallel to his E.P. Taylor Foundation Inc. in Canada, through which he is today giving away more money than ever before, he established the E.P. Taylor Bahamas Foundation. On Sunday, February 15, 1970, a beaming Edward Taylor stood beside Marguerite Pindling, wife of the Bahamian Prime Minister, while she cut a symbolic gauze bandage to officially open the new medical centre which Taylor's Bahamas

---

*A real estate taxation scheme was implemented by the Pindling government in 1977.

Foundation had built to serve the western portion of New Providence Island. The centre contained a well-equipped operating theatre, an X-ray room with the most modern equipment available, a film darkroom, dispensary and laboratory, examination and consulting rooms, and other facilities. This was phase one of the medical facilities. Phase two was to be a hospital of twenty beds, also to be built by the E.P. Taylor Bahamas Foundation.

Unfortunately for Taylor's New Providence construction plans, the worldwide depressed economic conditions of 1971, together with a shortage of mortgage funds and reduced revenue in his company, forced Taylor into a slow-down in construction. He had to put off the building of the 120-room hotel which he was required to build under his agreement with the government. He had already received an extension of the originally required opening date of June 1971. The servicing of lands for sale for housing would also be deferred. The government was unhappy, but recognizing the difficult economic situation and Taylor's heavy personal commitment to the Bahamas, it accepted the delay.

Notwithstanding the slow-down in development, the new South Ocean Golf Club, a 6,868 yard, championship, eighteen-hole course with an official U.S.G.A. par rating of 72, was ready to open in the first week of January 1971, complete with a first-class clubhouse. Taylor thinks that because of the need to move so much rock in order to create hills and contours on an otherwise flat expanse of land it is one of the most expensive golf courses ever built.

The residential development Taylor had in mind for the Bahamas had to be inexpensive. Most of the native people of the island could afford only a minimum of cost for housing. The question was what building techniques could be developed that would minimize housing costs and yet provide solid, durable, acceptable accommodation. During the slow period of 1971, Taylor put his New Providence Development team to work to research the elusive method of reducing the costs of residential housing to an economic level. Taylor would find the answer that same year, not through research, but during a visit to Mexico for the opening of Daniel Ludwig's Acapulco Princess Hotel. That trip to Mexico would later put Taylor on a new international business path.

Taylor kept his Lyford Cay interests separate and apart from the business of the New Providence Development Company. Lyford

Cay Investments Limited, which had been formed a few years earlier by Taylor and a group of Lyford Cay Club members, held a substantial acreage of undeveloped real estate and was building speculative houses. One of its major assets was the magnificent clubhouse and other associated buildings, tennis courts, and the superb eighteen-hole golf course. An energetic, seventy-five-year-old Roy Little, a member of the Lyford Cay Club, described the place as "the finest resort club anywhere in this hemisphere–beautiful clubhouse, fine marina, excellent golf course–everything done with taste and style." Little, a human dynamo in his own right, who had been and was then an enormously successful expansionist entrepreneur and a man after Taylor's own heart, approached Taylor suggesting that in order to perpetuate the club and at the same time provide the best possible management, the club and its facilities ought to be sold to the members themselves.

Taylor, who still owned 73 per cent of Lyford Cay Investments, together with a huge mortgage back which his own family company had taken at the time of his original funding of the construction and development of Lyford Cay, thought Little's idea was excellent, as did Taylor's fellow shareholders. The deal was closed on July 31, 1971. The purchase price was $3 million, of which $500,000 was paid in cash and the balance contributed as a gift to the new Lyford Cay Members Club Limited, which then raised operating capital by issuing debentures to its own members and through a long-term, low-interest mortgage.

An important addition to Taylor's Bahamian organization was made in 1973 in the person of Michael Dinnick, a thirty-four-year-old Torontonian graduate of McGill University (which gave him a plus in Taylor's assessment), with a degree in economic geography. He spent seven years in the marketing department of McLeod, Young, Weir (another plus), and joined Marathon Realty, the C.P. Rail land development arm, in 1968. Taylor needed a bright, fast-moving, experienced executive with an entrepreneurial background to assist him in the day-to-day monitoring of the various enterprises on New Providence Island, ranging from the stone-crushing plant, dairy farming, house building, hotel management, golf course operations, sale of water, to Taylor's own continuing involvement in Lyford Cay. Taylor started off giving Dinnick a little responsibility, then a little more, and kept increasing it as he became more and more satisfied with his young deputy's ability.

Once E.P. Taylor is happy with the performance of someone who works closely with him as part of his personal staff, his normal tendency is to give that person his full confidence, as much responsibility as he can, and above all, loyalty. People who join Taylor tend to stay with him and become an integral part of everything he does. Two examples of people with this type of close working relationship are Tom D'Arcy, the financial vice-president of Windfields Farm Limited, Taylor's financial adviser, who has been with him for the past twenty-one years, operating out of the Taylor base, the gatehouse cottage at Windfields. The other is Mrs. Beth Heriot, his long-time secretary, who has carried much of the responsibility of keeping his business life and calendar in working order. With Taylor spending about 200 days a year in the Bahamas, another fifty in Maryland with his horses, about seventy in Canada, and the rest of the year trudging around the world, both Beth Heriot and Tom D'Arcy frequently find themselves meeting E.P. Taylor at Lyford Cay or wherever else he happens to be when he needs one or the other of them, or both.

At the beginning of April 1973, Sir Etienne Dupuch, the owner and publisher of the *Tribune*, a Nassau newspaper, who had left the Bahamas the year before alleging that the government of Prime Minister Pindling was "callously destroying the economy of the islands, and the character of the people," told the Freedom of the Press Committee of the Inter-American Press Association at its mid-year meeting in the United States that government harassment was forcing him either to sell his newspaper for half its worth or to close it down. He said he had been told by "a highly reliable source" that the Pindling government intended to enact restrictive press laws after the Bahamas became independent on July 10.

Dupuch's allegations were immediately repudiated by the Prime Minister who said, "The government denies any harassment whatsoever of the *Tribune*. The government denies that it is forcing the editor to sell at all, to sell at half price or to close down."

Dupuch had also said publicly that in January an American firm had approached him to buy the *Tribune* at $3 million. While he was willing to sell for that price, Dupuch did not want to sell to foreigners. Furthermore, the government would not permit it.

As soon as the news broke of Dupuch's speech, Taylor, concerned that the *Tribune* should not stop publication and that it should not fall into foreign hands, decided that he, as a Bahamian, would attempt to purchase the newspaper. The day after Dupuch's disclosure, he gathered up the managing director of the RoyWest Banking Corporation, H.F. Dinner, and Mrs. Eileen Carron, the daughter of Sir Etienne Dupuch, and the trio flew to Miami in Taylor's jet to meet with Sir Etienne. Taylor indicated to the seventy-four-year-old publisher that it might be possible to put together a group in the Bahamas to purchase the newspaper. Taylor had in mind a syndicate of Bahamian companies and selected individuals to participate in the purchase, along with a percentage of the shares being offered to the Bahamian public. No rock bottom price was discussed with Sir Etienne. However, by April 13, Dupuch indicated his agreement to sell at $2 million. Taylor could have until May 15 to accept or reject the deal. Taylor then sat down and made a list of fourteen steps that had to be completed if the deal was to go forward.

The last item was really the first: "All of the above, subject to governmental approval." He immediately made contact with the Secretary to Pindling's Cabinet asking for an appointment to see the Prime Minister. When they met on the morning of April 26, he made it clear that his plan of purchase envisaged 100 per cent Bahamian ownership of the new company which would be formed to take over the *Tribune*, "with possibly an exception that the government might be asked to give permission that some very reputable financial institutions, incorporated or licensed in the Bahamas, might be permitted to become shareholders." There would be a strict limitation that no shareholder should own, at any time, more than 10 per cent of the capital of the company.

That afternoon, Taylor wrote to Eileen Carron reporting the results. "I had hoped that the Prime Minister would be enthusiastic about the plan. To my sorrow, I found out that this was not the case although he made it crystal clear that I was free to proceed with it if I should so decide. I had previously received a promise of substantial support from a few sources, but this was only given on the understanding that the Prime Minister would be pleased if a new change of ownership could be effected." The Prime Minister was not pleased and E.P. Taylor gave up on this third attempt –albeit the first two were as a reluctant Argus participant–to become one of the owners of a newspaper. It may not be his last try.

On July 10, 1973, the Bahamas, its 700 islands and 185,000 inhabitants, became an independent nation within the British Commonwealth. The light-hearted Prince Charles represented the royal family at the celebration of the event which brought with it a White Paper on independence dealing with the terms of the new constitution. In particular, it outlined the rules for obtaining citizenship in the new country, a matter which was of great interest to Winnie and Eddie Taylor, who had been "belongers" for several years. Their objective was to become fully qualified. They filed applications as soon as the new legislation and regulations came into effect, and in 1975 they became citizens of the Bahamas.

Chapter XVIII

Argus Divested
1975

E.P. Taylor's proclaimed "retirement," which was in reality nothing of the sort, nevertheless had moved him away from his former day-to-day involvement in the widespread affairs of Argus Corporation and the host of companies under its surveillance. Since Phillips' death in 1964, the Argus board had seen fit to leave the post of chairman vacant. In 1967, when E.P. Taylor became a "belonger" of the Bahamas, it seemed appropriate that, in the interests of the shareholders of Argus, an on-the-scene president should be appointed. On June 3, 1969, the man who had been seen many years before as the "crown prince" of Argus, John A. McDougald, moved into the post of president, while Taylor went upstairs to the long-vacant chairmanship and away from the firing line. It was a natural progression for each of these long-time friends, associates, and partners. Even so, Taylor's tenure as chairman of the Argus board of directors would be short-lived.

E.P. Taylor was seventy on January 29, 1971. At the annual meeting of Argus Corporation on March 11, Canada's "Mr. Big Business" gave up the post of chairman. He would remain a director and a member of the company's executive committee, but the complete mantel had finally been passed to Bud McDougald, who became chairman as well as president. Henceforth, the press references would be not to Taylor's, but to McDougald's "Argus Empire." The *Financial Times* commented on Taylor's departure: "The difficult process of retiring gradually and happily was completed last week by one of the few men who had been accepted by the Canadian public as a genuine Canadian tycoon. The occasion was notable, but it does not call for eulogy. Mr. Taylor remains alive and well in Lyford Cay, Bahamas; and E.P. Taylor alive is E.P. Taylor active."

Consistent with his resignation as Argus chairman, Taylor also gave up his membership on the board of both Domtar and Dominion Stores, the executives of each of which honoured him with dinners, gifts, and speeches praising his splendid work on their behalf. However, he stayed on as a director and chairman of the executive committee of Massey-Ferguson and on the board of the Royal Bank. Even that irascible senior citizen and famous broadcasting figure, Gordon Sinclair, got into Taylor's birthday act. On his "Let's Be Personal" program of February 1, Gordon noted Taylor's birthday, lamenting:

I heard very little said, and saw little written about Mr. Taylor's birthday, although on my own seventieth . . . last June . . . the day was set in my honour and soon afterwards a similar salute was given to Elizabeth, the Queen Mother.

This neglect is a shame. It is a shame to Ontario because Edward Plunket Taylor has been, and is, one of the greatest of all Canadians, and certainly one of the most unselfish. Despite the idea of the success story, the word rich . . . now . . . seems tarnished. Canada will desperately need help if it has no rich people, more desperately than ever before. Especially the "unselfish" rich, like Edward Plunket Taylor, who has certainly spent more of his time doing things for others, without pay or reward, than he has spent in the massing of personal fortune, if he has one. Knowing something about money, I doubt if Taylor is all that rich. He's certainly not one of the big rich of Canada.

What's more, his will is written in such a way that little part of his estate . . . perhaps no part whatsoever . . . will be inherited by kinfolk. The money will go to a trust; a Canadian trust. Some who have said that Taylor moved to the Bahamas to save taxes. This is untrue, but too complicated for me to explain in four minutes, and people probably wouldn't believe me anyhow. They've already made up their minds.

Taylor was also making up his mind about the future of Argus in which he had a substantial personal investment. The corporation, of which McDougald was now chairman and president was in Taylor's opinion doing little by way of expansion and growth. He was getting restive about its lack of activity, even though the earnings were acceptable. A *Financial Post* article of the day, reporting on the posture of the company, said, "Closed–End Investment Argus Corp ($19) is not noted for any flashing acts of legerdemain, preferring to sit and watch over its six massive holdings . . . last week shaking the cobwebs from its corporate image, Argus sold 500,000 shares–half its position–in B.C. Forest Products."

Between 1963 and 1972 the corporate assets of Argus grew by about 34 per cent, or 3 per cent compounded annually, while income level was only 5.5 per cent higher in 1972 than in 1963, a lacklustre performance.

So Taylor the expansionist entrepreneur wanted out. His New Providence Development could use the share of his cash that was locked up in the Argus treasury. But if anything was to be done, it would, of course, be with the unanimous concurrence of the Argus principals.

Taylor formulated a proposition, had the tax implications researched, and on October 15, 1972, wrote a letter to McDougald, suggesting a series of "steps which might eventually lead to the winding up of the Argus Corporation and the distribution of its assets." He pointed out that Massey-Ferguson's future profit position was not encouraging,* and the federal government was likely to impose full Canadian corporate rates of taxation on the profits of Massey-Ferguson's foreign subsidiaries where it made the bulk of its income. "I suggest that we do not delay the selling of our holdings in this company for cash if we can obtain a reasonable offer within the next ninety days (before Ottawa is liable to legislate)." Taylor calculated that that would put "more than $56 million in the till."

He was also worried about Dominion Stores. "We are all aware of the very substantial market value of our holding in this company and I shall always be grateful to you for introducing the ori-

---

*Massey-Ferguson reported a 1970 loss of over $19.5 million. Taylor and McDougald had seen what was coming and the reason for it and kept pressing the Massey executives for changes. In the three years up until 1970, "the management presented an estimate for the year which proved to be entirely unrealistic in sales and in the amount of business they were going to do. And we put our foot down and said, 'Let's get down to earth boys. You're operating too expensively. You must cut back and bring things into line.' " The heavy 1970 loss drove home the points Taylor and McDougald had been making. The necessary cuts and changes were made with the result that in the following year Massey-Ferguson was back in the black with a $9.25 million profit.

ginal piece of business to Argus before, I believe, you became a director of Argus." Profits would increase but at a slow rate, and there was the likelihood of periodic price wars. In addition, further competition was certain to be met everywhere in eastern Canada, "by the announced expansion of the new Safeway organization into eastern Canada which is our stronghold." Could Argus not look into the possibility of selling out to Safeway?

"Finally, should we not think seriously of winding up the Argus Corporation and distributing the portfolio to our shareholders on a pro rata basis after the debentures and preferred shares have been redeemed? Winding up in this fashion would give the equity shareholders cash and securities having a value of $4 to $6 a share above the then market value of the Argus shares."*

At that moment the public record showed the "control" voting shareholders of Argus were Ravelston Corporation with 776,000 common (voting) shares (45.8 per cent). Ravelston was defined in the corporation's proxy circular as an "associate" of Messrs. McDougald, Black, Matthews, and the Canadian General and Investment Companies (Max Meighen). Shawinigan Industries represented a Power Corp.-Desmarais interest with 175,484 common (10.37 per cent) and Windfields Farm Limited, 169,278 (10 per cent). In addition to the common, Taylor, through Windfields Farm, owned well over a million of the non-voting preference shares. His stake was high but the future of Argus was out of his hands and firmly in the grasp of McDougald and his associates.

At the conclusion of his letter to McDougald, Taylor suggested that the two of them might have an informal meeting with Meighen, George Black, and Bruce Matthews. This meeting took place at George Black's house early in November. The group unanimously approved that a report should be made on the tax implications of selling the Massey-Ferguson and Dominion blocks and also the winding up of Argus. Nevertheless, Taylor could not detect any enthusiasm for the proposal.

By the end of the year arrangements had been made for Taylor to retire as chairman of the executive committee of the board of Massey-Ferguson, and he was waiting patiently for the decision of his Argus colleagues on his winding up proposal.

---

*The then market price for the Argus shares was Class 'C', $11; and common, $15 against a net asset value of $18.83, as reported May 4, 1972.

Quite correctly assessing the mood of his colleagues, Taylor did not really believe that Argus would be broken up and interred. The annual report of December 19, 1974, clearly demonstrated that Argus Corporation was alive and doing very well, with income before taxes of almost $12 million, nearly double the year before, reflecting earnings on the Class 'C' preference and common shares of $1.20. Messrs. McDougald, Black, Matthews, and Meighen elected to keep Argus Corporation going rather than accept the liquidation idea. Taylor had no choice but to respect their opinion, so there the matter sat. However, the events of 1975 would provide E.P. Taylor with the answer to his dilemma.

Taylor had long been aware of the continuing acquisition of Argus shares by the young Canadian financier, Paul Desmarais, through Shawinigan Industries Limited, a subsidiary of Desmarais' Power Corporation of Canada.* He was pleased to know that Desmarais had enough faith in Argus to buy on the open market 175,484 voting shares of Argus, representing 10.27 per cent of its outstanding shares of that class. But Taylor had no idea that Desmarais had a takeover bid in mind. It was difficult to see how he could be successful unless he could convince Bud McDougald and his colleagues to sell. After all, their holding company, the Ravelston Corporation Limited, of which McDougald was chairman and president, held 861,000 voting shares, representing 50.86 per cent of the stock and therefore a clear majority control. †

Paul Desmarais knew the Argus situation. Nevertheless, by March 1975, he had decided to go ahead with a takeover bid. But before going to McDougald, he wanted to talk with the man who had put Argus together in the first place, E.P. Taylor. The two men knew each other. Taylor, who was at Lyford Cay, had no hesitation in agreeing to see Desmarais, who immediately flew down.

---

*Desmarais was a forty-one-year-old expansionist entrepreneur who had emerged out of a Sudbury, Ontario, bus line to create a new corporate complex called Power Corporation, which, like Argus, controlled sizable chunks of major Canadian businesses such as Alcan, Bell Telephone, Canadian Chemicals, Chemcell, Cominco, Consolidated Paper, Distillers-Seagrams, Imperial Oil, I.B.M., International Nickel, Metropolitan Stores, Union Carbide, Steel Company of Canada, George Weston (Loblaws) and other firms, the assets of all of which when added together then totalled more than $4 billion.

† In July 1973, McDougald ensured absolute majority control of Argus for his Revelston group by buying sufficient Argus voting shares to increase its position to just over 50.86 per cent. Prior to that move Revelston was required to obtain the support of Taylor's 10 per cent voting share block for an absolute majority.

As Taylor recalls the visit, "Desmarais came here to tell me what he was going to do, not for the specific purpose of making me an offer for my shares. He said, 'I'm going to make a bid for Argus Corporation.' And I said, 'I don't think you'll be successful.' I told him that the controlling shares were pooled. He said he was just informing me that he was going to make an offer. I don't remember whether he asked me if I would oppose the offer. I didn't encourage him in any way. He went on entirely on his own, and he kept chasing Bud McDougald in Florida."

On Sunday, March 23, Desmarais found McDougald at his Palm Beach home. McDougald agreed to see him, not knowing what was on Desmarais' mind. When they met at McDougald's house that same day, Desmarais quickly laid it on the line. Power Corporation was going to make a takeover bid on Argus Corporation and he wanted McDougald to agree to his offer of $22 for each voting share (they were then trading at $15.25/$16.50 and $17 for each Class 'C' non-voting share, against a market value of about $12.75). Taken aback, McDougald told Desmarais in no uncertain terms that he was not interested in such a deal and to forget it.

McDougald thought Desmarais had the message. But he hadn't. The next conversation between the two men was on March 24, when Desmarais called McDougald to tell him that Power Corporation lawyers had advised him to report their "negotiations" to the Securities Exchange Commission. McDougald denied that any negotiations had taken place.

The next morning, Tuesday, March 25, Power Corporation announced that it had begun a takeover bid for control of Argus Corporation, saying it would pay $22 a share for each of the 1,692,736 issued voting shares of Argus it did not already own through Shawinigan Industries Limited. Also, Power would pay $17 a share for all the 6,770,944 issued Class 'C' non-voting shares of Argus. If all the shares were tendered, the bid would cost Power Corporation $148.5 million, plus expenses. The bid was conditional on acceptance by the holders of at least 80 per cent of both classes of shares.

Bud McDougald's response was blunt and irate. "Control of the company is not for sale." Desmarais "has approached us on numerous occasions seeking to buy Argus and we have said 'no.' It just drives you crazy to have these various groups come along who would like to buy it. They just don't seem to believe us. My associates in Ravelston are all of one mind. We have control of Argus and we intend to keep it."*

The question was whether they would continue to be of one mind when faced with the lure of the considerable premium over the market price that Desmarais was prepared to pay. The Power Corporation head was gambling against long odds, especially since McDougald had gone public with his negative statements immediately after the takeover bid was announced. That afternoon, Desmarais went to see E.P. Taylor at his Windfields estate to present his offer personally for the Taylor family's shares, both voting and Class 'C' non-voting.

"The market for the Class 'C' non-voting shares at the time was about $12. He paid $17 for them and I accepted it. I told him I wouldn't sell him the voting shares without first offering them to my colleagues. They would have one year if they wanted to buy. I felt perfectly free to sell the other shares." In fact, Taylor was delighted to have the proposal for the Class 'C' shares. It couldn't have come at a better time. "I didn't know anybody else who would offer the same price. Frankly, I wanted the money, which was some $22 million, to use in the south. As to the voting shares, Desmarais said to me, 'I'll be back to see you in a year.' I wasn't part of the Ravelston group, but we had a cross agreement whereby we'd offer each other our shares. I didn't formally offer the voting shares to McDougald, but I discussed it with him and he said, 'Well, it's a free country.' He was sitting there with control of Ravelston and he wasn't prepared to find $4 or $5 million."

At the time of the formal offer, the press was speculating on whether E.P. Taylor was willing to sell to Desmarais, but he was remaining non-committal, refusing to say whether he approved or disapproved of Power's takeover bid. In an interview he said, "I'm deliberately not commenting on the Power Corporation bid because everything Argus has to say has been said by Mr. McDougald." While the battle over Argus raged between Montreal, Toronto, and McDougald's Palm Spring base, Taylor was sitting comfortably at Lyford Cay with Desmarais' firm $22 million offer for his Class 'C' Argus shares in his pocket. Furthermore, that offer was not conditional on the outcome of the takeover bid.

---

*Globe and Mail, Toronto, March 26, 1975.

No counter-offer was made for Taylor's Class 'C' shares by McDougald or his group.

Finally, on April 17, Taylor prepared a terse press release which Desmarais approved. It was delivered to Clarke Davey, managing editor of the *Globe and Mail*. It said:

> We are now going to deposit all of our Argus Class 'C' preferred shares owned by Windfields Farm Limited and subsidiary companies under the terms of the Power Corporation offer. We are doing this because we consider the price offered by Power Corporation for the Preferred 'C' shares to be fair and equitable.
>
> Insofar as our common share holding is concerned, we have an agreement with the Ravelston Company which prevents us from depositing such shares.
>
> This is the only statement I will make and I will not answer any questions.

Nor did he.

There was speculation that the Taylor sale would give an enormous psychological boost to Power Corporation in its takeover attempt, which was rapidly arriving at the cut-off date of April 25. But it would take far more than psychological impact to change the minds of the Argus principals. A letter, dated April 8, was sent to all the shareholders of Argus Corporation Limited, signed by John A. McDougald, chairman and president. The letter outlined the shareholdings in Ravelston and its holdings in Argus. Two statements made it crystal clear that the refusal to sell to Power Corporation was firm "Ravelston has stated that it will not accept the offer of Power Corporation in respect of the Argus common shares which it owns, [and] . . . the shareholders of Ravelston . . . will not be accepting the offer of Power Corporation for their Class 'C' shares." There was a statement that to E.P. Taylor confirmed Bud McDougald's position that it was a "free country": "The Board of Directors of Argus has decided that it will not make any recommendations to the holders of Class 'C' preference and common shares regarding the acceptance or rejection of the offer from Power Corporation. Each holder of these shares is, of course, free to take whatever course of action appears best to such shareholder." Which is exactly what Taylor did.

On April 22, just three days before the expiry of the Power

Corporation offer, Prime Minister Trudeau appointed a Royal Commission on concentration of corporate power in Canada. The potential of a successful Power/Argus merger was behind his move. In making the announcement in the House of Commons, the Prime Minister said, "With current activity suggesting that further large-scale concentration of corporate power in Canada may be taking place, particularly in relation to conglomerate enterprises, the government has decided that it is necessary at this time to enquire into whether and to what extent such concentrations of corporate power confer sufficient social and economic benefit to Canadian society as to be in the public interest."

When the Power Corporation offer expired on April 25, it had acquired 50 per cent of the equity in Argus, but only 14 per cent of the voting shares. Desmarais had waived the condition that at least 80 per cent of both the voting and the 'C' non-voting shares must be tendered for the offer to be binding. The price, $68.9 million.

At the Power Corporation annual meeting held on April 30, 1975, Desmarais said there was no special agreement of any kind between Power Corporation and E.P. Taylor bearing on the disposition of Taylor's holding of 10.34 per cent of the Argus voting shares at the termination of the agreement which Taylor had with Ravelston. Desmarais also reported that he had talked with Taylor who had said he "is not prepared to discuss" disposition of the block of voting shares he controlled. Nevertheless, Desmarais was optimistic. "It is obvious that I hope he is going to sell it to me."

At the end of 1975, when he sat down to take stock and to sort out his priorities for the next year, three questions were in Taylor's mind about Argus: Would Bud McDougald and his group buy his voting shares or would they let them go by? If they did let them go by, would Paul Desmarais be back to make an offer for them? And if he did, should he accept it? Taylor knew that if he did sell, it would be the end of his association with the company that he had founded a generation before.

The Ravelston first right of refusal on Taylor's voting shares expired at the end of May 1976. Taylor was free to sell. True to his word, Desmarais returned and offered market price, then $30 per share. The deal was closed and on Tuesday, June 8, 1976, the announcement was made that E.P. Taylor had sold to Desmarais.

Edward Plunket Taylor had just retired from the Massey-Ferguson board of directors after thirty-four years of continuous service.

338

Now he was out of Argus Corporation, the firm he had founded, just as he was out of every other Canadian firm he had founded or that Argus had acquired. He had "retired" from the Canadian corporate financial and industrial scene.*

*Even though Taylor was out of the Canadian corporate boardrooms, his family-controlled companies still held blocks of shares in Dominion Stores, Massey-Ferguson, and other companies in the Argus portfolio with which he had had such a long association.

Chapter XIX

Looking Ahead

Did E.P. Taylor move to the Bahamas to avoid taxes? Did he take all his money with him?

Had he taken his fortune out of the country as many Canadians would have liked to believe when they read that he had been granted Bahamian citizenship in 1975? He maintains that there would at no time have been any tax advantage to him in doing so. His large investments at Lyford Cay and in New Providence Development required him to move a substantial amount of his capital into the Bahamas. But there is no doubt that a large portion of his fortune remains in Canada, as may be seen in the substantial gifts made by the E.P. Taylor Foundation to worthy and charitable Canadian causes.

Over the last five years the philanthropic donations made by E.P. Taylor and his family through the foundation exceed $1.5 million.* This does not include the gift of the Windfields Estate land and home to the Borough of North York. Although Taylor will not give an evaluation of his Canadian holdings, it is apparent that to generate enough income to permit donations of this magnitude, his capital within Canada must be considerable, in the multi-millions. Moreover, he strongly maintains that he has at no time abandoned Canada, and that he did not become a Bahamian citizen to avoid paying taxes in Canada.

With the era of Argus behind him and his place at the Canadian corporate boardroom tables now occupied by others, and with the

---

*Since its beginnings in 1955, the amount the E.P. Taylor Foundation has given exce
$3 million.

financial liquidity which he had built up over the years in hand, it could reasonably be expected that this septuagenarian would be content. He could be fully occupied with the affairs of New Providence Development and its subsidiary businesses. The running of the complicated business of thoroughbred horseracing, in which he had become the most successful breeder in the history of the sport of kings, would be time-consuming enough by itself. One thing that is not to be expected of a man in his position is to embark on a major new business venture at the age of seventy-three and at the age of seventy-seven to be expanding it into global horizons. But that is exactly what Taylor has done.

In 1973, "I was looking around for a project for my old age when this deal came along. It's a well-known fact that I hate holidays. I enjoy working!" His friend, the little-known American billionaire, Daniel K. Ludwig, had made a major development investment at Freeport, on Grand Bahama Island. As a young man, Ludwig had started off with no money, but a lot of native intelligence, a willingness to work, and a banker who was prepared to take a big risk. He bought a ship and started his immense fortune from there. His holdings now spread into many other countries. He was developing an enormous port site in Brazil where he planned as well to grow pulp trees and rice and build a new town.

Ludwig also had a major land development in Acapulco, Mexico, the centrepiece of which was a new hotel, the Acapulco Princess, which was opened in November 1971 amid much publicity and fanfare. Taylor accepted Ludwig's invitation to attend the opening and to take a look at the low-cost concrete houses being built in the emerging residential development. Taylor was keenly interested in the special system Ludwig was using. It might be the very thing he was looking for to use in the Bahamas.

Ludwig had formed a holding company in Bermuda called International Housing Limited, which was jointly owned by him and an American named Robert Stout, who had invented a simple construction system for the rapid building of low-cost housing. Stout called his system ConTech. His patented light-weight aluminum forms are set up in two parallel rows with spaces between into which concrete is poured. The aluminum forms for an entire house can be set up in one day by unskilled labour. The required plumbing and electric fixtures are set in place and the material poured. The completion of a house by an experienced crew takes five days.

341

When the forms are stripped off, both sides of the wall have either a brick-like textured surface, or one that resembles stucco, depending on the forms used. The system is used for assembly-line techniques which are low-cost and at the same time utilize labour native to the place of construction. "It normally saved more than 30 per cent on the cost of building a house. So I purchased the rights for the Bahamas from Ludwig."

The system produced exactly the kind of inexpensive buildings Taylor had been looking for for his New Providence development. By 1973, he was in the process of building 134 ConTech system houses. "We successfully tested the system in the Bahamas and were developing a nice little business when Ludwig called from New York to arrange a meeting with me there." Taylor went to see Ludwig within a few days. "I almost fell off the chair when he said he wanted to sell me worldwide rights to the system. At the time, International Housing Limited was selling in six countries and the operation was losing money." He wanted to unload the International Housing firm because he was spending far too much time on its business. Ludwig had already bought out Stout, so he owned the entire company himself. Would Taylor be interested?

E.P. Taylor looked ahead and abroad. He could see the enormous potential of the ConTech system throughout the areas of the world that required good shelter at the absolute minimum cost. The need for shelter and housing among the poor and developing nations of the world was not debatable. Here was a chance to do something for people, to create, to build. Furthermore, the system was versatile enough that it could be used to build first-class residential units in the developed nations where the standard of living is high.

Yes, Taylor was very interested. In short order, the "retired" Taylor was transformed into the world's largest house builder, putting up thousands of dwelling units and office buildings in countries which range all over the world and especially those developing countries where the need is critical and urgent and the government must see to the shelter of its people. By 1978, Taylor's burgeoning International Housing Limited had units going up in some forty countries, all of them in the scale of hundreds, including Panama, Costa Rica, Nicaragua, Mexico, El Salvador, Honduras, Guatemala, Brazil, Aruba, Chile, Nigeria, Ecuador, Jordan, Iraq, Syria, Saudi Arabia, and the Arab Emirates, the Ivory Coast, and the Bahama Islands. E.P. Taylor and his representatives jet around the world dealing with heads of state, governments, and the people he understands best–businessmen.

The one thing that pleases Taylor most about his global housing operation is that through it he is playing a direct part in providing shelter for people in the underdeveloped countries of the world. This is of enormous importance to him and was the principal motive that pushed him into taking International Housing off Ludwig's hands in the first place.

For the Ottawa boy, Eddie Taylor–who became the ultimate Canadian expansionist entrepreneur industrialist of his time, and who is now the world's leading breeder of thoroughbred racehorses–to become, in his mid-seventies, the world's largest builder of houses should be a surprise to no one who knows anything about E.P. Taylor.

And, in Canada, the Bahamas, and the world of horseracing, there are few people who don't.

Appendix 1

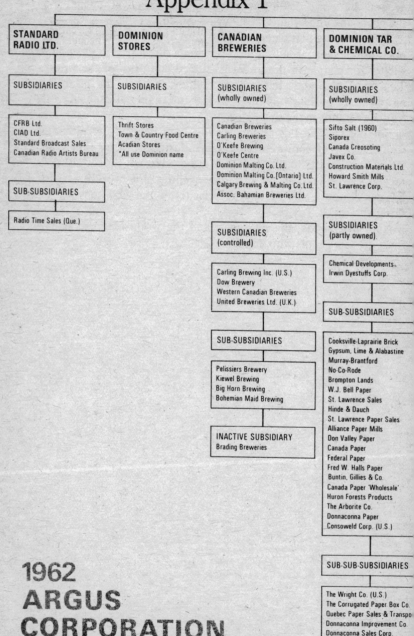

STANDARD RADIO LTD.	DOMINION STORES	CANADIAN BREWERIES	DOMINION TAR & CHEMICAL CO.

STANDARD RADIO LTD.

SUBSIDIARIES

CFRB Ltd.
CIAD Ltd.
Standard Broadcast Sales
Canadian Radio Artists Bureau

SUB-SUBSIDIARIES

Radio Time Sales (Que.)

DOMINION STORES

SUBSIDIARIES

Thrift Stores
Town & Country Food Centre
Acadian Stores
*All use Dominion name

CANADIAN BREWERIES

SUBSIDIARIES
(wholly owned)

Canadian Breweries
Carling Breweries
O'Keefe Brewing
O'Keefe Centre
Dominion Malting Co. Ltd.
Dominion Malting Co. [Ontario] Ltd.
Calgary Brewing & Malting Co. Ltd.
Assoc. Bahamian Breweries Ltd.

SUBSIDIARIES
(controlled)

Carling Brewing Inc. (U.S.)
Dow Brewery
Western Canadian Breweries
United Breweries Ltd. (U.K.)

SUB-SUBSIDIARIES

Pelissiers Brewery
Kiewel Brewing
Big Horn Brewing
Bohemian Maid Brewing

INACTIVE SUBSIDIARY
Brading Breweries

DOMINION TAR & CHEMICAL CO.

SUBSIDIARIES
(wholly owned)

Sifto Salt (1960)
Siporex
Canada Creosoting
Javex Co.
Construction Materials Ltd.
Howard Smith Mills
St. Lawrence Corp.

SUBSIDIARIES
(partly owned)

Chemical Developments
Irwin Dyestuffs Corp.

SUB-SUBSIDIARIES

Cooksville-Laprairie Brick
Gypsum, Lime & Alabastine
Murray-Brantford
No-Co-Rode
Brompton Lands
W.J. Bell Paper
St. Lawrence Sales
Hinde & Dauch
St. Lawrence Paper Sales
Alliance Paper Mills
Don Valley Paper
Canada Paper
Federal Paper
Fred W. Halls Paper
Buntin, Gillies & Co.
Canada Paper 'Wholesale'
Huron Forests Products
The Arborite Co.
Donnaconna Paper
Consoweld Corp. (U.S.)

SUB-SUB-SUBSIDIARIES

The Wright Co. (U.S.)
The Corrugated Paper Box Co.
Quebec Paper Sales & Transpo
Donnaconna Improvement Co.
Donnaconna Sales Corp.

1962
ARGUS
CORPORATION

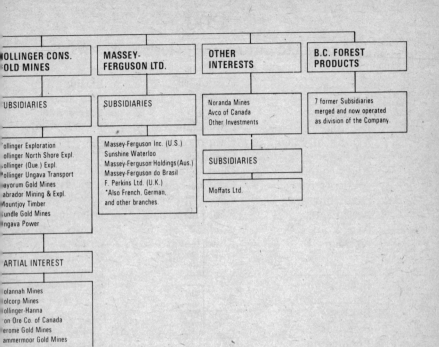

HOLLINGER CONS. GOLD MINES	MASSEY- FERGUSON LTD.	OTHER INTERESTS	B.C. FOREST PRODUCTS
SUBSIDIARIES	**SUBSIDIARIES**	Noranda Mines Avco of Canada Other Investments	7 former Subsidiaries merged and now operated as division of the Company.
Hollinger Exploration Hollinger North Shore Expl. Hollinger (Que.) Expl. Hollinger Ungava Transport Mayorum Gold Mines Labrador Mining & Expl. Mountjoy Timber Bundle Gold Mines Ungava Power	Massey-Ferguson Inc. (U.S.) Sunshine Waterloo Massey-Ferguson Holdings (Aus.) Massey-Ferguson do Brasil F. Perkins Ltd. (U.K.) *Also French, German, and other branches.	**SUBSIDIARIES** Moffats Ltd.	
PARTIAL INTEREST			
Holannah Mines Holcorp Mines Hollinger-Hanna Iron Ore Co. of Canada Jerome Gold Mines Hammermoor Gold Mines			

Appendix 2

A Complete Listing of Taylor's Stakes Winners

A

Acadian
Accumuli
Acushla
Against All Flags
Air Page
All Canadian
Arctic Actress
Arctic Blizzard
Artic Feather
Avec Vous
Axeman

B

Backstretch
Banqueroute
Battling
Belonger
Bennington
*Blue Light
Board of Trade
Boot Hill
Breezy Answer
Bright Monarch
Britannia
Brockton Boy
Buckstopper
Bulpamiru
Bull Vic
Butter Ball
Butterbump

C

*Canadiana
*Canadian Champ
Canadian Jerry
Canadian Victory
*Canebora
Cangal

Castleberry
Censor
Chomiru
Chopadette
Choperion
Chopine
Ciboulette
Cool Reception
Cool Ted
Cool Spring Park
Coulisse
Court Royal
Crown Count
Cut Steel

D

Dance Act
Deep Meadow
Des Erables
Dobbinton
Dr. Em Jay
Down North
Drama School
Dress Circle

E

Eltoro the Great
*Epic
Epic Queen
*Epigram

F

Fanfaron
Far North
Festivity
Fire N Desire
*Flaming Page
Flamme d'Or

Flashing Top
Flirt
Free Trade
French Wind

G

Gambler
Gay Jitterbug
Gay North
Giboulee
Golden Answer
Gracefield
Grand Garcon
Great Gabe
Greek Answer

H

Happy Harry
Happy Victory
Heroic Age
Hop Hop

I

Ice Palace
Icy Note
Imperial March
Impressive Lady

J

June Brook

K

King Gorm

L

La Belle Rose
Lady Victoria
Laissez Passer
L'Alezane

Le Grand Rouge
Lively Action
Lord Durham
Lost Majorette
*Lyford Cay

M

Maid O'North
Majestic Hour
*Major Factor
May Combination
*McGill
Meadowsweet
Menantic
Men At Play
Menedict
Military Bearing
Minsky
Miss Snow Goose
Momigi
Monarch Park
Myanna
Mystery Guest
My Wind

N

Nangela
Native Victor
Navy Wyn
Nearctic
Nearna
New Pro Escar
*New Providence
New Tune
Nijinsky II
Noble Answer
No Parando
Norcliffe
Norland
*Northern Dancer
Northernette
Northern Fling

Northern Minx
Northern Queen
Northern Taste
North of the Law
Nuclear Pulse

O

Our Sirdar

P

Perfect Sonnet
Peter's Chop
Petrus
Pierlou
Presidial
Pro Consul
Pryority D.

Q

Queen's Own
Queen's Reigh
Quick Selection
Quintain

R

Regal Alibi
Regal Dancer
Regal Gal
Regent Bird
Right Chilly
Royal Maple

S

Sea Service
Sherwood Park
Shine Ever
Silly Lilly
Snow Time
Solar Park
Solometeor
Son Blue

Song of Even
Sound Reason
South Ocean
Speedy Zephyr
Square Angel
Sunday Sail
Swain
Swinging Apache

T

Takaring
Tanzor
The Minstrel
*Titled Hero
Top Tourn
Tularia

V

Viceregal
Vickie's Champ
Victego
*Victoria Park
Victoria Regina
*Victoria Song
Victorian Era
Victorian Image
Victorian Prince
Victorian Queen
Victorianette

W

Willowdale Boy
Windfields
Windsor Field
Windspray
Windy Answer
Windy Ship
Winford

Y

Yummy Mummy

*King's/Queen's Plate winners

Index